Bob Dylan

A Life in
Stolen Moments

A Life in Stolen Moments

Day by Day: 1941-1995

CLINTON HEYLIN

Schirmer Books
An Imprint of Simon & Schuster Macmillan
New York

Prentice Hall International
London Mexico City New Delhi Singapore Sydney Toronto

To my mother

Acknowledgments

As Conrad Russell once wrote, "A preface, like a wedding speech, must necessarily be composed largely of thanks." There are many people without whose assistance this book would not be what it is, whatever that may be. Though I can't say I've maintained cordial relations with everyone who has stuck their oar in during the last fifteen years ("you are right from your side . . ."), I thank you one and all:

Kenny Aaronson, Bill Allison, Rod Anstee, Eddie Arno, Graham Ashton, Ivan Augenblink, John Bauldie, Andy Bell, Bob Bettendorf, Joel Bernstein, Mitch Blank, Graham Barrett, Ken Buttrey, Paul Cable, Bert Cartwright, Chris Cooper, Jay Craven, Dalton Dielan, Norbert Dierks, Dave Dingle, Peter Doggett, Glen Dundas, Tim Dunn, Michelle Engert, Susan Fino, Erik Flannigan, Roger Ford, Raymond Foye, Rob Fraboni, Geoff Gans, Terry Gans, Sandy Gant, Bruce Gary, Simon Gee, Roger Gibbons, Ellen Gilbert, Allen Ginsberg, John Green, Dennis Grice, Larry Hansen, John Hinchey, Nick Hill, Chris Hockenhull, Pete Howard, Rick Howell, Patrick Humphries, Ira Ingber, Markus Innocenti, Anthea Joseph, Steve Keene, Ken Kieran, Robby King, Al Kooper, Reid Kopel, Glen Korman, Harvey Kornhaber, Michael Krogsgaard, Russ Kunkel, John Lattanzio, Val Lawlan, Mick Lawson, Tony Legge, Spencer Leigh, Richard Lewis, Dennis Liff, John Lindley, Jorgen Lindstrom, Shelly Livson, Rod MacBeath, Greil Marcus, Elliott Mazer, Faridi McFree, Barry Miles, Blair Miller, Colin Moore, Jonathan Morley, Andy Muir, Harald Muller, John Owen, Bill Pagel, Freddie Patterson, Stephen Pickering, Scarlet Rivera, Arthur Rosato, Pete Seeger, Rani Singh, Wes Stace, Brian Stibal, Rob Stoner, Bob Strano, Dave Tulsky, Robert Van Estrick, Jacques Van Son, Peter Vincent, John Way, George Webber, A.J. Weberman, Brian Wells, Rob Whitehouse, Roy Whittaker, Paul Williams, Markus Wittman, Craig Wood, Ian Woodward, Howie Wyeth, Shane Youl.

Cheers.

CLINTON HEYLIN

Photo credits: Every effort has been made to trace the copyright holders of the photographs in this book but one or two were unreachable. We would be grateful if the photographers concerned would contact us.

Copyright © 1996 by Clinton Heylin

Book designed by Robert Carangelo

Schirmer Books
An Imprint of Simon & Schuster Macmillan
1633 Broadway
New York, NY 10019

Library of Congress Catalog Card Number: 96-16748

Printed in the United States of America

Printing Number
1 2 3 4 5 6 7 8 9 10

Library of Congress Cataloging-in-Publication Data

Heylin, Clinton.
    Bob Dylan : a life in stolen moments : day by day. 1941-1995 Clinton Heylin.
    p. cm.
    Includes bibliographical references and index.
    ISBN 0-02-864676-2 (hardcover : alk paper)
    1. Dylan, Bob, 1941- --Chronology 2. Singers--United States--Biography. I. Title
ML420.D98H48   1996   96-16748
782.42162'0092--dc20   CIP
[B]   MN

This paper meets the requirements of ANSI/NISO Z39.48-1992 (Permanence of Paper).

Contents

Introduction

"do not create anything/it will be misinterpreted."
—Bob Dylan (1964)

ithin thy grubby mitts is the first of a series of reference books about major popular music artists of the last 30 years. This volume deals specifically with the most prolific figure from the first 25 years of "rock" music, because this "tome" is about the career of Bob Dylan. And about Dylan it is, just about every documented Dylan concert, recording session, interview, rehearsal, personal appearance, publication, release, or composition should be found documented within, for this claims to be the Ultimate Bob Dylan Reference Guide. The core of the book is fact, although not without the odd irreverent opinion, prejudice, or comment thrown in for good measure.

The book is designed to bring together in one reference volume as much factually accurate information about Dylan's career as current research allows; although hard facts do sometimes have to give way to logical supposition. Nevertheless, everything here should "fit"; making sense in its attributed date. Indeed, I hope that at the end some worthwhile picture of Dylan's career does emerge, not to say the sheer scale of his many achievements. Of course there is undoubtedly some information here that is trivial, but I have not deemed it my role to decide for the reader which information about Dylan's activities should be excluded."

from the original introduction to *Bob Dylan: Stolen Moments* (1988)

Well, it's back to the starting point. *Stolen Moments,* the original version of the "tome" now within thy grubby mitts, was my first book proper (a few home-brewed pamphlets notwithstanding). Written in 1987, published in 1988, just as Dylan embarked on his ongoing Never Ending Tour (700 gigs-plus and still going strong), *Stolen Moments* did not, of course, presage a whole "series of reference books about major popular music artists" (the grandiose scheme of my original small-time publisher, who never even ended up publishing my effort), but it did spur me on to complete my own Dylan biography, *Behind the Shades,* and generally trying to make a go of being a rock historian of the non-igneous variety.

Stolen Moments was only ever published in the UK, in a single print run of 3,200 copies, and, despite the assurances of its original publisher, was never even copy-edited. Yet it got widely reviewed (even getting an enthusiastic half-page review in Australian *Rolling Stone*) and, in the interim, has become my most requested book (I even found bootleg copies on sale at a Pasadena swap-meet in 1991). I always promised that, one day, I would revise the damn thing (typos and all) and bring it bang up-to-date (at one point Random House even gave me $7,000 to do so, and then said keep the money, we've changed our minds). But the ol' codger just kept gigging, and no suitable opportunity ever seemed to arise.

Until 1995 when, between books (so to speak), I agreed to add a Dylan volume to St. Martin's's *Recording Sessions* series. Inevitably, in the process of unearthing not quite the motherload but certainly a shitload of good info about Mr. D. in the studio, I dug up a lot of ancillary stuff, ideal for a chronology, irrelevant to *Bob Dylan: The Recording Sessions 1960–1994*. I went back to my antiquated but uncorrupted 3-inch computer disk to see where *Stolen Moments* Mk stood. 2. May 1991, to be precise. Since I was already in Dylan mode, I mentioned the idea of a resurrected *Dylan Day by Day* to Schirmer and voila, eight years down the road of false starts and stopovers, the first and final volume in my very own Dylan trilogy, a no-dancing, all-singing *Bob Dylan: A Life in Stolen Moments*.

As a scholar who prides himself on getting things right, I am kinda embarrassed to admit how much information from *Stolen Moments* I have had to correct for this new edition. Inevitably, the studio information in the original book was more than a little off-kilter at times. But then, with new tapes and new info still emerging out of the ether, many a theory, measured and considered, has crumbled. In my biography, I poured a little scorn on Robert Shelton for suggesting that Dylan's first meeting with folksinger Cynthia Gooding was in the fall of 1959. (How could an experienced folkie like Ms. Gooding be impressed by the callow youth of 1959?) One year later, though, Murphy kicked in my door, laughed in my face, and dropped a tape on the mat: a March 1962 radio show compered by a gushing Gooding, in which she talks about first meeting Dylan in 1959 and "at that time you were thinking of being a rock & roll singer." Mea culpa.

Ditto the legendary "Royal Albert Hall 1966" tape, which for years has been misattributed, misdated, and misassigned. So it really is Manchester, all eight tracks. I even found out how, and how early, the error occurred. I saw that original three-track box, on which some doubtless-ignorant Cockney had written "Royal Albert Hall 17th May, 1966." No town: just "Royal Albert Hall," as if every town in England has its own Albert Hall. The date, though, was Manchester and the venue that night was the Free Trade Hall, home of the world-famous Halle Orchestra. (A similar error occurs on *Biograph* where the live "I Don't Believe You" is assigned to May 6, 1966, as stated on the original tape box, although the sheet also suggests more plausibly that the venue is Dublin, which was May 5, 1966.)

Of course, if Dylan scholars had the decency to let the man see his coffin coming before starting their own digging, perhaps a lot more information would be to hand. But by then perhaps as much will have been lost, mislaid, or buried 'neath a mountain of papers. Certainly at least one esteemed Dylan expert of not-so-tender years seems determined to await Dylan's demise before publishing his own research into the man's early gigs. And there is no guarantee that Dylan's people will become any more forthcoming once his work is at an end. Perhaps the Mr. Rosens of this world will continue to see themselves as the guardians of the man's work, the overseers of all legitimate Dylan output (a terrifying thought), continuing to decide who may or may not peek beyond the portals, as if it is up to them (or even Dylan himself) to decide who may, or may not, be his most fastidious chronicler(s).

No matter. Personally, I'm a firm believer in letting the documentation begin. But then, I'm documenting the man's career/life for myself (and other fans), not trying to keep Mr. Dylan (or his cronies) sweet. I raise this point because clearly there are several so-called authorities whose primary concerns are not upsetting Dylan (and friends), providing scoops for their fanzines, and not checking and corroborating their work with other recognized authorities, i.e., generally behaving like groupies, not academics. Equally there are plenty of people who would pour scorn on the notion of treating a mass-media artist like Dylan with the same academic methodology as the existing canon of non-oral literary artists. For them I reserve as much time as they doubtless donate to understanding Dylan.

Even those who would admit the man's importance often feel more than a little intimidated by the sheer scale of his output. Rather than admit to their own sense of inadequacy and deal with it (preferably in therapy, not in the *Village Voice*), these most dangerous of sloppy writers can't resist the subtle sleight at "obsessive factoids . . . performing major factual operations . . . to set things righter or straighter for others who would have them so." The implication is that their own ineptitude and general lack of inclination to get the facts of Dylan's career straight is nothing but a realization that such fact-hunting is trivial and reveals nothing of importance. "Only Dylan's official product is worth examining," cries the critic who only owns a few official albums; "Dylan's interviews are invariably a stream of put-ons and reveal nothing about his art," proclaims the writer who has neither the wish nor the wit to track down Dylan's 200-odd interviews. This lack of serious scholarship undermines many a worthwhile theory expounded by would-be authorities. I am not suggesting that getting the date right for Dylan's first attempt to record the *Desire* songs in the studio is the be-all and end-all of understanding his art. I leave it to the reader to decide the significance of the bric-a-brac of information within *Bob Dylan: A Life in Stolen Moments*. But nudging that bit closer to getting the facts straight before the man finally passes from view might just allow the analysis of this huge body of performance-literature to be a little more measured than the state of current Dylan scholarship (with certain notable exceptions) might suggest. (And if analysis is what you're looking for, there's always *Dylan Behind the Shades* and/or *Bob Dylan: The Recording Sessions*.) So feel no shame wallowing in the overload of data within. May it be just grist for thy own mill.

CLINTON HEYLIN
OCTOBER 1995

Prehistory
1902-1959

1902

Fall
Benjamin Harold Edelstein, his wife Lyba, and their children travel from Lithuania to North Hibbing, MN. Their eldest daughter, Florence, will be Bob Dylan's grandmother.

1907

Zigmar Zimmerman, having traveled from Odessa in Russia to Duluth, MN, sends for his wife, Amy, and their two children.

1911

October 19
Amy Zimmerman gives birth to her sixth child, Abraham H. Zimmerman.

1915

The erstwhile Florence Edelstein, now wife of Ben Stone, gives birth to Beatrice, third of their four children.

1934

June 10
Abraham H. Zimmerman and Beatrice Stone are married in Duluth.

1940

October 31 to November 1
Shirley Noznisky is born. She later changes her name to Sara Lowndes.

1941

May 24
At 9:05 PM a son, Robert Allen, is born to Beatty and Abraham Zimmerman, at Saint Mary's Hospital, Duluth.

1946

February
The birth of David Zimmerman, the younger brother of Robert Zimmerman.

May
Robert gives his first public performance, singing "Some Sunday Morning" and "Accentuate the Positive," on Mother's Day. He repeats the performance at an aunt's wedding two weeks later.

1947

The Zimmerman family moves from Duluth to Hibbing.

1948

The Zimmermans move into 2425 7th Ave., Hibbing.

1951

May 13
Robert gives his mother, Beatty, a poem for Mother's Day.

June 17
Robert gives his father, Abraham, a poem for Father's Day.

1952–1954

A poem purporting to be by a teenage Robert Zimmerman is later published in issue 44 of the Dylan fanzine *Isis*. Entitled "The Drunkard's Son," the curious thing about the poem (one that may suggest another hand at work) is that it is very self-consciously modeled on the structure of a million traditional ballads. Containing lines like, "I'm hiding with Jesus/who I'll always be by," it certainly reads like the work of a juvenile.

1953

January 1: The death of Hank Williams, Bob Dylan's first important musical influence.

Robert Zimmerman begins to play the family piano, on which his brother is already taking lessons.

Summer
Robert spends the first of five summer holidays at Camp Herzl in Wisconsin. There he befriends Louis Kemp, later organizer of the Rolling Thunder Revues, and Judy Rubin, an early girlfriend.

1954

May 22
The bar mitzvah of Robert Allen Zimmerman. Dylan would later say that the rabbi who conducted his bar mitzvah used to teach him his lines upstairs from a "rock & roll cafe."

Fall
Robert discovers the music of Hank Williams, his first idol.

1955

Fall
Zimmerman starts playing (presumably on piano) with a high school band consisting of Chuck Nara, Tony Connors, Bill Marinac, Larry Fabro, and John Shepard.

1956

Zimmerman gets his first motorcycle, a Harley Davidson 74.

ROW 1: John Milinovich, Mike Minelli, Bob Zimmerman, Frank Sherman. ROW 2: Pat Lamprecht, Carole Del Grande, Marsha Banen, Verlene Carpenter, Bonnie Schoenig, Sally Jolowsky, Carol Tappero, Mary Jane Svigel. ROW 3: Pierina Maracchini, Helen Taylor, Colleen Schulz, Barbara Rostvold, Barbara Satovich, Darlene Solinger, Jean Wright, Donna Urbia, Pat Baumgardner.

High School Yearbook, 1955

or their great treasure

Shirley Zubich

Members of †
who are not †

Janice Ander
Louis Barker
Russell Bergs
James Brekke
Richard Eric
William Este
Lawrence Fu
Arthur

Barbara Yeshe
Diane Zezel

Robert Zimmerman
Betsy Zozgornik

High School Yearbook, 1955

Summer to Fall
Robert Zimmerman, Chuck Nara, Bill Marinac, and Larry Fabro start rehearsing together, intending to audition for College Capers, a talent contest put on by Hibbing Junior College. The band is called The Shadow Blasters, and their one and only performance is loud and largely incomprehensible but shocking nonetheless for being full-blown rock & roll. Needless to say, the audition is unsuccessful.

Fall
Zimmerman forms his second band, The Golden Chords, with Le Roy Hoikkala and Monte Edwardson. Their set includes Johnny and Jack's "I'll Be Home."

1957

Winter
The Golden Chords make their debut at a talent show intended to select who would play at the high school Jacket Jamboree Talent Festival. Playing to a crowd of 1,500 pupils and parents, the performance shocks the parents, although fellow pupils apparently respond positively.

Spring (1957) to Winter (1958)
The Golden Chords begin to play regularly in Hibbing at a small snack bar, Van Feldt's, and at a barbecue joint called Colliers on Sunday afternoons. Although the performances are more jam sessions than concerts, teenagers come to watch the band at both venues.

Summer

Zimmerman and his friend John Bucklen start to regularly visit disc jockey Jim Dandy in Virginia, MN. He introduces the two teenagers to many of the black roots of rock & roll.

October

Zimmerman meets Echo Helstrom, his first regular girlfriend, who is later credited as one of the inspirations for "Girl from the North Country." The two of them discover they have a mutual interest in rhythm & blues.

1958

February 14

The Golden Chords play the Winter Frolic Talent Contest in the Little Theater in Hibbing's Memorial Building. Playing to a largely teenage audience of 250, the Chords apparently receive by far the best response of all the acts, but are awarded second place by an adult jury less-enamored with the idea of a rock & roll band. The Golden Chords break up shortly after this.

1956–1959

According to his music teacher, Zimmerman often performed solo at school shows.

• In 1986, Dylan said that during this period he was in a band with Bill Marinac, Chuck Nara, and Monte Edwardson. Possibly Dylan has confused the members of the Golden Chords with those of the Shadow Blasters.

[1956]–1958

Robert Zimmerman and his friend John Bucklen make at least a couple of home tapes at this time on an old wire recorder. Fragments of four songs appeared in a BBC documentary about *Highway 61,* one seemingly original ("Hey, Little Richard"), the others being the Hollywood Flames's "Buzz, Buzz, Buzz," Little Richard's "Jenny, Jenny" (both with Bucklen sharing vocals), and "Blue Moon," presumably learned from Elvis's version.

High School Yearbook, 1957

1958

Spring
Zimmerman has his first motorcycle accident when a three-year-old child runs out from between two parked cars. Although the child is all right, Zimmerman clearly is badly shaken by the incident.

Summer
According to comments Dylan made in 1986, one of his bands formed in Hibbing is called Elston Gunn and the Rock Boppers, although no more details of this band are known. Elston Gunn appears to have been Zimmerman's first alias.

• Zimmerman starts making regular trips to St. Paul and Minneapolis, sometimes alone, sometimes with his friends from Hibbing and Camp Herzl.

Fall
Echo Helstrom breaks up with "Bob," angry at his constant weekend trips to Minneapolis, alone on his motorcycle. Robert Zimmerman joins a band called the Satin Tones; apparently his cousin recruited him. I assume that it is with this band that Zimmerman plays the St. Louis County Fair in Hibbing. The band clearly enjoys some local success; playing a concert at the relatively prestigious Hibbing Armory, and recording a session for a local radio station.

Fall (1958) to Winter (1959)
On his regular sojourns to Minneapolis, Zimmerman starts to hang around the Ten O'Clock Scholar coffeehouse on the university campus.

1959

January 31
Buddy Holly plays the Duluth Armory three days before his death. A 17-year-old Robert Zimmerman is in the audience.

Winter
Zimmerman and Bill Marinac jam together on miscellaneous folk material. According to Marinac, Zimmerman has "started dabbling in folk [music] very seriously."

June 5
Robert Zimmerman graduates from Hibbing High School.

June
It would appear that Zimmerman left the Satin Tones at this point. According to Bobby Vee, Zimmerman was working as a busboy at the Red Apple Cafe in Fargo when he was recruited to play piano with Vee's band. Zimmerman only lasts a couple of gigs before Vee concludes that they do not really need a pianist. Zimmerman had apparently requested that his stage name be Elston Gunn.

Summer

At some point in the summer of 1958 or (more likely) 1959, Robert Zimmerman was sent by his parents to Deveraux, a boarding school in Pennsylvania. He seems to have only been there a few weeks, although the school's strict regime may well have later inspired his 1963 composition, "Walls of Red Wing."

September 29

Having secured a place at the University of Minneapolis, Zimmerman moves into a Jewish fraternity house, Sigma Alpha Mu.

October

Robert Zimmerman, so legend has it, walks into a Minneapolis coffeehouse, the Ten O'Clock Scholar, and asks the owner if he can play there. He announces his wish to be a folksinger. When asked his name, he replies, "Bob Dylan." According to the owner, David Lee, his early repertoire included folk songs like "Sinner Man," "St. James Infirmary," "Golden Vanity," and the occasional Carter Family song.

October (1959) to May (1960)

Dylan performs regularly at the Ten O'Clock Scholar before making the mistake of asking for a pay increase.

Fall

Dylan meets folksinger Cynthia Gooding in Minneapolis. He informs her he wants to be a rock & roll singer, although, according to Gooding, he is performing Johnny Cash songs at the time.

Mid- to Late December

Dylan remains in Minneapolis for some of the Christmas vacation, pining for girlfriend Judy Rubin. When he returns to Hibbing, he informs John Bucklen that he is a folksinger now, and plays him a series of songs he has learned from Odetta albums.

1960

Winter
Dylan leaves Sigma Alpha Mu and moves to a communal flat above Gray's
Drugstore on 7th Street Southeast. He stops using the name Zimmerman al-
together.

January (?)
Dylan starts to perform regularly at the Purple Onion Pizza Parlor in St.
Paul. [According to Terri Wallace this did not occur until Spring 1960.]

February
Dylan performs regularly with "Spider" John Koerner at the Ten O'Clock
Scholar. Their sets include songs like "They Called the Wind Maria." Dylan
begins to spend a lot of time with a local girl, Gretel Hoffman. Hoffman
furthers his education in folk music and the beatnik way of life.

> *Guitarist/vocalist "Spider" John Koerner became a leading blues
> revivalist in the mid-'60s, often performing with harmonica player,
> "Tony" Glover (see May 1960).*

Mid-March
Gretel Hoffman and Dylan attend a party in St. Paul, where they meet Dave
Whitaker. Dylan and Whitaker quickly become friends, and Hoffman mar-
ries Whitaker.

May
Dylan meets Dave "Tony" Glover at a party at the Whitakers.
  • One night, after he had played at the Purple Onion Pizza Parlor, Dylan
makes his first "extant" recording as Bob Dylan, in the apartment of Karen
Wallace in St. Paul. The recording shows a singer whose voice resembles
more the country twang of Hank Williams than the harsh nasal sound of
Woody Guthrie. The 27 songs are apparently recorded one song at a time,
being a mixture of obvious folk classics and more obscure traditional material. Only one or two of the performances hint at latent promise.
    After opening with Paul Clayton's "Gotta Travel On," a song Dylan has
returned to on a couple of occasions, he performs "Rovin' Gambler," Ewan
MacColl's "Go Down You Murderers," a regular feature of his act at the time,
the traditional "Bay of Mexico," the Child ballad "The Twa Sisters" (hint-

ing at Dylan's later approach to phrasing), John Jacob Niles's "Go 'Way From My Window," Guthrie's "This Land Is Your Land," the old spiritual "Go Tell It On The Mountain," "Fare Thee Well," Guthrie's "Pastures of Plenty," the traditional "Rock a Bye My Saro Jane," "Take This Hammer," "Nobody Loves You When You're Down and Out," Guthrie's "The Great Historical Bum," "Mary Ann," "Every Night When the Sun Goes In," "Sinner Man" (a particular favorite of Karen's sister, Terri), "Delia" (presumably either Blind Willie McTell's song of the same name or Blind Blake's "Delia's Gone"), a Yiddish folksong "Wop Da Alano," the folk perennial "Who's Gonna Shoe Your Pretty Little Feet," "Abner Young" (the source of which is unknown, although it includes a line about "falling in the world, boys and girls all skating"), "900 Miles," and "Muleskinner Blues."

At this point Dylan sings his earliest known composition, "One Eyed Jacks," before completing the tape with Guthrie's "Columbus Stockade Blues," and an incomplete version of the traditional "Payday at Coal Creek." The tape displays a folksinger with only a most rudimentary technique on guitar (and no harmonica). Karen Wallace (now Moynihan) has not seen fit to release the full tape. Incomplete circulating copies suggest little intrinsic aesthetic merit, even if the tape has undoubted historical importance.

> *Paul Clayton was a folk song revivalist who is best-known for his song "Gotta Travel On," a hit in the early '60s for Peter, Paul, and Mary, among others.*
>
> *Ewan MacColl was a British folksinger/songwriter popular in the '60s; his wife was Peggy Seeger.*
>
> *John Jacob Niles was an early folk-revivalist, popular in the late '40s, who played Appalachian dulcimer and sang in a high, falsetto voice. He popularized and reworked many traditional folk ballads.*
>
> *Blind Willie McTell and Blind Blake were both blues performers of the '20s who recorded extensively.*

May to Early Summer

Having quit playing the Ten O'Clock Scholar, Dylan begins to appear regularly at the Purple Onion and The Bastille, St. Paul. His set at this time includes the likes of "Go Down You Murderers," "Sinner Man," "House of the Rising Sun," "Timber," "Jerry," "Another Man Done Gone," "1913 Massacre," "San Francisco Bay Blues," "Columbus Stockade," "Omie Wise," "Car, Car," "I'm Gonna Sit at the Welcome Table," "I Thought I Heard That Casey When She Roll," "Blackjack Blues," and "Man of Constant Sorrow." He also starts to write his own compositions, which include "Greyhound Blues," and an adaptation of "Every Time I Hear The Spirit." Dave Whitaker refers to another composition written at this time, "Bob Dylan's Blues," although this may well have been an alternate title for "One Eyed Jacks."

Summer

Dylan travels to Denver, where he has been told to look up Walt Conley, a folksinger who performs at a local club called The Satire. He asks if he can play a couple of songs, although he is not well-received. However, Conley puts him up until he secures a gig playing piano in a strip joint called The Gilded Garter, in Central City, CO, where according to the man himself he played "Muleskinner Blues" between strip acts. During his time in Central City, Dylan lives with one of the strippers, making regular trips into Denver to hang out at the Exodus, where he meets Judy Collins, then a local talent on the Denver folk scene, Kevin Krown, and blues performer Jesse Fuller, who is playing there. Dylan is much impressed by the way Fuller uses a harmonica rack. However, Dylan is not well known enough to play the Exodus himself. He leaves Denver after an incident involving the theft of some of Conley's and Dave Hamil's record collection, returning to Minneapolis.

Early September

David Whitaker suggests that Dylan read Woody Guthrie's autobiography, *Bound for Glory.* Dylan eagerly devours the contents of the entire book, apparently carrying it around for weeks afterward, stopping people he knows in the street to read passages from it. The book temporarily focuses Dylan's search for identity on Woody Guthrie.

Mid-September

Dylan meets Ellen Baker, whose father has an extensive collection of both records and printed matter related to folk music. He visits their house a couple of days later. One song he discovers there, "These Brown Eyes" by Woody Guthrie and Cisco Houston, he plays over and over again. Dylan continues to visit the Bakers for the remainder of his stay in Minneapolis.

September

Bonnie Beecher records the earliest of several Minneapolis Dylan home recordings at his house on 15th Ave South. Primitively recorded, the tape features voice and guitar (no harmonica, suggesting it dates from shortly after his return from Denver). Dylan has begun to adopt Guthrie as his guru and to take on Guthrie's inflections in his singing. The half-hour tape features four songs in the talkin' blues genre popularized by Guthrie: Woody's "Talkin' Columbia" and "Talkin' Merchant Marine," as well as "Talkin' Inflation Blues," and an improvised song for/about Dylan's roommate, "Talkin' Hugh Brown." Also recorded, aside from Guthrie's "Jesus Christ," are the traditional "Streets of Glory," "Muleskinner Blues," "Red Rosey Bush," "Johnny I Hardly Knew You," "I'm a Gambler," and the Memphis Jug Band's "K.C. Moan."

Fall

Dylan meets Odetta, a key influence at this time, who convinces him that he has real potential as a folksinger.

Odetta was a popular folksinger of the late '50s and early '60s who recorded and performed extensively. Her vocal style showed hints of classical training, and her guitar accompaniments were fairly simple, on a selection of traditional folk and blues number.

Dylan participates in a jam session with "Spider" John Koerner and Rolf Cahn at the Ten O'Clock Scholar one evening.

• Dylan continues to perform at the Purple Onion and The Bastille, St. Paul. Some of the shows at the Purple Onion are with Cynthia Fincher, a banjo player and banker's daughter (who can be heard in the background on the September 1960 Minneapolis tape). Dylan also plays several gigs with Tony Glover accompanying on harmonica. Throughout the fall Dylan develops his harmonica skills, having started playing the instrument in earnest on his return from Denver.

• Dylan again jams with Bill Marinac in Minneapolis. He is now playing with guitar and harmonica, and, according to Marinac, has "started to write some music."

Early to Mid-December
According to his uncle, Dylan returned to Hibbing at this point to inform his parents that he was going to New York.

Mid- to Late December
Dylan leaves Minneapolis and heads straight for Chicago, where he tracks down Kevin Krown (Krown had invited Dylan to "look him up" when they had met in Denver that summer). Dylan shows up just before Christmas (possibly around the 21st), staying a couple of weeks, crashing on people's floors.

Late December
Dylan plays coffeehouses, dorms, and student parties in Chicago, generally hanging out with the folk crowd. One night he plays a sorority house at the University of Chicago. His set apparently consists entirely of Guthrie songs. While in Chicago, Dylan later related, he spent one night in the company of a 60-year-old, red-haired woman.

1961

Early January
Dylan stops over in Madison, WI, uncertain of which direction to take. He stays with Marshall Brickman and Eric Weissberg, and plays harmonica with Danny Kalb at a coffeehouse, before finally securing a ride to New York with a guy called Dave Berger. According to Berger, Dylan insisted on singing and playing all the way to New Jersey, until Berger finally told him to, "Shut the fuck up."

> *Brickman and Weissberg later moved to New York and played in a variety of folk revival groups. They are most famous for recording "Dueling Banjos," used as the theme for the film Deliverance. Kalb was a blues guitarist who later formed the blues-rock band The Blues Project.*

January 24
Dylan arrives in a snowbound New York, accompanied by his friend Fred Underhill. He heads for the Cafe Wha. It is a hootenanny night, and he performs a couple of songs. The Wha's owner, Manny Roth, asks the audience to provide them with a place to stay for the night.

January 25
Dylan travels out to Greystone Hospital in New Jersey to meet the ailing Woody Guthrie, crippled by the hereditary disease, Huntingdon's Chorea.

January 26
Probably the day when Dylan first called on Bob and "Sid" Gleason in East Orange, NJ. Woody Guthrie is allowed to stay with the Gleasons on weekends. Dylan presumably attempts to secure an invitation to the following Sunday's gathering.

Late January (27?)
Dylan visits Guthrie's family in Howard Beach. Guthrie's wife, Marjorie, is not there but Dylan manages to coax his way in and proceeds to teach young Arlo some harmonica tricks.

Late January

Dylan sends a card to the Whitakers in Minneapolis, telling them that he has actually met Guthrie.

January 29

Dylan performs at Izzy Young's Folklore Center. According to *Village Voice* journalist J. R. Goddard, he sang "Muleskinner Blues." He then heads out to Bob and Sid Gleason's home in New Jersey to spend the weekend with Woody Guthrie and some of his friends. The Gleason home provides a focal point on weekends for those in the New York scene still drawn to the Guthrie tradition.

> *From the late '50s through the mid-'70s, Israel G. "Izzy" Young ran New York's Folklore Center, a tiny shop that sold folk records and supplies, and also served as a concert promoter and general gadfly on the folk scene.*

February to December

Dylan continues to visit Guthrie at Greystone Hospital on a weekly basis. He occasionally takes friends along, although Guthrie's condition only tends to depress them. On one occasion he takes Bonnie Beecher, and Guthrie attempts to play "Hard Travelin'" for her.

February 1961

Dylan is performing at The Commons (later renamed the Fat Black Pussycat), the Cafe Wha, and The Gaslight.

February 1961

Dylan is taped on Bob and Sid Gleason's recording machine at their East Orange home, apparently while singing to their young daughter Kathy. This is a very different singer from the one heard performing on the 1960 Minneapolis recordings. The whole performance has power, the first Dylan recording to suggest real potential. Also for the first time on tape he plays a chugging harmonica. The tape begins with "San Francisco Bay Blues" and "Jesus Met a Woman at the Well" before he slips into Guthrie mode with "Gypsy Davey," "Pastures of Plenty," "Trail of the Buffalo," and "Jesse James." After toying briefly with the notion of singing "Southern Cannonball," he wraps up the set with a delightful plaintive ballad, "Remember Me (When the Candlelights Are Gleaming)," hinting at some strong "country" influences.

February to March

Dylan starts to supplement his meager solo work by accompanying the likes of Fred Neil, Mark Spoelstra, Ramblin' Jack Elliott, and Dave Van Ronk on harmonica. At the same time he expands the venues he is able to play. The Mill's Tavern, the Limelight, the Lion's Head, and Art D'Lugoff's Village Gate all provide him with "a dollar a day."

> *Fred Neil was a folk revivalist best known later in his career for the song "Everybody's Talkin'."*
>
> *Mark Spolestra was a blues revivalist, as was Dave Van Ronk, one of the most influential and successful of the Greenwich Village folksingers. Van Ronk was the elder statesmen of the Village folkies, the oldest and most successful of the bunch, and served as an early mentor for Bob.*
>
> *Van Ronk's then-wife, Terri Thal, managed many folk acts, including Dylan in the early days (see May to September 1961).*
>
> *Ramblin' Jack Elliott was a Brooklyn-born folk revivalist who emulated the sound and style of Woody Guthrie. He dressed and spoke as if he was raised in the wild west.*

February 6 (possibly January 30)
Dylan turns up at Gerdes Folk City on hootenanny night and asks owner Mike Porco if he can play. Porco, thinking he looks too young, asks him to return the following week with proof of age.

February 12
Dylan sends a second postcard to the Whitakers. In it he states that he visits Guthrie four times a week and that he has been playing The Commons "where people clap for me."

February 13
Dylan turns up at Gerdes Folk City with his birth certificate and gets to play. It is very likely that he now starts to play every Monday night at the Gerdes hootenannies, until Porco finally books him for a paying gig.

February 14
Dylan composes his first major composition, "Song to Woody," this Tuesday. He subsequently gives the Gleasons the dated, handwritten manuscript.

February 20
Gerdes Folk City, hootenanny night.

Late February
Dylan attends a concert by Ramblin' Jack Elliott at Carnegie Recital Hall. Afterward, he heads downtown to see Cisco Houston give his last performance at Gerdes Folk City. Houston then returns to California, where he dies on April 29. Dylan later claimed that he had the opportunity to play with Cisco at a "party or something."

> *Cisco Houston frequently performed with Woody Guthrie in the late '40s and early '50s before embarking on a career on his own. He died of cancer in 1961.*

February 27, Gerdes Folk City, hootenanny night

March 6, Gerdes Folk City, hootenanny night

March 13, Gerdes Folk City, hootenanny night

March 20, Gerdes Folk City, hootenanny night

March 27, Gerdes Folk City, hootenanny night
This is probably the night that Porco offered to book Dylan as a supporting act to John Lee Hooker. He is understandably elated. From this point, Dylan becomes a less regular fixture at the Folk City hootenannies, although he would continue to make regular appearances until the spring of 1963.

John Lee Hooker is a blues guitarist/singer whose career was revived in the early '60s. He performed on acoustic guitar at this point, although later he returned to playing electrified instruments.

April 3
Mike Porco takes Dylan down to get his union card, advancing him the $46 necessary to "pay his dues," and even signing as his guardian. Presumably Dylan shows up that evening for the weekly Folk City "hoot."

April 4–10
John Lee Hooker starts his residency at Gerdes Folk City. Dylan turns up every night to listen and watch, awaiting the start of his own supporting slot the following week.

April 5
Dylan plays his first paid concert, at the Loeb Music Center for the New York University Folk Society. He is paid the sum of $20. In the audience is a young Suze Rotolo, soon to be his girlfriend.

April 9
The entire Greenwich Village community demonstrates in Washington Square against local attempts to ban their Sunday afternoon gatherings, including impromptu music sessions. Dylan participates and subsequently writes a song about the event, called "Down At Washington Square."

April 11
The first night of a two-week stint supporting John Lee Hooker at Gerdes Folk City. Dylan is extremely nervous but performs his five songs creditably. His set includes "Song to Woody" and Dave Van Ronk's arrangement of "House of the Rising Sun," taught to Dylan by Van Ronk himself.

April 12–23 (except the 17th)
Dylan continues his stint supporting John Lee Hooker at Gerdes Folk City. By the end of the two weeks he is bored with the rigors of a regular nightly gig and decides to leave New York for a respite.

Gerdes flyer, 1961

Early May

Dylan goes to the Folkways office to try to get a recording contract with them. They are less than interested. Unperturbed, Dylan approaches the folk labels Vanguard and Elektra, again without result.

> *Folkways Records was the largest folk label in the country at the time. Moses Asch, the label's infamously difficult founder, made the mistake of rejecting Dylan on sight; ironically, Asch later issued Dylan's recordings made for* Broadside *magazine (see February 1962). Dylan was credited as "Blind Boy Grunt" on these albums, probably to avoid the wrath of Columbia (although no one could have possibly been fooled by this stunt).*

• Dylan writes "Talkin' New York," a sardonic view of his first three months in the Big City, jotting down the words as he hitchhikes on the New Jersey Turnpike.

May 6, Indian Neck Folk Festival, Montowesi Hotel, Branford, CT

Dylan performs three Guthrie originals, "Talkin' Columbia," "Slipknot," and "Talkin' Fisherman." He also gets the opportunity to jam with Bobby Neuwirth (whom he meets here for the first time), Mark Spoelstra, Jim Kweskin, and Robert L. Jones on several "obscure Woody Guthrie and Hank Williams songs." There is a party in the evening, which he attends.

Jim Kweskin was a popular performer in the Boston folk scene, playing music of the '20s and '30s; he later formed his Jug Band, a group that included Geoff and Maria (d'Amato) Muldaur.

Mid-May

On returning to Minneapolis, Dylan is anxious to play for his old friends. At least two informal sessions at Bonnie Beecher's apartment are recorded by Tony Glover. The 25 songs thus recorded constitute the so-called "Minneapolis Party Tape." The first session appears to consist of "Ramblin' Blues," "Death Don't Have No Mercy," "It's Hard to Be Blind," "This Train," an extemporized harmonica solo, "Talkin' Fish Blues," and "Pastures of Plenty." The second part/session (which sounds marginally superior sonically) includes "This Land Is Your Land," "Two Trains Runnin," "Wild Mountain Thyme," "Howdido," "Car, Car," "Don't You Push Me Down," "Come See," "I Want My Milk," "San Francisco Bay Blues," "Lang a Growin'," "Dev'lish Mary," "Railroad Bill," "Will the Circle Be Unbroken," "Man of Constant Sorrow," "Pretty Polly," "Railroad Boy," "James Alley Blues," and "Bonnie, Why'd You Cut My Hair," a whimsical original written in response to a particularly devastating haircut administered by Bonnie the previous year.

• Contemporaries have referred to Dylan playing a concert at Kaufman Union on his return to Minneapolis. This may refer to either the May or the December visit. (Dylan certainly played at the university in December.)

May to September

There are several accounts of Dylan demo recordings from his early months in New York. According to Dylan biographer Robert Shelton, Terri Thal, Van Ronk's then-girlfriend and Dylan's part-time manager, took an informal demo tape with her when trying to secure bookings in Boston, Springfield, and Cambridge, MA, in May 1961. In June and July of the same year, Terri and Kevin Krown were apparently "doing the rounds" of record companies with some Dylan demos, which may well be the same as those Thal used to obtain out-of-town gigs.

• Later in the summer, Sybil Weinberger and Carla Rotolo were trying to get a demo tape together comprising half a dozen of the up-and-coming folksingers. How far the project got is unknown, although Weinberger did enthuse to John Hammond Sr. about Dylan before their first meeting. According to Bob Spitz, Thal taped one of Dylan's April Folk City shows and attempted to attract the interest of specialist "folk" labels like Prestige and

Folkways. Thal is also quoted by Spitz talking about an(other) audition tape that is self-evidently the First Gaslight Tape (see September 6, 1961). This could not have been the same tape Thal was touting around in May.

> *John Hammond, Sr., was the legendary jazz fan and record producer who "discovered" Billie Holiday, Count Basie, Benny Goodman, Aretha Franklin, Dylan, and, later, Bruce Springsteen. Dylan was nicknamed "Hammond's Folly" around the Columbia offices because the other executives felt the singer/songwriter was so incredibly bad. Only Hammond's sponsorship saved him in his early days at the label.*

June

According to Shelton, Dylan played three dates at Cambridge's prestigious Club 47 at this time. This seems very unlikely, although he is certainly in Cambridge in June, where he is introduced (by Robert L. Jones) to Eric Von Schmidt. In Von Schmidt's apartment Dylan is introduced to several songs, including two that become part of the nascent Dylan repertoire, "He Was a Friend of Mine," and "Baby Let Me Follow You Down."

> *Eric Von Schmidt was a blues revivalist guitarist/vocalist who later became a well-known painter.*

Terri Thal manages to secure Dylan a booking for two nights at Cafe Lena in Saratoga Springs, NY. The gigs are poorly attended and he is not well received. However, club owner Lena Spencer is sufficiently impressed and agrees to rebook him.

• *New York Times* music critic Robert Shelton catches Dylan for the first time at a Monday night Gerdes hootenanny. The most memorable song in his set at this point is the recently composed "Talkin' Bear Mountain Picnic Massacre Blues."

Late June to Early July

Dylan plays a week's residency at The Gaslight with Dave Van Ronk. After one set Robert Shelton introduces Dylan to Albert Grossman who, some months down the line, will become manager.

> *Albert Grossman became one of the most powerful, and notorious, managers of the late '60s; besides representing Dylan, he also handled Janis Joplin. He founded his own label and recording studio, Bearsville Records, located in Woodstock, NY (see also May 1962).*

July

Dylan plays for a Kiwanis Club meeting at the Fifth Avenue Hotel. Distracted by clowns performing while he plays, he proceeds to kick one of them "in the nuts."

July 29
Dylan is part of a 12-hour hootenanny at the Riverside Church in New York, broadcast live (in its entirety) by WRVR-FM who present it as "all that is best in contemporary folk music." He comes on stage midway through the afternoon and performs three songs, all indicative of his repertoire at the time, "Handsome Molly," "Deep Water" (aka "Omie Wise"), and "Po' Lazarus." He returns later to play harmonica for Danny Kalb on "Mean Ol' Southern Railroad," and duets with Ramblin' Jack Elliott on a spoof of teen angst pop songs "Acne (Teenager in Love)." After the hootenanny, there is a party at Anna Bird's apartment. Dylan spends most of the evening with Suze Rotolo, her sister Carla, and journalist Pete Karman, although he detaches himself long enough to provide guitar accompaniment for John Wynn, who improvises an epic satire called "The Beautiful People."

Early August
Dylan meets Carolyn Hester and Richard Farina in Boston. He spends the day on the beach with Hester, Farina, and Eric Von Schmidt. He then accompanies the trio to Club 47, where Hester is due to perform that night. During her set she takes the opportunity to invite him on stage, and he performs four or five songs, including "Talkin' Bear Mountain Picnic Massacre Blues."

Carolyn Hester was a sweet-voiced folk performer who achieved some popularity in the early '60s. Her then-husband was singer/songwriter Richard Farina, who later married Mimi Baez (Joan's sister) and recorded a series of albums with her for Vanguard, a medium-sized folk label.

August
Dylan visits Minneapolis again.

Summer
Dylan writes many songs while staying at the home of the McKenzies. Several of the manuscripts he left behind are subsequently auctioned and include half a dozen songs for which no known recording exists: "California Brown Eyed Baby," "Rocking Chair," "Colorado Blues," "Over the Road," "I'll Get Where I'm Going Someday," "Dope Fiend Robber," and "V.D. Seaman's Last Letter" as well as an embryonic version of "Talkin' New York," and a polished version of "Talkin' Bear Mountain Picnic." The manuscripts also contain versions of traditional songs, like "Mary of the Wild Moor," "I'll Be a Bachelor 'Till I Die," "Satisfied Mind," "Southern Cannonball," something called "Mississippi River Blues," and "Omie Wise," all in Dylan's hand and presumably songs he was intending to add to his repertoire. Also apparently written around the same time are four other "lost" songs,

"Big City Blues," "The Preacher's Folly," "Dead for a Dollar," and "Red Travelin' Shoes."

One of the set lists Dylan had written out at this time and left at the McKenzies contains some very unusual choices. The list reads: "The Cuckoo [Is a Pretty Bird]," "Snow White Dove" (presumably "Railroad Boy" aka "Died for Love"), "[Will the] Circle Be Unbroken," "Pretty Polly," "On My Journey Home"(?), "[Man of] Constant Sorrow," "Great Divide," "Trying to Get Home"(?), "Highway 51," "Battleship of Maine"(?), and "Lady of Carlyle."

Late Summer
Dylan plays at bluesman Brother John Sellers's birthday party at Gerdes Folk City. He performs the ever-popular "Talkin' Bear Mountain Picnic Massacre Blues" (after a long "shaggy dog story" preface), and "Song to Woody." The set is recorded by Cynthia Gooding, although the tapes appear to have been lost.

September
Carolyn Hester apparently tried to cut an album live at the Club 47 prior to her first Columbia album and Dylan was allegedly to have sat in on harmonica.

September 6
Dylan's set at the Gaslight Cafe is recorded, and subsequently appears on assorted quasi-official European albums. The six-song tape features his three strongest original compositions at the time, "Talkin' Bear Mountain Picnic Massacre Blues," "Song to Woody," and "Man on the Street," plus Dylanesque arrangements of "He Was a Friend of Mine," and "Pretty Polly" and a raucous singalong on Woody Guthrie's "Car, Car" (with Dave Van Ronk). Apparently, this tape was recorded at Terri Thal's request.

Early September
Carolyn Hester visits Dylan at Suze Rotolo's mother's apartment on Sheridan Square. He teaches her "Come Back Baby," which she decides to include on her forthcoming sessions for Columbia.

September 12
Victoria Spivey and Lonnie Johnson start a two-week residency at Gerdes Folk City. Dylan is in attendance most nights.

Victoria Spivey and Lonnie Johnson both had long and distinguished careers as blues artists, dating from the '20s. Spivey founded her own label in the early '60s, and used Dylan as a sideman on a session with Big Joe Williams (see March 2, 1962).

September 14
Dylan attends a rehearsal this afternoon at the West 10th St. apartment where Carolyn Hester and her then-husband Dick Farina are residing. The informal session has been set up to run through some of the songs Hester

intends to record for Columbia. John Hammond Sr., who is due to produce Hester, attends the afternoon run-through and is suitably intrigued by Dylan. At this point, according to Hammond, he asks Dylan if he would like to come into Columbia and cut a couple of demos.

Mid- to Late September
According to biographer Anthony Scaduto, Dylan cut some demos, one of which was "Talkin' New York," with John Hammond prior to signing with Columbia. There is no record of any such session in the CBS archives, but Hammond always insisted that he did formally "audition" Dylan.

September 24
Dylan makes a guest appearance at a concert by Paul Clayton at the Showboat Lounge in Washington, DC.

September 26
Robert Shelton reviews the opening night of another two-week residency at Gerdes Folk City for the *New York Times*. Although the Greenbriar Boys are the headliners, Shelton is wholly focused on Dylan, whose first set includes "Talkin' Bear Mountain Picnic Massacre Blues," "Talkin' New York," "Talkin' Hava Nagilah," "House of the Rising Sun," "See That My Grave Is Kept Clean," and "Black Girl (in the Pines)." After the set, Shelton interviews Dylan, who cannot resist spinning a series of increasingly fantastic tales. Shelton, though, is not put off by Dylan's verbosity and writes a highly enthusiastic review of his performance.

Late September (28?)
Folksinger Jean Redpath turns up at Miki Issacson's apartment one Thursday afternoon to find Dylan, Jack Elliott, and the Greenbriar Boys having their own private hootenanny.

September 29
Shelton's endorsement of Dylan appears in *The New York Times*. In the afternoon, Dylan attends his first session at Columbia's Studio A in New York, although in this instance he is just a harmonica player working on Carolyn Hester's first Columbia album. He contributes to three songs, "Swing and Turn Jubilee," "I'll Fly Away," and "Come Back, Baby," the latter two of which also generated alternate takes that appeared in 1994 on the CD reissue of *Carolyn Hester*.

• A nervous Dylan enters Gerdes Folk City this evening to continue his residency. In an attempt to keep himself interested, he changes his sets from night to night. Tonight his set(s) include "Ranger's Command," "San Francisco Bay Blues," and "The Great Divide" (both with Jack Elliott), "See That My Grave Is Kept Clean," "Ain't No More Cane" (prefaced with a rap about the *Times* review), "Dink's Song," "He Was a Friend of Mine," "Pretty Boy Floyd," "Black Girl (in the Pines)" (with Jim Kweskin), and "Sally Gal." According to Shelton, Dylan informed him during this evening that Hammond had offered him a contract with Columbia but asked him to keep it secret as it had yet to be ratified by the powers-that-be.

September 26 to October 8, Gerdes Folk City, NY

Two sets a night. One night the set is "Sally Gal," "Sporting Life Blues," "900 Miles," "Talkin' New York," "Dink's Song," an unknown blues song, "Hard Travelin'," "Talkin' Bear Mountain Picnic Massacre Blues," "Talkin' Hava Nagilah," and "Song to Woody." His sets at this time also often featured "Po' Lazarus," "It's Hard to Be Blind," and "Gospel Plow" (Dylan's own arrangement of the traditional "Hold On").

October 3

The famous photo of Dylan singing at Gerdes that hung in the club for many years, attributed to his April 11, 1961 show, is taken at tonight's show.

Early Fall (October?)

Dylan plays harmonica at a Harry Belafonte session. He plays on just one song, "Midnight Special," which becomes the title track of Belafonte's next album, having grown quickly exasperated at the multiple takes Belafonte tends to insist upon.

Note: There is considerable dispute as to when this session occurred, although the resultant album was released in March 1962, suggesting that the session may predate Dylan's first Columbia session.

Fall

Dylan plays a two-week residency at The Gaslight with fellow folksinger Jim Kweskin, performing two sets a night. Among the songs they perform is a duet of "San Francisco Bay Blues."

Late October (20 or 23?)

Dylan performs "Fixin' to Die" with Dave Van Ronk and John Gibson at Izzy Young's Folklore Center. A recording is made by Cynthia Gooding but appears to have been lost. The performance probably dates from one of the two days Izzy Young was interviewing Dylan at the Folklore Center.

October 20

Izzy Young conducts a written interview with Dylan intending to glean some material for a program to accompany his forthcoming Carnegie Recital Hall concert. In this first interview, Dylan spins his usual tales of living in New Mexico, Iowa, South Dakota, Kansas, and North Dakota. Between mentions of all the famous people he has met on his travels, he finds time to refer to the popularity of his adaptation of "Columbus Stockade Blues," "California Brown Eyed Baby."

October 23

During a second, longer interview with Izzy Young at the Folklore Center, Dylan discusses such esoterica as the "dead man's hand," "aces backed with eights," his thoughts on first arriving in New York, meeting Jesse Fuller in Denver, going up to Folkways Records to ask for a contract, beatniks, and flunking out of college.

October 26

Dylan officially signs with Columbia Records.

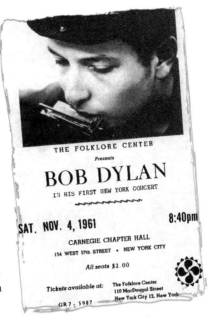

THE FOLKLORE CENTER

Presents

BOB DYLAN

IN HIS FIRST NEW YORK CONCERT

SAT. NOV. 4, 1961   **8:40pm**

CARNEGIE CHAPTER HALL
154 WEST 57th STREET • NEW YORK CITY

All seats $2.00

Tickets available at: The Folklore Center
110 MacDougal Street
New York City 12. New York
GR 7 - 5987

October 29

Dylan appears on Oscar Brand's "Folksong Festival," a weekly program on the WNYC radio station. He sings two songs, "Sally Gal" and a unique rendition of "The Girl I Left Behind," which he insists he learned firsthand from a farmer. Dylan's appearance was obviously intended to publicize the show at Carnegie Recital Hall on November 4, and was arranged by Izzy Young.

October 30

Robert Shelton, in his biography, states that there was a "run-through" session with John Hammond. If so, it was not at Columbia's Studios as there is no record of any such session in the Sony archives.

November 4

Izzy Young presents Dylan at the 200-seater Carnegie Recital Hall. The concert is judged something of a flop, with only 53 people traipsing uptown, while Dylan sounds extremely nervous and uncertain of himself. The set includes "Pretty Peggy-O," "Black Girl (in the Pines)," "Gospel Plow," "1913 Massacre," "Backwater Blues," "Young but Daily Growin'," "Fixin' to Die," and "This Land Is Your Land." A. J. Weberman also attributes a version of "Standing on the Highway" to this show, although tape collectors still await the second half of the show (only the first seven songs circulate on tape).

November 20

Dylan begins recording his first album for Columbia, with John Hammond producing, at Columbia's Studio A in New York. Despite Hammond complaining of his poor microphone technique, Dylan lays down usable versions of "You're No Good," "Fixin' to Die," "House of the Rising Sun," "Talkin' New York," "Song to Woody," "Baby Let Me Follow You Down," and "In My Time of Dyin'" at the three-hour afternoon session. He also records an introduction about a Connecticut cowboy for "You're No Good," which ends up unused, attempts an incomplete "Man of Constant Sorrow," and cuts a lovely "He Was a Friend of Mine," which eventually appears on *The Bootleg Series.* All in all, a successful start to his Columbia career.

November 22

Dylan completes his eponymous first album in just two afternoons, cutting a further nine songs this afternoon at Columbia Studio A. Of the six cuts from the 22nd that appear on *Bob Dylan,* "Freight Train Blues," "Gospel Plow," and "Highway 51 Blues" are cut in single takes, "Pretty Peggy-O" in two, "Man of Constant Sorrow" in two plus one false start, and "See That My Grave Is Kept Clean" in three plus one false start. Two of the three outtakes cut on the 22nd have now been released on *The Bootleg Series,* "Man on the Street" and an exhilarating "House Carpenter." Two complete takes of

Woody Guthrie's "Ramblin' Blues," the only Guthrie song attempted at the sessions, still remain in the vaults.

November 23

On Thanksgiving Day 1961, Dylan and his new girlfriend Suze Rotolo dine with Eve and "Mac" MacKenzie. After the Thanksgiving meal, Dylan plays for his friends, who record his performance on a reel-to-reel. The Thanksgiving tape features a new Dylan composition based on the traditional "Down on Penny's Farm," called "Hard Times in New York Town." Also apparently recorded on this day were "Wayfaring Stranger," "(I Heard That) Lonesome Whistle," "Worried Blues," "Baby Let Me Follow You Down," "Fixin' to Die," "San Francisco Bay Blues," "You're No Good," "House of the Rising Sun," and "This Land Is Your Land."

Late November

Dylan is interviewed by Columbia publicist Billy James, who is hoping to acquire some background material for the CBS files. Unfortunately, Dylan continues to construct a childhood far more glamorous than real life, and his wild stories become part of the standard Dylan biography for many years to come. Material from the interview, which is quite extensive, subsequently appear in the most disparate of sources, whiles Billy James himself becomes one of Dylan's staunchest advocates at the label.

December 4

A date attributed by discographer Michael Krogsgaard to one of the Dylan tapes made at the home of the Eve and "Mac" MacKenzies. There is no evidence such a session took place.

December

Dylan and Gil Turner visit Toronto together. Dylan apparently composes a song in Toronto entitled "Strange Rain."

According to Shelton, Dylan performed at a coffeehouse in Toronto.

December 22

The date of the most famous of Dylan's many "home" tapes, the so-called "Minneapolis Hotel Tape." Recorded by Tony Glover at Bonnie Beecher's apartment in Minneapolis, whimsically dubbed The Beecher Hotel by Dylan (hence the title of the tape), large portions of this tape appeared on the first Dylan bootleg album, the legendary *Great White Wonder*. Even more songs appeared on the quasi-official Italian triple-album set, *A Rare Batch of Little White Wonder*.

The 26-song tape consists of: "Candy Man," "Baby Please Don't Go," "Hard Times in New York Town" (now released on *The Bootleg Series*), "Stealin'," "Po' Lazarus," "Ain't Got No Home," the superlative "Dink's Song," "Man of Constant Sorrow," a peculiar monologue of indefinite origins entitled "East Orange, New Jersey," "Deep Water/Omie Wise," an outstanding "Wade in the Water," "I Was Young When I Left Home," which Dylan introduces as "I sorta made it up on a train" and Greil Marcus describes as having "a maturity youth deserves to be spared," "In the Evening,"

"Baby Let Me Follow You Down," "Sally Gal," "Gospel Plow," "Long John," "Cocaine Blues" (with parts of "Cocaine Bill and Morphine Sue" thrown in for good measure), a medley of Guthrie's VD songs, "VD Blues," "VD Waltz," "VD City," "VD Gunner's Blues," "See That My Grave Is Kept Clean," Guthrie's "Ramblin' Blues," and finally "Black Cross," a withering monologue Dylan presumably learned from Lord Buckley, ending this remarkable 90-minute tape "as high as a pigeon."

According to Scaduto, Dylan gave copies of this tape to several friends, suggesting that he felt it was a good representation of his development as an artist. According to Shelton, Glover also taped Dylan at this time "doing [some] r&b-type Chuck Berry songs." There is no evidence to support Shelton's assertion, although Dylan and Glover may well have jammed together on those kinds of songs.

Mid- to Late December
Dylan plays a concert at the University of Minnesota.
• According to Tony Glover, he and Dylan recorded an instrumental for an independent film that was being made in Minneapolis at the time. One assumes the film was never completed.

Late December, Rutgers University, New Brunswick, NJ
On Dylan's return to New York, Robert Shelton conducts an interview with Dylan to garner information for the liner notes to Dylan's debut album. Although not as extensive as Billy James's, it contains similar wild stories, as well as references to the blues singers Dylan most admires, his extracurricular reading at university, and the composition of a song called "The Ballad of the Ox-Bow Incident," which he wrote after watching the film on TV.

December 31
Dylan is at a large New Year's Eve party at Robert Shelton's place in the Village.

Date Unknown
At some point after he left Minneapolis, Dylan writes a song for Bonnie Beecher. "Song to Bonny" is clearly modeled on "Song to Woody" (which it presumably postdates). The handwritten manuscript is reproduced in *The Telegraph 46*.
• According to Bob Fass, Dylan's first appearance for New York's subscription radio station WBAI was on a show called "Radio Unnameable," and that he and John Herald "did some kind of comic improvisation about folksingers." Perhaps Fass is mistaken about who accompanied Dylan, perhaps it was John Wynn, and the song was "The Beautiful People" (see July 29, 1961).

1962

January

Between the recording and the release of Dylan's debut album, John Hammond arranged a music publishing deal for him with Leeds Music. Although the album features only two originals, by the time of its release Dylan is writing at a prolific rate, evidenced by the demo tape he makes for Leeds Music at the outset of 1962. Aside from stalwarts of his club set, like "Hard Times in New York Town," "Talkin' Bear Mountain Picnic Massacre Blues," and "Man on the Street," Dylan records four brand new "originals," "Poor Boy Blues," "Standing on the Highway," "Ramblin' Gamblin' Willie," and "Ballad for a Friend" (originally entitled "Reminiscence Blues").

• Dylan and Suze Rotolo spend an afternoon looking for a one-bedroom apartment. They finally find one on West 4th St.

January 13, The San Remo Coffeehouse, Schenectady, NY

January 13–16

Dylan stays at the home of Joe Alper in Schenectady, playing the piano and working on new songs. Alper takes several photos of Dylan performing in Schenectady and Saratoga Springs, as well as leafing through his record collection at home.

January 14–15, Cafe Lena, Saratoga Springs, NY

January 29

Dylan is recorded at the home of Eve and Mac MacKenzie. After accompanying their son, Peter, on a couple of songs (one of which is "San Francisco Bay Blues"), he plays them a couple of his newer originals, "Hard Times in New York Town" and "The Death of Emmett Till."

February

At Dylan's suggestion, Mike Porco books blues shouter Big Joe Williams at Gerdes Folk City for three weeks. Dylan shows up most nights and on several occasions jams onstage with Big Joe.

• Columbia are apparently already considering dropping Dylan. The somewhat less prestigious Prestige Records are interested in taking up his contract.

• Pete Seeger introduces Dylan to "Sis" Cunningham at her West Village apartment. Cunningham is in the process of setting up a new mimeographed magazine for topical songs to be called simply *Broadside.*

> *Pete Seeger was one of the leading voices in the folk revival. An original member of the Almanac Singers and the Weavers in the late '40s and early '50s, Seeger was one of the founders of* Sing Out! *magazine, the premier journal of the revival. As a solo banjo player, he was active both in political causes and as a performer; he recorded extensively for Folkways and then Columbia Records. Seeger was an early fan of Dylan's, but turned against the singer when he "went electric" at Newport.*
>
> *Agnes "Sis" Cunningham was a politically radical singer/songwriter who first performed with Seeger and his friends in the '40s. She edited and published* Broadside, *along with her husband, Gordon, to promote socially conscious singer/songwriters, including Dylan, Phil Ochs, Tom Paxton, and many others. She also produced a series of recordings on her own label that were pressed and distributed by Folkways Records.*

Broadside publishes its first edition. The magazine is devoted to new songs by young songwriters emerging from the ongoing folk revival. Dylan quickly becomes a regular contributor, his first offering being a new talkin' blues about the John Birch Society.

February 1
Dylan visits the Folklore Center, enthusing to Izzy Young about the imminent publication of his first songbook, *Bob Dylan Himself* (the songbook would not actually be published until 1965). He also talks about a new composition, "Death of Emmett Till," he has written for a CORE (Congress of Racial Equality) benefit concert, and another song he is working on called "The Death of Robert Johnson."

February 7
Dylan plays Izzy Young a song called "Strange Rain" at the Folklore Center. Young considers the lyrics obscure but still "dug the song."

February 22
Dylan plays "Let Me Die in My Footsteps" for Izzy Young.

February 23
Dylan plays a benefit concert for CORE at City College in Manhattan. At this time Suze Rotolo is doing volunteer work for CORE.

February 28
Dylan makes another home tape at Eve and Mac McKenzie's.

March 2
Dylan contributes harmonica and backing vocals to four songs recorded at Cue Recording Studios by Victoria Spivey and Big Joe Williams. None of the tracks are released until 1964, when two appear on Spivey's own label,

Spivey Records. The highlight of the session is a superb "Sitting on Top of the World," featuring some exemplary harp work from Dylan. The other songs cut are Big Joe Williams's "Wichita," Spivey's "It's Dangerous," and an instrumental jam simply dubbed "Big Joe, Dylan, and Victoria." Dylan's harp playing at this session certainly illustrates why he was a prized accompanist at the time.

Note: The accredited date for this session was always October 21, 1961 until Shelton suggested that it really took place on the above date. A subsequently published photo from the session is also credited to March 1962, the time of Big Joe Williams's residency at Gerdes. Presumably the October 1961 date was an attempt on Spivey's part to attribute the session to a period before Dylan signed to Columbia (otherwise permission for Dylan's appearance might have been required from CBS).

March 11

One of the most remarkable finds of recent years has been a one-hour radio program of Dylan in March 1962 on Cynthia Gooding's "Folksinger's Choice," which circulated for the first time in 1992 on a bootleg CD of the same name, on the Yellow Dog label. The show features a very gushing Gooding, a very self-conscious Dylan, embarrassed to be reminded of their first meeting in 1959, and 11 Dylan performances, some of them unique: "(I Heard That) Lonesome Whistle," "Fixin' to Die," "Smokestack Lightnin'," "Hard Travelin'," "The Death of Emmett Till," "Standing on the Highway," "Roll on John," "Stealin'," "(It Makes) a Long Time Man Feel Bad," "Baby, Please Don't Go," and "Hard Times in New York Town."

Note: During the show, Dylan refers to his debut album being released "next month." *Bob Dylan* was released just eight days after the attributed date of this broadcast. This has led to some ingenious suggestions as to an actual recording date for the program, including turning 3-11-62 into 1-13-62, although this would be too early for "Emmett Till." However, the March 11 date may well refer to a broadcast date and the actual recording may date from early to mid-February (before he wrote "Let Me Die in My Footsteps").

March 14

Dylan plays "Ballad of Donald White" for Izzy Young at the Folklore Center.

March 19

Dylan writes a poem for Izzy Young called "Talkin' Folklore Center." He signs a handwritten draft of the poem, "Bob Dylan of Gallup, Phillipsburg, Navasota Springs, Sioux Falls, and Duluth." The song is published as a song-sheet by the Folklore Center at the time, and is subsequently included in *Bob Dylan: In His Own Words.*

Bob Dylan Columbia (CL 1779/CS 8579): "You're No Good," "Talkin' New York," "In My Time of Dyin'," "Man of Constant Sorrow," "Fixin' to Die," "Pretty Peggy-O," "Highway 51," "Gospel Plow," "Baby Let Me Follow You Down," "House of the

Risin' Sun," "Freight Train Blues," "Song to Woody," "See That My Grave Is Kept Clean"

March 23, Gerdes Folk City, New York, NY

Spring 1962

Dylan travels to the CBS-TV production center on West 57th St. to audition for "The Ed Sullivan Show." He apparently performs material from his debut album, including "Pretty Peggy-O," "Man of Constant Sorrow," and "Song to Woody," but is met with a wall of incomprehension and leaves baffled by the lack of response, positive or negative. On the way back to Greenwich Village, he wanders down 42nd St. "to visit the flea circus and see the man from Borneo again," before proceeding to McGowan's Bar in the Village.

• Dylan is recorded by Cynthia Gooding at her apartment, performing versions of "Ballad of Donald White," "Wichita Blues," "Acne (Teenager in Love)," "Rocks and Gravel," and "(It Makes) a Long Time Man Feel Bad." This was presumably shortly after his appearance on "Folksinger's Choice."

• Henrietta Yurchenco interviews Dylan on WNYC's "Adventures in Folk Music" radio program shortly after the release of his debut album.

Early to Mid-April

According to biographer Bob Spitz, Mikki Issacson organized regular Sunday afternoon parties at this time, where the itinerant folksingers of the Village were encouraged to play their new songs in return for a plentiful dinner. One Sunday Dylan plays "Blowin' in the Wind."

April 9

After Dylan teaches Gil Turner the chords to "Blowin' in the Wind" backstage at Gerdes, Turner performs the new song at the Monday night hootenanny, having taped the words to the microphone. This version features only the first and last verses.

April 12

A dated, signed fragment of "Blowin' in the Wind," which refers to the "cannonballs fly" line and chorus, was recently auctioned, bearing this date.

April 16

A mid-April Dylan live recording, generally attributed to Gerdes Folk City, features "Deep Elem Blues," "Blowin' in the Wind" (still two verses long but prefaced by a rap about how it is not a protest song—a sign of early flak?), "Honey Just Allow Me One More Chance," "Corrina, Corrina," and "Talkin' New York" (which now contains a verse from "Talkin' Folklore Center").

Note: This is the only possible date for a Gerdes set given the Ann Arbor shows and April 24 recording of "Corrina, Corrina," which surely postdates this performance.

April 20–22, Goddard College, Ann Arbor, MI
Dylan shares the bill with Jesse Fuller.

April 24 to May 6
Dylan plays his first residency at Gerdes Folk City as a headliner.

April 24
Between 2:30 PM and 4:55 PM, Dylan begins recording his second album for Columbia at the ubiquitous Studio A, with John Hammond again producing. Two songs from the 24th, "Ramblin' Gamblin' Willie" and "Talkin' John Birch Society Blues" are slated for the original version of *The Freewheelin' Bob Dylan,* but are pulled when legal problems arise. The other five songs remain unreleased except for "Death of Emmett Till" (on *The Bootleg Series*). The remaining songs, all non-original, include two adaptations: "Sally Gal," a version of Guthrie's "Sally Don't You Grieve," and a bluesy rewrite of the traditional "Corrina, Corrina," plus unimpressive renditions of the traditional "Going to New Orleans" and Hank Williams's "(I Heard That) Lonesome Whistle." Jazz bassist Bill Lee accompanies Dylan on some of the songs.

April 25
Dylan records a further eight songs during another two-and-a-half hour afternoon session at Studio A. Once again, the bulk of material ends up unreleased, only "Let Me Die in My Footsteps" being scheduled for inclusion on the original *Freewheelin'* (albeit with one verse edited out). It later appears on *The Bootleg Series* (still edited), along with versions of the absurdist "Talkin' Hava Nagilah Blues" and a surprisingly workmanlike "Talkin' Bear Mountain Picnic Massacre Blues." An acoustic "Rocks and Gravel," a remake of "Sally Gal," a "Baby, Please Don't Go" several notches down from its Hotel Tape forerunner, and takes of both "Milk Cow Blues" and "Wichita Blues" all remain in the can.

Late April to Early May
Dylan performs "Blowin' in the Wind" (now with three verses) at Sis Cunningham's apartment, so it can be transcribed for publication in the next issue of *Broadside.*

May
Albert Grossman assumes management of Dylan's career. Possibly it was the composition of "Blowin' in the Wind" that finally convinced him of Dylan's potential. The first order of business is to extricate Dylan from his contract with Leeds Music and place him with Artie Mogull at Witmark Music.

   • Dylan takes part in the recording of a radio program promoting *Broadside* magazine on the subscription radio station WBAI. When not talking about his ability to write five songs before breakfast, he sings three songs, "Ballad of Donald White," "Death of Emmett Till," and "Blowin' in the Wind," the first two of which are subsequently released on *Broadside Reunion* (where Dylan is billed as Blind Boy Grunt). Sis Cunningham, Pete Seeger, and Gil Turner are also featured on the show.

Mid-Year
On a trip to Virginia with Paul Clayton, Dylan plays some songs at the Charlottesville Gaslight Club.

June 8
Suze Rotolo leaves for Perugia, Italy. Dylan departs for Minneapolis on the same day, after seeing her off at the docks.

Late June
Dylan records a publishing demo for Witmark Music of "Blowin' in the Wind."

Summer
Dylan attends a Mahalia Jackson concert with Robert Shelton.
  • Dylan meets John Henry Faulk at a party held by Theodore Bikel. He is greatly impressed with the man. Presumably, it is this meeting that inspires him to compose a song about Faulk. The song, quoted in Gil Turner's *Sing Out* profile of Dylan (but now lost), is called "Gates of Hate."

> *Theodore Bikel was a folksinger who had a career as a character actor in the '50s and '60s.*
>   *Gil Turner was another folk revivalist, active on the board of* Sing Out!

Edwin Miller interviews Dylan for a brief profile in *Seventeen* magazine. Dylan is already disavowing his first album as being unrepresentative of his work.
  • Gil Turner interviews Dylan for a major profile in folk's premier quarterly, *Sing Out.* For the first and last time Dylan seems happy to discuss the composition of songs like "Ballad of Donald White" and "Blowin' in the Wind."

Summer 1962
According to Nat Hentoff's notes to Canadian duo Ian and Sylvia's debut album, their arrangement of "C.C. Rider" "was arrived at in the course of a long afternoon session with Bob Dylan last summer."

June 28 to July 1, The Potpourri, Montreal, Quebec

July 2, The Finjan, Montreal
Finjan regular Jack Nissenson has the foresight to record this performance for posterity. Ten of the 11 songs that he recorded subsequently appear on the quasi-official *Historical Archives Vols. 1 & 2.* Dylan's set consists of four originals "Blowin' in the Wind," "Quit Your Lowdown Ways," "Let Me Die in My Footsteps," and "Death of Emmett Till," his own arrangements of "Rocks and Gravel" and "He Was a Friend of Mine," folk standards "Hiram

Hubbard," "Stealin'," and "Muleskinner Blues," and two classic blues tunes, "Two Trains a-Runnin'" and "Ramblin' on My Mind." According to the club's owner, "The place was empty when he finished."

July 9
Dylan resumes recording at Columbia Studio A, with John Hammond producing. The session only lasts from 2:30 to 4:25 PM, but in that time he cuts seven songs, four of which survive the transition to the final *Freewheelin'*. "Honey, Just Allow Me One More Chance" and "Down the Highway" are cut in single takes, whereas "Bob Dylan's Blues" and "Blowin' in the Wind" are third takes. (According to press reports, the *Highway 61 Interactive* CD-ROM was originally going to include the first take of "Blowin' in the Wind." However, it was not on the released disc.) The other three songs at this July session have also now appeared on official Sony product, take four of "Babe, I'm in The Mood for You" appearing on the *Biograph* boxed set (an alternate take circulates among collectors), whereas "Quit Your Lowdown Ways" (drawing heavily on Kokomo Arnold's "Milk Cow Blues" for its "original" lyrics) and the beautiful "Worried Blues" are part of *The Bootleg Series*.

July 13
Dylan officially signs with Witmark Music.

August 2
Robert Allen Zimmerman legally changes his name to Bob Dylan.

August
Broadside publishes another new Dylan composition. "Ain't Gonna Grieve," a typical "protesty" effort, is based on the old spiritual, "Ain't Gonna Grieve My Lord No More." Presumably Dylan gives Cunningham the song shortly before departing for Minneapolis.

August 11
Tony Glover tapes another Dylan home session, at the apartment of Dave Whitaker. Dylan plays his friends four brand-new original songs: "Tomorrow Is a Long Time," "Talkin' Hypocrite," "Long Ago, Far Away," and "Long Time Gone." These he intersperses with interpretations of "This Land Is Your Land," "Motherless Children," "Blue-Eyed Babe," "Worried Blues," "Deep Elem Blues," and "Corrina, Corrina."

Mid-August
FM Stereo-Guide's Rachel Price interviews Dylan on his return from Minneapolis. He once again dismisses the first album, but admits that Elvis Presley was "a good singer . . . in the beginning."

September
During a three-song performance at The Gaslight, Dylan premiers a new song based on Child ballad No. 12, "Lord Randall," the epic "A Hard Rain's a-Gonna Fall."
• Cafe Yana, Boston, MA.

September 22

Dylan appears for the first time at Carnegie Hall, part of an all-star hootenanny. Aside from reviving "Sally Gal," "Talkin' John Birch Society Blues," and "Highway 51 Blues," Dylan showcases two major new compositions, "A Hard Rain's a-Gonna Fall" and "Ballad of Hollis Brown." According to one correspondent to *Sing Out,* he also performed "Talkin' Bear Mountain Picnic Massacre Blues," although it is absent from the audience tape of the event.

October

Dylan appears on Cynthia Gooding's radio show, performing at least one song with John Gibbons (possibly "TB Blues").

• Dylan appears on folk banjoist Billy Faier's show on WBAI, chatting amiably and playing four songs: "Baby Let Me Follow You Down," "Talkin' John Birch Society Blues," "Death of Emmett Till," and a unique performance of the traditional "Make Me a Pallet on the Floor."

Note: At one point, there is a reference to Dylan's appearance on Cynthia Gooding's show the previous week.

October 5

Dylan headlines a "Travelin' Hootenanny" at New York's Town Hall. As well as performing the same three originals played at the Carnegie Hall hootenanny, he does "Talkin' New York." Shelton reviews the show positively for *The New York Times.* Although his article suggests that there will be other "Travelin' Hootenanny" events, there is no evidence that any more took place.

Mid- to Late October

A performance at the Gaslight Cafe is recorded for posterity's sake. This so-called "Second Gaslight Tape" is subsequently released in quasi-official form in Italy, first on LP and then on CD, as *The Gaslight Tapes.* The originals performed at this show include an unfinished "Don't Think Twice, It's All Right," the turgid "John Brown," "Ballad of Hollis Brown," and "A Hard Rain's a-Gonna Fall." The remainder of the set comprises traditional fare, like "Barbara Allen," "Handsome Molly," "The Cuckoo Is a Pretty Bird," "No More Auction Block" (included on *The Bootleg Series*), "Motherless Children," "Going Down to West Texas," "Cocaine Blues," "Ain't No More Cane," and "See That My Grave Is Kept Clean," as well as more adventurous material, like "Black Cross," "Kind Hearted Woman," "Moonshine Blues," and the ubiquitous "Rocks and Gravel." Some of the shows at the Gaslight in this period Dylan co-headlines with the New World Singers.

Fall

BBC producer Philip Saville sees Dylan performing at a club called Tony Pastor's Place on West 4th St. He approaches him, asking whether he would be interested in appearing in a BBC play. Dylan refers him to his manager, Albert Grossman.

October 26

With Dick Wellstood on piano, Howie Collins and Bruce Langhorne on guitars, Leonard Gaskin on bass, and Herb Lovelle on drums, Dylan undertakes his first electric session at Studio A. Under Hammond's guidance, they attempt just three songs in a three-hour session. Although the ostensible purpose of the session seems to have been to cut a single, the only released cut proves to be an electric "Corrina, Corrina," which appears on *Freewheelin'*. The bulk of the session is taken up with five recorded attempts at "Mixed Up Confusion," a curious attempt to replicate the Sun Sound. Dissatisfied with the results, Dylan and the band then run through a single take of r&b singer Arthur Crudup's "That's Allright Mama," an appropriate riposte to the fakery of "Mixed Up Confusion." The session ends at 5:28 PM.

November 1
Unwilling to give up producing his very own Sun single, Dylan returns to Columbia's Studio A with Hammond to attempt a further five takes of "Mixed Up Confusion" and three more stabs at "That's Allright Mama." This time Art Davis is on bass, while jazz guitarist George Barnes replaces Howie Collins on guitar. Once again, though, the only cut from this session under consideration for official release is a solitary "Rocks and Gravel" cut at the end of the session, seemingly an afterthought. This rollicking arrangement of Brownie McGhee's "Solid Road," was in fact scheduled for inclusion on the original *Freewheelin'*.

November
Dylan makes the first, and indeed the most productive, set of recordings for *Broadside* magazine at their "offices" in New York. Since the idea was to provide songs that can be transcribed for the magazine, Dylan concentrates exclusively on originals, laying down earliest known versions of "I'd Hate to Be You on That Dreadful Day," "Oxford Town," "Paths of Victory," "Walkin' Down the Line," "Train a-Travelin'," "I Shall Be Free," and "Cuban Missile Crisis."
- At what appears to have been a separate session, but certainly contemporaneous, Dylan records "Ye Playboys and Playgirls," also for *Broadside*.
- Dylan records a new song for Witmark Music, "Long Ago, Far Away."

November 14
Still unable to give up on a bad idea, Dylan returns to Studio A with John Hammond and the band, hoping to come up with a usable version of "Mixed Up Confusion." Utilizing his third bassist, Gene Ramey, Dylan begins by rerecording "Corrina, Corrina" (this version is used as b-side to the "Mixed Up Confusion" 45). He then sets about "Mixed Up Confusion" with a vengeance, cutting four versions of the song, including (at least according to legend) a Dixieland-style version. He finally succeeds in cutting a piano-driven version he is happy to put out as a single. However, when the song is subsequently collected on album, first on the Japanese *Masterpieces* set and then on *Biograph*, an alternate take, dominated by an insistent acoustic strum is used. At this point in the session, which runs from 3 PM until 5:30 PM, a virtuoso guitar performance of "Don't Think Twice It's All Right," is cut in a single take. Then, accompanied by Bruce Langhorne on second guitar, he cuts embryonic versions of "Ballad of Hollis Brown," "Whatcha Gonna

Do?," and his own rewrite of "Who's Gonna Shoe Your Pretty Little Feet?," entitled "Kingsport Town." This final track subsequently appears on *The Bootleg Series.*

December 3
Dylan visits Izzy Young at the Folklore Center and discusses the recording of "Mixed Up Confusion," which had clearly frustrated him.

Early December
Dylan records a substantial number of demos for his new music publishers, Witmark Music. A single session spans an entire year of compositions, from "Death of Emmett Till" and "Let Me Die in My Footsteps," through "Babe I'm in the Mood for You" and "Quit Your Lowdown Ways" to such hot-off-the-press ditties as "Ballad of Hollis Brown," "A Hard Rain's a-Gonna Fall," and the gorgeous "Tomorrow Is a Long Time."

December 6
Resuming work on *Freewheelin'*, Dylan is back at Columbia Studio A for what proves to be his last session with John Hammond. The session occupies a mere hour and a half, running from 5:30 until 7:00 PM, yet Dylan manages to record some five songs, three of which he deems good enough for *Freewheelin'*. These include at least one epic performance, the six-and-a-half-minute "A Hard Rain's a-Gonna Fall," which he dispatches in a single take. Also taken care of in a single run-through is "Oxford Town," which elicits Hammond's stunned response, "Don't tell me that's all." The "I Shall Be Free" on *Freewheelin'* is also a first take. However, uncharacteristically, Dylan perseveres with the song, cutting two more complete takes, both with quite different lyrics, before deciding that take one was fine after all. He also attempts "Whatcha Gonna Do" again, this time as a solo performance. However, the song that he finds hardest to get down on tape is a brand-new tirade against women who want someone (him) to live up to some romantic ideal, "Hero Blues." Having opened the session with one complete run-through, he returns for a couple more takes midsession (he returns to the song at the *Times They Are a-Changin'* sessions, but it again ends up discarded). Nevertheless, a most remarkable session.

December 13
Suze Rotolo sets sail from Naples, on the liner Leonardo da Vinci, returning to New York. She arrives in New York five days later, but Dylan has already flown to England.

December 14: The release of Dylan's first US single, "Mixed Up Confusion/Corrina, Corrina" (4-42656), which is quickly withdrawn by CBS.

December 17 or 18
Dylan arrives in London for the very first time. Although booked into the Mayfair hotel by the BBC, who have brought him over to appear as a

folksinger in a TV play called "Madhouse on Castle Street," he prefers the more homey charms of the Cumberland Hotel, around the corner from Marble Arch. His manager, Al Grossman, is already in London with another of his proteges, Odetta.

December 18

Dylan arrives at the Troubador, where he has been told by Pete Seeger to look up Anthea Joseph, the organizer of the club on Tuesdays. She recognizes him and asks him to perform, which apparently he does. Later in the evening he is introduced to English folksinger Martin Carthy.

> *Martin Carthy is a British folk revivalist whose guitar playing and repertoire greatly impressed visiting American folk artists, including Dylan and, a year or two later, Paul Simon. Carthy's version of "Scarborough Fair" was lifted by Simon, whereas Dylan borrowed several melodies he heard Carthy perform for future compositions.*

December (19?)

Dylan arrives for the first reading for his part in "Madhouse on Castle Street." Seemingly incapable of reading his lines, he asks Saville, "Why can't I just be a singer? Can't I just scat a couple of things?"

December (20–22?)

Dylan stays at Philip Saville's house for a couple of days. One night he plays "Blowin' in the Wind" for Saville and his two children. Saville decides to use the song over the opening credits of "Madhouse on Castle Street."

December 22

Dylan performs at the Singers Club in London, apparently singing "Ballad of Hollis Brown." According to Anthea Joseph, who had taken him to Singers, the crowd was enthusiastic but owners Peggy Seeger and Ewan MacColl "sat there in stony silence."

December 23

Dylan sings three songs at the King and Queen pub in London's West End, including "Talkin' John Birch Society Blues" and "Ballad of Hollis Brown."

Mid- to Late December (19–27)

Dylan spends some time with Martin and Dorothy Carthy as well as hanging around the Soho folk clubs. He is thought to have put in an appearance at three clubs during this week: Bunjies Coffee House, where he returns with Dick Farina and Eric Von Schmidt in January, Les Cousins on Greek Street, and The Establishment, which he visited but did not play.

December 28

Dylan goes up to the offices of *Melody Maker* hoping to find journalist Max Jones, a contact suggested by Ramblin' Jack Elliott. Jones, though, is absent. (They are subsequently introduced by Anthea Joseph.)

December 29

Dylan plays the Troubador again. The audience includes several notable English folksingers: Martin Carthy, Bob Davenport, Nigel Denver, Jim McLean, and Louis Killen among them. The response is mixed. Dylan then heads over to the "Ballads and Blues," a weekly shindig at The Roundhouse pub on Wardour Street, accompanied by Carthy.

December 30

On the first day of filming "Madhouse on Castle Street," Dylan records versions of "Blowin' in the Wind" (which is broadcast in two parts), "Hang Me Oh Hang Me," "The Cuckoo Is a Pretty Bird," and "Ballad of a Gliding Swan" (which he had supposedly written especially for the play). Dylan is also required to provide two minutes of incidental guitar music. There is a brief photo session after today's filming.

December 31

Dylan and Carthy go down to the King and Queen pub, where they both perform a few songs. Dylan seems to have felt more accepted at the King and Queen than the more established Singers and Troubador clubs.

1963

January 1
According to Ron Gould, Dylan returns on New Year's Day to the King and Queen pub, where he shouts assorted insults at Nigel Denver, who is performing at the time. Denver and Dylan had apparently fallen out at some point after their first meeting.

Early January (1–3)
Dylan is interviewed for the English performing arts magazine *Scene*. In the interview, he comes across as very brash and more than a little overbearing. At one point he proclaims that he is "consciously trying to recapture the rude beauty of a Southern farmhand musing in melody on his porch."

Early January (2–3)
While visiting Rory McEwen, Dylan meets up with fellow compatriots, Eric Von Schmidt and Dick Farina. Dylan plays Farina "Don't Think Twice, It's All Right," which greatly impresses him. McEwen also takes Dylan to meet the poet Robert Graves, presumably at Dylan's request. He was apparently reading Graves's 'grammar of poetic myth' *The White Goddess* at the time. Graves is not, however, greatly impressed by Dylan.

January 2 (or 9)
One of two possible dates for a long-rumored appearance at the Surbiton and Kingston Folk Club, held weekly at the Surbiton Assembly Rooms. Because of the Christmas recess, the club only met twice during Dylan's visit. On January 2, The Strawberry Hill Boys, fronted by Dave Cousins, were scheduled to appear. (They were also the scheduled act the night that Dylan first visited the Troubador.) On the ninth it was to be Bob Davenport, whom Dylan had already met on at least two occasions. Davenport insists that Dylan did not appear with him in Surbiton. The *Scene* interview also implies that Dylan was not due to return from his trip to Rome until the 10th.

January 4
The second (and final) day of recording for "Madhouse on Castle Street," delayed by a technicians' strike.

January 5
Dylan flies to Rome to join Odetta. During his brief stay he performs at the Folkstudio Club, as well as composing "Girl from the North Country" and

"Boots of Spanish Leather," both of which take a large part of their melodies from Martin Carthy's arrangement of "Scarborough Fair."

January 10
Dylan attends Odetta's London show at the Prince Charles Theatre in Leicester Square.

January 12
Dylan, Eric Von Schmidt, Dick Farina, and Ethan Signer join Martin Carthy onstage at the Troubador for a relaxed jam session.

January 14
In the basement of Dobell's Jazz Shop on the Charing Cross Road, Dick Farina and Eric Von Schmidt record an album for Doug Dobell's folk label. When the ostensible producer, Tom Costner, arrives, it is with Dylan in tow, carrying a crate of beer. After emptying a bottle of Guinness on the floor, Dylan contributes some backing vocals and harmonica. The session lasts about three hours. Farina, Schmidt, and Dylan then adjourn to the Troubador where they gerrymander the stage—much to the chagrin of the two "folkies" due to perform that night, Judy Silver and Nigel Denver, Dylan proceeds to give a strangely controlled, albeit stoned, performance.

January 15
Recording continues in the basement of Dobell's. These two sessions subsequently appear on Folklore Records as *Dick Farina & Eric Von Schmidt*. Dylan, under the alias Blind Boy Grunt, contributes to six tracks: "Glory, Glory," "Cocaine Blues," the 1927 Memphis Jug Band's "Overseas Stomp," Furry Lewis's "You Can Always Tell," and two Farina originals, "Christmas Island" and "London Waltz." Dylan, Farina, and Schmidt then descend on Bunjies Coffee House, where they perform a few songs.

January 16
Dylan and Eric Von Schmidt fly back to New York.

Mid- to Late January
Dylan composes an original song called "Liverpool Gal" based, it would appear, on the traditional ballad "When First Unto This Country." Although a handwritten version of the lyrics (part of the Margolis & Moss manuscripts) reads "by Bob Dylan 1962," the song appears to have been written during Dylan's last few days in London—there is a reference in the final verse to "now leavin' London"—or shortly after his return to New York (the only known recording would not be made until July 1963).

Early Winter
A poor audience recording from this period, features just three songs: "Ramblin' Down Thru the World," "Freight Train Blues," and "Walls of Redwing." It probably dates from a Gerdes Folk City hootenanny.

• Dylan writes a poem on nuclear weapons, creatively called "Go 'Way Bomb." It is intended for a book that Izzy Young is trying unsuccessfully to compile.

January 19

Dylan records a couple of new songs at the *Broadside* "offices," a brief "talkin' blues" called "Talkin' Devil" and an original based on the traditional "Leaving of Liverpool," called "Farewell." The latter is somewhat decimated by super-flat backing "harmonies" by Gil Turner.

January 21

Dylan plays his first Gerdes Folk City hootenanny in some time, premiering a new antiwar anthem, "Masters of War," based around the English ballad "Nottamun Town."

• The notorious "Banjo Tape" was recorded on this day at the home of Gil Turner. Both Dylan and Happy Traum, who contributes some banjo and sporadic backing vocals, sound a little the worse for wear on what is, after all, an informal jam session. The set includes a healthy smattering of the kind of traditional songs Dylan was beginning to transcend—"Lonesome River Edge," "Back Door Blues," "Keep Your Hands Off Her," "Honey Babe," and "Stealin'"—as well as several songs new to his friends: "Masters of War," "Bob Dylan's Dream," "Farewell," "All Over You" (described appositely by Paul Cable as "the nearest thing to a rugby song that has yet come out of America"), and what appears to have been a wholly improvised work called "Going Back to Rome."

> *Happy Traum was a then-New York based folksinger/guitarist who later relocated to the artist's community of Woodstock, NY. He recorded with Dylan three songs that appeared on Dylan's* Greatest Hits, Vol. 2 *(see September 24, 1971).*

Late January

Dylan performs on the campus of New York University.

February

Continuing to demo songs for *Broadside,* Dylan records "John Brown" and "Only a Hobo," both of which are published in the mimeographed magazine the following month, and subsequently included on the first Folkways album of *Broadside* material—*Broadside Ballads Vol. 1.*

• Dylan appears on Skip Weshner's New York radio show. Between some gushing monologues from Weshner, Dylan performs three of his most recent compositions, "Bob Dylan's Blues," "Masters of War," and "Tomorrow Is a Long Time."

• Dylan and his now-reconciled girlfriend Suze Rotolo are photographed walking together down a snowbound 4th St. for the front cover of his new opus, *The Freewheelin' Bob Dylan.*

Late Winter

Dylan records demos of "Bound to Lose," "All Over You," and "I'd Hate to Be You on That Dreadful Day" for Witmark Music. All three songs are belatedly copyrighted.

Scene interview, 1963

Nat Hentoff interviews Dylan for the liner notes he has been commissioned to write for *Freewheelin'*. The sleeve notes for the original version of the album include Dylan quotes about three of the songs later cut from the album. Hentoff is impressed enough by Dylan the folksinger to make him the key figure in a profile on new folk music for the June 1963 issue of *Playboy* magazine.

Winter (?)
A scrap of a Dylan lyric published 30 years later in the fanzine, *Isis,* appears to date from this period. Entitled "That California Side," the unfinished song looks authentic, predating Dylan's other anti-California song, "California," by a good two years.

March
Dylan records at least five demos for his music publishers, Witmark Music: "Don't Think Twice, It's All Right," "Long Time Gone," "Masters of War," "Oxford Town," and "Walkin' Down the Line." This version of "Walkin' Down the Line" subsequently appears on *The Bootleg Series.*

• Dylan records three songs for a one-hour TV special on folk music for the Westinghouse Broadcasting Company. The songs he performs for the special, which is hosted by John Henry Faulk, are the mandatory "Blowin' in the Wind," "Ballad of Hollis Brown," and "Paths of Victory."

• Dylan is a surprise guest on folksinger Oscar Brand's "World of Folk Music." Arriving at the studio with scheduled guest Barbara Dane, he agrees to perform a couple of new songs for the syndicated radio show, "Girl from the North Country" and "Only a Hobo"; both of which he prefaces with spoken introductions.

> *Davey Moore is knocked out by Sugar Ramos in a boxing match. He dies two days later without ever regaining consciousness. On April 12, Dylan premieres "Who Killed Davey Moore."*

April
Dylan records four demos for Witmark Music: "I Shall Be Free," "Bob Dylan's Blues," "Bob Dylan's Dream," and "Boots of Spanish Leather."

April 12

According to Columbia records, there was a 4:00 PM soundcheck for Dylan's Town Hall show, which was recorded and includes the following songs: "Ramblin' Round" (presumably "Ramblin' Down Thru The World), "Bob Dylan's Dream," "Walls of Redwing," "Boots of Spanish Leather," "Hero Blues," "Tomorrow's a Long Time," "Dusty Old Fairgrounds," "Who Killed Davey Moore," "Highway 51 Blues," "New Orleans Rag," "With God on Our Side," and "Masters of War."

In the evening, some nine hundred hip souls attend Bob Dylan's first solo concert at a major New York venue, the Town Hall. *Billboard* and *The New York Times* have both sent reviewers, the latter being Robert Shelton, of course. For the first time, Dylan showcases nothing but his own material. Indeed, only three songs will appear the following month on his second album: "A Hard Rain's a-Gonna Fall," "Bob Dylan's Dream," and "Masters of War" ("Blowin' in the Wind" is a surprising absentee). Opening the show with "Ramblin' Down through the World," a new song largely based on Guthrie's "Ramblin' Round," Dylan closes with an eight-minute recital of a poem about his "last hero," "Last Thoughts on Woody Guthrie," now released on *The Bootleg Series*. In between are a whole series of premieres: "Dusty Old Fairgrounds," "Bob Dylan's New Orleans Rag," "Walls of Redwing," "Who Killed Davey Moore," "All Over You," "Tomorrow Is a Long Time," "Hero Blues," "With God on Our Side," and a curiously misguided "talkin' blues" presumably called "You've Been Hiding Too Long." There are just two holdovers from his Fall '62 club set, "John Brown" and "Ballad of Hollis Brown."

According to a recent listing obtained from Sony, Dylan also performed "Talkin' New York," "Talkin' John Birch Paranoid Blues," "Boots of Spanish Leather," "Blowin' in the Wind," "Seven Curses," "Highway 51 Blues," "Pretty Peggy-O," and "Don't Think Twice, It's Alright." This would make for a two-hour plus show, which strikes me as extremely unlikely. The inclusion of songs soundchecked and one song surely not written in April 1963 ("Seven Curses") suggests to me that this information comes from composite reels, and that some or most of these additional songs were not performed at the Town Hall show, particularly as Robert Shelton's review refers to Dylan performing a mere sixteen songs—that would be quite a miscount.

The concert program also features a new Dylan poem, "My Life in a Stolen Moment," destined to be regularly reprinted in the ensuing years. After the show, Dylan is an elated guest of honor at a party at Peter (of Peter, Paul, and Mary) Yarrow's mother's plush Midtown apartment.

Mid-April

Dylan meets with Tom Wilson, producer of Sun Ra and John Coltrane, after Al Grossman has orchestrated the removal of John Hammond as his producer. Grossman phones Columbia the following day to confirm Dylan's endorsement of Wilson as his new producer.

April 18
Dylan makes his final home recording at Eve and Mac McKenzie's.

April 19–20, Cafe Yana, Boston, MA

April 21, Club 47, Cambridge, MA
Dylan appears at a Sunday hootenanny, performing with Eric Von Schmidt and Ramblin' Jack Elliott. After the "hoot" Dylan and his fellow performers, including the likes of Joan Baez, Bobby Neuwirth, Carolyn Hester, and Jim Kweskin, adjourn to Sally Schoenfeld's apartment for a party-cum-continuation of the "hoot." Joe Boyd seems to recall Dylan performing "A Hard Rain's a-Gonna Fall" at Schoenfeld's.

April 24
The decision having apparently already been made to delete four of the tracks scheduled for *Freewheelin'*, Dylan goes into StudioA with his new producer, Tom Wilson, to cut some songs as possible replacements for the deleted cuts. The session runs from 10:00 AM till 1 PM and results in four of the finer tracks on the rejuvenated *Freewheelin'*: "Girl from the North Country," "Masters of War," "Talkin' World War III Blues," and "Bob Dylan's Dream." Also recorded at this session is a version of "Walls of Red Wing." According to the notes accompanying *The Bootleg Series,* it is this version that appears on that set. However, all other evidence indicates that it is the *Times* version, not the *Freewheelin'* outtake, that ended up on *The Bootleg Series.*

April 25
Dylan plays at a newly opened club in Chicago called The Bear. Grossman is one of the partners in this venture, which presumably explains Dylan's appearance. Since this is less of a showcase than the Town Hall concert, Dylan reintroduces some older material. "Talkin' John Birch Society Blues" and "Honey, Just Allow Me One More Chance" reappear alongside "A Hard Rain's a-Gonna Fall," "Ballad of Hollis Brown," "With God on Our Side," "Bob Dylan's Dream," "Walls of Redwing," and the mordant "Talkin' World War III Blues." After the show Dylan jams with local blues guitarist, Michael Bloomfield.

Mike Bloomfield was an electric blues guitarist from Chicago, who soon came to prominence as a member of Paul Butterfield's Blues Band. He later sessioned on Dylan's folk-rock albums.

April 26
Dylan records seven songs for "Stud Terkel's Wax Museum," a regular feature of Chicago's WFMT radio schedule. Aside from obvious choices like "A Hard Rain's a-Gonna Fall," "Blowin' in the Wind," and "John Brown," Dylan manages to slot in new works like "Farewell," "Bob Dylan's Dream," "Who Killed Davey Moore," and "Boots of Spanish Leather," as well as talking to Terkel about long-term projects like a novel he's in the process of writing.

Early May

Dylan is interviewed by "The Ed Sullivan Show's" producer Bob Precht (probably on the fifth). He strums a few songs to help Precht decide whether they can slot him into such a family-oriented show. Having passed the audition, he is instructed to turn up for a dress rehearsal the following week.

May

Dylan records three demos for Witmark Music: "Girl from the North Country," "Seven Curses," and "Hero Blues."

May 10

Dylan performs on the opening night of the two-day Brandeis University Folk Festival in Waltham, MA. His set immediately precedes the intermission, although he stays around for the statutory communal finale. Despite poor acoustics, he is well received. After the show, Eric Von Schmidt takes Dylan, Suze Rotolo, and Robert Shelton to a select party.

May 12

In the afternoon, Dylan rehearses four songs for his scheduled appearance on "The Ed Sullivan Show," including the satirical "Talkin' John Birch Society Blues." Even though Sullivan himself approves the choice, Dylan is instructed by the editor of "program practices" to drop the song. Rather than agree to this blatant act of censorship, Dylan storms out of the studio.

Mid-May

Izzy Young circulates a mimeographed broadsheet condemning the censoring of "Talkin' John Birch Society Blues." The version of the song's lyrics printed on the broadsheet includes two verses absent from any other published or recorded version. At the same time, Dylan records a new version of the song for Witmark Music under the title, "Talkin' John Birch Paranoid Blues."

Mid-May (17?)

Dylan drives up to Monterey from Los Angeles in the company of Elektra Records president Jac Holzman and Jim Dickson.

May 18, Monterey Folk Festival

Dylan performs a three-song set comprising a talkin' blues (surely "Talkin' John Birch Society Blues"), "Masters of War," and "A Hard Rain's a-Gonna Fall." Joan Baez then joins him to duet on "With God on Our Side."

> May 27: *The Freewheelin' Bob Dylan* (CL 1986/CS 8786): "Blowin' in the Wind," "Girl of the North Country," "Masters of War," "Down the Highway," "Bob Dylan's Blues," "A Hard Rain's a-Gonna Fall," "Don't Think Twice, It's Alright," "Bob Dylan's Dream," "OxfordTown," "Talkin' World War III Blues," "Corinna Corinna," "Honey Just Allow Me One More Chance," "I Shall Be Free"

Mid- to Late May
Dylan stays at Joan Baez's home for a couple of weeks, writing and consorting.

June to July
Dylan and Suze Rotolo spend a few weeks with Peter Yarrow at his cabin in Woodstock, writing, painting, and swimming.

July 5
Dylan flies through the night, changing planes in Atlanta, in order to attend a voter-registration rally in Greenwood, MS.

July 6
During the voter-registration rally in Greenwood, Dylan performs a brand-new song "Only a Pawn in Their Game"—about the murder of civil rights leader Medgar Evers—on the back of a truck, temporarily transformed into a makeshift stage. Part of this performance is later inserted into D. A. Pennebaker's *Don't Look Back* documentary.

July 8
Dylan flies back to New York from Greenwood, MS.

> *July 13, 1963: Peter, Paul, and Mary score a number two hit with their version of "Blowin' in the Wind."*

Mid-July
Dylan makes an appearance at the Columbia Records Convention in Puerto Rico. At a salesmen's dinner at the Hotel Americana in San Juan he performs "With God on Our Side" and "Only a Pawn in Their Game," the latter clearly targeted at those salesmen from the south. He is accompanied by Suze Rotolo and her sister, Carla. One night he is refused admission to the hotel restaurant because he is not wearing a tie. The Columbia Record Division president Goddard Lieberson intervenes on his behalf.

July 17
Tony Glover makes his final home tape of Dylan. The tape is divided into two parts, both recorded at the apartment of Dave Whitaker. The first part comprises six Dylan originals, all compositions from the preceding six months: "Only a Pawn in Their Game," "With God on Our Side," "Girl from the North Country," "Boots of Spanish Leather," "Eternal Circle," and "Who Killed Davey Moore?" The second part shows that Dylan is still very much a product of his influences, beginning with an instrumental jam with "Spider" John Koerner, followed by "What Did the Deep Sea Say?" "Hero Blues" and the only known recording of "Liverpool Gal." Next are two songs on which Tony Glover plays harmonica: "West Memphis" and "Death Letter Blues." Dylan then reverts to a little showing off, performing "Only a Pawn in Their Game" (again), "New Orleans Rag," "Ballad of Hollis Brown," "With God on Our Side" (again), and "Tomorrow Is a Long Time." Interspersed between songs are Dylan's recollections of the Ed Sullivan affair and

a discussion with Paul Nelson about "protest songs." Sadly, this recording remains in the sole possession of Mr. Glover.

Mid-July
Dylan visits Hibbing.

July 26
On the first afternoon of the Newport Folk Festival, Dylan duets with Joan Baez on "With God on Our Side" to a small workshop crowd. In the evening he performs his own set on the main stage, comprising "Bob Dylan's Dream," "With God on Our Side," "Talkin' John Birch Society Blues," and "A Hard Rain's a-Gonna Fall." He returns at the end of the evening to join the assembled multitude in ensemble versions of "We Shall Overcome" and his very own "Blowin' in the Wind."

July 27
Dylan makes a second appearance at one of the Newport Folk Festival afternoon workshops, this time dueting with Pete Seeger on "Ye Playboys and Playgirls."

July 28
During Joan Baez's evening set at the Newport Folk Festival, Dylan joins her for the now mandatory "With God on Our Side."

July 30
Having arrived at the WNEW-TV studio in New York with Joan Baez in tow, Dylan records two songs—"Blowin' in the Wind" and "Only a Pawn in Their Game"—for a program called "Songs of Freedom." He huddles conspiratorially with Baez throughout the taping.

Late July (31?)
Dylan and Baez head for the peace and solitude of Woodstock for a couple of days.

Summer
Dylan is a guest on NBC's "The Tonight Show," then hosted by Johnny Carson. He sings one song and chats briefly with Carson but is clearly uncomfortable and is gone after the commercial break.

   • Dylan contributes prose-poem sleeve notes to two albums by friends of his: The New World Singers' (self-titled) album and Peter, Paul, and Mary's *In The Wind.*

August
Dylan records two demos for Witmark Music: "Gypsy Lou" and "Whatcha Gonna Do."

"Blowin' in the Wind"/"Don't Think Twice, It's Alright" (4-42856)

Newport, 1963

Early August

Dylan and Baez perform the jointly composed "Troubled and I Don't Know Why" at Gerdes Folk City.

• Dylan is interviewed by Jack Smith for the radical newspaper, *The National Guardian*. The interview reveals some of his feelings at an early stage of mass acceptance. However, Dylan is understandably upset at the way the published article makes him appear to be some kind of spokesman for the Left, even if statements like "The same guy who sucked up my town wants to bomb Cuba" and "I'd like to visit Russia someday, see what it's like," suggest a Dylan happy to play along with Smith's line of questioning. Nevertheless, he also explicitly states in the interview that "there is nobody that looks like me or represents the way I feel." The interview is also reprinted in *Broadside*.

August

Dylan attends a reception for Pete Seeger at Carnegie Hall.

August 3, Camden Music Fair, NJ

Dylan appears as Joan Baez's guest. He plays a short solo set, before dueting with her on a couple of his own songs.

August 6

Dylan commences work on his third album at Studio A, with Tom Wilson now firmly installed as his producer. Although he cuts some eight tracks in the afternoon, just one of them makes it to the album, "North Country

Blues." Evidently this is more of a warmup session, given that four of the outtakes are first attempts at songs later earmarked for the album: "Boots of Spanish Leather," "Only a Pawn in Their Game," "Ballad of Hollis Brown," and "With God on Our Side." Of the three remaining songs, "Seven Curses" is eventually given air on *The Bootleg Series.* "New Orleans Rag" and "Farewell" continue to languish in the vaults.

August 7
Another three-hour afternoon session at Studio A with Tom Wilson results in satisfactory takes of four songs first attempted on the sixth: "Boots of Spanish Leather," "Only a Pawn in Their Game," "Ballad of Hollis Brown," and "With God on Our Side," as well as another unsatisfactory take of "New Orleans Rag." Also recorded at this session are versions of "Eternal Circle" and "Walls of Red Wing," both of which were lodged with Witmark Music for copyright purposes. The latter song later appeared on *The Bootleg Series* (incorrectly assigned to the April session).

August 10, Asbury Park, NJ
Dylan again appears as Baez's guest.

August 12
Dylan begins this afternoon's session at Studio A playing the piano, still attempting to cut a usable "New Orleans Rag," as well as two songs already demoed for Witmark, "Paths of Victory" (now on *The Bootleg Series*) and "Hero Blues." When he reverts to guitar, the intensity level jumps a notch with one of his most inspired arrangements of a traditional song, "Moonshiner Blues." "Eternal Circle" is also attempted again, before Dylan wraps up the final August session with his own rewrite of "Only a Miner," "Only a Hobo" (this version appears on *The Bootleg Series*).

August 13–16
Dylan guests at a Joan Baez concert in Connecticut and one in Massachusetts. He also composes "When the Ship Comes in" one night after being refused admission to a hotel.

August 17, Forest Hills Stadium, Forest Hills, NY
Introduced to 15,000 fans as Baez's "special guest," Dylan performs "Only a Pawn in Their Game" and "A Hard Rain's a-Gonna Fall" before being joined by Baez. They perform "Farewell," "Troubled and I Don't Know Why," and "Blowin' in the Wind." "Troubled and I Don't Know Why" is subsequently included on Baez's boxed-set retrospective, *New, Live and Rare.*

Late August
Suze Rotolo moves out of Dylan's 4th St. apartment and in with her sister Carla.
  • Dylan records three demos for Witmark Music: "Ain't Gonna Grieve," "John Brown," and "Only a Hobo."
  • Dylan is given important exposure in an interview by Sidney Fields in *The New York Mirror.*

- Tony Glover visits Dylan at his apartment on 4th St. while in town to cut Elektra's *Blues Project* album. Dylan is working on "The Times They Are a-Changin'."

- Dylan attends the session for Elektra's *Blues Project* album (featuring many prominent New York-based blues revivalists), which is apparently cut in a single 13-hour session at Masterhouse Studios in New York. He contributes piano to a single song, "Downtown Blues," credited as Bob Landy on the album sleeve.

August 28

Dylan is one of the performers at the Washington Civil Rights March. Photographs of the historic march show him perched on the steps of the Lincoln Memorial, singing with Baez. He also accompanies folk revivalist Len Chandler on the traditional "Hold On," as well as performing solo versions of "Only a Pawn in Their Game" and "Blowin' in the Wind." "Only a Pawn in Their Game" appears in bastardized form on the Folkways's *We Shall Overcome* documentary album, largely obliterated by some ill-considered polemic superimposed over the song.

Late August to Early September

Dylan records two brand-new demos for Witmark Music. Playing the piano for the first time on a Witmark demo, he lays down versions of "The Times They Are a-Changin'" and "When the Ship Comes in," both of which are later utilized on *The Bootleg Series, Vols.1–3*.

- Dylan visits Sis Cunningham and plays her his two newest songs: "The Times They Are a-Changin'" and "When the Ship Comes in." However, neither song appears in *Broadside*.

September

Dylan stays with Joan Baez at her home in Carmel. He composes at least two new songs, "Lay Down Your Weary Tune" and "The Lonesome Death of Hattie Carroll." This stay also presumably resulted in Dylan's extensive prose-poem sleeve notes that accompanied *Joan Baez in Concert Part Two*.

October 9

Dylan is the "surprise" guest at Joan Baez's Hollywood Bowl concert. Certain sections of her right-on audience are upset by an extended rendition of his new paean to nature, "Lay Down Your Weary Tune." After the concert, Dylan and Baez visit author Henry Miller at Pacific Palisades, where he and Miller end up playing table tennis. Dylan also presumably guests at a couple of other West Coast Baez shows at this time.

Fall

Dylan meets beat-scribe Lawrence Ferlinghetti in New York, and they discuss the possibility of a Dylan book for Ferlinghetti's City Lights publishing house in San Francisco.

Mid-October

Dylan is interviewed by journalist Michael Iachetta at Grossman's Park Ave.

office. The interview, published in the *New York Daily News,* once again portrays him as a spokesman for the young.

October 19, Hill Auditorium, Ann Arbor, MI
Dylan returns to solo performances.

October 23
Returning to Columbia Studio A, hoping to finish his third album, Dylan quickly lays down usable versions of "Lonesome Death of Hattie Carroll" and "When the Ship Comes in." However, the session bogs down as Dylan works long and hard (but without success) on "The Times They Are a-Changin'." Finally, despairing of getting a workable take, Dylan runs through a lengthy new protest song, "Percy's Song," before switching to the piano for a little fun and games. "East Laredo Blues," a highly derivative instrumental, is followed by Big Bill Broonzy's "Key to the Highway" and another Columbia version of "That's Allright Mama" which is threatening to segue into "Sally, Free and Easy" just as Dylan's voice gives out.

October 24
Dylan manages two more cuts for *The Times They Are a-Changin'* at his second October Studio A session: the title track and the sublime "One Too Many Mornings," part of a generally inspired day in a studio. Aside from these cuts, Dylan manages the best "Eternal Circle" he can muster, a "Percy's Song" transformed overnight in melody and drama into a major work, and, most significantly, a breathtaking single-take version of his first hymn to the mysteries of creation, "Lay Down Your Weary Tune." The latter two songs appear on *Biograph,* while "Eternal Circle" is on *The Bootleg Series,* along with a minor instrumental called "Suzy" (oft-bootlegged as "The Cough Song"). Dylan closes out the session with one more piano-driven "New Orleans Rag" that easily surpasses its August antecedents.

October 23 or 24
After trying to arrange an interview with Dylan for some time, *Newsweek* reporter Andrea Svedburg finally gets her wish, although only after digging up parts of Dylan's past that he (and Grossman) would prefer to keep hid (i.e., his middle-class Hibbing background). The interview, arranged by publicist Billy James, rapidly turns sour as Dylan realizes that this woman is intent on a "hatchet job." Subsequently *Newsweek* publishes her vindictive piece, which leads Dylan to write at least one retaliatory prose-poem directed at Svedburg and include it on the rear sleeve of his third album. He also composes a new finale for the album that targets those seeking to bury him in a "dust of rumors." The whole affair sours his relationship with Billy James and colors his attitude to *Newsweek* and *Time* for many years to come.

October 25, Town Hall, Philadelphia, PA

October 26
Six months after his Town Hall appearance, Dylan has been elevated to the plush surroundings of Carnegie Hall. Just five songs remain from that night,

Dylan unveiling a dozen new songs in his 18-song set: "Masters of War," "The Lonesome Death of Hattie Carroll," "When the Ship Comes in," "North Country Blues," "A Hard Rain's a-Gonna Fall," "Talkin' World War III Blues," "Don't Think Twice, It's Allright," "With God on Our Side," "Only a Pawn in Their Game," "The Times They Are a-Changin'," "Ballad of Hollis Brown," "Who Killed Davey Moore?" (which now has a tune), "Boots of Spanish Leather," "Talkin' John Birch Society Blues," "Lay Down Your Weary Tune," "Blowin' in the Wind," "Percy's Song," "Seven Curses," and "Walls of Red Wing." Although only the version of "Talkin' John Birch" has been released officially (on *The Bootleg Series*), the entire show was recorded by Columbia, and five songs—"When the Ship Comes in," "Who Killed Davey Moore," "Lay Down Your Weary Tune," "Percy's Song," and "Seven Curses"—were intended for a *Bob Dylan in Concert* album that Columbia planned to release in 1964. After the show, Harold Leventhal hosts a celebratory party at his West 96th St. residence.

Harold Leventhal was a prominent manager and publisher in the folk world. He handled Woody Guthrie's music publishing and managed Pete Seeger.

October 31
One suspects that Dylan's return to Studio A with Tom Wilson on this date was an unscheduled one. However, he has a new song he wants to record. "Restless Farewell," the only long cut, is self-evidently targeted at Ms. Svedburg and her fellow *Newsweek*ers.

November 2, Jordan Hall, Boston, MA

November 3, Regent Theater, Syracuse University, NY
This concert is presented by CORE.

November 4
Dylan is photographed, early in the morning, down on the Hudson River.

November 4–23
Dylan "goes underground" for three weeks after the *Newsweek* story appears, spending a lot of time with the Van Ronks and folk guitarist Barry Kornfeld. If he is writing a lot, it is not songs but prose-poems that occupy his time.

October 1963 to January 1964
Dylan contributes to Robert Shelton's short-lived *Hootenanny* magazine, providing poems for the December 1963 and March 1964 issues. He also writes a prose-poem for a January 1964 issue of *Broadside,* which he dedicates to editors "sis and gordon." Also composed at this time are all 11 outlined epitaphs that will constitute the sleeve notes for *The Times They Are a-Changin'* (requiring an insert for the album). Epitaphs eight to 11 evidently post date Andrea Svedburg's *Newsweek* story. Even assuming the epitaphs were writ-

ten chronologically (which seems probable), the first seven probably also date from after his trip to the West Coast and were probably written in Woodstock.

A typescript of all 11 outlined epitaphs, complete with corrections in Dylan's own hand, constitute part of the Margolis & Moss manuscripts, sold to Graham Nash in 1990, most of which appear to date from the Fall of 1963. Aside from the outlined epitaphs and published prose-poems, there is an untitled, unfinished 15-page play, proof positive that Dylan was no playwright. (He mentions working on a play in various interviews in the early months of 1964.) There are also several unpublished poems in this collection, including a whole series that have as their theme the Kennedy assassination, tying them to late November/early December. There is also one two-page poem that deals with his first Christmas in Minneapolis, a bio-poem that alludes to both his Sigma Alpha Mu fraternity brothers and to Judy Rubin. There are also poems about a political rally, racial strife, and "bullshit," as well as a six-line fragment of a poem that includes a quartet of lines directly anticipating the third verse of "Chimes of Freedom." These presumably date from late December 1963 to early January 1964.

November 22
The assassination of President John F. Kennedy. Dylan and Suze sit at home throughout the weekend watching events unfold on TV.

November 23
Dylan gives one of his most reluctant performances at a theater in New York state, opening the show with the now bitterly ironic "The Times They Are a-Changin'."

Late November, Princeton, NJ

November 30, Mosque Theatre, Newark, NJ
After performing in Newark, Dylan attends one of Lenny Bruce's shows (presumably the late one) at the Village Theater in New York.

December
Dylan demos rewritten versions of "Paths of Victory" and "Farewell," for Witmark Music.

December 13
Dylan receives the Tom Paine award at the annual Bill of Rights dinner organized by the Emergency Civil Liberties Committee at the Hotel Americana's Grand Ballroom. Unfortunately, his discomfort at his surroundings leads him to drink heavily. He delivers a very uptight acceptance speech, in which he questions the validity of the issues his wealthy liberal audience are supporting. Afterward, he is profoundly embarrassed by his behavior and offers to make up any shortfall in donations resulting from his outburst (something he apparently failed to deliver on).

December 14, Lisner Auditorium, Washington, DC
Includes "Girl from the North Country."

Mid- to Late December

Dylan sends a lengthy prose-poem to the Emergency Civil Liberties Committee, attempting to explain his feelings at the time of the Bill of Rights dinner. In the poem, entitled "A Message to ECLC," he once again offers to recompense the ECLC for any financial loss.

December 24

Dylan has a Christmas Eve dinner with Suze Rotolo and her mother at Mrs. Rotolo's home in Hoboken, NJ.

December 25

Dylan and Suze hold a party at her apartment on Avenue B.

December 26

Al Aronowitz takes Dylan to the Lower East Side apartment of beat poet Allen Ginsberg. Dylan and Ginsberg hit it off, and Dylan invites Ginsberg to fly with him to Chicago the following day. Ginsberg declines, owing to other commitments, but they resolve to keep in touch.

December 27, Orchestra Hall, Chicago, IL

The set includes "Restless Farewell." Dylan attends an after-show party, where he again meets blues guitarist Michael Bloomfield.

Late December

Dylan visits Robert Shelton, who is struggling to keep his new magazine, *Hootenanny,* afloat. Dylan expresses dissatisfaction with the direction of the magazine, which folds shortly afterward.

December 31

Dylan and Suze attend a small party at Terri and Dave Van Ronk's apartment.

1964

Winter
Under the pseudonym Tedham Porterhouse, Dylan contributes harmonica on "Will the Circle Be Unbroken" for Ramblin' Jack Elliott's new album, *Jack Elliott*.

> January 13: *The Times They Are a-Changin'* (CL 2105/CS 8905): "The Times They Are a-Changin'," "Ballad of Hollis Brown," "With God on Our Side," "One Too Many Mornings," "North Country Blues," "Only a Pawn in Their Game," "Boots of Spanish Leather," "When the Ship Comes In," "The Lonesome Death of Hattie Carroll," "Restless Farewell"

January, Zanesville, OH

January, New York, NY
Dylan makes his final visit to the tiny Witmark studio to record demos of "Guess I'm Doing Fine" and his arrangement of "Baby Let Me Follow You Down" (whose copyright has to be subsequently withdrawn, presumably because of Von Schmidt's *a priori* claim).

January 31
Dylan is in Toronto to film a TV special for the Canadian Broadcasting Company. Helen McNamara interviews Dylan for the *Toronto Telegram* newspaper. He refers to writing both a novel and a play that "will be an extension of the ideas he has put into his songs."

February 1
Dylan records a half-hour program as part of the CBC-TV series "Quest." The half a dozen songs he sings—"Talkin' World War III Blues," "Hard Rain's a-Gonna Fall," "Girl from the North Country," "The Times They Are a-Changin'," "The Lonesome Death of Hattie Carroll," and "Restless Farewell"—are all performed within the most incongruous of settings, a log cabin filled with working men pretending to pay attention. On the same day, he is interviewed for *Gargoyle* magazine. Once again he refers to his novel, admitting he doesn't "know when it's ever going to be done," and the ubiquitous play, which he wants "to see . . . get done."

February 3
Dylan, Victor Maimudes, Pete Karman, and Paul Clayton set out from New York on a cross-country jaunt by car, intending to make it to San Francisco via New Orleans in just three weeks. They stay in Charlottesville, VA this first evening.

February 4
On leaving Charlottesville, Dylan and entourage head for Harlan County, picking up a miner, somewhere near Abingdon, VA. Arriving in Harlan County, they give clothes collected in New York to the leader of the striking miners before moving on, stopping overnight in a motel in Pinesville, KY.

February 5
Dylan and company travel on, stopping over in Asheville, NC.

February 6
The happy band drive to Hendersonville, NC, where they manage to track down poet/folklorist Carl Sandburg. After an unsatisfactory meeting with Sandburg—who is unimpressed by Dylan's bravura—they head on through South Carolina, arriving in Atlanta, GA the same evening.

February 7
During the day, Dylan looks around Atlanta before playing his scheduled concert at Emory University in the evening. After the gig, there is an impromptu party in Dylan's motel room.

February 8
Dylan visits two old friends, civil rights activists Bernice Johnson and Cordell Reagon, in Atlanta.

February 9
With his head in Mississippi, Dylan sits in the back of the car working on a new song called "Chimes of Freedom." They stop overnight in Meridian.

February 10
Arriving in New Orleans, Dylan and his companions discover that they have only one room awaiting the four of them. After briefly sampling New Orleans nightlife, the quartet retire for the night.

February 11
The annual New Orleans Mardi Gras. Dylan is determined to experience the festivities to the full. At one point during the revelries, Dylan encounters schoolteacher/poet Joe B. Stuart and they jointly stagger from club to club, ending up at the Athenian Room at 3:00 AM.

February 12
Heading out of New Orleans in the morning, the happy band arrive in Tougaloo, MS by midafternoon. Dylan proceeds to play an unscheduled one-hour set at Tougaloo College. After a brief chat with various civil rights ac-

tivists, they move on. In 1985, Dylan would recall beginning to write "Mr. Tambourine Man" on leaving New Orleans.

February 13–14
Dylan and company drive on to Denver. When they reach Dallas, they pull over in Dealey Plaza and examine the site of Kennedy's assassination. After this macabre diversion, they drive via Fort Worth through the Panhandle, and onto Wichita Falls. In southern Colorado, they stop in Ludlow, scene of a notorious massacre immortalized in one of Woody Guthrie's ballads.

February 15
Arriving in Denver, Dylan hangs out at the Denver Folklore Center and briefly does the rounds of the coffeeshops he had frequented in the summer of 1960. In the afternoon, he plays the Civic Auditorium to an enthusiastic, if not sellout, audience. The fortunate few are treated to the premiere of a major new composition, "Chimes of Freedom."

February 16
Dylan takes his friends up to Central City, where he had spent a few weeks back in 1960. They then start the long trek toward San Francisco, where he is scheduled to perform on the 22nd. The night is spent in Grand Junction, CO.

Mid-February
While driving to San Francisco, Dylan hears "I Wanna Hold Your Hand" on the radio. It is already number one on the American charts. He is instantly intrigued by what the Beatles are trying to do.

February 17–18
Dylan and his companions drive from Grand Junction to Reno, NV, where they arrive at 8:00 AM on the 18th.

February 19–20
The foursome drives from Reno to San Francisco, arriving on the 20th. Dylan turns up at Lawrence Ferlinghetti's house, but he is not at home. He leaves a note inviting Ferlinghetti to the show on the 22nd.

February 22
Dylan gives one of his most legendary performances at the Berkeley Community Theatre. He receives the ecstatic approval of a largely student audience and the barely more restrained plaudits of Ralph J. Gleason in the *San Francisco Chronicle* and Richard Farina in *Mademoiselle*. Aside from the likes of "One Too Many Mornings," "Restless Farewell," "North Country Blues," and "Only a Pawn in Their Game" from his latest album, Dylan also provides a smattering of unreleased originals, ancient and modern, from "Who Killed Davey Moore," "Walls of Redwing," and "Eternal Circle," through the newly composed "Chimes of Freedom." Joan Baez proves to be a popular "surprise guest" performing a handful of duets with Dylan, including "With God on Our Side" and "Blowin' in the Wind."

February 23–24
Dylan, Victor Maimudes, Bobby Neuwirth, and Paul Clayton stop over at Joan Baez's home in Carmel, where they dine on the 23rd with Baez, her mother, her sister Mimi, and Mimi's husband Richard Farina. In the morning they drive to Los Angeles in their station wagon.

February 25
Dylan appears on "The Steve Allen Show," broadcast nationally from CBS's Hollywood studios. He sings "The Lonesome Death of Hattie Caroll," looking visibly nervous throughout.

Late February
During a show in Riverside, CA, Dylan dedicates his encore to Baez. While in LA, he stays at Hollywood's Thunderbird Motel, drifting out to parties and local nightclubs between engagements.

February 27, Fox Theatre, San Diego

February 29, Santa Monica Civic Auditorium
The show is advertised as "The Freewheelin' Folk Songs of Bob Dylan."

March 7, Cousen's Gym, Tufts University, Medford, MA

Early to Mid-March
Dylan writes the first of four letters to Tami Dean (they are later published in issue 16 of *The Telegraph*). The letter refers to time spent in Dallas three weeks earlier (February 13).

March
Chris Welles, after repeated efforts, finally manages to get Dylan to sit down for a five-page profile, which appears in a forthcoming issue of *Life* magazine (April 10). He again refers to "working on two plays and a book," the latter of which he describes as "a rambling travelogue."

- Dylan is alleged to have played at the Taft Auditorium in Cincinnati at this time.

Late March
The final breakup with long-time girlfriend Suze Rotolo awaits Dylan on his return to New York. His version of the night in question is told in the maudlin "Ballad in Plain D." The breakup will color the majority of songs on *Another Side of Bob Dylan*. The Rotolos's version of the evening's events are relayed in considerable detail in Bob Spitz's biography.

- Dylan and Robert Shelton attend a Simon and Garfunkel concert at Gerdes Folk City.

March to April
Information about a tape purporting to be from a home session at Eric Von Schmidt's house in Sarasota, FL, and featuring Von Schmidt and Dylan (with Joan Baez in attendance though absent from the tape) appeared in issue No. 44 of *The Telegraph*. However, according to Von Schmidt, Dylan never vis-

ited him in Sarasota, and there is no obvious gap in Dylan's and Baez's schedules when this trip would have been practical. The tape, though, remains and contains Dylan and Von Schmidt trading vocals on "Black Betty," "Come All Ye Fair and Tender Ladies," two takes of "Long Johnny Coo Coo," a fragment of Von Schmidt's "Joshua Gone Barbados," "Money Honey," "More and More," "Mr. Tambourine Man" (a request from Von Schmidt, suggesting he was already conversant with the song, which may well suggest a later recording date), "Susie Q," "Glory, Glory," "Stoned on the Mountain," and "Walkin' Down the Line." The session ends with Von Schmidt singing "Joshua Gone Barbados" in its entirety, with Dylan contributing some back-up vocals and harmonica.

Mid-April

Dylan plays Providence, RI. The set includes "Chimes of Freedom" and "The Times They Are a-Changin'."

Mid-April, Symphony Hall, Boston, MA

Mid-April, Brandeis University Folk Festival, Waltham, MA

Mid-April

Dylan makes a surprise appearance at Club 47, Cambridge.

Mid- to Late April

Dylan travels from Cambridge to Amherst, where he plays at Amherst College. According to a letter he wrote to Ferlinghetti, he was accompanied by "15 friends from Cambridge." While in Cambridge, Dylan stays with Betsy and Bob Siggins, who run Club 47. Also part of the regular retinue on this New England trip are record producer Paul Rothschild, Victor Maimudes, folksinger John Sebastian, Charlie Frizell, and John Cooke, who walks around with a camera in hand, snapping shots. According to Rothschild, after the Amherst show, Dylan, Maimudes, and he drove directly back to Woodstock, where Dylan was first introduced to the LSD experience (two months after writing "Mr. Tambourine Man").

April 28

Dylan sends a letter to Lawrence Ferlinghetti. He briefly recounts his trip to New England, and assures Ferlinghetti that he would still like to write a book for City Lights, but is uncertain what he wants it to be. He also says he is traveling to France the following day, although, in fact, he is due to fly to the west coast to perform at the Monterey Folk Festival.

Early May, Monterey Folk Festival,
Monterey County Fairgrounds, Monterey, CA

May 9

Having been due to fly into England on the seventh, Dylan finally arrives at Heathrow Airport on the ninth, where he is met by publicist Ken Pitt.

May 11

Dylan is scheduled to appear on BBC's radio show "Saturday Club" on this date. However, he does not make an appearance.

May 12

Originally due to appear on the English "Tonight" program on the eighth of May, Dylan appears on the program on the 12th, introduced by Cliff Michelmore. He performs a very hesitant version of "With God on Our Side." The TV footage is obviously a video insert, so it was presumably filmed earlier in the day. Dylan is interviewed by Maureen Cleave for the London *Evening Standard.* The interview is published under the headline, "If Bob can't sing it, it must be a poem or a novel or something." He was also apparently interviewed by Julian Holland of the London *Evening Post.*

May 14

Dylan is filmed for "Hallelujah," a Sunday program on ATV, one of ITV's regional TV stations. Hosted by Sidney Carter, the show is recorded at Didsbury Studios in Manchester. Dylan sings three songs on the show: "The Times They Are a-Changin'," "Blowin' in the Wind," and "Chimes of Freedom." He stays at the Parrs Wood Hotel.

May 17

Max Jones of *Melody Maker* interviews Dylan at lunchtime in Dylan's Mayfair Hotel room. Dylan refers to having "written a play, well I'm working on it when I have the time." He also refers to working on a book with Barry Fenstein: "It's just pictures and . . . words that . . . somehow fall into the same direction or mood."

May 17, Royal Festival Hall, London

Dylan plays to a sellout audience on a fine Sunday afternoon. The London *Times* reviewer compares Dylan to Segovia in the way he holds an audience spellbound throughout a two-hour show. After a rehearsal early in the afternoon, Dylan unveils three new compositions to the London audience: "Chimes of Freedom," "Mr. Tambourine Man," and "It Ain't Me, Babe." "Walls of Redwing," "Eternal Circle," and "Who Killed Davey Moore" remain in the set.

Perhaps as a concession to the English audience, with *The Freewheelin' Bob Dylan* just entering the UK album charts, he also includes a surprising number of songs from that album. These include the only known live version of "Down the Highway," plus "Honey, Just Allow Me One More Chance," "Bob Dylan's Dream," "Talkin' World War III Blues," "A Hard Rain's a-Gonna Fall," "Don't Think Twice, It's Alright," "Masters of War," and probably "Girl from the North Country." However, "Blowin' in the Wind" was not performed, much to the surprise of the *New Musical Express* reviewer. The show is recorded by Columbia. After the show, a delighted Dylan signs autographs at the front of the stage. As he leaves the hall by the stage door, Dylan is mobbed and forced to return inside until an alternative escape route can be organized.

May 20
Polly Devlin interviews Dylan in London at the behest of *Vogue* magazine. However, the interview is never published.

May 21 to Early June
Dylan leaves England, heading for Paris with Ben Carruthers. While there, he stays with French singer Hughes Aufray and meets an Austrian chanteuse called Nico, for whom he plays his new composition "It Ain't Me, Babe." Having stayed in Paris nearly a week, he travels to Berlin, where he stays with writer Mason Hoffenburg for a couple of days. He then heads on to Vernilya, a village just outside Athens, where he composes the majority of *Another Side of Bob Dylan* in a week of intensive writing.

Early to Mid-June
Dylan signs a petition of artists, poets, etc., supporting Lenny Bruce in his fight against charges of obscenity. The petition is published in several newspapers on June 13.

June
Dylan attends his brother David's high school graduation in Hibbing.

June 9
With just Tom Wilson at the Studio A console, Dylan proceeds to cut an album in a single night. Columbia have decided that they want an album in time for the Fall sales convention, and so in one prolific burst Dylan tapes his fourth solo album. He has invited old friend Nat Hentoff, who is doing a profile for the *New Yorker,* to attend the session. As the evening progresses, he makes a couple of observations to Hentoff regarding the change of direction the new songs represent. Aside from the 11 cuts on the album, just three outtakes were recorded. Limbering up on the piano results in the amusing, but slight, "Denise, Denise." Halfway through the session Dylan attempts a complete version of the song he had been working on since New Orleans, "Mr. Tambourine Man." With Jack Elliott harmonizing on the choruses and Dylan prefacing the verses with an extended harmonica solo, the performance has much to recommend it. However, Dylan stumbles over a couple of lines and there is a general hesitancy that causes him to file the song away for another day. "Mama, You Been on My Mind" is perhaps the more surprising omission from *Another Side.* It is one of the more successful love songs from this era, and a song that Dylan has never entirely dropped from his repertoire. The *Another Side* version is now available on *The Bootleg Series.* Of the album cuts, the only song that proves unduly problematic is "I Shall Be Free No.10," which has to have a whole three-verses edited out and substituted with an insert. "Chimes of Freedom" also gets bogged down by false starts before being cut in a single full take. The session is wrapped up at 1:30 AM with one last take of "My Back Pages."

June 16
Nat Hentoff interviews Dylan's for his *New Yorker* profile, their first conversation having taken place during the *Another Side* session. A week on, they

meet for lunch, and the interview includes a long explanation by Dylan of his feelings at the Emergency Civil Liberties Committee dinner in December 1963.

Mid- to Late June

John Hammond Jr. records his *So Many Roads* album in a couple of sessions in New York. The musicians featured include Chicago blues guitarist Michael Bloomfield (supposedly on piano, according to the sleeve notes!), Robbie Robertson, Garth Hudson, and Levon Helm of Canadian bar band, the Hawks, and Charlie Musselwhite on harmonica. According to Hammond, Dylan attended both sessions and "flipped out" at the sound these guys were creating.

• The probable date for three crudely recorded piano demos, subsequently lodged with Witmark Music for copyright purposes. The three songs are all mid-1964 compositions, "Mr. Tambourine Man," "Mama You Been on My Mind," and "I'll Keep It with Mine."

Mid-year

Throughout this period, Dylan is working on a book with Barry Fenstein who is providing photos while Dylan provides the captions.

Summer

Dylan composes a series of poems, five of which are published on the rear sleeve of *Another Side of Bob Dylan* under the heading, "Some other kind of songs." However, a further six remain unpublished until 1973 when *Writings and Drawings* includes all 11 poems. Presumably these six poems were omitted from *Another Side* for reasons of space.

Summer to Fall

Dylan writes three more letters to Tami Dean (see Early to Mid-March 1964), all later published in *The Telegraph 16*. The letters directly anticipate *Tarantula*'s style, with a clear development in wordplay and narrative style over the four letters. The second of these three letters is signed "Aleu, the goodest god," and stylistically seems to postdate the sleeve notes for *Another Side,* as does the third letter that closes with a 29-line, freeform poem, and is signed "uh huh." This letter introduces the marvelous character Doctor Zen as well as the likes of "maggy . . . [who] caught a duck the other day."

Mid-July, Ann Arbor High School Auditorium, Ann Arbor, MI

After a standard first-half set featuring favorites like "Walls of Redwing," "Who Killed Davey Moore," and "With God on Our Side," Dylan unveils a wealth of new songs during the second part, including the first known live version of "To Ramona," "Mr. Tambourine Man" (which was performed at the Royal Festival Hall in May), and the only known live version of "Ballad in Plain D."

• According to A. J. Weberman, Dylan played the Detroit Masonic Temple (Auditorium) the night after Ann Arbor.

July 24, Newport Folk Festival

Dylan appears at an afternoon topical-song workshop. He performs two new songs: "It Ain't Me, Babe" and "Mr. Tambourine Man." In the evening, he joins Joan Baez during her set, and they duet on "It Ain't Me, Babe." During the day, Dylan jams with Johnny Cash in Joan Baez's hotel room at the Viking Motor Inn.

July 26, Newport Folk Festival

As the major performer on the closing night of the festival, Dylan presents a completely new image to the audience of over 15,000. His brief set features "All I Really Want to Do," "To Ramona," "Mr. Tambourine Man," and "Chimes of Freedom." For the encore Dylan returns Baez's gesture, inviting her on stage for "With God on Our Side." Critical response to his performance is mainly unfavorable, *Sing Out!* attacking all his new songs as "maudlin," and even longstanding supporter Robert Shelton considers the Sunday night set lackluster. Audio evidence contradicts his assessment.

August 1, Waikiki Shell, Waikiki, HI

Early August

Dylan invites Joan Baez, her sister Mimi, and Mimi's husband, Richard Farina, to Woodstock for a couple of weeks.

August

At Macmillan's New York offices, Dylan has his first meeting with editor Bob Markel. He is now contracted for a book of unspecified writings. Joan Baez accompanies him. They discuss possible titles for the book, which at this stage is provisionally called *Side One.*

August 8, Forest Hills Stadium

Dylan once again joins Joan Baez during her show at the annual Forest Hills Music Festival. Aside from the perennial "With God on Our Side," they duet on "It Ain't Me, Babe" and the first known performance of "Mama, You Been on My Mind." Shelton's harsh review of this performance in *The New York Times* angers Dylan.

Another Side of Bob Dylan (CL 2105/CS 8905): "All I Really Want to Do," "Black Crow Blues," "Spanish Harlem Incident," "Chimes of Freedom," "I Shall Be Free No. 10," "To Ramona," "Motorpsycho Nitemare," "My Back Pages," "I Don't Believe You," "Ballad in Plain D," "It Ain't Me, Babe"

August 21

Dylan writes a lengthy, hilarious letter to Joan Baez's mother, which Baez later includes in her autobiography *And a Voice to Sing With.*

August 27

Probable date for the first of several photo sessions in Woodstock with Daniel Kramer.

August 28
Al Aronowitz drives Dylan from Woodstock to New York to meet the Beatles. Dylan and Aronowitz end up introducing the Beatles to the delights of cannabis at the Delmonico Hotel in New York.

August 29
Dylan returns to the Delmonico Hotel to spend some more time with the Beatles.

September 8
According to Joan Baez's autobiography, *And a Voice to Sing With,* Dylan's fall 1964 tour started on this date.

September 20
Dylan attends the Beatles's New York concert at the Paramount Theater and afterward meets with them.

Late September, Philadelphia Town Hall
Dylan performs the last acoustic versions of "Chimes of Freedom" and "Only a Pawn in Their Game" in a set that combines old favorites like "Girl from the North Country," "Ballad of Hollis Brown," and a solo "With God on Our Side," with new songs like "Mr. Tambourine Man" and "It's Alright, Ma."

September to October
Miles Davis gives a party for Robert Kennedy, who is running for senator of New York, at his house in New York that Dylan attends.

Fall
Dylan is interviewed by an unknown interviewer who publishes the results in the *New York Post* in January 1965.
   • Stuart Crump interviews Dylan for the *Brown University Daily Herald.* This is subsequently reprinted in *Comment* magazine.

October
Dylan plays concerts in Detroit, MI, and Kenyon, MN. By Kenyon he is performing another new song, "Gates of Eden."

October 24, Symphony Hall, Boston

October 31, Philharmonic Hall, NY
Dylan's first New York concert in a year is a complete sellout, and once again CBS has the tapes rolling, recording the show for a possible live album. The concert program features a new poem from Dylan, "Advice to Geraldine on Her Miscellaneous Birthday." Still in the set are "Who Killed Davey Moore" and "Talkin' John Birch Society Blues," along with four new songs: the surreal triad, "Mr. Tambourine Man," "It's Alright, Ma," and "Gates of Eden"; and the lightweight "If You Gotta Go, Go Now." From the recently released *Another Side* Dylan includes the only known live version of "Spanish Harlem

Incident" along with "To Ramona" and "I Don't Believe You." After "The Lonesome Death of Hattie Carroll," he introduces Joan Baez, with whom he performs "Mama, You Been on My Mind," "Silver Dagger" (sung by Baez, with Dylan accompanying on harmonica), "With God on Our Side," and "It Ain't Me, Babe." The show concludes with a solo "All I Really Want to Do."

November, Yale University, New Haven, CT

November 13, Massey Hall, Toronto, Ontario
The set includes "The Lonesome Death of Hattie Carroll," "The Times They Are a-Changin'," and "Talkin' World War III Blues."

November 25, Civic Auditorium, San Jose, CA
Joan Baez appears as a guest.

November 27, Masonic Memorial Auditorium, San Francisco, CA
Ralph Gleason of the *San Francisco Chronicle* enthusiastically reviews a show that is very similar to the New York concert except for the omission of "Spanish Harlem Incident" and the inclusion of a fifth song with Joan Baez, again featured as a "surprise" guest.

November 29, Sacramento Auditorium, Sacramento, CA

December 1, Men's Gymnasium, San Mateo College, CA

December 4, Peterson Gym, State College, San Diego, CA

December 5, Wilson High School, Long Beach, CA

December 6, Royce Hall Auditorium, UCLA, Pasadena, CA

December 7, University of CA, Santa Barbara
Bob Blackmar interviews Dylan on the University of Santa Barbara campus, later broadcasting the results on the local KCSB radio station. Blackmar subsequently writes to *Sing Out!*, bemoaning Dylan's detachment from his fans and criticizing him for surrounding himself with an entourage of sycophants.

December 8
Tom Wilson goes into Columbia's 30th St. studio, without Dylan's approval, and attempts to overdub electric instrumentation onto versions of "Mixed Up Confusion," "Rocks and Gravel," and "House of the Rising Sun." The "House of the Rising Sun," which self-evidently copies the Animals's electric arrangement of the song (a hit the previous August), is subsequently included on the *Highway 61 Interactive CD-ROM*, credited to 1962, some two years before the Animals recorded their version!

1965

Winter

Dylan takes members of the pop combo the Animals down to the club, the Kettle of Fish, in Greenwich Village. According to Eric Burdon, they had previously met Dylan at the Copper Rail or Odine's.

January

Throughout 1965, Dylan works on his book *Tarantula.* However, the first *Tarantula*esque prose piece to be published is in *Sing Out!* in January 1965, supposedly drawn from a book entitled *Walk Down Crooked Highway.* By April 1965 the book has its eventual title, and much of its content. Indeed, it would appear that the book is all but complete by September 1965. Needless to say, the published book is only a small part of a very large manuscript. Moreover, the nature of the book seems to have altered on a couple of occasions since it was first conceived in the winter of 1964.

• Robert Shelton conducts another interview with Dylan, this time for *Cavalier,* a men's magazine Shelton regularly contributed to at the time.

Early January

Dylan makes a surprise appearance at the Playhouse on MacDougall Street, performing some of the material he is due to record for *Bringing It All Back Home.*

January 13

Dylan begins the landmark *Bringing It All Back Home* sessions. Accompanied by just producer Tom Wilson and, on a couple of tracks, John Sebastian on bass, he spends most of the afternoon laying down solo tracks, none of which are destined to make the album in this form. Of the 12 songs cut on the 13th, six appear in electric guise on *Bringing It All Back Home* "Love Minus Zero/No Limit," "She Belongs to Me," "Subterranean Homesick Blues," "Bob Dylan's 115th Dream," "California" (rewritten as "Outlaw Blues" between sessions), and "On the Road Again," and one appears in a different acoustic form, "It's All Over Now, Baby Blue" minus the light embellishment of Sebastian's bass. "If You Gotta Go, Go Now," which became a blasting foray into rock & roll two days later, is also attempted acoustically, as are two key omissions from *Bringing It All Back Home,* "I'll Keep It with Mine" (included on *Biograph*) and "Farewell Angelina" (on *The Bootleg Series*). A half-formed fragment called "You Don't Have to Do That" and another incomplete effort conclude the four-hour session.

January 14

Today's first session at Studio A translates all but one of six songs attempted acoustically on the 13th into electrically augmented form. With session regulars Bobby Gregg on drums, Bruce Langhorne on electric guitar, Kenneth Rankin, also on guitar, Paul Griffin on piano, and Joseph Macho Jr., and William E. Lee on bass, Dylan slides easily from one song to the next, getting bogged down just once, on "Outlaw Blues." In the evening, Dylan continues to experiment, cutting six or seven songs with John Hammond Jr. and Bruce Langhorne (on guitars), and John Sebastian and John Boone (on bass), none of which ends up on the album. The six songs that are logged are "Love Minus Zero," "I'll Keep It with Mine," "Its All Over Now, Baby Blue," "Bob Dylan's 115th Dream," "She Belongs to Me," and "Subterranean Homesick Blues." This is also presumably the "next to last session" that Kramer attributes a version of "Mr. Tambourine Man" to.

January 15

The majority of the work done today at Studio A involves songs scheduled for the (acoustic) second side of *Bringing It All Back Home.* "It's Alright Ma," "It's All Over Now, Baby Blue," and "Gates of Eden" are recorded solo. Langhorne adds some tasteful touches to "Mr. Tambourine Man," which Dylan finally nails in the studio after seven months of performing the song live. Just three songs are cut with today's band. William E. Lee has been replaced by Joseph Macho, Jr., who along with pianist Paul Griffin and guitarists Al Gorgoni and Kenny Rankin bolster the sound on "Maggie's Farm," "On the Road Again," and "If You Gotta Go, Go Now," the last of which is only released as a single in Europe in 1967. An alternate version is used on *The Bootleg Series* in 1991.

January 22

Dylan is photographed at Sheridan Square by Fred W. McDarrah for the *Village Voice.*

February

Daniel Kramer travels up to Woodstock to ask Dylan to provide some captions for a photo profile he has prepared for *Pageant* magazine. Dylan writes the necessary captions in less than two hours, all in a suitably *Tarantula*esque style. When they are published, Dylan claims the captions are from his forthcoming book.

February 17

Dylan gives a hilarious performance on Les Crane's one-hour show for WABC-TV, singing a song at the beginning ("It's All Over Now, Baby Blue") and end of the show ("It's Alright, Ma"), accompanied by Bruce Langhorne on second guitar. Between the songs, Dylan chats with Crane and his other guests. Crane finds it difficult to deal with Dylan's razor-sharp repartee. Asking Dylan what his main message is, he is told: "Eat . . . Be. Period."

Late February, State College, Bridgewater, MA

The start of a joint tour with Joan Baez.

Late Winter (probably March)

D. A. Pennebaker meets Dylan and Bobby Neuwirth at the Cedar Tavern in New York to discuss the idea of a film documentary of the forthcoming English tour.

March

Dylan tells *Melody Maker*'s Max Jones during a telephone interview that he has "four or five songs . . . about recorded" for the follow up to *Bringing It All Back Home.* Although there is no evidence Dylan recorded anything between January and May 1965, he does write "Love Is Just a Four Letter Word" when staying with Baez in Carmel, presumably at the time of his early spring West Coast concerts. Dylan describes his new single, "Subterranean Homesick Blues," to Jones as "just a little story."

• Maura Davis interviews Dylan in Woodstock on the subject of his necktie. The interview is subsequently published by *Cavalier* magazine, along with a photo by Daniel Kramer of Dylan wearing the offending item.

• As the pressures of fame start to grow, Dylan becomes the master of the put-on. With J. R. Goddard, a *Village Voice* journalist, he devises a wholly spurious press conference entitled "Dylan Meets the Press," at which he "consented to answer all those deep, meaningful, searching questions he's been bombarded with by reporters." The results are published by the *Village Voice.*

"Subterranean Homesick Blues"/"She Belongs to Me" (4-43242).

March 5, Convention Hall, Philadelphia, PA
(with Joan Baez)

March 6, J. I. New Haven Arena, New Haven, CT
(with Joan Baez)

March

Dylan and Baez continue their joint tour, playing a series of shows in Trenton, Princeton, the University of New Jersey, Newark, and Buffalo, NY. To warm up for the shows, Dylan and Baez often do a duet of "You've Lost That Loving Feeling." Among songs in their set is a version of "Wild Mountain Thyme."

March 14

The probable date for a photo session at Albert Grossman's cabin in Woodstock with Daniel Kramer and Sara Lowndes. The intention is to get a photo for the cover of the book of prose Dylan is working on. The famous shot of Dylan and Sara at the cabin is rejected by Dylan and/or Macmillan as too much like the sleeve for *Bringing It All Back Home.* It is later included in Kramer's own book of Dylan photos.

March 22: *Bringing It All Back Home* (CL 2328/CS 9128): "Subterranean Homesick Blues," "She Belongs to Me," "Maggie's Farm,"

"Love Minus Zero/No Limit," "Outlaw Blues," "On the Road Again," "Bob Dylan's 115th Dream," "Mr. Tambourine Man," "Gates of Eden," "It's Alright Ma (I'm Only Bleeding)," "It's All Over Now Baby Blue"

March 24
Dylan and Baez perform two concerts in Pittsburgh, probably the last shows of their joint tour.

March 26
Paul Jay Robbins, a writer for the *Los Angeles Free Press,* meets Dylan at a promotion party thrown by Columbia Records. They jointly compose a brief absurdist interview that includes such profound statements as "I know a lot of people that are really President Johnson in a crash helmet when they say they're really Mickey Rooney in a jock strap." They agree to meet the next afternoon for a proper interview. It is at this party that Dylan poses for a photograph on the outside steps with the Byrds, who are also in attendance at the party.

Late March (26?)
Dylan guests on harmonica for the Byrds during one of their sets at Ciro's in Los Angeles (presumably the day of the promotion party). He apparently played on "All I Really Want to Do."

March 27
The afternoon of the Santa Monica show, Paul Jay Robbins conducts an extensive and surprisingly serious interview with Dylan. It is not published until September 1965, but is subsequently extensively reprinted. It includes much that is informative, including an extensive discussion about Dylan's book, which he describes as "something that had no rhyme, all cut up . . . except something happening which is words." Dylan is also clearly no longer just a folksinger: "Sure you can make all sorts of protest songs and put them on a Folkways record. But who hears them?"

March 27, Santa Monica Civic Auditorium
Dylan gives his first solo concert since the recording of *Bringing It All Back Home.* The set thus includes the first-known live performances of "Love Minus Zero/No Limit," "She Belongs to Me," and "It's All Over Now, Baby Blue."

April 3
Dylan returns to the Berkeley Community Theater.

Early April
Between the Berkeley (April 3) and Vancouver (April 9) shows, Dylan plays a concert in Seattle.

April 7
Dylan is rumored to have guested at a Joan Baez concert at the Berkeley

Community Theater, the last time they would appear on stage together for 10 years.

April 9, Queen Elizabeth Theatre, Vancouver, BC
A solo performance.

Mid-April
In a brief respite before his English tour, Dylan returns to Woodstock, accompanied by Joan Baez and Mimi and Dick Farina. According to Mimi Farina, after a few days Baez has to return to the west coast to play some shows, joining Dylan again at the end of the month to fly to London for his English tour.

April 26
Arriving at London Airport at 9:35 PM, Dylan is immediately subjected to a press conference in the VIP lounge. His arrival and the subsequent press conference represent the opening scenes in *Don't Look Back,* during which he is seen brandishing a large industrial light bulb. When asked the inevitable "What is your real message?" he replies, "Keep a good head and always carry a light bulb." After the conference, Dylan is seen to shrug and proclaim, "Oh, to be a simple folk singer again." He is also interviewed by telephone at the airport, for the BBC radio program "Teen Scene."

The program is presented by Mike Hurst, who conducts the interview, broadcast live between 10:35 and 11:15 that evening. When questioned about "Subterranean Homesick Blues," Dylan describes it as "early, authentic folk music." Afterward, he is driven to the Savoy Hotel where he arrives to find that a cocktail party, arranged by Al Grossman for assorted press officers, has been in full swing since 5 PM. The party continues until 2:30 AM and turns into an impromptu press conference, Dylan being subjected to questions for most of the evening.

April 27
After a light breakfast, there are more interviews. Most important, there is an afternoon press conference in the Manhattan room at the Savoy, which receives extensive press coverage. By this point, however, Dylan has lost interest in the interminable questions, appearing bored throughout. In *Don't Look Back,* he is seen at the end of the conference parrying questions about the Bible from Maureen Cleave. Unimpressed, Cleave's write up in the *Evening Standard* is headlined, "So very, very bored . . . the curious Mr. Dylan." At least one other interview is recorded on this day for radio broadcast. It is conducted by Jack de Manio and is broadcast on the BBC's early morning "Today" program the following day. Also conducted on the 27th is an interview with Michael Hellicar of the *Daily Sketch* in which Dylan reveals that the proposed title for his book is *Tarantula.* After a full day of interviews, he visits John and Cynthia Lennon for dinner at their house in Weybridge, staying there until 4 AM.

April 28
Dylan conducts further interviews until 3 PM, when he and Joan Baez de-

cide to visit the West End boutique Annello and Davide, where he orders three new pairs of boots. In the late afternoon, they visit London's Regent Park Zoo before heading back to the hotel for a meeting with the Beatles.

April 29

While at the Savoy Hotel, Dylan agrees to review the current single releases for *Melody Maker*'s "Blind Date" column. Clearly not the most serious of reviewers, his comments on one unfortunate singer are: "I think she's singing in a pool of water and she's got a thermometer in her ear." He also gets to hear Donovan's single, "Catch the Wind," which he thinks is "a great record," although Donovan apparently sounds "a bit like he's holding on to a tree trunk, wearing a patch over one eye." He is also interviewed for the BBC's African Service, the preparation for which is included in *Don't Look Back*. Later, there is a CBS reception at the Dorchester Hotel, which Dylan attends with his court jester Bob Neuwirth, and Alan Price of the Animals.

Late April to Mid-May

The Beatles and the Rolling Stones are both in regular attendance at Dylan's suite at the Savoy Hotel throughout his English tour.

April 30

Dylan arrives at Sheffield's Grand Hotel at 6 PM, where he is photographed in his room, feet up, with an iris in his hand.

April 30, City Hall, Sheffield

Dylan opens his first English tour to unprecedented publicity. The set throughout this eight-date tour remains standard, featuring: "The Times They Are a-Changin'," "To Ramona," "Gates of Eden," "If You Gotta Go, Go Now," "It's Alright, Ma," "Love Minus Zero," "Mr. Tambourine Man," "Talkin' World War III Blues," "Don't Think Twice, It's Alright," "With God on Our Side," "She Belongs to Me," "It Ain't Me, Babe," "The Lonesome Death of Hattie Carroll," "All I Really Want to Do," and "It's All Over Now, Baby Blue." Excerpts from the first two songs at the City Hall are featured in *Don't Look Back*. After the concert, Dylan meets a local band, the Freewheelers, and is clearly very interested in their attempts to perform his songs with electric backing. He is also interviewed by Jenny De Yong and Peter Roche, reporters from the Sheffield University paper *Darts*. Apparently "very tired but willing to talk," Dylan gives a surprisingly straight interview, talking about his new songs as "more three-dimensional . . . there's more symbolism, they're written on more than one level." Also from his stay at the Grand Hotel is the incident in *Don't Look Back* where the hotel manager asks Albert Grossman to keep the noise down, and Grossman tells the "fop manager" to call a constable.

May 1, The Odeon, Liverpool

A microphone failure at the start of the concert is later featured in *Don't Look Back*. After the concert, Dylan visits the Blue Angel club, where he meets Paul McCartney's younger brother, Mike McGear, and Scouse poet Roger McGough. They adjourn with him to the Adelphi Hotel.

May 2, De Montfort Hall, Leicester

A fragment of "The Lonesome Death of Hattie Carroll" is included in *Don't Look Back*. After the show, Dylan is driven back to London's Savoy Hotel, although not until a girl who has climbed onto his car has been removed. Dylan's departure is included in *Don't Look Back*.

May 4

Dylan sits at the typewriter in his London hotel room, typing a prose piece entitled "Alternatives to College." It is later to be offered for publication to *Esquire* magazine, but is not used (it is not actually published until its surprise inclusion in *Lyrics 1962–1985*). In attendance at the hotel are Marianne Faithfull, Al Grossman, Bobby Neuwirth, and Joan Baez, who insists on playing some songs while Dylan types. Her set includes "Percy's Song," "Love Is Just a Four Letter Word," and "What a Friend I Have in Jesus." At this point, Dylan picks up a guitar himself and plays his own instrumental version of "What a Friend I Have in Jesus." He follows this by singing several country songs accompanied by Baez: "I Forgot More (Than You'll Ever Know)," "Remember Me," "More and More (I'm Forgettin' 'Bout You)," "Blues Stay Away from Me," "Weary Blues from Waitin'," "Lost Highway," and "I'm So Lonesome I Could Cry." Pennebaker films the session, and part of the final two songs appear in *Don't Look Back*. In the early evening Dylan goes for an Indian curry at a London restaurant with Marianne Faithfull, Joan Baez, John Mayall, and Al Grossman. Afterward, there is a party at the Savoy Hotel, where they are joined by Donovan. At one point in the evening, Dylan, annoyed by Baez's shrill voice, holds up a glass and challenges her to break it.

May 5, Town Hall, Birmingham

Dylan is accompanied by John Mayall and Joan Baez on the 120-mile drive to the show. Dylan stays at the Grand Hotel in Birmingham.

May 6

Clearly sick of the obvious and pointless questions he is repeatedly asked, Dylan's interviews with the English press have become a stream of verbal put-ons. Interviewed in the afternoon by a reporter from the *Newcastle Evening Chronicle,* he at one point retorts, "Why should you want to know about me, I don't want to know about you." He admits that the book he is working on is "a book of confusion." Later on, in the dressing room of Newcastle City Hall, there is another interview, this one with Terry Ellis, the Social Secretary at Newcastle University. Immortalized by Pennebaker's camera in *Don't Look Back*, Ellis finally blows his cool, proclaiming, "You're the artist. You're supposed to be able to explain [everything] . . . in two minutes." Dylan is considerably more polite to the High Sheriff's lady, who comes backstage with her three "sons." This is also featured in *Don't Look Back*. Dylan stays at the Royal Turk's Head Hotel.

May 6, City Hall, Newcastle

A fragment of "Don't Think Twice, It's Alright" from this show is included in *Don't Look Back,* and the entire song is subsequently broadcast on a syndicated radio show, "Retro Rock," as part of a tribute to D. A. Pennebaker.

May 7, Free Trade Hall, Manchester

After the show, Dylan returns directly to London. An exemplary soundboard of the entire show has recently been issued on bootleg CD by Swingin' Pig. The 72-minute show fits very snugly onto the single CD, entitled *Now's the Time for Your Tears.*

May 8

Dylan, Allen Ginsberg, Bobby Neuwirth, and D. A. Pennebaker shoot the promotional film for "Subterranean Homesick Blues" at the side of the Savoy Hotel, set back from the Strand. They are aided by Donovan, Alan Price, and Joan Baez, who all help Pennebaker paint the placards held up by Dylan in this famous sequence. Dylan, Donovan, and Price adjourn to the Soho district, where they turn up at the club Les Cousins, meeting up with Anthea Joseph. However, they are forced to leave as teenyboppers soon converge on the place, and they flag down a taxi back to the Savoy. In the evening, there is a party in Dylan's hotel room, attended by the likes of Donovan, Darroll Adams, Bobby Neuwirth, and Howard Alk. It is at this party that Dylan has the tantrum about "Who threw the fucking glass?," which he surprisingly allowed to be included in *Don't Look Back.* Later on in the party, when things have quieted down a bit, Donovan plays "To Sing for You," which Dylan appears to appreciate. Donovan then requests that Dylan sing "It's All Over Now, Baby Blue," and he duly obliges, followed by performances of "Love Minus Zero" and "She Belongs to Me." Only the first of these songs is featured in *Don't Look Back.*

May 9, Royal Albert Hall, London

There is a party at the Savoy after tonight's concert, which all four Beatles attend.

May 10, Royal Albert Hall, London

Dylan's last solo concert is taped in its entirety by a member of the audience. Fragments of this second show, added after the first show had sold out in a matter of hours, are also featured in *Don't Look Back.* The last sequence in *Don't Look Back* is of Dylan in a taxi after the concert, saying, "God, I feel like I've been through some kind of . . . thing, man . . . something was special about it." The Beatles attend both concerts.

May 9–10

Having returned to the Savoy Hotel in time for two shows at the Royal Albert Hall, Dylan is again subjected to a battery of interviewers. Still resentful toward *Time* and *Newsweek,* Dylan rips into Judson Manning of *Time* before one of the shows. At one point Dylan reminds Manning that one day he'll be dead: "You do your job in the face of that." This verbal onslaught is later a highlight of *Don't Look Back.*

May 10–12

Rehearsals take place for a BBC drama called "Man Without Papers," for which two of Dylan's poems ("Jack of Diamonds" and "Go Joshua Go") have

Newport, 1965

been put to music, sung by his friend Ben Carruthers. It is likely that Dylan attends one or more of the rehearsals. He is even rumored to have contributed some (incidental) music for the play. The exact degree of his involvement remains unknown.

Mid-May (11?)
Dylan reportedly performed with Lee Hazelwood at the Marquee Club on Wardour Street during his stay(s) in London through late April to early May. It has been suggested that the most likely date would be the 11th.

May 12
Dylan is interviewed by Laurie Henshaw of *Disc and Music Echo* but is extremely uncooperative. However, Henshaw is not put off, later writing in *Disc* how much he enjoyed interviewing a pop musician not prepared to simply play the yes man. At one point Dylan claims he made his first record in 1935, "a race record," and that "John Hammond discovered me . . . sitting on a farm." If increasingly hostile to most of the UK press, Dylan is still happy to talk to *Melody Maker,* and Ray Coleman conducts the lengthiest interview of the tour on this or the previous day. Clearly in an expansive mood, Dylan denies being a poet. But he says, "I like to think of myself as the one who carried the lightbulb."

• In the evening, Dylan attempts to record some songs with John Mayall and his band, the Bluesbreakers's, Eric Clapton, John McVie, and Hughie Flint, at Levy's Recording Studio in London. The studio had recently been purchased by CBS and Tom Wilson has flown into London to produce the session. The whole saga proves something of an embarrassment, however, as Dylan and Wilson consume large quantities of wine. After recording a suitably crass message for the 1965 CBS convention in Miami, an attempt is made at "If You Gotta Go, Go Now," which soon collapses. According to Flint, Dylan seemed to take a lot of interest in Clapton. However the session soon fizzles out, with Wilson and Dylan departing arm in arm, clearly the worse for drink. Marc Bolan of T. Rex fame subsequently claimed four songs were recorded at the session, but there is no hard evidence to support his assertion. In attendance throughout the session were Nadia Catouse, Sidney Carter, Paul Jones, and Sally and Al Grossman.

Mid-May (13?)
Dylan again visits Cynthia and John Lennon at their house in Kenwood, Hampstead, probably on the 13th.

Early to Mid-May
New Musical Express asks Dylan to contribute to one of its features, a questionnaire with sections like "Most Thrilling Experience" and "Taste in Music." Dylan returns the form with two of the four pages answered. His replies are somewhat more surreal than *NME* expected. In reply to the above two questions Dylan wrote: "Getting my birthday cake stomped on by Norman Mailer" and "Sort of peanut butter."

May 14 (–21)
Dylan flies to Paris where he meets up with the lovely Sara Lowndes. They then travel to Portugal for a few days holiday, before returning to London Airport on May 21.

May 23
Dylan is due to attend Joan Baez's London concert, but is struck down by a viral complaint shortly after returning from Portugal and is too ill to attend.

May 24
Dylan is due to film for the BBC but is again too ill, and so the recording has to be delayed.

May 26
After several days lying sick in the Savoy Hotel, Dylan finally decides to admit himself to hospital. Consequently, he is transferred to St. Mary's Hospital in Paddington.

May 29
Dylan is discharged from St. Mary's Hospital and returns to the Savoy Hotel for a couple of days of recuperation before the rescheduled filming of two TV specials for the BBC.

June 1

Dylan records two 35-minute TV programs for the BBC, which had outbid Granada for a Dylan TV special, only to then have a delay brought on by Dylan's illness. During the rehearsals for the show, he tries an acoustic "Maggie's Farm," but decides not to attempt it for the shows. The BBC film one of the songs at rehearsal, "Mr. Tambourine Man," but the footage is later destroyed. The two programs feature 12 songs, including three not featured in the then-current repertoire: "Ballad of Hollis Brown," "One Too Many Mornings," and "Boots of Spanish Leather." Except for these three songs, the shows concentrate on newer material, featuring only "The Lonesome Death of Hattie Carroll" and "It Ain't Me, Babe" from the first four albums. The bulk of the shows are taken up with five songs from *Bringing It All Back Home*: "Mr. Tambourine Man," "Gates of Eden," "Love Minus Zero," "She Belongs to Me," and "It's All Over Now, Baby Blue," plus the unreleased "If You Gotta Go, Go Now," which Manfred Mann obtain a copy of for their next single. Also recorded on the same day is a brief interview with Dylan by Sarah Ward, which is subsequently broadcast on BBC 2's "Late Night Line-Up," although the whole sequence, including a clip of "It Ain't Me, Babe" from the TV special, lasts less than five minutes.

June 2

Dylan flies out of London Airport with Sara, having completed his TV special for the BBC.

> June 5, 1965: The Byrds's folk-rock version of "Mr. Tambourine Man" hits number one on the *Billboard* charts.

Mid-year

Dylan moves into his own place near Grossman's house in Byrdcliffe, NY.

Early June

According to Dylan, "Like a Rolling Stone" was written on his return from England, initially in the form of a "long piece of vomit." He invites Mike Bloomfield up to Woodstock at this point to work on some new songs.

June 15

According to legend, this is the date of the famous "Like a Rolling Stone" session, and indeed Dylan does record "Like a Rolling Stone"on the 15th, along with two other songs, in the familiar confines of Studio A in New York, with the reassuring visage of Tom Wilson at the controls. However, a whole series of frustratingly brief snippets of the song on the *Highway 61 Interactive* CD-ROM confirm that, rather than cutting the song in a single take, as Al Kooper long maintained, Dylan labored over "Like a Rolling Stone" longer than just about any song from his recorded works. With Paul Griffin on keyboards, Bobby Gregg on drums, Chicago blues maestro Mike Bloomfield on guitar, and Russ Savakus on bass, Dylan warms up for the session with a fast blues, "Phantom Engineer." Dylan himself is at the piano for "Sitting on a Barbed Wire Fence," and it is presumably Griffin who is

playing those outrageous organ vamps. Both these cuts were extensively bootlegged in the early 1970s and are now featured on *The Bootleg Series,* although a very different, piano-dominated alternate take of "Sitting on a Barbed Wire Fence" remains available only in bootleg form. Then it is on to the real business of the day, cutting "Like a Rolling Stone." At what point Griffin switches to piano and Al Kooper is brought in on organ is not clear, but that is surely Dylan on piano on the incomplete version included on *The Bootleg Series.* Assuming that this is the last of four false starts (and the boxed-set notes are very unhelpful on this point) it is after this take that Dylan abdicates the piano to Griffin and Kooper is given the opportunity to trademark a whole style of organ playing. The final take of the day, with Kooper, is complete but the sound is only just beginning to gel. The entire ensemble, Kooper included, are required to return the following day.

June 16
Work on "Like a Rolling Stone" continues at Studio A. Having figured out the sound he wants, Dylan cuts the definitive version of the song as the second complete take of the day. However, seemingly unconvinced that "Like a Rolling Stone" was now in its most powerful state, Dylan continues to cut versions of the song, nine of them, four complete, until he has driven the band, the song, and the producer to the edge of despair. Finally, playbacks of the session extract the diamond issued as a single just four weeks later. No further finished songs are cut on the 16th, although Dylan and the band do briefly jam on a half-idea he has about someone with a head full of gasoline.

Mid- to Late June
A brief interview in *KRLA Beat* offers to reveal "The mystery man . . . on today's pop scene." Dylan pleads, "Don't put me down as a man with a message."

Late June to Early July
Dylan and Tom Wilson have a major disagreement, resulting in Wilson being replaced for the remaining *Highway 61 Revisited* sessions.

> July 20: "Like a Rolling Stone"/"Gates of Eden" (4-43346)

July 24, Newport Folk Festival
Dylan performs "All I Really Want to Do" during an afternoon workshop. The song subsequently appears in a documentary film of the Newport Folk Festivals 1963–1966, *Festival.*

July 25
Having rehearsed through the night and soundchecked in the afternoon Dylan, backed by Michael Bloomfield on guitar, Sam Lay on drums, Jerome Arnold on bass (all from the Paul Butterfield Blues Band), Al Kooper on organ, and Barry Goldberg on piano, alienates a large Newport crowd by appearing with electric instruments. He deliberately plays music more akin to r&b than folk, opening with a raucous "Maggie's Farm," following it with

the chart-bound "Like a Rolling Stone," and concluding with "Phantom Engineer," a fast prototype for "It Takes a Lot to Laugh, It Takes a Train to Cry." Booed by sections of the audience and, legend has it, with tears in his eyes, he then leaves the stage, but is coaxed back with his "folk" guitar in hand. He bids adieu to the folkies with a poignant "It's All Over Now, Baby Blue" and "Mr. Tambourine Man" (in F). Critical reaction is harsh: Irwin Sibler of *Sing Out!* condemns him and Robert Shelton, in his *Cavalier* review, considers Dylan has misunderstood his audience. Both later recant their initial views. At a party afterward, Dylan sits in the corner, talking with old friends, still clearly shaken by the venom of the audience's response. A hint as to Dylan's state of mind at the time had already been provided in the festival's program, where his contribution was a surreal prose piece entitled "Off the Top of My Head." The performance of "Maggie's Farm" and part of "Mr. Tambourine Man" are included in the film, *Festival.* Accounts of the events of this fateful day seem to be mutually contradictory.

July 26
According to Michael Bloomfield, he met Dylan at a party the day after Newport. Dylan is no longer dismayed by the response at the festival.

July 29
Dylan resumes work on *Bringing It All Back Home*'s successor at Studio A in New York with the same band that brought "Like a Rolling Stone" home. However, he has a new producer in Bob Johnston, a Nashville-based Columbia man. Once again, Dylan warms up for the session ahead by running down "Phantom Engineer," one of the three songs for which he had been roundly condemned at Newport. At some point during this session, Russ Savakus is replaced by Harvey Brooks on bass, probably after "Phantom Engineer." "Tombstone Blues" is cut (a version with the Chambers Brothers was under consideration for *Highway 61 Revisited* but remains unreleased) before it is time for a lunch break, during which Dylan stays behind and reworks "Phantom Engineer" into a slow blues, which they immediately cut on the band's return, as "It Takes a Lot to Laugh, It Takes a Train to Cry." The final song of the session is Dylan's vitriolic riposte to the betrayed folkies, "Positively Fourth Street." An alternate take of this Dylan classic was originally scheduled for inclusion on *The Bootleg Series* but was pulled at the last minute.

July 30
Today's session at Studio A is not quite as productive as the previous day's. Nevertheless, Dylan and co. manage to rustle up an acceptable take of "From a Buick Six," dubbed "Lunatic Princess" on the studio log. In fact, because of a mispressing, an inferior alternate version (also cut on the 30th) appeared on some early pressings of *Highway 61 Revisited.* Also cut today are two versions of another of Dylan's vengeful digs at womanhood, "Can You Please Crawl Out Your Window?" The second of these versions was also mistakenly issued by Columbia when some engineer mistook the song for "Positively Fourth Street." The mispressed "Positively Fourth Street" was quickly withdrawn and remains one of the most collectible of Dylan singles. It is

Newport, 1965

also alleged by Tony Glover, an eyewitness at this session, that they attempted an electric version of "Desolation Row" on the 30th but that it was painfully bad. The log-sheets confirm this. After the session, Dylan, Tony Glover, and Al Kooper leave New York for a quiet weekend in Woodstock.

July 31
Dylan and Kooper spend most of the day writing out chord charts. However, still wired after the week's activities, Dylan buses back to New York at suppertime.

August 2
An epic burst of inspiration leads Dylan to all but complete *Highway 61 Revisited* in a single session at Studio A. After a weekend of furious (re)writing, Dylan begins today's session in audacious fashion, cutting the 11-minute "Desolation Row" in a single take accompanied by Charlie McCoy, specially drafted in from Nashville to play bass. If McCoy is more than a little disoriented by the whole vibe of the session, he apparently stuck around long enough to contribute to a version of "Highway 61 Revisited" before hotfooting it back to Tennessee. Dylan reverts to the ultra-reliable Bloomfield-Gregg-Griffin-Kooper-Brooks combination for the remainder of the session, resulting in four more cuts for *Highway 61 Revisited:* the title track, "Just Like Tom Thumb's Blues," "Queen Jane Approximately," and "Ballad of a Thin Man."

August 4
Dylan is back at Studio A, accompanied by just Bob Johnston and presumably Bruce Langhorne. He has decided to recut "Desolation Row," this time with a simple two-guitar accompaniment, Langhorne being required to provide appropriate flourishes.

Newport, 1965

Early August

Mary Martin, a secretary at Albert Grossman's office, takes Dylan to a New Jersey club to see Levon and the Hawks (soon to become just the Hawks and then The Band).

August 13–14

Dylan visits the Beatles twice at the Riviera Motel near Kennedy International Airport, spending half the night discussing music.

> August 14: "Like a Rolling Stone" peaks at number two on the *Billboard* charts.

Mid-August

Robert Shelton conducts a brief telephone interview with Dylan for his preview of the Forest Hills concert in the *New York Times*. "If anyone has imagination, he'll know what I'm doing," says Dylan.

Mid- to Late August

Dylan rehearses for two weeks at Bob Carroll's rehearsal hall with Robbie Robertson and Levon Helm of the Hawks, plus Harvey Brooks and Al Kooper from his recent studio ensemble.

August 28, Forest Hills Stadium

This time Dylan is determined to be prepared, and after arduous rehearsals with his new band, soundchecks with them on the afternoon of the concert. Although the weather is cold and windy, he has succeeded in selling out

15,000 seats. The format presented at this show is to remain constant throughout the next nine months of touring. The 45-minute opening set features Dylan solo, just guitar and harmonica, followed by a similar-length electric set with the band. The acoustic set he presents is a tour de force of some of his finest writings: "She Belongs to Me," "To Ramona," "Gates of Eden," "Love Minus Zero/No Limit," and his new 11-minute composition, "Desolation Row." He finishes with the same two songs performed solo at Newport: "It's All Over Now, Baby Blue" and "Mr. Tambourine Man." After the intermission Dylan returns with "an excellent rock & roll quartet" (Shelton observes in *The New York Times*), and launches straight into "Tombstone Blues." As if determined to compound the audience's confusion, half of the songs in the electric set are wholly new, and lyrically dense. "Tombstone Blues," "From a Buick Six," "Just Like Tom Thumb's Blues," and "Ballad of a Thin Man" all receive their first public airings. "I Don't Believe You" and "It Ain't Me, Babe" are both rocked up. "Maggie's Farm" and "Like a Rolling Stone" remain from the Newport set. A large contingent in the audience boo throughout the second half, and Dylan quickly exits the stage after "Like a Rolling Stone." The band had rehearsed two songs for possible encores, "Baby Let Me Follow You Down" and "Highway 61 Revisited." Shelton's review in *The New York Times* chastises the audience and extols Dylan's performance. The *Village Voice* considers the crowd reaction virulent enough to warrant a review of the show on its front page.

> August 30: *Highway 61 Revisited* (CL 2389/CS 9189): "Like a Rolling Stone," "Tombstone Blues," "It Takes a Lot to Laugh, It Takes a Train to Cry," "From a Buick Six," "Ballad of a Thin Man," "Queen Jane Approximately," "Highway 61 Revisited," "Just Like Tom Thumb's Blues," "Desolation Row"

Late August to Early September
After the controversy at Forest Hills, Nora Ephron and Susan Edmiston of the *New York Post* interview Dylan regarding his new sound. He talks about chaos, folk-rock, poets, and his new songs; he concludes the interview with, "It's not the bomb that has to go, man, it's the museums."

September 1
The probable date for an evening visit to Atlantic Records's New York studios to witness a Sonny and Cher recording session. This possibly ties in with a story in *New Musical Express* 10 days later suggesting that Dylan had offered to write Sonny and Cher's next single.

September 3, Hollywood Bowl, Los Angeles
With the same band and repertoire as at Forest Hills, Dylan plays a major west coast show. However, this time far more of the audience are enthusiastic about the show, and Dylan treats them to an encore. After the show, he attends a Hollywood-style party, along with 300 other guests, at which he meets a longtime idol, Marlon Brando.

September 4
A press conference is held in a bungalow at the Beverly Hills Hotel, the day after the Hollywood Bowl concert. Dylan arrives with Dave Crosby of the Byrds, a Columbia executive, and a barefoot woman. The conference lasts about an hour, and Dylan again plays his word games with the press, much to mass bemusement. At one point, he announces that his new book *Tarantula* will be "a book of words."

September 9
Dylan is named as a member of the committee organizing a "Sing-In for Peace" at Carnegie Hall on September 24. He does not appear at the actual benefit.

September 15
Dylan flies to Toronto to rehearse with the Hawks at Friars, a Toronto nightclub. Al Kooper has decided not to tour, so the remainder of the Hawks (Garth Hudson, Rick Danko, and Richard Manuel) are reunited with Robertson and Helen, becoming Dylan's backing band for the remainder of the historic 1965–1966 world tour. Dylan flies in by private plane, arriving in the early evening at the Four Seasons Hotel.

September 16
At about midnight on the 15th, Dylan goes to Friars to see the Hawks's late set. Afterward he rehearses with them until 6 AM.

September 17
Dylan again arrives at Friars in the early hours of the morning to catch the Hawks's late set and then to rehearse with them. He takes a break at 2 AM to be interviewed by Robert Fulford of the *Toronto Star* in a bar on Younge Street. In the interview, Dylan describes imitators like Barry McGuire as "not very honest." He is once again called upon to defend his new sound. After rehearsals, he flies back to New York, arriving at noon.

September 23
Dylan and the Hawks arrive in Austin, staying at the Villa Capra Motor Hotel.

September 24
Dylan holds a press conference before his concert in Austin, TX. Again he proves unresponsive to questions about his message. When questioned about God he proclaims that "God is a woman . . . you take it from there."

September 24, Municipal Auditorium, Austin, TX
This is Dylan's first concert backed by Levon and the Hawks, and they play to an enthusiastic crowd. Dylan is so delighted that, three months later, at the San Francisco press conference, he is still praising the Texan audiences. The version of "Maggie's Farm" features Dylan at the piano. Otherwise the show remains along the lines of the Forest Hills show.

Newport, 1965

September 25, Southern Methodist University Coliseum, Dallas, TX

The set, similar to the one in Austin, is greeted by an equally enthusiastic audience.

Late September

Dylan rehearses in Woodstock with the Hawks. According to Michael Krogsgaard, who says there is audio evidence, these include arrangements of "Maggie's Farm," "It Takes a Lot to Laugh," "It Ain't Me, Babe," "Can You Please Crawl Out Your Window?," "Like a Rolling Stone," "Mr. Tambourine Man," the standard "Blues Stay Away from Me," "Tombstone Blues," "Just Like Tom Thumb's Blues," "Ballad of a Thin Man," "I Don't Believe You," "Positively Fourth Street," and Fats Domino's "Please Don't Leave Me."

September to October

Frances Taylor interviews Dylan in his manager's Manhattan office, for a feature in the *Long Island Press*.

October 1, Carnegie Hall, NY

Dylan is again surprised by a favorable reception and performs a rare encore. After "Ballad of a Thin Man" Dylan says, "That was about Mr. Jones, this one's for Mr. Jones," and launches into "Like a Rolling Stone." This show is rumored to include an electric version of "Can You Please Crawl Out Your Window?"

October 2, Symphony Hall, Newark, NJ

October 5(–6?)

For the first time, Dylan enters Studio A with his touring band, the Hawks.

Their primary raison d'etre is to rerecord *Highway 61 Revisited* outtake "Can You Please Crawl Out Your Window?," now intended as the follow-up to the recently charted "Positively Fourth Street." Aside from coming up with the necessary bile to transform "Can You Please . . ." into a hit single, Dylan also attempts to work on three other songs at this session, none of which evolve beyond the half-ideas they had been to start with. "Jet Pilot," which subsequently appears as filler on *Biograph,* is cut last, preceded by the one-verse "Medicine Sunday" (now available on the *Highway 61 Interactive* CD-ROM in inferior quality to the bootlegs) and a song listed as "I Don't Want to Be Your Partner," self-evidently a parody of the Beatles's "I Wanna Be Your Man."

Note: The session may have carried over to the following day. Equally "Can You Please Crawl out Your Window?" may not have been completed until the 20th.

October 9, City Auditorium, Atlanta, GA

Dylan is interviewed before the show by Ann Carter for *The Atlanta Journal.*

October 15 or 17, Civic Center, Baltimore, OH, and McCarter Theatre, Princeton, NJ

Dylan performed at these venues either on the 15th or the 17th (exact date unknown).

October 16, Memorial Auditorium, Worcester, MA

Dylan continues to open the electric half of his concerts with "Tombstone Blues."

October 20

Back at Studio A, Dylan records a complete version of the "I Don't Want to Be Your Partner" fragment previously recorded on the fifth and now entitled "I Wanna Be Your Lover." With Bob Johnston producing and the Hawks playing along, it takes Dylan six attempts to get the song on tape. The final take appears on *Biograph.* An alternate take, presumably also from the 20th, has been bootlegged many times.

Note: Krogsgaard has disputed that such a session ever took place. Possibly, the completed versions of "I Wanna Be Your Lover" date from a session on the sixth.

October 22, Auditorium, Providence, RI

October 23, University of Vermont, Patrick Gymnasium, Burlington, VT

Some time around the middle of October, the electric set undergoes a major change. By Burlington, "Maggie's Farm" and "From a Buick Six" have been dropped from the set. In their place, Dylan is performing versions of "Baby Let Me Follow You Down" and "Positively Fourth Street." The order of the acoustic set has also changed, although the songs remain the same.

October 24, Cobo Hall, Detroit, MI

Dylan is interviewed by Allen Stone for radio station WDTM as he prepares for this evening's concert. The interview lasts some 15 minutes.

October 27

The Rolling Stones arrive in New York, about to embark on their fourth American tour. Dylan visits Brian Jones at the City Squire Hotel, where the Stones are staying, after the Warwick Hotel has declined to give them their customary accommodation.

October 29, Back Bay Theater, Boston, MA

October 30, Bushnell Memorial Auditorium, Hartford, CT

This concert is reviewed for the English music paper *New Musical Express,* which reports that Dylan was mocked with cries of "Go back to England" and "Get rid of the band."

October 31, Back Bay Theater, Boston, MA

October to November

Nat Hentoff, a long-time supporter of Dylan, interviews him for *Playboy.* Dylan responds to the questions without recourse to put-ons. It is his most extensive interview to date, both in length (lasting over two hours) and in the amount of ground covered. At one point Dylan even says, "I guess everybody's smoked pot." The interview is never published officially, although a transcript of the circulating tape is issued as a bookleg in 1986.

October to Early November

A brief interview is conducted by Mary Merryfield for the *Chicago Tribune.* It is, however, an unrevealing affair, with the interviewer more interested in asking Dylan about "The Times They Are a-Changin'" and "Blowin' in the Wind" than his current work.

Note: Although published in November 1965, it is possible that this interview dates from some time earlier, given the nature of the questions.

November

Dylan attends one of the sessions for Tom Rush's album, *Take a Walk with Me.*

November 4

Dylan arrives in Minneapolis, visiting the Ten O'Clock Scholar, McCosh's Bookstore, and several bars in search of his old friend Tony Glover.

November 5, Minneapolis Auditorium, Minneapolis, MN

Dylan and the Hawks perform a nine-song electric set. The ninth song, according to one reviewer, was "Subterranean Homesick Blues" (unlikely).

November 6, Kleinhans Music Hall, Buffalo, NY

November 7

Around midnight on the sixth, Dylan joins with the Rolling Stones at a club called the Phone Booth. Dylan takes Brian Jones around various Greenwich Village clubs until 2 AM, when they totter along to a Wilson Pickett recording session. According to a contemporary report, Dylan and Jones worked on lyrics together at the session. Any results remain unknown.

November 9
Bob Dylan, Robbie Robertson, Brian Jones, and Bobby Neuwirth jam in the City Squire Hotel in New York as a power failure blacks out the whole city.

Early to Mid-November
One night, Dylan, photographer Jerry Schatzberg, and Brian Jones go out to dine together. Presumably Dylan and Schatzberg had been shooting a photo session during the day. Schatzberg would be responsible for the photos on both the front and inside covers of *Blonde on Blonde,* as well as the cover of *Tarantula.* A publicity shot, presumably from this session, is published on the cover of *Publishers Weekly* in December 1965, and is clearly part of the session that produced the cover for *Tarantula.*

November 12, Music Hall, Cleveland, OH

November 14–15, Massey Hall, Toronto, Ontario
On the 15th, Dylan is alleged to have performed an electric version of "Queen Jane Approximately" at one of the Toronto shows. Prior to this show, he is interviewed in his hotel room at the Inn on the Park by Margaret Steen for the Toronto *Star Weekly.* It is a lengthy interview, and Dylan is very forthcoming, even talking about, "the music, the rhyming and rhythm, what I call the mathematics of the song." He also discusses aspects of "She Belongs to Me," "My Back Pages," and "Love Minus Zero/No Limit."

November 18, The Music Hall, Cincinnati, OH

November 19, Veterans Memorial Auditorium, Columbus, OH

November 20, Rochester, NY

November 21, Onodago County War Memorial Auditorium, Syracuse, NY
The set includes "Positively Fourth Street."

November 22
Dylan marries Sara Lowndes at a private ceremony in Nassau County, NY. The wedding is kept secret for several months, even to close friends. Sara is very pregnant.

November 30
While Bob Johnston is working on a stereo mix for "Can You Please Crawl Out Your Window," Dylan and the Hawks (with Bobby Gregg on drums, Helm having quit at the end of November, tired of the booing) take the opportunity to convene at Studio A and cut the man's latest (and probably greatest) magnum opus, the magnificent "Freeze Out" (later to be renamed "Visions of Johanna"). This exhilarating rock version of the song gives perhaps the most accurate reflection of how Dylan and the Hawks sounded live at this point, although "Freeze Out" was apparently never performed live with the Hawks. Despite the undeniable quality of this recording, Dylan decides to return to the song at a later date.

December 1, University of Washington, Seattle, WA

December 2
Arriving in San Francisco, Dylan has supper with beat poets Allen Ginsberg, Peter Orlovsky, and Lawrence Ferlinghetti at a Japanese restaurant. They then head to La Tosca cafe, before ending the evening at Mike's Bar.

December 3
The famous San Francisco press conference takes place at the studios of KQED, an educational TV station in the bay area, at 1 PM. KQED films the entire proceedings, which are broadcast later that evening. A transcript of the full conference is published two years later in *Rolling Stone.* By this point in his career, Dylan has become an expert at only answering those questions he wants to. At one point, to much general amusement, Allen Ginsberg asks Dylan, "Can you ever envisage being hung as a thief?" Ralph J. Gleason is present to stage-manage the press conference. In the evening, Dylan plays the Berkeley Community Theater. After the show, Dylan has supper at Robbie's Bar before attending a party where he is briefly interrogated by writer Ken Kesey.

December 4, Community Theater, Berkeley
Ralph Gleason reviews both Berkeley shows for the *San Francisco Chronicle.* On both nights, Dylan performs a new song during the electric set, "Long Distance Operator." He also premiers a new song during tonight's acoustic set. It is introduced as "Freeze Out," which had also been mentioned during the press conference the previous day.

December 5 and 11, Masonic Memorial Auditorium, San Francisco, CA

December 7, Civic Auditorium, Long Beach, CA

December 10, Community Concourse Theater, San Diego, CA

December 12, Civic Auditorium, San Jose, CA

Early to Mid-December
Dylan, actress/Warhol groupie Edie Sedgwick, and probably Bobby Neuwirth stay at the Castle, a mansion in Hollywood, during the west coast tour.

• While on the west coast, Dylan renews his friendship with *San Francisco Chronicle* jazz critic Ralph J. Gleason. They spend some time together discussing Dylan's new-found fame. Several quotes from these conversations are later included in Gleason's major profile of Dylan in the March 1966 issue of *Ramparts.*

December 16
Dylan's second west coast press conference in two weeks takes place in Los Angeles. His mood is far less amenable than it had been in San Francisco. The conference lasts just over half an hour. Again it is filmed and, although

primarily intended as news coverage, some eight minutes of black and white footage is in circulation, showing an increasingly annoyed Dylan coming clean, "I have none of those feelings: pain, remorse, love . . ."

December 18, Civic Auditorium, Pasadena, CA

December 19, Civic Auditorium, Santa Monica, CA

Dylan flies back to New York shortly after the Santa Monica show, probably on the morning of the 20th.

Late December

After spending the day at a photo session with Jerry Schatzberg (probably the outdoor shots used on the *Blonde on Blonde* inner sleeve); the evening sees Dylan launch into one of his so-called truth-attacks on Phil Ochs, who has unwisely expressed disappointment with Dylan's new single "Can You Please Crawl Out Your Window?" while still sitting in Dylan's limousine. After the verbal onslaught Dylan orders Ochs out of the car.

• Dylan sits for a filmed portrait by Andy Warhol, taking as payment one of Warhol's paintings of Elvis Presley. The filming takes place at the Factory and is apparently "a fifteen minute study in silence."

• Dylan meets with Brian Jones and Anita Pallenburg at the Chelsea Hotel. Dylan asks Brian, "Where's your paranoia?"

• Shortly before Christmas, Dylan crashes a party being thrown by Paul and Betty Stookey at their home in Greenwich Village. He leaves just before 3 AM and drives to the Clique club with Phil Ochs, David Blue, and Robert Shelton.

Paul Stookey was, of course, Noel Paul Stookey of Peter, Paul, and Mary.

Phil Ochs was a topical singer/songwriter who, in folk circles at least, was considered to be on a par with Dylan. "From a Buick" later crossed over into popular folk music, but never was terribly successful. Depressed by his failure to make it big, he committed suicide in 1976.

David Blue (born David Cohen) was another singer/songwriter who had brief fame in the late '60s early '70s.

"Can You Please Crawl Out Your Window"/"Highway 61 Revisited" (4-43477)

December 28, 1965

Dylan, Andy Warhol, and Edie Sedgwick are out partying at the New York club Arthur. Dylan spends several evenings in late December in the company of Edie Sedgwick and Bobby Neuwirth.

1966

Early January
Dylan visits the Village Vanguard.

January
The birth of Jesse Byron Dylan.

• After a heavy-handed editor at *Playboy* edits Nat Hentoff's Dylan interview, a furious Dylan calls Hentoff. Although Hentoff initially suggests scrapping the interview, Dylan suggests they make answers up. So a spoof interview is composed over the phone, with Hentoff writing the "script" by hand. The new interview is forwarded to *Playboy* with no indication that it is one of Dylan's put-ons. Many of the quotes from the article are instantly memorable, and the piece is the most oft-quoted of all Dylan interviews. Although designed to reveal little, the article features marvelously surreal responses to the sort of questions the baffled media continually asked Dylan through 1965 and into 1966. Through the whole charade, Hentoff plays an admirable straight man.

January 21
Dylan and the Hawks have booked four days at Studio A, hoping to cut a successor to *Highway 61 Revisited.* With Bobby Gregg on drums, they spend the first session working on two major works, "Freeze Out" and a new song called "She's Your Lover Now." Dylan records a solo piano version of the latter, before proceeding to cut the song with the Hawks. For reasons we do not know, an electric version is never completed, although a superb take, that breaks down during the final verse, is later included on *The Bootleg Series.*

January 25
Dylan and the Hawks return to Studio A with producer Bob Johnston to continue working on new songs. Although it would be hard to fault Garth Hudson's input on the 21st, Dylan has decided to draft in Al Kooper on organ for this session, which results in versions of "Leopard-Skin Pill-Box Hat" and, after much work, "One of Us Must Know," which is destined to become Dylan's next single. However, Dylan seems to have very little in reserve songwise.

January 26
Dylan and friends (Al Kooper, alias Roosevelt Gook, and Victor Maimudes, alias Pete the Suede) appear on Bob Fass's early morning WBAI radio show,

participating in a two-hour phone-in. Both Dylan and Fass sound extremely stoned. When asked to "turn on the telephone" Dylan replies, "Your telephone is very infamous." The whole phone-in becomes a series of hilarious verbal confrontations with Dylan. When one caller says he is hungry, Dylan retorts, "Tell me, are you hungry as a man in drag?" At the end of the show, Dylan talks about the single he has just recorded, and the sessions that are taking place. A session scheduled for the 26th is canceled.

January 27
A final January session at Studio A fails to yield any releasable goodies. "Leopard-Skin Pill-Box Hat" is once again attempted, and then discarded. As evidence of Dylan's desperation to come up with album tracks at this point, they attempt "I'll Keep It with Mine," although it is never fully realized. It is still one of the more pleasant surprises on *The Bootleg Series*.

January 31
According to A. F. of M. records, a session was booked for this day at Studio A. Possibly it was a mixing session.

> February: "One of Us Must Know"/"Queen Jane Approximately" (4-43541)

February 5, Westchester County Center, White Plains, NY
For the winter 1966 leg of Dylan's world tour, the acoustic set remains the same as Forest Hills, save for the replacement of "Gates of Eden" with "Freeze Out." The electric set, however, has a new opening song, called "Tell Me Momma." According to Dylanologist A. J. Weberman, "One of Us Must Know" is also played at Westchester. "Leopard-Skin Pill-Box Hat" replaces "It Ain't Me, Babe" in the 1966 set. "Positively Fourth Street," "Ballad of a Thin Man," "Like a Rolling Stone," "Baby Let Me Follow You Down," "I Don't Believe You," and "Just Like Tom Thumb's Blues" are all retained. However, there is a new drummer for this leg of the tour, Sandy Konikoff replacing Bobby Gregg.

February 6, Syria Mosque, Pittsburgh, PA
A member of the audience has the foresight to record (parts of) tonight's show, which includes "Positively Fourth Street" with the Hawks.

February 7(–9?), Louisville, KY

February 10, Ellis Auditorium Amphitheater, Memphis, TN

February 11, Shrine Mosque, Richmond, VA

February 12, Municipal Auditorium, Norfolk, VA

February 14
Dylan arrives in Nashville for his first session at Columbia's renowned Mu-

sic Row Studios with Al Kooper and Robbie Robertson in tow. Bob Johnston has assembled the "A" list of Nashville musicians for these sessions, which result in *Blonde on Blonde.* Wayne Moss, Jerry Kennedy, and Charlie McCoy all contribute their guitar licks, Joe South plays bass, Ken Buttrey is the drummer, and Hargus "Pig" Robinson plays piano. No one seems entirely aware of Dylan's stature. On day one, Dylan finally cuts the versions required of two songs attempted in January, "Visions of Johanna" and "Leopard-Skin Pill-Box Hat," Dylan even playing lead guitar himself on the latter. He also records "Fourth Time Around," complete with strange harmonium-like noises. An auspicious start to Dylan's first Nashville sessions.

February 15

Aside from an instrumental listed on the studio log as "Keep It with Mine," only one song is cut at today's session at Music Row Studios. According to Buttrey and McCoy, this song was cut in a single take. In fact the studio records confirm that the song was attempted four times, and that three of the takes were marked as complete. The idea of two complete, alternate "Sad-Eyed Lady of the Lowlands" is certainly an intriguing thought. In fact, Dylan spends the bulk of the session writing and rewriting whole chunks of the song he intends to record. When the tapes finally start rolling, "Sad-Eyed Lady of the Lowlands" clocks in at 12 minutes, eventually occupying the whole of side four of *Blonde on Blonde.*

February 16

Another long, drawn-out session at Music Row Studios is spent writing and rewriting, carrying over into the morning of the 17th. It is the early hours of the morning before Dylan and the bemused musicians realize a usable take of "Stuck Inside of Mobile." Dylan leaves Nashville early on the 17th.

February 18

According to Shelton, Dylan played in New Haven between the Norfolk and Ottawa shows. This is the only possible date, given the recording sessions in Nashville. However, a late February date, around the time of the Hempstead show, seems a tad more likely.

February 19, Ottawa Auditorium, Ottawa, Ontario

The sound at this concert is so poor that the reviewer for the *Ottawa Citizen* thought Dylan performed an electric version of "Only a Pawn in Their Game."

February 20, Place des Arts, Montreal, Quebec

Prior to the show, Dylan is interviewed by Martin Bronstein for CBC radio. The 12-minute interview is later unearthed when Dylan returns to Montreal in 1974, at which point it is published in British literary magazine *Bananas.* The most important (and quoted) part of the interview is when Dylan discusses the composition of "Like a Rolling Stone": "I found myself writing this song, this story, this long piece of vomit, about twenty pages long, and out of it I took 'Like a Rolling Stone.'"

February 24–25, Academy of Music, Philadelphia, PA

February 26, Island Gardens, Hempstead, NY
After "She Belongs to Me," Dylan has replaced "To Ramona" with "Fourth Time Around." "Freeze Out" is now "Visions of Johanna." In the electric half Dylan has added another song to the set, a magnificently atmospheric version of "One Too Many Mornings."

March 3, Miami Convention Hall, Miami, FL
Dylan is the subject of a very brief interview by 14-year-old Louise Sokol before this Miami concert. It is later published by *Datebook* in their series, "Teens Interview Stars."

March 8
Dylan has three more days of sessions booked at Nashville's Music Row Studios, hoping to complete a worthy successor to *Highway 61 Revisited.* In the three weeks between Nashville visits, Dylan has been letting the songs pour out. At this first session, with the same grade A Nashville musicians (plus Henry Strzelecki, contributing some bass), Dylan cuts two of his catchiest melodies, "Absolutely Sweet Marie" and "Just Like a Woman." He also allows himself an obligatory slow blues, "Pledging My Time," driven by some wailing harmonica.

March 9
The sessions at Music Row Studios have at last reached a plateau where the musicians no longer need to second guess their bandleader, and Dylan is more concerned with getting the best take than throwing the guys a curveball or two. Today's session results in "Most Likely You Go Your Way" and "Temporary Like Achilles."

March 10
The final *Blonde on Blonde* session, at Music Row Studios, gives Dylan the three songs he needs to make his next album one of rock's first double sets. "Obviously Five Believers," "I Want You," and "Rainy Day Women" make a fitting end to the Nashville experiment. Dylan also attempts his fourth "Leopard-Skin Pill-Box Hat" this one apparently complete with doorbell noises, although it is the version cut at the first February session that ends up on *Blonde on Blonde.*

March 11, Kiel Opera House, St. Louis, MO

**March 12, Pershing Memorial Auditorium,
University of Nebraska, Lincoln, NE**
Dylan is apparently well received at this show.

March 12–13
Robert Shelton's most exhaustive interview with Dylan takes place before and during a midnight flight between Lincoln, NE, and Denver, CO. Dylan is in physically poor condition by this point in the 1966 tour, and much of what he has to say comes across as unconnected and rambling. Nevertheless,

the interview proves to be one of the few notable surprises in Shelton's biography, *No Direction Home.* When Dylan and Robbie Robertson arrive at their Denver hotel at 3 AM, they jam in Dylan's hotel room for an hour. Shelton tapes the session on his portable reel-to-reel. Although it is just three days after Dylan completed *Blonde on Blonde,* Dylan and Robertson work on three new songs that, had they been given titles and not simply forgotten by Dylan, might have been called "Positively Van Gogh," "Don't Tell Him," and "If You Want My Love." Dylan then plays "Just Like a Woman" and "Sad-Eyed Lady of the Lowlands" for Shelton's benefit, before deciding it is time to get some sleep.

March 13
During the afternoon, Dylan travels with Robert Shelton along Highway 58 from Denver to Central City. They walk around Central City before Shelton continues the interview back at Dylan's Denver motel room.

March 13, Civic Auditorium, Denver, CO

Mid- to Late March
While staying in the Hollywood Hills, Dylan has his first meeting with Jules Siegel, who is writing a profile on him for the *Saturday Evening Post.*
   • Dylan supposedly plays a show in San Jose and possibly another show in the San Francisco area at this time.

March 24, Paramount Theater, Portland, OR

March 25, Seattle Center Arena, Seattle, WA

March 26, Pacific National Exhibition Agrodome, Vancouver, BC
The sound is horrendous. "Love Minus Zero" is removed from the acoustic set in favor of "Just Like a Woman." "Positively Fourth Street" makes its last documented appearance in the 1966 set. Dylan is in quite a talkative mood, introducing "Just Like Tom Thumb's Blues" with, "This song is about a painter. Not too many songs are about a painter. This one lived in Mexico City. I know it's a long way away but some of you might have been there sometime. He lived with Indians in the jungle." He also states, after "Ballad of a Thin Man," that "Mr. Jones lives in Lincoln, Nebraska . . . he hangs around bowling alleys there. He also owns watermill rights. But we don't talk about that when we're in Nebraska. We just let Mr. Jones have his little way." After six months touring the States, this is Dylan's final North American tour date. Jules Siegel, who met Dylan in Los Angeles, accompanies and interviews him on the last couple of concerts. Siegel's profile is published the day after Dylan's fabled motorcycle accident.

March 27, Tacoma, WA

March 30
Dylan and "his group" spend the evening at Columbia's Studio D in Los Angeles according to AF of M records, entering the studio at 10:25 PM.

The notes indicate the session was "rehearsal only, no mike or engineer [required]." Presumably the session was a run-through for new drummer, Mickey Jones.

Early April

Dylan attends a screening of *Don't Look Back,* which Pennebaker has now completed to his satisfaction. The private screening is in Hollywood, and afterward Dylan says there will have to be major changes, which he will propose after another screening the following day. However, at the next day's screening, Dylan decides the film is fine as it is.

"Rainy Day Women #12 & 35"/"Pledging My Time" (4-43592)

April 6

Still in Los Angeles, Dylan has a photo session with Art Kane on a rooftop above Sunset Strip.

April 7

Dylan, due to fly out to Hawaii, delays the trip "to do extra work on a long-playing album." Presumably this relates to the mixing of *Blonde on Blonde.*

April 8

Dylan attends an Otis Redding show at the Cafe Au Go-Go, Los Angeles. Afterward he ventures backstage and offers Otis some unreleased songs.

April 9

Dylan and the Hawks embark on their world tour with a concert at the Honolulu International Center Arena. Mickey Jones has replaced Sandy Konikoff on drums for this leg of the tour.

April 10

Dylan, Al Grossman, and the Hawks fly from Honolulu to Australia. It is a 36-hour flight.

April 12

Dylan arrives at Sydney Airport and is greeted by a curious Australian press. The airport press conference prepares him for the blank incomprehension he is to meet from most journalists in Australia. Faced with questions like "Why have you gone commercial?" and "Are you a professional beatnik?," Dylan resorts to his usual series of put-ons. After this farce, he is interviewed for a national television program due to be broadcast that Thursday (April 14). The bland interviewer seems unable to cope with Dylan's surreal responses, and the interview rapidly grinds to a halt. Amused by the whole circus, Dylan improvises an interview with himself, to the great amusement of the band, Al Grossman, and Craig McGregor, an Australian journalist. Dylan is then driven to the King's Cross Hotel in Sydney, where he has to undergo another press conference. Both conferences receive extensive coverage the following day. Dylan appears on the front pages of both Sydney

Leopard-Skin Pill-Box Hat, Sheet Music, 1966

dailies, and the tour receives worldwide coverage in *Newsweek,* *Variety,* and *Melody Maker.* The hotel press conference features typically obscure responses from Dylan. He claims to have been a thief, and when asked whether he was ever caught, replies, "Yes, once by a priest. He converted me and I became a folksinger." When asked about a general theme in his songs, he says, "They're all about the Second Coming." It would also appear that he was interviewed on a one-to-one basis in his hotel room by Ron Saw of the *Sydney Daily Mirror* and Uli Schmetzer, for an unknown Australian paper.

Mid-April
While in Australia, Dylan is interviewed for the Australian music paper, *Music Maker.* He is also apparently interviewed by John Cornell for *The West Australian.*

April 13 and 16, Sydney Stadium, Sydney

April 15, Festival Hall, Brisbane
When Dylan arrives at Brisbane, he is interviewed, one-to-one, in the VIP lounge of the airport. The interview is intended for either radio or TV. There is also a press conference held in the lounge, presumably before the one-to-one interview.

April 17
Dylan conducts a press conference in the VIP lounge of Melbourne international airport. One reporter also endeavors to interview him on the tarmac.

April 18
In the afternoon, local beat poet Adrian Rawlins provides a tour of Fitzroy, Melbourne's slum area, for Dylan, Robbie Robertson, Victor Maimudes, and soundman Richard Van Dyke. They then head down to the university campus, stopping a succession of girls, each of whom fails to recognize Dylan.

April 19–20, Festival Hall, Melbourne
One of the two Melbourne shows is broadcast on Australian radio. A radio station acetate later emerges with (part of) "She Belongs to Me," "Fourth Time Around," "Visions of Johanna" (introduced as "Mother Revisited"), "It's All Over Now, Baby Blue," and "Desolation Row." In 1978, a further song from the acoustic set is broadcast on Australian radio, a truly remarkable version of "Just Like a Woman." Dylan sounds extremely stoned. Part of the same Melbourne concert is also filmed, and is shown on Australian television in January 1967. It comprises three songs from the electric set: "Tell Me Momma," "Baby Let Me Follow You Down," and "Just Like Tom Thumb's Blues," which is introduced as a song about a 124-year-old Mexican artist called Tom Thumb. Dylan's voice is extremely rough, but the performance is, if anything, even more intense than the English shows. After the first concert, Dylan goes to a disco club called Pinocchio's. In the early hours of the 20th, in his hotel suite, Dylan and Adrian Rawlins talk about college and Dylan's early years. Smoking hash constantly, Dylan at one point picks up his guitar and sings "Sad-Eyed Lady of the Lowlands" for Rawlins's benefit.

April 21

Dylan faces a press conference in Adelaide. Part of it is broadcast on local radio. Dylan is also interviewed by Brian Taylor for the TV channel ADS7. The interview is subsequently part of the "News Report" program.

April 22, Palais-Royal, Adelaide

April 23

The final press conference on the Australian leg of Dylan's world tour takes place at Perth Airport. Dylan, dressed in striped trousers, polka dot shirt, and bare feet, views the whole proceedings with detached amusement.

April 23, Capitol Theater, Perth

After the show, Dylan meets Rosemary Gerrette, an actress, who hangs around with him for the last couple of days in Australia. She later recounts her experiences to biographer Anthony Scaduto.

"Rainy Day Women" reaches number two on the *Billboard* charts, Dylan's biggest hit single.

April 25–26

Australian actress Rosemary Gerrette sits in on an all-night session with Dylan and Robbie Robertson, who are staying up to ensure that they are tired enough to sleep through the 27-hour flight to Stockholm. According to Gerrette, Dylan and Robertson work on six new songs for which "the poetry seemed already to have been written." At 7 AM, Dylan reads parts of *Tarantula* to her.

April 26

Dylan and the Hawks fly from Australia to Stockholm, possibly via Copenhagen, to begin the European leg of their arduous world tour.

April 27

Dylan arrives at Stockholm airport. Newsreel footage shows him walking across the tarmac carrying one of his little props (what looks like a child's umbrella). During his stay in Stockholm, he resides at the Flamingo Hotel.

April 28

Dylan conducts his first European press conference at a small restaurant in Solna, a suburb of Stockholm. He is in top form, although the questions are numbingly predictable, for example: "How much money do you have?" "I have about 75 million dollars, all sewn into my jacket-lining."; "Are you a protest singer?" "No, I sing mathematical songs . . . I deal with subjects like hunger and thirst. . . " Later, he is interviewed by a few journalists at a small gathering at the Flamingo Hotel. On this occasion he plays an acetate of *Blonde on Blonde*. One journalist complains "that it sometimes can be really difficult to hear and understand what he sings on his records." Dylan, though, is more helpful than at the earlier conference, confessing at one point, "What I'm doing would exist whether people looked on or not." Among those in attendance are journalists Jan Persson, Bjorn Larsson, and Carsten Crolin.

April 29

In the morning Dylan visits Gulins, a clothes shop, and Sandbergs, a book-shop, where he tries to buy a version of Rimbaud's poetry in English. After lunch, Dylan and the Hawks soundcheck, rehearsing a version of "Just Like Tom Thumb's Blues." During the day, Dylan is interviewed at the Swedish Radio Building in Stockholm by Klas Burling. The interview lasts some 12 minutes. The evening show at the Stockholm Konserthaut apparently features a rare encore.

April 30

Flying into Copenhagen airport in the morning, Dylan is driven to Vaed-baek, a village 20 miles north of Copenhagen, to conduct a press conference at the Hotel Marina. A brief segment from this conference appears in the 1966 tour documentary, *Eat the Document.* Dylan practices answering questions with questions, at one point taking out a notebook and asking a jour-nalist, "When does the sun rise in the country?" then jotting an answer down. Dylan's other questions range from "When does the sun set?" to "Where is the nearest cow?" One poor woman when asked by Dylan what her favorite music is, replies, "Beethoven's symphonies." Dylan retorts, "Yes, but I was thinking about your favorite music." After the conference Dylan visits Kronberg castle, the home of Hamlet. His film crew shoots footage throughout, although none of it is included in *Eat the Document.*

May

A live recording of "Tell Me Momma," taped during the European shows, is subsequently lodged with Dwarf Music as a demo. The recording appears to be a composite of two versions, although neither location is known.

May 1, KB Hallen, Copenhagen, Denmark

May 2

While filming footage for the 1966 tour documentary at Copenhagen's docks at dawn, Dylan meets the captain of an American destroyer who claims to have once written a book called *One Too Many Mornings,* shakes a bemused Dylan's hand, and takes his leave. Flying into London in the afternoon, Dy-lan meets Beatles's road manager Neil Aspinall and Paul McCartney at Dol-ly's Club in the evening. Dylan arrives at the club with Keith Richards and Brian Jones of the Rolling Stones.

May 3

Dylan, staying at the Mayfair Hotel in London, gives his 15th press confer-ence in a year. Again the press is totally bemused, leading to headlines like "At Least in His Songs Mr. Dylan Has Something to Say" and "Cliff Richard Was Never Like This." The questions are all fairly obvious, although when asked what his book is about, Dylan replies: "It's about spiders . . . it's an insect book." Asked to explain the title "Rainy Day Women," he says he can't unless "you been down in North Mexico for six straight months." A couple of excerpts from this conference are included in *Eat the Document*. After the conference, Dylan obligingly climbs out onto the balcony of the Mayfair so that he can be photographed, shades in hand, peering down upon the people.

• In the evening, Dylan, Dana Gillespie, and Paul McCartney go to see John Lee Hooker perform at the London club, Blaises. Afterward they return to Dylan's hotel room at the Mayfair where McCartney plays him the *Revolver* album and Dylan plays the acetates of *Blonde on Blonde*.

May 5, Adelphi Theatre, Dublin, Ireland

CBS records this concert. A PA recording of the acoustic half of the show is subsequently widely bootlegged. The extant tape features "Visions of Johanna," "Fourth Time Around," "It's All Over Now, Baby Blue," "Desolation Row," "Just Like a Woman," and "Mr. Tambourine Man" (but not "She Belongs to Me," presumably performed). Although the acoustic set seems to be well received, the audience is hostile throughout the electric set. One review of the show is headlined "Night of the Big Let Down." According to Robbie Robertson, some of the audience were even holding up placards saying "Stop the War." A recording of "I Don't Believe You" from the electric set is eventually released on the *Biograph* set, incorrectly assigned to Belfast.

May 6, ABC Theatre, Belfast, Northern Ireland

May 7

Dylan returns to London from Belfast.

May 10, Colston Hall, Bristol

Amid shouts of "Turn it down," and people walking out, Dylan plays his first electric set on English soil. The headline in the *Bristol Evening Post* reads: "Day of Disillusionment for Dylan Fans."

May 11, Capitol Theatre, Cardiff, Wales

The probable location for Dylan and Johnny Cash's meeting. Part of their backstage duet on "I Still Miss Someone" appears in *Eat the Document*.

May 12

Dylan, escorted by Steve and Muff Winwood of the Spencer Davis Group, spends the afternoon visiting a haunted farmhouse in Solihull.

May 12, The Odeon, Birmingham

Dylan reacts to audience hostility during the electric half by sarcastically introducing the vamped-up "Baby, Let Me Follow You Down" with, "If you want some folk music, I'll play you some folk music . . . this is a folksong my granddaddy used to sing to me . . . it goes like this . . ."

May 14, The Odeon, Liverpool

A truly demonic "Just Like Tom Thumb's Blues" from this show is issued (in mono) as the b-side of "I Want You." For many years, this would be the only official evidence of the power of Dylan and the Hawks in performance.

May 15, De Montfort Hall, Leicester

May 16, Gaumont Theatre, Sheffield
After the show, Dylan and his entourage return to the Grand Hotel, where they listen to a tape of tonight's performance. A reporter who is present describes this as "a nightly ritual."

> *Blonde on Blonde* (C2L 41/CS8 841): "Rainy Day Women Nos. 12 & 35," "Pledging My Time," "Visions of Johanna," "One of Us Must Know (Sooner or Later)," "I Want You," "Stuck Inside of Mobile," "Leopard-Skin Pill-Box Hat," "Just Like a Woman," "Most Likely You Go Your Way," "Temporary Like Achilles," "Absolutely Sweet Marie," "Fourth Time Around," "Obviously Five Believers," "Sad-Eyed Lady of the Lowlands"

May 17, Free Trade Hall, Manchester
CBS records this concert for a possible live album, and it is this show that is mistakenly labeled "Royal Albert Hall" by the engineer, leading to dozens of bootleg versions of the electric set being misattributed to the London venue. Post-concert interviews with angry members of this audience are included in *Eat the Document*.

May 18 or 19
Dylan and Robbie Robertson are filmed by Pennebaker in a Glasgow hotel room during one of their jam sessions. They are clearly working on some new material. Three songs are included in *Eat the Document:* "What Kind of Friend Is This?," "I Can't Leave Her Behind," and "On a Rainy Afternoon" (the copyrighted title of a song usually referred to as "Does She Need Me," a joking reference to the reason for the hotel jam session, rather than an explanation of the contents of the song). "What Kind of Friend Is This" is (very) loosely based on Koko Taylor's "What Kind of Man Is This?" but remains a very Dylanesque reinterpretation. "I Can't Leave Her Behind" seems to require the most effort, and at least two versions of the song are filmed, *Eat the Document* featuring an edit of both. Dylan seems to be directing operations while behaving severely stoned, yet the results remain as moving as anything already recorded in Nashville.

Blonde on Blonde, advertisement 1966

May 19, The Odeon, Glasgow

The Scottish *Daily Mail* reports: "Folk Fans Walk Out on Dylan." Pennebaker films this concert from the stage for *Eat the Document,* however very little footage in the film dates from this concert.

May 20, ABC Theatre, Edinburgh

The Scottish *Daily Mail* is once again on hand to report that "Dylan faces [a] second night of cat calls." Two songs recorded by the film crew, "One Too Many Mornings" and "Like a Rolling Stone," are subsequently broadcast in New York on the WNEW radio station.

May 21, The Odeon, Newcastle

May 22

Dylan flies into Le Bourget airport in Paris, before heading for the George V Hotel on the exclusive Champs-Elysees. In the evening, he visits a nightclub in St. Germain de Pres and at 12:45 PM goes to Pastel's Club for a prearranged meeting with French pop singer Johnny Halliday.

May 23

The final press conference of Dylan's 1966 world tour takes place at the George V Hotel in Paris. Dylan arrives with a marionette doll, which he perches on his knee throughout the conference. Asked what it represents, he replies, "It's a religion of tears and wailing." Asked the doll's name, he responds Finian. Asked what he is certain of, "The existence of ashes, doorknobs, and windowpanes."

May 23 or 24

Dylan is visited at the George V by Mike Porco, the owner of Gerdes Folk City, the man who gave him his first major break in New York.

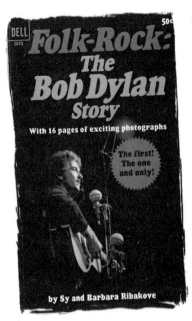

May 24, L'Olympia, Paris

Dylan, who is having genuine trouble tuning his guitar throughout the first half of the show, receives an unusual crowd response: hostility during the acoustic set. According to one report in *Pop* magazine, Dylan's standard seven-song set lasted 65 minutes. Clearly frustrated, Dylan tells the hecklers, "Go to the bowling-hall until I'm finished!" When he returns with the Hawks for the second half, the curtains open to reveal a massive American flag draped across the back of the stage. The French press respond with predictable fury. The concert is recorded for French radio but it is not broadcast. According to one source, Dylan vetoed it at the last minute.

The first book on Bob Dylan, 1966.

May 26, Royal Albert Hall, London, England

In circulation from this show are three acoustic songs and three electric songs, part of the widely bootlegged *Gelston* acetates. Before "Leopard-Skin Pill-Box Hat" someone shouts something at Dylan, and he threatens, "Come up here and say that!" The offer is not taken up.

Before a nine-minute "Like a Rolling Stone," which Dylan dedicates to the Taj Mahal, he introduces the Hawks for the first and only time on the tour.

Late May (26?)

Dylan visits the fashionable Cromwellian club in London, probably in the company of members of the Rolling Stones and/or the Beatles.

May 27

It is presumably on this day that Dylan and John Lennon are filmed by Pennebaker in the back of a taxi cab driving around London, a brief snippet of which appears in *Eat the Document.* They are self-evidently smacked out of their heads. The Beatles attend tonight's show.

May 27, Royal Albert Hall, London

The final show of the 1966 world tour. Thankfully the entire acoustic half has emerged on acetate. CBS in fact recorded both nights at the Royal Albert Hall for a possible live album. Before performing "Visions of Johanna," Dylan launches into a verbal attack on those critics who accuse him of writing drug songs, informing them the next song, "is not a drurg [sic] song. It's just vulgar to think so." But the highlight of this, the final 1966 acoustic set is a six-and-a-half minute "Just Like a Woman," Dylan veering in and out of control of his phrasing. During the electric set, tempers, both on and off the stage, become frayed. Before "I Don't Believe You," Dylan announces, "I get accused of dismissing my old songs. That's not true. I luuurve my old songs." At the time critics are divided as to the merits of the two London shows. Ray Coleman, in *Disc and Music Echo,* felt that Dylan, "insults his own talents . . . [with] a shamble of noise." The London *Times* reviewer, writing up the first London show, much preferred the acoustic set, entitling his article, "The Better Half of Dylan." After Dylan's motorcycle accident, though, the shows will quickly achieve mythic status.

Late May

Dylan and his new wife, Sara, head down to Spain for a brief holiday.

June

Dylan travels to New York from Woodstock to discuss some last minute changes to *Tarantula* with Macmillan editor Robert Markel. Publication has been set for late summer, and the publicity machine has been put in gear, with *Tarantula* shopping bags and badges being distributed to bookshops.

"I Want You"/"Just Like Tom Thumb Blues" (4-43683); the B-side was recorded live in Liverpool.

June 23 or 24

Dylan attends a John Hammond Jr. recording session. Robbie Robertson is playing guitar and Bill Wyman of the Rolling Stones has volunteered to play bass. The resultant songs appear on the *I Can Tell* album.

Early July

Dylan's Chelsea Hotel apartment is the venue for a party whose guests include painter Brice Marden, actress Edie Sedgwick, Robbie Robertson, Brian Jones, and Mick Jagger.

Note: Dylan biographer Bob Spitz attributes this party to late July but the Stones were already touring the United States. The only possible dates are the last week of June and the first five days of July.

July

After Neuwirth and D. A. Pennebaker have worked on the film footage from the European tour, Dylan spends two or three days with Pennebaker watching the rushes in a film studio.

• Robbie Robertson joins Dylan in Woodstock with the ostensible purpose of helping him edit the 1966 tour documentary. The remainder of the Hawks will soon join him there, renting a house painted pink, in West Saugerties.

Saturday Evening Post, 1966

July 29
Dylan falls off his motorcycle while riding around Albert Grossman's estate in Woodstock. He is taken to Middletown Hospital, where x-rays reveal a cracked vertebra. Although not a serious accident, Dylan is in poor physical shape at the time. The accident affords him time to recuperate and relax after months of living a pressure-cooker existence.

August: "Just Like a Woman"/"Obviously Fire Believers"
(4-43792)

August 3: Lenny Bruce dies of a drug overdose.

Early August
In a 1987 interview, Dylan claimed to spend some time recuperating at a doctor's house in Woodstock after leaving hospital. Biographer Spitz refers to Dylan being treated by Dr. Ed Thayler in Middletown and, on one occasion, staying at Thayler's for a while. However, he implies that this was a couple of months after the accident.

Mid- to Late August
A few days after Dylan's motorcycle accident, D. A. Pennebaker visits him in Woodstock to discuss the 1966 tour documentary. Dylan is walking around in a neck brace.

August 19
Allen Ginsberg visits Dylan in Woodstock. According to Ginsberg, Dylan was still in bed recuperating from his accident. Ginsberg brings him some light reading material: Emily Dickinson, Bertolt Brecht, Arthur Rimbaud, William Blake, and Percy Shelley.

October 13
CBS announces that Dylan "has not scheduled any performance before March 1967."

December
Dylan's office attempts to place an injunction on Citadel Press to stop the publication of Daniel Kramer's book of photographs of Dylan, claiming an infringement of his privacy. The legal plea is rejected, however, and the book is rescheduled for publication in March 1967.

1967

Winter

Mort Nasatir visits Dylan at his home in Woodstock to discuss the likelihood of Dylan signing with MGM now that his contract with CBS is about to expire. Dylan seems in good health and keen to leave CBS.

> March 27: *Bob Dylan's Greatest Hits* (KCL 2263/KCS 9463): "Rainy Day Women Nos. 12 & 35," "Blowin' in the Wind," "Subterranean Homesick Blues," "Like a Rolling Stone," "Positively 4th Street," "The Times They Are a-Changin'," "It Ain't Me Babe," "Mr. Tambourine Man," "I Want You," "Just Like a Woman."

March and April

Dylan spends several evenings at his home in Byrdcliffe with Tiny Tim, discussing the virtues of crooners like Rudy Vallee.

Spring

Al Aronowitz, an old friend of Dylan's, visits him in Woodstock and witnesses him working on some songs with Robbie Robertson. One song quoted by Aronowitz includes the lines, "you can change your name but you can't run away from yourself." Dispelling rumors of inactivity, Aronowitz writes: "Dylan [is] writing 10 new songs a week, rehearsing them in his living room with . . . the Hawks."

Late Spring to Early Summer

According to Mort Nasatir, MGM sent a recording crew up to Woodstock to record Dylan and the Hawks performing some of Dylan's new material. It seems far more likely that MGM was simply sent some of the songs that Garth Hudson had already recorded in the Big Pink basement.

May 6

Michael Iachetta of the *New York Daily News* tracks Dylan down at his Woodstock retreat, securing the first interview since his accident. Their conversation is quite brief, but Dylan talks freely, emphasizing his commitment to making music and how he has been "thinkin' about where I'm goin'."

May 17: Don't Look Back *premieres at the Presidio Theatre, San Francisco.*

June 19: Rubin Carter and John Artis receive life sentences for allegedly shooting three white people in a bar the previous year. The saga is later documented by Dylan and Jacques Levy in their song "Hurricane," part of a 1975 campaign to free the wholly innocent Carter and Artis.

May to June

Dylan begins "daily" sessions with Garth Hudson, Richard Manuel, Robbie Robertson, and Rick Danko, easing himself back into music making again. The initial sessions take place at Dylan's home, in the Red Room. These sessions probably account for some of the basement tape material that has come down to collectors. Certainly Hudson soon began recording these sessions on an Ampex reel-to-reel machine. Among the songs likely to come from the Red Room are improvisations like "Silouette," "Bring It on Home," "King of France," "Lock Your Door," "Baby Won't You Be My Baby," "Try Me Little Girl," and "Don't You Try Me Now," as well as many covers. These include "I Can't Make It Alone," "Young But Daily Growin'," "Bonnie Ship the Diamond," "The Hills of Mexico," "Down on Me," "I'm Alright," "One Single River," "People Get Ready," "I Don't Hurt Anymore," "Stones that You Throw," "Baby Ain't that Fine," "Rock, Salt and Nails," and "A Fool Such as I." There are virtually no originals on these recordings save for the purely improvised, although two new songs may have been worked out in advance, "One for the Road" and "One Man's Loss." However, the normal daily distractions of family life soon begin to impinge on the sessions and it is decided that a relocation is required.

June to August

When sessions resume at the home of the Hawks in West Saugerties, a house dubbed Big Pink, the reel-to-reel is set up in the basement. These basement tape sessions last some three to four months, with one obvious break. If the bulk of the basement tapes come from a heady summer of inspiration, the early Big Pink sessions seem to have been largely concerned with continuing Dylan and the guys' exploration of all forms of American popular music. At what may have been the first Big Pink session, they recorded the traditional "900 Miles" and "Spanish Is the Loving Tongue" as well as what appear to be two improvised originals, "No Shoes on My Feet" and "On a Rainy Afternoon." A second session on the same reel continues the process, two originals "I Can't Come in with a Broken Heart" and "Under Control" being broken up by a falsetto version of "Come All Ye Fair and Tender Ladies." The next session appears to be resolutely traditional, covering everything from "Ol' Rosin the Beau" to "Banks of the Royal Canal," as well as "I'm Guilty of Loving You," "Johnny Todd," "Cool Water," and "Po' Lazarus."

There appears to be a strong country flavor to the next reel as Dylan runs through Johnny Cash's "Belchezaar," "Big River," and "Folsom Prison Blues" plus some older country fare: "I Forgot to Remember to Forget Her," "You Win Again," "Still in Town, Still Around," and "Walkin' with Sin." The reel concludes with a most unusual arrangement of "Bells of Rhymney."

The next reel has more of a mixture of originals and covers, containing the first of the "basement tape" material that Dylan bothers to copyright. The opening song, "I'm a Fool for You," does not warrant its own copyright. However "Tiny Montgomery" and "Sign on the Cross," two of the best basement cuts, share the same reel, as does Dylan's radical reworking of Bobby Bare's "All American Boy" (which was copyrighted on Dylan's behalf in 1973, presumably by someone unaware of the song's origins). The reel also has its share of raucous improvisations, "See You Later, Allen Ginsberg," "I'm in the Mood For Love," and "I'm Your Teenage Prayer" being some of the guilty parties. Spirited covers of "The Big Flood," "You Gotta Quit Kickin' My Dog Aroun'," "The Spanish Song," "Next Time on the Highway," "Joshua Gone Barbados," "The French Girl," and an exquisite "Four Strong Winds" take up the bulk of the reel.

At this stage in the sessions there are a handful of reels whose full details remain unknown, although they presumably contain the likes of "It's Just Another Tomato in the Glass," "Don't Ya Tell Henry," "Bourbon Street," "Silent Weekend," "Santa Fe" (now on *The Bootleg Series*), and "Wild Wolf."

What appear to be the final three reels of these summer sessions contain the bulk of copyrighted basement songs and are exclusively concerned with new, original songs. The first reel is devoted to "Million Dollar Bash" and "Yea! Heavy and a Bottle of Bread," for which there are two takes each. The second reel opens with one of Dylan's most obtuse works, "I'm Not There," which was not copyrighted until 1970 and remains unreleased. "Please Mrs. Henry" is a single take, whereas "Crash on the Levee" and "Lo and Behold" both require second takes to achieve their fully honed state, although the first take of "Crash on the Levee" has a crashing fury all its own. The third reel, only recently reconstructed, appears to contain four songs in all. "You Ain't Going Nowhere" take one has no verses in common with take two, from which it seems to be separated by "This Wheel's on Fire," on which Robertson is demoted to drums. "I Shall Be Released" achieves perfection in a single take, although the nth generation mono tape utilized for *The Bootleg Series* makes it hard on the ears. "Too Much of Nothing" requires two takes, although it is the tuneless first take that Robbie Robertson preferred to include on *The Basement Tapes*.

August 21

Columbia Records News announces that Dylan has signed a new contract with CBS. Dylan had originally been anxious to leave CBS, but after they offer an unprecedented royalty rate, without any advance for signing, he agrees to continue to record for them.

Summer

The birth of Anna Dylan.

• Dylan invites Tiny Tim, who has been working with the Hawks, to his house in Woodstock one evening. Dylan ends up singing "Cool Water" to Tiny Tim, who sings Dylan "one of the Irving Kaufman songs of 1922" in return.

• Dylan's parents visit him in Woodstock. It is to be the last known occasion that he sees his father alive.

September

Bob Johnston visits Dylan in Woodstock. Although Dylan has little to say, he indicates a willingness to record a new album.

• After an interruption in their basement sessions during which the Hawks went into New York and cut their own demos Dylan and the guys resume their musical deliberations. The tapes from this period concentrate exclusively on original Dylan songs. The first reel yields up "Tears of Rage" and that most unlikely of hit singles, "Quinn the Eskimo." "Tears of Rage" requires three takes, take two being incomplete. Take one appears on the original 14-song acetate his music publishers sent out in 1968, but take three is the one that appears on *The Basement Tapes.* "Quinn the Eskimo" is tried twice. The second reel has "Open the Door Homer" getting the three-take treatment, although take one is again preferred for copyright purposes. The two takes of "Nothing Was Delivered" are both of equal merit, although the rarer, second take has Dylan improvising his very own middle-eight monologue. The final reel of these sessions also includes a fragment of "Nothing Was Delivered," sandwiched between two takes of "Odds and Ends." The last three songs return the basements to the sort of light-hearted fare recorded earlier in the summer. "Get Your Rocks Off," "Clothesline Saga," and two takes of "Apple Suckling Tree" all seem to bear the mark of some serious imbibing of local moonshine.

Fall

Indian wandering minstrels, the Bengali Bauls, are invited to the United States by Allen Ginsberg, where they are in turn invited by Al Grossman to stay in a converted barn on his Woodstock estate. They meet Dylan, who spends some time with them; he is photographed with minstrels Purna and Lakhsman Das for the cover of *John Wesley Harding.* According to Purna Das, the Bauls rehearsed with Dylan for a day, for a concert they were going to play together at the Cornelli Mansion. Purna also claims the rehearsal was recorded.

October 3: Woody Guthrie dies after 15 years of constant suffering from Huntington's chorea.

October to November

Because none of the basement tape reels is dated, definitively assigning the various reels remains a pipe dream. However, it would appear that at least a couple of the Dylan/Hawks sessions postdate the first *John Wesley Harding* session (and therefore Levon Helm's return to the fold) and take place at the home of Danko, not at Big Pink. One song, "All You Have to Do Is Dream," for which two takes are known sounds like Dylan has the full backing of the Band. Helm also sounds present on "Going to Acapulco" and its companion track, "Gonna Get You Now." Finally, there is a session with a more down-home feel on the same reel on which Dylan sings "Wild Wood Flower," "See That My Grave Is Kept Clean" (in a *Nashville Skyline* voice!), "Comin' Round the Mountain," "Flight of the Bumble Bee," and "Confidential to Me." These appear to have been the final 'basement' sessions.

October 17–18

Although the studio reels attribute the first three songs cut for *John Wesley Harding* to a session on the 17th, according to Columbia's job records the 17th was a warm-up session (Robert Shelton refers to a warm-up session in his biography), and it was on the 18th that the real work began on Dylan's follow up to *Blonde on Blonde*. What is not in doubt is that the session(s) took place at Columbia's Music Row Studios, that Bob Johnston was again the producer, and that Dylan cut "The Drifter's Escape," "I Dreamed I Saw St. Augustine," and "The Ballad of Frankie Lee and Judas Priest" with drummer Ken Buttrey and bassist Charlie McCoy providing the only musical embellishments, save for Dylan's guitar and harmonica.

November 6

The *John Wesley Harding* sessions continue at Nashville's Music Row Studios. This session runs from six until 10 PM. In that time, Dylan, Buttrey, and McCoy cut two usable versions of the title track, two more of "All Along the Watchtower," as well as takes of "As I Went Out One Morning," "I Pity the Poor Immigrant," and "I Am a Lonesome Hobo."

November 21

Dylan, Buttrey, and McCoy complete *John Wesley Harding* at Columbia's Music Row Studios. Again the session runs from 6 until 10 PM. Pete Drake is brought in to play steel guitar on two songs, "Down Along the Cove" and "I'll Be Your Baby Tonight." Also recorded on this evening are two of the album's darker tracks, "The Wicked Messenger" and "Dear Landlord," the latter a bitter tale of licensed servitude that many saw as an attack on Dylan's manager, Albert Grossman, as well as featuring some of Dylan's best piano-playing to date.

> *November 25: Peter, Paul, and Mary's version of "Too Much of Nothing" enters the* Billboard *charts, the first "Basement Tape" song to be heard publicly.*

December

Dylan asks Robertson if he (and presumably Garth Hudson) would add some musical embellishments to the sparse tracks he has just recorded for *John*

Wesley Harding. Robertson feels that the songs sound fine as they are, and the tracks remain untouched.

December 27: *John Wesley Harding* (CL 2804/CS 9604): "John Wesley Harding," "As I Went Out One Morning," "I Dreamed I Saw St. Augustine," "All Along the Watchtower," "The Ballad of Frankie Lee and Judas Priest," "Drifter's Escape," "Dear Landlord," "I Am a Lonesome Hobo," "I Pity the Poor Immigrant," "The Wicked Messenger," "Down Along the Cover," "I'll Be Your Baby Tonight"

1968

January
Dylan is apparently offered the part of Woody Guthrie in a film biography, but the project does not materialize.

January (19?)
There is a rehearsal/run-through at Carnegie Hall for the Woody Guthrie Memorial Concert.

January 20
Dylan's first live appearance in 20 months is also the first Woody Guthrie Memorial Concert at Carnegie Hall in New York. Backed by the Crackers (aka the Band), he rocks up three of Guthrie's finest songs: "The Grand Coulee Dam," "Dear Mrs. Roosevelt," and "I Ain't Got No Home." There is both an afternoon and an evening show, with Dylan performing the same set on both occasions. He also participates in ensemble versions of "This Land Is Your Land" at the afternoon show, and "This Train (Is Bound for Glory)" at the evening show (on which he temporarily fumbles the words). Between shows, Dylan relaxes at the Sheraton Plaza Hotel. His three-song performance is subsequently included on *Tribute to Woody Guthrie, Vol. 1*. After the show, he makes a brief appearance at a party at Robert Ryan's apartment.

Early Winter
At his home in Woodstock, Dylan is interviewed by Hubert Saal. He is happy to talk about his new songs, "a song is moral just by being a song." He is reluctant, however, to discuss the accident ("I stared at the ceiling for a long time"), *Tarantula* ("It didn't have a story"), or his family. He does open up about his so-called retreat: "You have to be let alone to really accomplish anything. I'm a country boy myself."

February
Dylan meets with Bob Markel of Macmillan at Al Grossman's house to discuss the current situation regarding the publication of *Tarantula*. Dylan is unhappy with the book and wishes to work on something entirely different.

June 5
Dylan's father, Abraham Zimmerman, dies of a heart attack.

June 6
Dylan flies into Hibbing-Chisholm airport to attend his father's funeral.

June 7
The funeral of Abraham Zimmerman.

June 11
Dylan returns to New York from Hibbing. Sara is expecting another baby, and he wants to be on hand.

Mid-June
The birth of Samuel Dylan.

June to July
Dylan agrees to a major interview with *Sing Out!* magazine. John Cohen and Happy Traum (then the magazine's editor) visit him at his home in Woodstock to conduct three interviews during June and July. When published, the interviews extend to 13 pages. As his first major interview since the accident, the article is widely circulated. Among topics discussed are *Eat the Document,* which Dylan and Howard Alk are putting the finishing touches to at the time of the interview, as well as *John Wesley Harding* and

its connection with traditional ballads and folk songs. Dylan also requests that two songs be included in the issue of *Sing Out!:* Robbie Robertson's "The Weight" and "Penal Farm Blues" by blues guitarist Scrapper Blackwell, "a truly great artist [who] deserve(d) more than was given him." According to Traum, Dylan actually asked to do the interview to help *Sing Out!* during a serious financial plight.

July
Dylan is asked to write some music for the film, *Midnight Cowboy.* He eventually delivers "Lay, Lady, Lay," but too late for inclusion.

Summer
Elliott Landy visits Dylan in Woodstock for a photo session to provide a cover shot for Al Aronowitz's article on Dylan in a forthcoming *Saturday Evening Post.* The chosen photo shows a clean-shaven, young looking man and is the first public indication of his new image.

Fall
Dylan forms a new music publishing company, Big Sky Music, presumably part of his endeavors to extract himself from Grossman's financial grip.

Fall 1968 to Early Winter 1969

While visiting backstage at one of their New York concerts, Dylan offers the Everly Brothers a new song, "Lay, Lady, Lay." He sings/mumbles the song to them, but Phil Everly is unimpressed and declines the offer.

October (23?)

Dylan meets Jann Wenner in a New York hotel to discuss the possibility of doing an interview for Wenner's magazine, *Rolling Stone.*

October 23

Dylan travels to New York to see Johnny Cash perform at Carnegie Hall. After the show, Dylan, Sara, and some friends have dinner with Cash.

Late November

George Harrison visits Dylan and Sara at their home in Woodstock, spending a few days over Thanksgiving (November 28) with them. A poor quality recording, purporting to be Harrison and Dylan, is presumed to date from this visit. It features "I'd Have You Anytime," a song they composed during Harrison's stay. It also features a song usually titled "Everytime Somebody Comes to Town," although the correct title would appear to be "Nowhere to Go," presumably another joint composition. Harrison also hears a new composition Dylan has written, "I Threw It All Away," which Harrison plays at one of the January 1969 Twickenham Beatles sessions. Indeed, he is apparently given a tape of some Dylan songs during his visit. The tape may well have contained "I Don't Want to Do It," another Dylan original that Harrison demoed for *All Things Must Pass* (it was eventually released in 1984 on the *Porky's Revenge* soundtrack). Elliott Landy photographs Dylan and George Harrison together during Harrison's visit.

Note: According to the Beatles's PR man, Derek Taylor, Harrison and Ringo Starr attended a Dylan recording session in Nashville in December 1968. Taylor cannot have confused this with the February 1969 sessions, as Harrison and Starr were working in England at the time. However, there is no record of any December session.

Bob Dylan in Woodstock,
Saturday Evening Post, 1968

1969

Winter
English folksingers John and Beverly Martin give a concert in Woodstock. Dylan attends and comes up at the end to say how much he enjoyed it.

January
Dylan and family vacation in the West Indies.

February 12
Bob Johnston goes over to the Nashville Ramada Inn, where Dylan is staying, so that Dylan can play him the songs he wants to record and discuss the musicians he wants to play on the forthcoming sessions.

February 13
Dylan begins recording his first album in 15 months at Columbia's Nashville Music Row Studios. Bob Johnston is again producing and Charlie McCoy and Ken Buttrey are once again the rhythm section, augmented by Bob Wilson on piano, Pete Drake on pedal steel, and Norman Blake and Charlie Daniels as the guitarists. Six songs are recorded on this first day, three of which will appear on *Nashville Skyline:* "To Be Alone with You," "One More Night," and "I Threw It All Away." "Lay, Lady, Lay" is attempted at this first session but Dylan is unhappy with the results. An untitled song and something identified simply as 'blues' occupy the remainder of the time.

February 14
Dylan returns to Music Row Studios to continue work on *Nashville Skyline.* This time around he gets a satisfactory "Lay, Lady, Lay," as well as three other candidates for the album: "Peggy Day," "Country Pie," and "Tell Me that It Isn't True."

February 15–16
Dylan writes "Tonight I'll Be Staying Here with You" on Ramada Inn notepaper in a Nashville hotel room.

February 17
A most curious day at Music Row Studios, Nashville, as Dylan divides between new originals and a couple of rehashed oldies. Dylan and the band warm up with an instrumental jam (which appears on the album as "Nashville Skyline Rag," although a warm up is just what it sounds like)

before beginning work on the song Dylan has written in the intervening days, "Tonight I'll Be Staying Here with You." At least two takes are required to get the finale to *Nashville Skyline.* At this juncture Johnny Cash joins Dylan and his band to attempt a few duets. Three songs are attempted with Cash on the afternoon of the 17th, two Dylan originals ("One Too Many Mornings" and "Don't Think Twice, It's All Right") plus "I Still Miss Someone." Although none of these songs appear on *Nashville Skyline,* the version of "One Too Many Mornings" appears in a documentary on Johnny Cash for NBC entitled "The Man and His Music."

February 18

Dylan and Johnny Cash resume their "experiment" at Music Row Studios, recording at least 15 Dylan/Cash duets in a single session. At one point there is talk of this session being released as a Dylan/Cash album. Thankfully, such rumors came to nothing, as there is very little of worth in among the ragbag of familiar country covers and Dylan oldies they record. Of the two Dylan originals, "One Too Many Mornings" is a repeat, but no advance, on yesterday's rendition. "Girl from the North Country" works better simply because it temporarily dispenses with that all-too-familiar Nashville session sound. The other songs have even less to recommend them as the band chung-chung their way through "Good Ol' Mountain Dew," "I Still Miss Someone" (again), "Careless Love," "Matchbox," "That's Alright Mama" (Dylan's third attempt in a Columbia studio), "Big River," "I Walk the Line," "You Are My Sunshine," "Ring of Fire," "Guess Things Happen That Way," "Just a Closer Walk with Thee," "T For Texas," and "Blue Yodel No. 4." Long rumored to have been recorded at this session (almost certainly erroneously) was a version of "Understand Your Man." However, several songs were also attempted at the session but never completed. The songs in question were "Mystery Train," "How High the Water," "Wanted Man," and "Amen." This incomplete "Wanted Man" remains the only Dylan recording of this original song. (Dylan donated it to Cash at the time.)

Late February

Jann Wenner speaks briefly to Dylan on the phone, discussing his forthcoming album *Nashville Skyline.* Dylan says, "The new songs are easy to sing and there aren't too many words to remember."

March

Dylan calls Elliott Landy to arrange a photo session to shoot the cover for *Nashville Skyline.* Initially, Dylan suggests shooting himself and two friends outside the Woodstock bakery, but finally the cover photo is of Dylan alone on his Woodstock estate, unsure whether to keep his hat on or take it off.

• Hubert Saal again interviews Dylan for *Newsweek,* the conversation inevitably concentrating on the new album, *Nashville Skyline.*

March 9: "The Mighty Quinn" performed by Manfred Mann reaches number 10 on the Billboard *charts.*

March 17
Dylan attends a Clancy Brothers concert in New York.

Spring
Dylan moves his family from the old Ben Webster place. Although they remain in Woodstock, the new home is the old home of Walter Weyl.

> April 9: *Nashville Skyline* (KCS 9825): "Girl of the North Country," "Nashville Skyline Rag," "To Be Alone with You," "I Threw It All Away," "Peggy Day," "Lay, Lady, Lay," "One More Night," "Tell Me That It Isn't True," "Country Pie," "Tonight I'll Be Staying Here with You"

April 24 and 26
Just two months after completing *Nashville Skyline,* Dylan is back at Music Row Studios in Nashville recording songs of a similar sensibility but older vintage. For the first time since his debut album, Dylan records almost exclusively covers at a Columbia session. With the same musicians (and producer) as on *Nashville Skyline* save for Bob Moore on bass, Bill Pursell on piano, and Fred Carter, Jr., as an additional guitarist, some seven songs are recorded on these two days. Only the first song cut, "Living the Blues," is a Dylan original. Of the six remaining songs, the three that appear on *Self Portrait* represent the best of the bunch: "Take Me as I Am," "I Forgot More (than You'll Ever Know)," and "Let It Be Me." Considerably worse are two other cuts from the 24th, "Spanish Is the Loving Tongue" and "A Fool Such As I," both of which are subsequently released on *Dylan.* "Running," which was also originally scheduled to appear on *Dylan,* remains unreleased.

April 30
Dylan spends the day looking at real estate in Nashville. He attends a rehearsal for "The Johnny Cash Show," before retiring to his motel, where he apparently writes some songs with Doug Kershaw.

May 1
Dylan records three songs for "The Johnny Cash Show" at the Ryman Auditorium, then-home of the Grand Ole Opry in Nashville. The songs are "I Threw It All Away," "Living the Blues" (which Dylan intends to issue as a single), and "Girl from the North Country," which is sung as a duet with Johnny Cash. The set is recorded twice (and "Living the Blues" a third time).

After the show, a relieved Dylan returns to Johnny Cash's house with famed bluegrass banjo player Earl Scruggs, Bob Johnston, and country songwriter Boudleaux Bryant for dinner. After dinner, they each perform a song, Dylan at his turn singing the old standard "These Working Hands." According to Graham Nash, who also recalls a dinner at Cash's, attended by, among others, himself, his then-girlfriend Joni Mitchell, Kris Kristofferson, and Eddy Arnold, Dylan sang four or five songs. Presumably it was the very same dinner. Nash recalls Sara sitting there crying at the drama of the moment.

May 3

Four songs are recorded at Dylan's last session in Columbia's Music Row Studios. Two are later included on *Self Portrait,* although neither "Take a Message to Mary" nor "Blue Moon" exactly redefine the famous originals. Dylan also attempts two of Johnny Cash's most famous recordings, "Ring of Fire" and "Folsom Prison Blues," although both are deemed unworthy of release, even on *Self Portrait.*

June 26

After a year of pursuit, Jann Wenner finally gets Dylan to do a major interview with *Rolling Stone.* Wenner obtains a lengthy feature but little is revealed. Dylan later says that his mind was on other things at the time, and it certainly comes across that way. Wenner tries to cover as many topics as possible, but the only subjects Dylan seems to open up on are his feelings toward A. J. Weberman and why *Tarantula* has not been issued. Perhaps the most perceptive comment in the whole piece is about "My Life in a Stolen Moment": "This thing wasn't written for hundreds of thousands of people . . . it was just a little game for whoever was going in [the Town Hall] and getting a ticket." The interview is poorly received. Many see it as proof that Dylan has lost touch with the real world.

June to July

Dylan is rumored to have visited Israel at this time.

Summer

Jazz musician/musicologist David Amram regularly goes to Dylan's place in East Hampton to accompany Dylan on the French horn. Amram later told *Rolling Stone* he was "jamming on Fire Island with Bob Dylan" and that "it was Dylan who got him into playing the guitar."

Early July: "Lay, Lady, Lay"/"Peggy Day" (4-44926)

July 14, Mississippi River Festival, Southern Illinois University, Edwardsville, IL

Under the alias of Elmer Johnson, Dylan is the surprise guest during The Band encore. Dylan and The Band perform four songs, three of which are documented: "I Ain't Got No Home," "Slippin' and Slidin'," and "Black Girl (In the Pines)." The set is taped at Dylan's behest.

Late July to Early August

Dylan and The Band rehearse in Woodstock in preparation for Dylan's live performance at the Isle of Wight Festival.

August 2

The Moose Lodge in Hibbing hosts a 10-year reunion for Dylan's year at Hibbing High School. Both Dylan and Sara attend, meeting (among others) Dylan's old flame, Echo Helstrom.

Early August

The first of a couple of brief interviews to publicize Dylan's appearance at the Isle of Wight is conducted by Don Short for the *Daily Mirror* newspaper. Short travels to Dylan's Woodstock home for the interview, but is not aware of Dylan's history and seems startled to discover he is married, believing Dylan's claim that, "Sara and I grew up together as kids in Minnesota." Short also believes it was a car crash that interrupted Dylan's career.

Early to Mid-August [9–12]

Ray Connolly travels to Woodstock to interview Dylan for the London *Evening Standard*. Although a brief interview, it is far more informative than Don Short's. Discussing the set he intends for the Isle of Wight, Dylan comments, "I'll be doing some of those old songs with just guitar and harmonica. . . . My range of songs should be much bigger this time [than in 1966]."

August 14

Dylan and his family are set to sail on the QE2 to England for the Isle of Wight festival when Jesse has an accident as they are boarding. This dissuades them from taking the trip.

Mid- to Late August

Dylan encounters engineer-producer Elliott Mazer at the Carnegie Deli. He asks him to come to the Isle of Wight to record the show.

August 25

Dylan and Sara fly to Heathrow Airport, where they are picked up by promoter Rickie Farr and driven to Portsmouth, arriving there about 1 AM. There they board a hovercraft for the Isle of Wight. They drive to Forelands Farm, where they remain throughout their stay on the island.

August 26

Dylan rehearses with the Band in a barn at Forelands Farm. He is visited by George Harrison and Beatles's roadie Mal Evans.

August 27

In response to pressure from the media, Dylan agrees to a press conference, which is staged at the Halland Hotel on the Wednesday afternoon. The conference receives extensive coverage on BBC news programs, although Dylan gives little away. At one point he claims his 1966 stage act "was all for publicity. . . . I don't do that kind of thing anymore." After the conference, which is shorter than expected (Dylan curtailing it with, "I think I've answered enough questions"), there is a brief photo session on the seafront, before Dylan is whisked back to Forelands Farm.

Late August

Chris White of the *Daily Sketch* manages to penetrate the security at Forelands Farms to ask Dylan a few questions. Although more a brief conversation than an interview, Dylan does at least state that the English "are the most loyal fans I have and that was one of the reasons that I wanted to come to England to make my comeback."

Isle of Wight, 1969

August 29
After a friendly game of tennis, Dylan, John Lennon, George Harrison, Ringo Starr, and The Band indulge in a jam session "in the barn where Bob had been rehearsing for the previous four days with the Band."

August 30
Dylan and the Band run through the material they have in mind for their set at the Isle of Wight Festival. The rehearsal apparently lasts four hours. Rumors abound that on this evening Dylan and the Band jammed in a pub on the island. Indeed, a contemporary report in *Disc* alleges a Saturday-night performance took place at Hector's Crab and Lobster Inn.

August 31, Ryde, Woodside Bay, Isle of Wight
After a long wait, Dylan takes to the stage at about 11 PM to close the second Isle of Wight Festival. Backed by The Band, Dylan opens with "She Belongs to Me," followed by his latest single "I Threw It All Away" and "Maggie's Farm." The members of the Band then take a well-earned rest (they had already played their own set) while Dylan does acoustic versions of the traditional "Wild Mountain Thyme" and his own "It Ain't Me, Babe," "To Ramona," and "Mr. Tambourine Man" (including only the briefest of bursts on harmonica). The Band returns to the stage to provide some appropriate backing on versions of "I Dreamed I Saw St. Augustine," "Lay, Lady, Lay," "Highway 61 Revisited," "One Too Many Mornings," "I Pity the Poor Immigrant," a runt of a version of "Like a Rolling Stone," "I'll Be Your Baby Tonight," and, finally, Dylan's own live version of "Quinn the Eskimo." The audience manages to cajole Dylan into returning for a two-song encore: a new Dylan composition entitled "Minstrel Boy," plus a delightful version of "Rainy Day Women #12 & 35." He leaves the stage barely an hour after his arrival, much to the disgust of certain members of the audience fed on tall tales of a three-hour set climaxing with a massive all-star jam session. Dylan and the three Beatles in attendance return to the farm for a small party after the show.

The concert is taped by Elliot Mazer for CBS, who were seriously considering a live album of the event. The project does not materialize, however, although four songs are featured on *Self Portrait* including the two most disappointing performances of the whole night, "She Belongs to Me" and "Like a Rolling Stone." Quite possibly Dylan was disappointed with his own performance when listening back to the tapes. Certainly talk of an American tour rapidly subsides, and Dylan's next paid performance is not until 1974.

September 1
Dylan and his wife board a hovercraft for the mainland. During their brief stay in London, Dylan is alleged to have played piano at a session with Lennon during which they attempted a version of "Cold Turkey."

September 2
Dylan and Sara fly from Heathrow to Kennedy airport, where Dylan tells waiting members of the press, "they make too much of singers over there."

September
Dylan moves back to New York's Greenwich Village with his family, buying a townhouse on MacDougal Street.

October
Dylan attends performances by Dr. John at the Fillmore East, and John Mayall at the Cafe A Go Go in New York.

October 21: The death of Jack Kerouac, author of On the Road *and* Mexico City Blues.

December 29
Dylan attends a Janis Joplin concert at Madison Square Garden. At a party afterward in Clive Davis's apartment, he chats with Joplin.

Isle of Wight, 1969

1970

March 3
Dylan enters Columbia Studio B in New York with Bob Johnston, Al Kooper (piano/organ), Dave Bromberg (guitar/dobro), and possible violinist Emmanuel Green, to resume work on *Self Portrait*. Fifteen songs are recorded at the session, which lasts a mere four hours. Everything, save the opening song, "Pretty Saro," is cut in single takes. "Pretty Saro" requires three full takes and three false starts. Of the remaining tracks, seven end up on *Self Portrait*: "Little Sadie," "In Search of Little Sadie," "Belle Isle," "Copper Kettle," "It Hurts Me Too," "The Boxer," and "Boogie Woogie." The other songs include two originals—"Went to See the Gypsy" and an unidentified track, which is almost certainly "If Not for You"—plus "Sitting on Dock of the Bay," "Universal Soldier," "When a Fellow's out of a Job," "These [Working] Hands," and "Spanish Eyes."

March 4
Dylan continues to record at Studio B with Kooper, Bromberg, and Green, augmented on two or more songs by drummer Alvin Rogers and bassist Stu Woods. Just eleven songs are recorded over the three sessions, which run from two-thirty in the afternoon until two-thirty in the morning, with two hour-and-a-half breaks. "Went to See the Gypsy" is again attempted, as are two other originals, the instrumental "Wigwam" and "Time Passes Slowly," though no complete take of the latter is achieved. Of today's covers, just two make it to *Self Portrait*: "Days of '49" and "Early Morning Rain." "Thirsty Boots," which Dylan attempts three times, "Annie's Gonna Sing Her Song," "House Carpenter," "Railroad Bill," "Little Brown Dog," and Tell Ol' Bill" all end up discarded.

March 5
For the final session at Columbia Studio B, Dylan brings in three female singers, Hilda Harris, Albertine Robinson, and Maeretha Stewart, to augment Kooper, Green, Bromberg, Rogers, and Woods. Dylan cuts two different arrangements of the traditional "Alberta," which will eventually open and close *Self Portrait* as "Alberta no. 1" and "Alberta no. 2." Also cut today are *Self Portrait* versions of "Gotta Travel On" and "All the Tired Horses," as well as versions of "Went to See the Gypsy" and "Time Passes Slowly" (this time complete), plus covers of "Little Moses," "Come All You Fair and Tender Ladies," "My Previous Life," and "Come a Little Bit Closer." The session runs from four-thirty in the afternoon to eight in the evening.

May 1

With Charlie Daniels on bass, George Harrison (and probably at the evening session, Ron Cornelius) on guitar(s), Russ Kunkel on drums, and Bob Johnston on keyboards, Dylan spends the day at Columbia Studio B in New York. Most of the three sessions consist of desultory run throughs of old Dylan songs and a bizarre selection of covers. "Gates of Eden," "I Threw It All Away," "I Don't Believe You," "Honey, Just Allow Me One More Chance," "Rainy Day Women," "Song to Woody," "Don't Think Twice, It's Alright," "Just Like Tom Thumb's Blues," "One Too Many Mornings," and "It Ain't Me Babe" are all given the gravel voice and nonarrangements that come to characterize the *New Morning* covers. Dylan also gives the same treatment to "Ghost Riders in the Sky," "Cupid," "All I Have to Do Is Dream," "Matchbox," "True Love, Your Love" (?), the seemingly spontaneous "When's My Swamp Gonna Catch Fire?," "I'm a-Goin' Fishin'," "Yesterday," and "Da Doo Ron Ron." All in all, pretty much a waste of tape. Returning in the evening with a more earnest purpose, Dylan records nothing but originals, his first such session since February 1969. Of the five originals recorded, "If Not for You" appears on *The Bootleg Series,* and "Working on the Guru" has been widely bootlegged. Four complete takes of "Sign on the Window," three full versions of "Time Passes Slowly," and a single take of "Went to See the Gypsy" remain unheard.

May to June

It would appear that Dylan intended to set up several sessions during this period, including one with Ringo Starr in Hollywood, one with Johnny Cash, and one with the Byrds (they failed to appear, much to Dylan's annoyance). It is not known if the sessions with Cash or Starr took place, although, according to the June 1970 *Beatles Monthly,* the session with Starr was scheduled for June. According to a report in an April 1970 issue of *Disc & Music Echo,* Dylan was also planning to record at a small studio in North Miami, Criteria Recording Studios.

June 1

Dylan arrives at Columbia's new Studio E in New York along with his producer Bob Johnston, keyboardist Al Kooper, drummer Russ Kunkel, guitarist Ron Cornelius, bassist Charlie Daniels, and backing singers Hilda Harris, Albertine Robinson, and Maeretha Stewart. This is the first of five daily sessions intended to result in a new album of original songs. Today's session, though, is exclusively devoted to covers, three of them to be precise: "Alligator Man," "Ballad of Ira Hayes," and "Lonesome Me."

June 2

Once again, Dylan spends the bulk of today's session at Studio E working on covers. A far more strenuous session than the previous day, Dylan records seven songs, beginning with a retake of "Alligator Man." "Mary Ann" is attempted eight times, including five complete takes, whereas "Rock a Bye My Saro Jane" generates seven attempts, three of them complete. As light relief, he then cuts the magnificent solo "Spanish Is the Loving Tongue" later released as b-side to "Watching the River Flow," before returning to a more workmanlike band arrangement of "Mr. Bojangles." Finally, Dylan attempts to cut two of the songs attempted with Harrison in May, "If Not for You" and "Time Passes Slowly" both of which appear on *New Morning*.

June 3
Repeating the pattern, Dylan cuts four more covers at Studio E before attempting another new song. Of the four covers, "Can't Help Falling in Love" and "Lily of the West" both subsequently appear on *Dylan*. "Jamaica Farewell," listed on the reels as "Kingston Town," and "Long Black Veil" both remain unreleased. At session's end they finally work up the *New Morning* version of "One More Weekend."

June 4
Five songs are recorded at Studio E, including a new arrangement of "Tomorrow Is a Long Time" that was sequenced for inclusion on *New Morning* but remains unreleased. "Big Yellow Taxi," with a harmonica insert, later appears on *Dylan,* while the other cover of the day, "Bring Me Water," remains unreleased, indeed unidentified (I assume that it is Leadbelly's "Bring Me Little Water, Sylvie"). "Three Angels" and "New Morning" are also cut today, both requiring just a couple of takes.

June 5
One of Dylan's mammoth sessions wraps up the bulk of the *New Morning* album. Today at Studio E he begins with the truly trite "If Dogs Run Free," cut in two complete takes. He then returns to "Went to See the Gypsy." Although it had already been cut in March and May, it requires three more takes before Dylan is happy. "Sign on the Window," perhaps the highlight of *New Morning,* requires half a dozen false starts but just two takes before Dylan nails the vocal. "The Man in Me," an instrumental listed simply as "Ah-ooh!," "Father of Night," and "Winterlude" make for seven new originals cut at this final session. That these originals run the gamut from genius to gauche suggests that Dylan is no longer the best editor of his own work. All but the instrumental "Ah-ooh!" appear on *New Morning* in some form. The session, though, ends with Dylan returning to covers, running down versions of "I Forgot to Remember to Forget" and "Lily of the West."

Early June (6?)
Dylan visits Dave Crosby and Graham Nash at the Warwick Hotel in New York. Dylan asks them to play him some of their new songs and Nash plays him "Southbound Train," which Dylan asks him to sing again.

June 7
Dylan attends the final Crosby, Stills, Nash, and Young show at the Fillmore East in New York, as well as the party afterward.

June 8
Dylan checks in at the Princeton Inn with Sara, David Crosby, and Ben Saltzman.

Self Portrait (C2X 30050): "All the Tired Heroes," "Alberta No. 1," "I Forgot More than You'll Ever Know," "Days of 49," "Early Morning Rain," "In Search of Little Sadie," "Let It Be Me," "Little Sadie," "Woogie Boogie," "Belle Isle," "Living the Blues," "Like a Rolling Stone," "Copper Kettle," "Gotta Travel On," "Blue Moon," "The Boxer," "Quinn the Eskimo," "Take Me as I Am," "Take a Message to Mary," "It Hurts Me Too," "Minstrel Boy," "She Belongs to Me," "Wigwam," "Alberta No. 2"

June 9
Dylan accepts an honorary doctorate in music at Princeton University.

June 30
At Columbia's Studio B, Dylan returns to the song he has spent many years disavowing, "Blowin' in the Wind." With a line-up comprising Al Kooper, Stu Woods on bass, Dave Bromberg on guitar, Rick Marotta on drums, and Thomas Cosgrove on backing vocals, Dylan records the song, although the purpose of the session remains unknown and this recording unreleased.

Summer
Dylan reportedly visits Israel.

• Naomi Saltzman, Dylan's lawyer, phones Robert Markel, Dylan's editor at Macmillan, and suggests that they finally publish *Tarantula*.

August 12
Dylan completes the *New Morning* album with one session at Columbia Studio E in New York. With Billy Mundi on drums, Buzzy Feiten on guitar, and presumably Charlie Daniels and Al Kooper on bass and organ respectively, Dylan rerecords versions of "Time Passes Slowly" and "If Not for You" before cutting three complete takes of a brand-new song, self-evidently inspired by the Princeton degree ceremony, "Day of the Locusts."

August
Dylan may have met George Harrison and Derek Taylor at Fire Island during this month.

September 11
Delaney & Bonnie play the Fillmore East, with Eric Clapton on guitar. Dylan joins Clapton after the show, their first meeting since the famous May 1965 session (see May 12, 1965).

September 18: The death of Jimi Hendrix.

Fall
Dylan plays organ at a session for Happy and Artie Traum. They cannot get the sound right, however, and the session is abandoned.

• The birth of Jakob Dylan.

October 4: The death of Janis Joplin.

October 7

In a letter to his publisher, Archibald MacLeish outlines recent attempts to produce "a play with songs by Dylan" called *Scratch*. Unfortunately, MacLeish observes, Dylan "proved simply incapable of producing new songs." Dylan refers to the project in the notes to *Biograph*, and says that several of the songs on *New Morning* were intended for the play.

October 21: *New Morning* (KC 30290): "If Not For You," "Day of the Locust," "Time Passes Slowly," "Went to See the Gypsy," "Winterlude," "If Dogs Run Free," "New Morning," "Sign on the Window," "One More Weekend," "The Man in Me," "Three Angels," "Father of Night"

November: Tarantula *is finally released.*

November 20

Dylan attends a concert by Elton John at the Fillmore East in New York, along with members of The Band. He visits backstage after the show.

November 21

Dylan, this time in the company of his wife, returns to the Fillmore East to see Elton John.

December

Dylan records two songs with Randy, Gary, and Earl Scruggs at the New York home of Thomas B. Allen, for a documentary on Earl Scruggs. Playing harmonica and guitar on "Nashville Skyline Rag," he then duets with Earl on "East Virginia Blues." The first song is later released on *Earl Scruggs Performing with His Family and Friends,* both are included in a documentary of the same name screened by NBC in January 1971.

(Late?) December

Dylan arranges to meet members of the revolutionary Black Panthers, specifically Huey Newton and David Hilliard. The meeting does not go well and both sides part without finding any common ground.

Late Fall 1970 to Early Winter 1971

Sometime shortly after the release of *New Morning* Dylan is alleged to have rehearsed a band supposedly comprising Al Kooper, Harvey Brooks, and Russ Kunkel with a view to going back on the road. Apparently the rehearsals go badly, and Dylan changes his mind. Neither Kooper nor Kunkel recall such an experiment.

1971

Early January
Dylan finally encounters self-appointed Dylanologist A. J. Weberman outside his New York home. They talk, and the next day Dylan phones Weberman to invite him over to his studio to hear some tapes and chat some more.

January 6
Dylan phones Weberman regarding his intended article on his meetings with Dylan. He is clearly unhappy with the idea of an article about such informal discussions, and offers Weberman a proper interview. He asks to see a copy of the text before publication, because the feature is wholly composed from Weberman's recollections.

January 9
Dylan phones Weberman after perusing a copy of the intended article on their meetings. He claims Weberman has misquoted him on several matters, notably whether "Dear Landlord" is about Al Grossman. At one point, Weberman starts claiming Dylan sings "Don't expose me" backward on one of the songs on *New Morning.* This clearly fazes Dylan, who exclaims, "Oh, fuck man. Jesus!" Toward the end of their phone conversation, Dylan says, "You don't have my permission to do any of this shit, man." Clearly, by this point, he has no intention of continuing his dialogue with Weberman.

Winter
Dylan is interviewed by longtime friend, Tony Glover. At the last moment, however, he withdraws his permission to publish the interview.

January to February
Dylan finally agrees to an interview with Anthony Scaduto, who is working on a biography of Dylan, after Weberman has told Dylan that Scaduto's book will be an expose. After a brief telephone conversation, they meet the following day at Dylan's Village studio. Dylan is quite helpful, seemingly anxious to add his own comments about major changes in his career to other voices in Scaduto's book. They meet on several occasions over the next few weeks, Scaduto gaining much valuable material for his biography.

March
Dylan visits the Gaslight to see Bobby Neuwirth perform.

March 16–18

At Leon Russell's invitation, Dylan records with Russell and friends at Blue Rock Studios in New York for three days. With Russell producing and playing piano, Joey Cooper and Don Preston on guitars, Carl Radle on bass, and Chuck Blackwell on drums, he records a new single on the first day of sessions, a rollicking shot of r&b called "Watching the River Flow." Also recorded at these sessions is another major new Dylan composition, "When I Paint My Masterpiece." Clearly enjoying the atmosphere, Dylan and the band also record several covers, including "That Lucky Ol' Sun," Ben E. King's "Spanish Harlem," "Alabama Bound," "Blood Red River," and even apparently "Rock of Ages."

Mid-May

Dylan attends a Hasid wedding around the second week of this month.

May 21

Dylan meets Robert Shelton at the Henry Hudson Hotel for a formal interview to provide further material for Shelton's biography. Dylan is quite talkative and, according to Shelton, the interview was a long one. Dylan mentions that he is going to Israel in two days, so presumably the interview is conducted on or around May 21.

May 23

Dylan and his wife fly into Lod Airport, Jerusalem, and then travel to the Sharon Hotel.

May 24

Dylan is photographed by a UPI photographer at the Wailing Wall in Jerusalem on his 30th birthday. According to what Dylan said to Catherine Rosenheimer later, Sara and he "went to see a Gregory Peck movie" that evening.

Late May

Dylan and Sara visit the Kibbutz Givat Haim to discuss the possibility of the family moving there for a period of time.

• Dylan and Sara walk through Old Jerusalem and visit Mount Zion Yeshiva.

May 31

Dylan is interviewed on Herzliyya Beach by Catherine Rosenheimer of the *Jerusalem Post.* According to Rosenheimer, Dylan had been in Israel eight days.

Summer

Dylan attends a bluegrass festival in San Francisco, where he sees the Greenbriar Boys, with whom he had shared that bill at Gerdes Folk City 10 years earlier.

July 31

Rehearsals for the two Bangladesh benefit concerts at Madison Square Garden include Dylan and Harrison dueting on "If Not for You." The briefest of snippets of this rehearsal appears in the film of the shows.

August 1, Madison Square Garden, "The Concerts for Bangladesh"

Dylan performs at both the afternoon and evening shows, backed only by Harrison's understated guitar and Leon Russell on bass. At the afternoon show, he opens with "A Hard Rain's a-Gonna Fall," followed by "Blowin' in the Wind," "It Takes a Lot to Laugh," "Love Minus Zero," and "Just Like a Woman." He is rapturously received by the audience. Both concerts are recorded by Phil Spector for a benefit album (or three). Spector subsequently broadcasts the afternoon versions of "A Hard Rain's a-Gonna Fall" and "Love Minus Zero" on

US radio in unmixed form. For the evening show, Dylan drops "Love Minus Zero" and replaces it with "Mr. Tambourine Man." This set is subsequently issued as side five of the *Concert for Bangladesh* set. However, when the film is released "Mr. Tambourine Man" is excluded. Dylan's performance is well received by fans and critics alike, and is again used as evidence that Dylan is about to abandon his self-imposed exile from live performances.

September

Dylan visits Anthony Scaduto at his New York apartment and plays him an acetate of *Greatest Hits Volume Two*.

• Dylan attends performances at the Bitter End by Tony Joe White and Steve Goodman.

September 24

Dylan records at Columbia Studio B with Happy Traum, hoping to record some new versions of old originals for his forthcoming *Greatest Hits* package. Three of the four songs cut appear on *Greatest Hits Vol. 2* are: "I Shall Be Released," "Down in the Flood," and a drastically rewritten "You Ain't Going Nowhere," which appears to aim a couple of digs at one Mr. McGuinn. Dylan and Traum also attempt four takes of "Only a Hobo," which remains unreleased.

Early Fall

Dylan helps George Harrison to edit the documentary film of *The Concert for Bangladesh*.

October

Dylan physically attacks A. J. Weberman on Elizabeth Street after Sara catches Weberman and an Associated Press reporter rummaging through their garbage, despite previous assurances from Weberman that he would desist. Dylan is eventually pulled off Weberman by some passing hippies.

October 4

Dylan attends a Crosby and Nash concert at Carnegie Hall. During the second half of the show, both Stephen Stills and Neil Young join the duo on stage.

October 11

Dylan attends a Frank Zappa concert at the Fillmore East in New York.

Late October

Dylan attends a reading of improvised poetry by Allen Ginsberg and Peter Orlovsky with the theme, "Why write poetry down on paper when you have to cut down trees to make poetry books?" Dave Amram accompanies him. Later that evening, Dylan phones Ginsberg to discuss the idea of improvising poetry and music.

October 31

Dylan goes over to Ginsberg's Lower East Side apartment. With Dylan on organ and Peter Orlovsky, Ginsberg, and David Amram all joining in, they improvise "Vajraguru." They then talk about specific chords, before recording versions of "Infant Joy" (two), "Holy Thursday," and "The Fly" using an organ drone. Dylan reverts to guitar for versions of "Spring," "Merrily to Welcome in the New Year," "A Dream," and "Om Mani Padme Hum." Dylan continues the lesson on chords, before suggesting they book a studio and record some improvised material.

Early November

Allen Ginsberg appears on New York educational TV station channel 13 on a program called "Free Time" with friends Peter Orlovsky, Gerard Malanga, and Anne Waldman, all reading and singing along. Musical accompaniment is supplied by Happy Traum and a denim-clad Bob Dylan. At least five songs are performed by Ginsberg and friends, including a mantra, two William Blake poems, "A Dream" and "Nurse's Song," and a major new poem by Ginsberg, "September on Jessore Road." The first mention of Dylan's low-key appearance is in Scaduto's major profile in *The New York Times* on November 28.

November 2

Dylan finishes reading *Soledad Brother* by George Jackson.

November 3

Dylan composes "George Jackson." He then phones Columbia and asks them to book a studio for the following day.

November 4

Dylan returns to Blue Rock Studios to record a new single with Leon Russell on bass, Ben Keith on steel guitar, Kenneth Buttrey on drums, and two backup singers, Joshie Armstead and Rose Hicks. As well as recording "George Jackson" with this lineup, Dylan also records the song solo, just guitar and harmonica. Also recorded at this session is another new Dylan composition, "Wallflower," which shows an enduring interest in country music. At around this time, and therefore presumably at this session, Dylan is reported to have recorded a version of John Prine's "Donald and Lydia."

November 9

Dylan and Allen Ginsberg, in the company of the likes of Happy and Artie Traum, Peter Orlovsky, and David Amram, resume their improvisatory experiments at Record Plant studios in New York with a view to producing a joint album. On this first day, they warm up with "Mantras" and "Merrily to Welcome in the New Year," before attempting "September on Jessore Road," a song Ginsberg had written "to offer Dylan a text equal to his own genius and sympathy." William Blake's "Nurses Song" follows. The session concludes with the wholly improvised "Gimme My Money Back," on which Dylan sings the first verse.

> November 12: "George Jackson" (big band version)/"George Jackson" (acoustic version) (4-45516)

Mid-November

Dylan has a couple of conversations with Anthony Scaduto who is writing a profile on him for *The New York Times Magazine.* However, he does not refer to his recording of "George Jackson."

November 17

The second Dylan/Ginsberg session at Record Plant results in another Blake poem set to song, "A Dream," another attempt at "September on Jessore Road" and a series of improvised ditties, "Raghupati Rashava," "Many Loves," "Vomit Express," "Jimmy Berman Rag," "Going to San Diego," "Om My Soul Shalom," "Walking Down the Street," and another Dylan/Ginsberg duet, "(Oh Babe) for You," which is attempted twice.

> *Bob Dylan's Greatest Hits, Vol. 2* (KG 31120): "Watching the River Flow," "Don't Think Twice It's Allright," "Lay, Lady, Lay," "Stuck Inside of Mobile," "I'll Be Your Baby Tonight," "All I Really Want to Do," "My Back Pages," "Maggie's Farm," "Tonight I'll Be Staying Here with You," "She Belongs to Me," "All Along the Watchtower," "Quinn the Eskimo," "Just Like Tom Thumb's Blues," "A Hard Rain's a-Gonna Fall," "If Not for You," "It's All Over Now, Baby Blue," "Tomorrow Is a Long Time," "When I Paint My Masterpiece," "I Shall Be Released," "You Ain't Goin' Nowhere," "Down in the Flood"

November 19
According to Ginsberg's own notes, there was something called a "Greaser Jam" with Dylan on this date. No further information is known.

November 25
A report in *The New York Times* outlines attempts by a fellow tenant on MacDougal Street to sue Dylan regarding the restricted use of his basement.

December
Dylan travels uptown to Harlem to see the Staple Singers play at the Apollo. He visits backstage afterward.
• Dylan buys a modest house on the Malibu coastline from Los Angeles sports writer Jim Murray. Dylan subsequently buys some of the connecting land.
• Several stories appear that Dylan is planning a one-hour TV special for Christmas 1971. Dylan had told Tony Scaduto in October that there would be a special and it would include "a lot of new stuff, from my new album."
• John Lennon, Yoko Ono, and Jerry Rubin publish an open letter in the *Village Voice* requesting that A. J. Weberman publicly apologize to Dylan for his campaign of "lies and malicious slander."
• Dylan and Terry Noble visit the *Village Voice* office to find out why the paper has not published a letter Dylan wrote criticizing Scaduto. They are informed that the letter was libelous. Dylan is filming the whole affair with a video camera. After threats by office personnel to call the police, Dylan, Noble, three other friends, and a dog depart peacefully.

> *The Concert for Bangladesh* (Apple 3885): "A Hard Rain's a-Gonna Fall," "It Takes a Lot to Laugh, It Takes a Train to Cry," "Blowin' in the Wind," "Mr. Tambourine Man," "Just Like a Woman"

December 28
Dylan goes backstage after the first of four concerts by The Band at the New York Academy of Music.

1971–1972
Dylan supervises what is intended to be a complete anthology of his lyrics, to be published under the title *Words*. After his late decision to illustrate the text with some of his drawings, the book is retitled *Writings & Drawings*. The endpapers inside the front and back cover feature drafts of unknown Dylan songs, presumably ones contemporary with the book's compilation.

1972

Unknown

Dylan writes a letter publicly supporting John Lennon and Yoko Ono in their pleas to the American immigration service for a green card. In the letter he states that they "help others to see pure light" and concludes, "Let them stay and live here and breathe."

• Dylan attends a reading by Russian poet Voznesensky at the Town Hall, in the company of his wife Sara, Ed Sanders, Peter Orlovsky, Allen Ginsberg, and aspiring poet Jim Carroll. After the reading, they adjourn to the Greenwich Village bar, the Kettle of Fish, with Voznesensky in tow.

January 1, Academy of Music, NY

With the Band recording a live set, *Rock of Ages,* at this New Year's Eve show, Dylan appears as a surprise guest after midnight. Playing rhythm guitar and singing lead, Dylan performs "Down in the Flood," "When I Paint My Masterpiece," "Like a Rolling Stone," and "Don't Ya Tell Henry." Unfortunately, although the tapes were certainly rolling, Dylan's part of the show is not part of the Band's double live album.

January

Allen Ginsberg visits Dylan and plays him three new songs, "CIA Dope Calypso," "New York Blues," and "New York Youth Call Annunciation." Dylan is impressed and suggests to Ginsberg that the poet is ready for his second album (although none of the November 1971 material has yet been released). Dylan volunteers to accompany Ginsberg again.

Early Winter

Dylan attends a show by Link Wray at New York's Max's Kansas City.
• Dylan attends a Jackson Browne concert at the Bitter End in New York.

> *Link Wray is a legendary "twangy" guitarist who recorded in the '60s.*
>
> *Jackson Browne is a singer-songwriter who was just gaining attention at this time; he would become a major recording star from the mid-'70s through the '80s.*

Winter to Spring

Dylan spends some time with his family in Arizona. He owns a ranch in north Phoenix, where he presumably spends most of his time. In *Biograph*, though, he says he started writing "Forever Young" in Tucson, AZ. He also refers to being in Arizona at the time of the release of Neil Young's "Heart of Gold," a song he disliked greatly. According to a story in *The Arizona Republic*, Dylan also played an impromptu concert while in Arizona on a riverboat "during a tubing party on the lower Salt River."

April 7: Joey Gallo is gunned down in Umberto's Clam House. Dylan's 1975 ballad, "Joey," will describe the incident in somewhat rose-tinted terms.

May 20

Dylan attends a recording session in Los Angeles by Joe Cocker who is working on his *Something to Say* album.

June

With his contract with Columbia due to expire, Dylan has discussions with Warner Brothers regarding a new contract. He appears bored and listless throughout the meeting.

June 9–11

Dylan attends one of Elvis Presley's shows at Madison Square Garden in New York.

July 18

Dylan attends a Grateful Dead/Allman Brothers show at Jersey City's Roosevelt Stadium.

July 23

Dylan attends, but does not perform at, the Mariposa Folk Festival on Toronto's Central Island. He stays at the King Edward Hotel in Toronto with Sara, who attends the festival with him. Throughout the day they socialize with Gordon Lightfoot, Dave Bromberg, Leon Redbone, and Bukka White. Although speculation is rife that Dylan will perform at the festival, the organizers are clearly worried about the chaos that a Dylan set would cause. Eventually Dylan, Sara, and Leon Redbone take a police boat off of the island.

Gordon Lightfoot was a well-known Canadian singer/songwriter.
    David Bromberg was a session musician from New York who worked with Dylan in the early '70s and then had a career on his own leading a folk-rock band.
    Leon Redbone is a blues revivalist known for his onstage persona.
    Bukka White was a traditional blues singer who originally recorded in the '30s and was "rediscovered" in the early '60s.

July 26
Dylan and Sara attend Mick Jagger's 29th birthday party in New York, where Dylan is photographed with Zsa Zsa Gabor.

Late August
Dylan and Dave Bromberg jam in a hotel room in Philadelphia while in the city to attend the Eleventh Annual Philadelphia Folk Festival.

September 9, The Bitter End, NY
At the late set Saturday of John Prine's residency at the Bitter End, Dylan walks onstage to perform three songs with Prine. He accompanies Prine on harmonica and some back-up vocals. Two of the three songs they perform are "Donald and Lydia" and "Sam Stone."

Mid-September
Under the alias of Robert Milkwood Thomas, Dylan contributes piano and harmony vocals on two songs recorded by Steve Goodman at Atlantic Recording Studios in New York: "Election Year Rag" and the title track for Goodman's album, *Somebody Else's Troubles.*

Late September
Dylan and Doug Sahm visit Jerry Wexler's home, where they presumably finalize some ideas for Doug Sahm's forthcoming album.

> *Doug Sahm is a Texas-born musician who led the Sir Douglas Quintet in the mid-'60s, scoring hits with "What'd I Say" and "She's About a Mover." He then went solo, and his since performed in various combinations through the '90s (most recently with The Texas Tornados).*

October (1–14)
Dylan sits in on sessions for the *Doug Sahm and Band* album, contributing some keyboards, some guitar, and even the occasional vocal. Dave Bromberg is also one of the session musicians. Dylan contributes vocals on three tracks: "(Is Anybody Going to) San Antone," "Blues Stay Away from Me," and "Wallflower," on which he largely drowns out Sahm's own vocals. "Me and Paul," which Dylan retakes because he is dissatisfied with his playing on the first take, and "Faded Love" feature Dylan on organ (and harmonica on the former). "Dealer's Blues" also features an uncredited organ player. Three songs recorded at these sessions are subsequently released on *Texas Tornado* and presumably also feature Dylan in some capacity, even though he is not credited on the sleeve. The three songs are "Tennessee Blues," "Ain't that Loving You," and "I'll Be There." Also recorded at these sessions, according to a report in *Rolling Stone,* is a version of "Just Like Tom Thumb's Blues" with Dylan and David Newman on guitars, plus several songs composed by the likes of Hank Williams, Atwood Allen, Johnny Bush, and Ray Price, all featuring Dylan on guitar. The sessions take place at the Atlantic Record-

ing Studios on New York's West 60th St. and are produced by Sahm, Arif Mardin (who also produced the Steve Goodman album), and Jerry Wexler.

October

Dylan attends one of the recording sessions at Atlantic Recording Studios for Bette Midler's debut album. Presumably this is at the time of the Doug Sahm sessions.

• Rudy Wurlitzer sends Dylan his screenplay for *Pat Garrett & Billy the Kid* in the hope that he will contribute a song for the soundtrack. Dylan duly obliges with an eight-verse ballad, entitled simply "Billy." Presumably the version of the song sent to Wurlitzer is also the version copyrighted in December 1972.

• Dylan attends a Loudon Wainwright III concert at Max's Kansas City, NY.

> *Loudon Wainwright III is a wry singer-songwriter often compared to Dylan.*

Fall

A story in the February 1973 *Creem* reports that Dylan has recorded a version of "It's Alright, Ma" with ex-Steppenwolf frontman John Kay for Kay's second solo album. No such track has ever emerged.

Early November

Dylan travels down to Durango in Mexico to meet director Sam Peckinpah to discuss the possibility of a role in Peckinpah's film of *Pat Garrett & Billy the Kid*. The first night there, they dine on roast goat. Dylan plays his new composition, "Billy," for Sam Peckinpah, James Coburn, and Kris Kristofferson.

November 23

Dylan arrives in Durango with Sara to start work on *Pat Garrett & Billy the Kid*.

Late November

The first day of shooting for *Pat Garrett & Billy the Kid* involves the turkey scene, featuring Alias (Dylan) and Billy the Kid (Kris Kristofferson).

• A cassette recording is made by Sam Peckinpah at his house of Dylan singing "Billy" and playing several instrumentals.

December 19

Filmed on or around the 19th is a scene where Billy prepares to ride out of Fort Sumner and head for Mexico. At this point, according to the shooting script, Dylan's character, Alias, still speaks with a stutter.

1973

January 2
Filmed on or around the 2nd is a scene where Chisum's cowhands murder Paco and are then in turn gunned down by Billy. In this version of the scene, Alias rides in at the end and asks Billy whether he is going back to Fort Sumner. Alias has lost his stutter.

January 6–7
Dylan and Sara visit George and Patti Harrison at their Surrey home and are seen shopping together in the center of London.

January 16
Filmed on or around the 16th is the scene where Alias is sharpening Paco's knife before Paco sets out for Mexico. Billy is musing about whether to leave for California.

January 18
Filmed on or around the 18th are the scenes that make up the final night of Billy the Kid's life. In one scene Alias, Eno, and Billy come out of the Fort Sumner saloon and meet Kip, who declares he has given up his badge. This scene does not appear in the final movie.

January 20
Dylan records soundtrack material for *Pat Garrett & Billy the Kid* at CBS's Disco Studios in Mexico City. The session starts at 11 PM. After limbering up with an instrumental run-through of "Billy," the first usable take of the evening is a nine-verse version of "Billy" with extended harmonica breaks. A second take features two alternate verses. At this stage in the proceedings, Dylan is augmented by Kris Kristofferson's band: Mike Utley on organ, Sammy Creason on drums, Stephen Bruton on guitar, and Terry Paul on bass. An instrumental called "Under Turkey" (not "Turkey Chase") is followed by a slow, syncopated version of the same instrumental with harmonica, segueing into a partial version of "Billy" (Dylan calls this "Turkey No.2,"). Next up is "Billy Surrenders," which appears in both the original version of the film and the "director's cut," although it is absent from the soundtrack album. A wailing chorus augments another instrumental, the second take of which is introduced in a gruff voice by James Coburn, "And He's Killed Me Too." The slow, gospelish "Goodbye Holly," which will be dropped from the film when Dylan comes up with "Knockin' on Heaven's Door," is next,

followed by two takes of an instrumental called "Peco's Blues," featuring two Mexican trumpeters. Part of the refrain is a dead ringer for Dylan's 1963 composition, "Troubled and I Don't Know Why." After listening to the playback, Dylan decides to try another take of "Billy," this time with bass, drums, and harmony vocals (from Terry Paul). The song is cut to eight verses, but Dylan decides to try one more take, this time accompanied by just Terry Paul. He is happy with this version, and the session breaks up at 7 AM. This final take is subsequently included on the soundtrack album as "Billy 4." However, as a reporter on the set noted, "It began to be apparent that the stuff would have to be redone, maybe in Los Angeles after the movie." The session is produced by Gordon Carroll.

January 21
Dylan sleeps until 10 PM at the Fiesta Palace Hotel, while his fellow actors watch the Super Bowl.

January 22
Michael Watts, while on assignment for a *Melody Maker* feature about the filming of *Pat Garrett & Billy the Kid,* has a brief conversation with Dylan at a bar in the Mexico City airport. They briefly discuss *Eat the Document* and Dylan hints at how unpleasant Durango is proving to be.

Late January
After the disappointing results in Mexico City, score arranger Jerry Fielding is brought in to help Dylan put together the musical soundtrack for *Pat Garrett & Billy the Kid.* He arranges two dubbing sessions to tape "Billy," which is then transcribed, and another song that he has asked Dylan to write to fill up the soundtrack. Dylan comes up with "Knockin' on Heaven's Door"; Fielding hates it.

February
During the filming of *Pat Garrett & Billy the Kid,* a couple of Dylan's children fall ill; they had previously joined their parents in Durango. Dylan takes them to Los Angeles for treatment and then decides to rent a home in Malibu.

• Dylan attends a Willie Nelson session at the Atlantic Recording Studios with Leon Russell and Kris Kristofferson.

• Dylan records the soundtrack for *Pat Garrett & Billy the Kid* at the Burbank Studios in California in two sessions. For some reason, different takes of a couple of the songs are used for movie and album. For the first California session, Dylan is backed by Terry Paul on bass, Roger McGuinn on guitar, and Jim Keltner on drums and bongos. Carol Hunter, Donna Weiss, and Brenda Patterson provide back-up vocals for "Knockin' on Heaven's Door" (both film and album versions) and "Final Theme." Also recorded at this session is "Billy 7," the "Bunkhouse Theme" (with Carol Hunter on second guitar), an instrumental version of "Knockin' on Heaven's Door" used in the director's cut of the film, an alternate "Billy 7," a brief original tune called "Billy Ride," and a couple of impromptu jams, "Amarillo" and "Rock Me Mama."

Roger McGuinn was one of the founders of the Byrds; Dylan helped him out on his first solo album, and McGuinn toured as part of the Rolling Thunder Revue in 1975–76.

• The second of the *Pat Garrett & Billy the Kid* sessions at Burbank Studios on Warner Boulevard is again produced by Gordon Carroll. Roger McGuinn contributes guitar and banjo, Bruce Langhorne plays guitar on his first Dylan session in eight years, Booker T. (Jones) is on bass, Russ Kunkel provides tambourine and bongos where necessary, and Byron Berline plays fiddle. Aside from a version of "Billy" used in edited form in the released movie (and in its entirety at the end of the director's cut of the film, in place of "Billy 4"), the remainder of the material is instrumental: "Main Theme," "Cantina Theme" (the film version of which is a different take from the album), "Billy 1," "Turkey Chase," and "River Theme."

Late Winter
Dylan contributes harmonica on "I'm So Restless," one of the songs on Roger McGuinn's first solo album, recorded at Wally Heider Studio #4 in Los Angeles. McGuinn and Dylan also apparently make some unrealized attempts at joint composition.

March
According to discredited Dylanologist Stephen Pickering, Dylan visits Israel shortly after the completion of *Pat Garrett & Billy the Kid.* Possibly Dylan's visit to Israel was at the beginning of January, when he made his brief trip to London.
• Dylan attends David Blue's set at the Troubador in Los Angeles and goes backstage afterward. He is in the company of actor Harry Dean Stanton. Dylan is also rumored to have performed at the Troubador this month, playing harmonica for Roger McGuinn.

March to April
In the company of Willie Nelson, Dylan attends a Waylon Jennings show at the Troubador.

April
Dylan attends a party in honor of Kris Kristofferson and Rita Coolidge at the Great American Food and Beverage Company in Santa Monica.

April 24
Dylan signs a one-month lease to rent 21336 Pacific Coast Highway, Malibu for the month of June.

June
Dylan demoes three new originals, "Nobody 'Cept You," "Never Say Goodbye," and "Forever Young," at his New York offices on a cheap reel-to-reel player. This version of "Forever Young," with traces of an unerased track leaking through, closes the 1985 *Biograph* set.

June to July
Dylan visits pianist/singer/songwriter Barry Goldberg at his home and they end up jamming for seven hours. He returns the next night. They play some old rock & roll, some of Dylan's songs, and some of Goldberg's, including "(I've Got to Use My) Imagination," "Stormy Weather Cowboy," and "Dusty Country." Dylan then invites Goldberg up to his house in Malibu, where they jam with The Band and Doug Sahm.

July: Writings and Drawings *is published.*

July 13: *Pat Garrett and Billy the Kid* (KC 32460): "Main Theme," "Cantina Theme," "Billy 1," "Bunkhouse Theme," "River Theme," "Turkey Chase," "Knockin' on Heaven's Door," "Final Theme," "Billy 4," "Billy 7"

Summer
Having also relocated to Malibu, Robbie Robertson discusses with Dylan the possibility of a Dylan/Band tour.

• As a condition of Barry Goldberg's contract, Atlantic Records requires Dylan to coproduce Goldberg's eponymous solo album. Dylan thus has his first collaboration with Jerry Wexler at Muscle Shoals Sound Studio. He also contributes backing vocals on four tracks—"Stormy Weather Cowboy," "Silver Moon," "Minstrel Show," and "Big City Woman," plays percussion on "It's Not the Spotlight," and contributes backing vocals for a take of the Goffin-Goldberg song, "(I've Got to Use My) Imagination," previously a hit for Gladys Knight, issued as a single at the time of the album's release.

Late Summer
Dylan rehearses with the Band for a possible "comeback" tour. The rehearsals take place in Malibu at Shangri-Las Studios. They purportedly run through some 80 songs.

August to September
Dylan has discussions with David Geffen, a fellow resident of Malibu, about recording for Asylum Records. Wise to Geffen's reputation, Dylan will not sign a long-term agreement, but agrees to record for Asylum on an album-to-album basis.

Late August: "Knockin' on Heaven's Door"/"Turkey Chase" (4-45913)

September 20–22
Dylan attends one of Neil Young's shows at the Roxy in Los Angeles with David Geffen and Robbie Robertson.

October

According to Rob Fraboni, Dylan went to New York at this time, staying for two and a half weeks, and composing the majority of the songs recorded for *Planet Waves*.

November 2

Dylan and the Band, minus Levon Helm, arrive at Village Recorder (Studio B) in Los Angeles to begin work on Dylan's first real album since 1970's *New Morning.* The album will be coproduced by Dylan, Robbie Robertson, and engineer Rob Fraboni. Richard Manuel plays drums throughout the session. According to Fraboni, some eight songs were recorded on the second. These include at least three attempts at "Nobody 'Cept You," one of which subsequently appears on *The Bootleg Series,* plus *Planet Waves* versions of "Never Say Goodbye" and (the fast) "Forever Young." Also attempted at this first session are an instrumental called "Crosswind Jamboree" and a less than successful run-through of "House of the Rising Sun." After the session, Dylan and Rob Fraboni go to the Whisky A Go-Go on Sunset Boulevard to see Bobby 'Blue' Bland perform.

November 5–6

The bulk of *Planet Waves* is completed over two very intense days at Village Recorder. Levon Helm is back on drums for the sessions, his only studio sessions with Dylan except for two October '65 all-nighters. Aside from recording the album versions of "On A Night Like This," "Going, Going, Gone," "Tough Mama," "Hazel," "Something There Is about You," the slow "Forever Young," and "You Angel You," Dylan also records acoustic versions of "Dirge" and "Forever Young," an entire vocal overdub on "Going, Going, Gone" (which ends up discarded), and a version of "Forever Young" with Garth Hudson on accordion. During the recording of "Forever Young," Dylan's old school chum Louis Kemp pops in to say hello.

November 9

The first mixing session for *Planet Waves* at Village Recorder also results in a new version of "Dirge," with Dylan on piano and Robertson playing some staccato guitar fills. After a quick warm-up, they cut the song in a single take with the tape running.

November 10

Once again Dylan cannot resist tinkering with an album at the mixing stage. Back at Village Recorder, Dylan informs Fraboni that he has written a song he wants to record solo. The song in question, "Wedding Song," he again cuts in a single take, completing the recording of *Planet Waves* in a mere five days.

November 16: *Dylan* (PC 32747): "Lily of the West," "Can't Help Falling in Love," "Sarah Jane," "The Ballad of Ira Hayes," "Mr. Bojangles," "Mary Ann," "Big Yellow Taxi," "A Fool Such as I," "Spanish Is the Loving Tongue"

Mid- to Late November
Dylan and Sara visit Mexico at this time.

December
Dylan visits Joni Mitchell in Laurel Canyon. She plays him her forthcoming album, *Court and Sparks,* but Dylan is not overwhelmed.

December 26–27
Dylan and the Band have their final rehearsals for the 1974 tour at the Inglewood Forum in Los Angeles.

1974

January 2

Dylan leaves Los Angeles for Chicago in a private plane, Starship 1, specially hired for the forthcoming tour. He has decided to keep a diary on the tour and his impressions on this first day end up appearing as the sleeve notes for his new album, *Planet Waves.* Their late addition requires a separate sheet to be shrinkwrapped with the album's first pressing.

• In the evening, he sees folksinger Fred Holstein perform at the Earl of Old Town, Chicago.

January 3, Chicago Stadium, Chicago

Dylan opens his first American tour in eight years at Chicago Stadium. Media interest is at an unparalleled height as Dylan, wrapped in a scarf, launches into the first song, a rewrite of his unreleased 1963 composition, "Hero Blues." Backed by the Band, the sound is raw and punchy, with Dylan chewing his fair share of gravel. "Lay, Lady, Lay," no longer tender-hearted, follows "Hero Blues." Then it is time for the first *Planet Waves* live performance, "Tough Mama." After this brief burst of activity Dylan turns the spotlight on the Band for three songs. After contributing harmonica on "Share Your Love with Me," Dylan is back to center stage with "It Ain't Me, Babe," "Leopard-Skin Pill-Box Hat," "All Along the Watchtower" (a la Hendrix), "Ballad of a Thin Man," and "I Don't Believe You." Mid-show comes Dylan's solo spot, during which he performs "The Times They Are a-Changin'," "Song to Woody," "The Lonesome Death of Hattie Carroll," the *Planet Waves* outtake "Nobody 'Cept You," and finally "It's Alright, Ma," with its prophetic line: "Even the President of the United States sometimes must have to stand naked." In light of the Watergate scandal, audiences respond dramatically to this line throughout the tour. The Band then return to the stage, performing two further songs from the yet-to-be-released *Planet Waves,* the hymnal "Forever Young" and "Something There Is About You" before closing the main set with an inevitable "Like a Rolling Stone." The Band returns (minus Dylan) for the first encore, "The Weight," before Dylan bids adieu with "Most Likely You Go Your Way." After much uncertainty regarding Dylan's ability to affirm his power in live performance *Rolling Stone* echoes most critical opinion with their headline: "Dylan opens to a hero's welcome." After the show, Maureen Orth of *Newsweek* obtains the first interview of the 1974 tour, a remarkably conciliatory gesture on Dylan's part considering his previous opinion of *Newsweek.* He is reasonably forthcoming, providing some great lines: "The singers and musicians I grew up with transcend nostalgia." Throughout the interview, he is at pains to dispel any attempt to make him a messiah once again: "Those carved pieces of wood . . . that's what an idol is."

January 4, Chicago Stadium, Chicago

Dylan again opens with "Hero Blues." Four songs are introduced into the set: "Just Like Tom Thumb's Blues," Dylan's most recent hit, "Knockin' on Heaven's Door," an acoustic "Love Minus Zero," and, as the encore, "Maggie's Farm" replaces "Most Likely You Go Your Way."

January 6, The Spectrum, Philadelphia

For the first time, Dylan and the Band play an afternoon *and* an evening show, at the Spectrum in Philadelphia. The afternoon show has a new opener for the set, "Ballad of Hollis Brown." It also includes the last live "Tough Mama." The real surprises, though, come during the acoustic set, when Dylan performs the only 1974 versions of "To Ramona" and "Mama, You Been on My Mind." There is no encore.

At the evening show, they try another opener, "Rainy Day Women." "Leopard-Skin Pill-Box Hat" also makes one of its rare 1974 appearances. Again, though, it is the acoustic set that provides the most notable variations. In a six-song acoustic set, "Song to Woody" makes its final 1974 appearance, "It's All Over Now, Baby Blue" makes its 1974 debut, along with the only solo "Mr. Tambourine Man" of the 1974 tour. "Most Likely You Go Your Way" is reinstated as the encore. David Devoss of *Time* uncovers little worthwhile information during an interview with Dylan backstage. It is a brief affair, even when compared with Maureen Orth's.

January 7, The Spectrum, Philadelphia

In his suite at the Sheraton Hotel, Dylan is interviewed in the afternoon by John Rockwell of *The New York Times*. In the evening, Dylan and The Band play their third and final show at the Spectrum. Although the sets with The Band have settled quickly into a rigid format, Dylan continues to ring the changes in the acoustic set, introducing "Just Like a Woman," "Girl from the North Country," and "Wedding Song" into his five-song solo slot. "Ballad of Hollis Brown" reappears, this time in the middle set with The Band.

January 9, Maple Leaf Gardens, Toronto, Ontario

An impromptu-sounding version of "It Takes a Lot to Laugh" is the one surprise in the opening set with The Band. "Girl from the North Country" makes its second and last appearance on the 1974 tour during the acoustic set. After the show, Dylan visits the Nickelodeon, before returning to his hotel, the Inn on the Park. In the early hours, he visits Gordon Lightfoot at Lightfoot's home.

January 10, Maple Leaf Gardens, Toronto, Ontario

A real surprise tonight is the only ever live version of "As I Went Out One Morning," featuring some fine understated backing from the Band. "Don't Think Twice, It's All Right" and "Gates of Eden" are introduced into the acoustic set. "Most Likely You Go Your Way" has replaced "Rainy Day Women" as the opener, completing a circle by opening *and* closing the shows.

January 11–12, Montreal Forum, Montreal
On the 12th, Dylan plays a solo version of "Blowin' in the Wind." On the same date, Ben Fong Torres, editor of *Rolling Stone,* conducts the only major interview of the 1974 tour in Dylan's room at the Chateau Champlain hotel in Montreal. It is a wide-ranging interview, revealing somewhat more than the infamous 1969 *Rolling Stone* interview.

January 14, Boston Gardens, Boston, MA
Afternoon and evening shows. At the afternoon performance, "Rainy Day Women" opens the show one last time. At the evening show, the acoustic set includes "Love Minus Zero" and "Blowin' in the Wind."

January 15
Tom Zito interviews Dylan at the Sheraton Hotel in Boston early in the morning. It is not a good interview. Zito is upset that Dylan will not bare his soul to him. At the end of the interview, Dylan asks Zito to delete a comment about George McGovern because, "the guy's sentiments were in the right place." Zito's failure to do so leads to a ban on further interviews during the tour.

January 15, Washington Capitol Center, Washington, DC
Includes the last 1974 version of "I Don't Believe You."

January 16
During the day Dylan visits the Philips Collection on 21st St., Washington.

January 16, Washington Capitol Center, Washington
Includes a solitary electric version of "One Too Many Mornings," and the last performance of "Nobody 'Cept You."

January 17, Charlotte Coliseum, Charlotte, NC
On the day of the release of *Planet Waves,* Dylan performs just two songs, "Forever Young" and "Something There Is about You," from his new album.

> *Planet Waves* (Asylum S 73 1003): "On a Night Like This," "Going Going Gone," "Tough Mama," "Hazel," "Something There Is about You," "Forever Young," "Dirge," "You Angel You," "Never Say Goodbye," "Wedding Song." (Reissued by Columbia in April 1982 as PC 37637)

January 18
Dylan visits Bubba's Folk & Blues Club in Miami, FL.

January 19, Hollywood Sportatorium, Miami, FL
Afternoon and evening shows. The afternoon show includes "Leopard-Skin Pill-Box Hat."

January 20
Dylan decides to join a religious rally at Peacock Park in Miami where he talks to organizer Arthur Blessitt.

January 21, OMNI Coliseum, Atlanta, GA
Includes the last 1974 version of "Leopard-Skin Pill-Box Hat." After the show, Dylan, the Band, and Bill Graham attend a post concert party at the mansion of Jimmy Carter, the governor of Georgia. The party ends at 1:30 AM, and Dylan returns to his hotel room.

January 22, OMNI Coliseum, Atlanta, GA
"Rainy Day Women" becomes the regular choice for the fourth song of the opening set. Dylan performs a rare 1974 "It's All Over Now, Baby Blue."

January 23, Mid-South Coliseum, Memphis, TN
Includes a truly horrendous acoustic rendition of "Fourth Time Around."

January 25, Tarrant County Convention Center Arena, Fort Worth, TX

January 26, Hofheinz Pavilion, Houston, TX
Afternoon and evening shows.

January 28–29, Veterans Memorial Coliseum, Nassau County
The show on the 29th includes "It's All Over Now, Baby Blue."

January 30–31, Madison Square Garden, NY
All three New York shows are recorded for a possible live album. The version of "Knockin' on Heaven's Door" from the first show is subsequently included on *Before the Flood.* The show also includes the last 1974 version of "Something There Is about You," and a second encore of "Blowin' in the Wind" with the Band, something that becomes a regular feature of the remaining shows.

   • On the 31st, Dylan performs afternoon and evening shows. The afternoon show features "Highway 61 Revisited" as a replacement for "Something There Is about You," and "Maggie's Farm" as first encore. Although both concerts are recorded for a possible live album, nothing from these concerts is featured on *Before the Flood.* After the show, Dylan attends a party on the roof of the St. Moritz Hotel in New York.

February 2, University of Michigan, Ann Arbor, MI

February 3, Indiana University Assembly Arena, Bloomington, IN

February 4, Missouri Arena, St Louis, MO
Afternoon and evening shows. The afternoon show includes two lengthy one-off additions to the solo set. Unfortunately, the versions of "Desolation Row" and "A Hard Rain's a-Gonna Fall" do neither song justice. At the evening show, "Wedding Song" is reintroduced into the solo set.

Los Angeles, 1974

February 6, Denver Coliseum, Denver, CO

Afternoon and evening shows. Again the afternoon show's solo set includes two surprises: "She Belongs to Me" is performed for the first time on the tour, while "Visions of Johanna" makes its only 1974 appearance.

February 7

Dylan and the Band indulge in mid-tour rehearsals at Denver's Playboy Club, presumably in preparation for the recording of a live album from the remaining concerts.

February 9, Seattle Coliseum, Seattle, WA

Afternoon and evening shows. "The Lonesome Death of Hattie Carroll" makes a reappearance at today's afternoon show. Both concerts are recorded for a possible live album.

February 11, Alameda County Coliseum, Oakland, CA

Afternoon and evening shows. At the afternoon show, the first encore is "Maggie's Farm." Again both concerts are recorded for a possible live album.

February 13, Inglewood Forum, Los Angeles, CA

"Love Minus Zero" makes its final appearance on the tour, as the tapes roll for the projected live album. Three songs from this show later appear on *Before the Flood*: "Rainy Day Women," "Lay, Lady, Lay," and (part of) "Blowin' in the Wind."

February 14, Inglewood Forum, Los Angeles, CA

Afternoon and evening shows. Both the final shows of the 1974 tour are recorded for the live album. Indeed they make up the bulk of the double album, *Before the Flood.* The afternoon show includes "It's All Over Now, Baby Blue," plus *Before the Flood* versions of "Ballad of a Thin Man," "All Along the Wachtower," and (part of) "Blowin' in the Wind." The evening show includes a first encore of "Maggie's Farm" as well as a unique version of "Mr. Tambourine Man," featuring Garth Hudson on accordion. However, the songs from this final show chosen for *Before the Flood* are decidedly unadventurous: "Most Likely You Go Your Way," "It Ain't Me, Babe," "Just Like a Woman," "Don't Think Twice, It's All Right," "Highway 61 Revisited," and "Like a Rolling Stone."

• The tour has been a tremendous commercial success; Dylan having reaffirmed his status as a major performing artist. But, in retrospect, Dylan would state that he "hated every moment of that 1974 tour," that he "knew that going through with the tour would be the hardest thing I had ever done."

February 15

Dylan attends the post-tour party at the Forum Club, leaving by 2 AM. He then returns to the Beverly Wilshire Hotel for a private party with The Band, family, and close friends.

February 21

Dylan attends David Geffen's 31st birthday party at the Beverly Wilshire Hotel. During the party, he performs a solo "Mr. Tambourine Man" and a version of "All I Really Want to Do" with members of The Band and Cher.

Robbie and Bob, Los Angeles, 1974

Late February to Early March

Dylan selects recordings for *Before the Flood.*

Mid-April

Dylan is staying with friends in Marin County, on the outskirts of San Francisco.

Mid- to Late April

Dylan attends Chick Edwards's wedding at the Hyatt Regency Hotel in Marin County, even apparently singing at the reception. Also in attendance are Paul McCartney and the Doobie Brothers.

April 24

Dylan flies from Los Angeles to New York, presumably to discuss contractual matters relating to the live album of the 1974 tour.

Spring

In Greenwich Village, Dylan runs into lyricist Jacques Levy, who had previously worked with Roger McGuinn, and they spend the evening together. They are to renew their acquaintance the following summer.

• Dylan studies under an artist/teacher named Norman Raeben in New York. According to Dylan, "Five days a week I used to go up there . . . I used to be up there from eight o'clock to four. That's all I did for two months." According to a fellow pupil, Dylan attended the classes for more than two months. If so, he must have returned to the classes after the summer. Dylan later credits Raeben with teaching him "to do consciously what I used to do unconsciously." The first result of this new approach is *Blood on the Tracks.*

Late April

Dylan attends a concert by Buffy St. Marie at the Bottom Line in New York. He is so impressed he returns the following two nights, and tells her he'd like to record her composition, "Until It's Time for You to Go."

May 6

Dylan runs into Phil Ochs in front of the Chelsea Hotel and they decide to go for a drink together.

May 7

Dylan visits Ochs at his apartment and agrees to perform at the "Friends of Chile" benefit Ochs has arranged at the Felt Forum. Tickets for the show had been selling very disappointingly.

May 9, Felt Forum, NY

Dylan appears at the "Friends of Chile" benefit. However, much sampling of Chilean wine before the show means that his performance leaves a lot to be desired. Staggering onstage, he proceeds to massacre "Deportees," "North Country Blues," "Spanish Is the Loving Tongue," and "Blowin' in the Wind." The last two songs are not helped by equally drunken contributions from Dave Van Ronk, Phil Ochs, and assorted "folksingers."

May 10

Dylan escorts Joan Jara, widow of Chilean activist-folksinger Victor Jara, to the New York Museum of Modern Art in the afternoon.

May 10–11

After the "Friends of Chile" benefit, Dylan and Ochs spend a couple of evenings in each other's company. On the 11th, they meet Ron Delsener at the Carnegie Hall Tavern. Dylan is already considering the possibility of a tour of small halls and clubs.

> *Ron Delsener is a prominent promoter of concerts in the New York City area.*

> June 20: *Before the Flood* (Asylum S 201): "Most Likely You Go Your Way," "Lay, Lady, Lay," "Rainy Day Women Nos. 12 & 35," "Knocking on Heaven's Door," "It Ain't Me Babe," "Ballad of a Thin Man," "Don't Think Twice, It's All Right," "Just Like a Woman," "It's Allright Ma," "All Along the Watchtower," "Highway 61 Revisited," "Like a Rolling Stone," "Blowin' in the Wind" (Reissued by Columbia in April 1982 as KC 37661)

July

Syndicated columns report that Dylan and Sara are breaking up. The reports link Dylan with John Sebastian's ex-wife Lorey, although she quickly refutes these stories. Dylan is also linked with a Columbia A&R executive, Ellen Bernstein, whom he had first encountered in February.

Mid- to Late July

Dylan heads for his farm in Minnesota, where he is joined by his children. They visit relatives and friends in Hibbing and the Mesabi Range. Dylan also works on the songs that will constitute *Blood on the Tracks*. The lyrics are written in a small, red notebook. The order that they appear in the notebook is: "Lily, Rosemary and the Jack of Hearts," "Tangled Up in Blue," "You're a Big Girl Now," "There Ain't Gonna Be any Next Time," "Shelter from the Storm," "Belltower Blues (Climbed Up the Bell Tower)," "If You See Her, Say Hello," "Church Bell Blues" (aka "Call Letter Blues"), "Where Do You Turn? (Turning Point)," "It's Breakin' Me Up," "Simple Twist of Fate (Fourth Street Affair)," "Idiot Wind," I "Don't Want No Married Woman," "You're Gonna Make Me Miss You When You Go," "Up to Me" I & II, "Ain't It Funny," "Little Bit of Rain," and "Idiot Wind" II. Presumably "Buckets of Rain" and "Meet Me in the Morning" are omitted because they had not as yet been written.

July 22

Dylan meets Dave Crosby at the St. Paul Hilton. Crosby, Stills, and Nash are playing the Civic Center that evening and he decides to attend the concert, afterward returning to the Hilton, where he sits in a hotel room jamming with Stephen Stills and Tim Drummond for two hours. He sings eight or nine new songs to Drummond and Stills.

August 2
Irwin Segelstein signs Dylan to an exclusive deal with Columbia Records at the annual CBS convention at the Century Plaza Hotel in Los Angeles.

August
While in San Francisco for a couple of weeks in the company of Ellen Bernstein, Dylan visits Michael Bloomfield in Marin County to play him some material from the yet-to-be-recorded *Blood on the Tracks.* He is considering the possibility of using Bloomfield on the sessions. The visit does not go well, however, and the atmosphere is tense as Dylan runs through song after song, without pause. Bloomfield is unable to follow the chord changes, and Dylan seems uninterested in helping him learn the songs. He also visits country songwriter Shel Silverstein on Silverstein's houseboat, playing him most of the songs that will make up the new album, as well as the home of guitarist Peter Rowan, who after Dylan has unveiled a few new works, insists on playing Dylan some of his songs.

September 16
Dylan begins work on one of the landmark albums of the 1970s, *Blood on the Tracks,* at A&R Studios (formerly Columbia Studio A) in New York. Dylan produces the sessions himself, Phil Ramone providing technical assistance as engineer. In attendance throughout the New York sessions will be Ellen Bernstein, the Columbia A&R lady with whom Dylan has become involved. The afternoon is spent running through songs acoustically, although there are few details of the songs so attempted. A solo "Up to Me" dates from this session and has a telltale clatter from Dylan's coat buttons. After a short break, Dylan resumes work in the evening, this time with Eric Weissberg and his band Deliverance providing some musical support. Of the songs cut at this evening session, three end up unused: "Lily, Rosemary & the Jack of Hearts," "Simple Twist of Fate," and "You're a Big Girl Now," all of which presumably feature some or all of Deliverance. Also cut at this session, and later included on *The Bootleg Series,* is a prototype version of "Meet Me in the Morning" called "Call Letter Blues," plus at least two versions of "Tangled Up in Blue" and "If You See Her, Say Hello." One take of each ends up on the original *Blood on the Tracks* test pressing, and inferior alternates on *The Bootleg Series.*

September 17
Dylan resumes work at A&R Studios. Dispensing with Weissberg's band, except for bassist Tony Brown, he is augmented by one of the key figures from the legendary 1965 sessions, Paul Griffin, on organ. He proceeds to rerecord "You're a Big Girl Now." This heart-rending performance is included on the original test pressing but has to wait until 1985's *Biograph* for an official release.

September 18

Tony Brown and Dylan continue their solitary progress at A&R Studios, cutting versions of "You're Gonna Make Me Lonesome When You Go" and "Shelter from the Storm." An alternate version of the former was originally scheduled for *The Bootleg Series* but was deleted at the last minute and remains unreleased.

• Dylan attends the second Little Feat concert at the Bottom Line, New York. He meets David Bowie for the first time at this show.

September 19

Tony Brown and Dylan recut the epic "Lily, Rosemary & the Jack of Hearts" and "Simple Twist of Fate," two songs attempted on the 16th with Deliverance but now pared down to guitar and bass. They are then joined by the New Riders of the Purple Sage pedal steel player Buddy Cage for the brand new "Buckets of Rain." Cage had been a suggestion of Ellen Bernstein's. Finally they cut at least two versions of "Idiot Wind," one of which will later be included on *The Bootleg Series*. A far superior take, with overdubs, is placed on the original *Blood on the Tracks* test pressing.

September 20

According to Columbia records, a session was scheduled at A&R Studios for this afternoon. Possibly the session was simply spent listening to playbacks.

September 23–25

Two to three days are spent mixing, overdubbing, and sequencing *Blood on the Tracks* at A&R Studios. With Tony Brown and Buddy Cage adding some of their own overdubs, Dylan takes the opportunity to rework the basic track for "Call Letter Blues," coming up with "Meet Me in the Morning." He and Brown also rerecord "Up to Me," which later appears on *Biograph*. "Idiot Wind" is subjected to some overdubs by Paul Griffin on keyboards, while Dylan "punches in" a new vocal on four lines. On the 25th, Ramone cuts a test pressing for Dylan that contains an approved sequence for the album. This will remain unchanged despite all the traumas the album must now go through.

December
Dylan attends George Harrison's concert at Toronto's Maple Leaf Gardens. They jam backstage, but Dylan does not join Harrison onstage.

Mid- to Late December
Dylan heads up to his farm in Minnesota to spend Christmas with his relatives. While there, he asks his brother David for his opinion of the new album.

December 27
On his brother's recommendation, Dylan enlists some local Minneapolis musicians to rerecord six songs scheduled for *Blood on the Tracks*. At Sound 80 Studios in Minneapolis, Dylan is backed by Ken Odegard on guitar, Chris Weber on 12-string, Bill Preston on bass, Greg Imhofer on keyboards, and Bill Berg on drums. They record (four takes of) "Idiot Wind" and "You're a Big Girl Now."

December 30
At Dylan's second session at Sound 80 Studios in Minneapolis, the local musicians play with considerably more flair, laying down usable takes of "Tangled Up in Blue," "Lily, Rosemary and the Jack of Hearts," and "If You See Her, Say Hello." Also supposedly recorded at one of these two December sessions is a version of "Meet Me in the Morning," but it is not deemed good enough to replace the September version.

1975

Early Winter
Dylan visits the New York club Reno Sweeney's with Bette Midler and David Bowie to see Dana Gillespie in concert.

Winter
Dylan and Phil Spector attend a concert by Leonard Cohen at the Troubador in Los Angeles.
• Dylan is again considered for the role of Woody Guthrie in a picture about Guthrie's life. He meets with Harold Leventhal and director Alan Arkin to discuss the role shortly before leaving for the West Indies, where he is vacationing with his wife and children. The role ends up being offered to David Carradine.

> January 17: *Blood on the Tracks* (PC 33235): "Tangled Up in Blue," "Simple Twist of Fate," "You're a Big Girl Now," "Idiot Wind," "You're Gonna Make Me Lonesome When You Go," "Meet Me in the Morning," "Lily, Rosemary and the Jack of Hearts," "If You See Her, Say Hello," "Shelter from the Storm," "Buckets of Rain."
> February: "Tangled Up in Blue/"If You See Her, Say Hello" (3-10106)

Late February
Dylan threatens legal action against Los Angeles radio station KMET-FM when disc jockey 'Obscene' Steven Clean segues "Idiot Wind" into a *National Lampoon* spoof of Dylan.

March
At the Greenhouse, in Los Angeles, Warner Brothers holds a party to celebrate the end of the Faces's US tour. Paul and Linda McCartney, Bryan Ferry, and Dylan attend.

March 10
Old friend Mary Travers convinces Dylan to give his first radio interview since 1966. He appears on "Mary Travers and Friends" on KNX-FM, recorded in Oakland, CA. He is not in a particularly talkative mood, although he does discuss the imminent release of *The Basement Tapes* and the critical reaction to *Blood on the Tracks*.

March 22

Dylan, Neil Young, and company spend the afternoon soundchecking in Golden Gate Park for tomorrow's SNACK benefit show. According to at least one eyewitness, Dylan's performance at the soundcheck is far less inhibited than the show itself.

March 23, Kezar Stadium, Golden Gate Park, San Francisco

Dylan is the surprise guest, billed as "the man from the Fairmont," at a benefit concert for SNACK (Students Need Athletic and Cultural Kicks). Along with three members of the Band, Neil Young, Tim Drummond, and Ben Keith, Dylan stays on stage for half an hour. He contributes vocals on "Are You Ready for the Country," "I Want You," (the slightly rewritten) "Knockin' on Dragon's Door," and "Will the Circle Be Unbroken." Unfortunately his microphone is turned way down in the mix, and he is barely audible on tapes of the show, even though the whole concert is broadcast on a local radio station. Dylan also provides backing on piano/guitar for the five other songs: "Ain't That a Lot of Love," "Lookin' for a Love," "Loving You Is Sweeter than Ever," "The Weight," and "Helpless." Sara Dylan accompanies him to the show. After the concert, Dylan (and presumably Sara) dine at the home of Francis Ford Coppola, along with Bill Graham and Marlon Brando.

March 24

Dylan and Sara attend a party given by Paul and Linda McCartney on the Queen Mary, at its permanent mooring in Long Beach, CA.

Early May

Dylan flies over to Saintes-Maries de-la-Mer in the south of France, where he stays with painter David Oppenheim, who had painted the rear sleeve for *Blood on the Tracks* (reissued in the spring of 1975 minus Peter Hamill's sleeve notes). He remains there for six weeks.

May 24

Dylan attends a gypsy festival in Saintes-Maries de-la-Mer on his 34th birthday. The festival inspires the song "One More Cup of Coffee." Dylan introduces the song on the US 1978 tour with a rap about the gypsy festival.

Mid-June

On his return from France, Dylan visits Rubin "Hurricane" Carter in prison, having previously been moved by Carter's autobiography, *The Sixteenth Round,* which recounts the story of his unjust imprisonment for murders he did not commit.

• Dylan moves back to Greenwich Village alone, living in a borrowed loft on Houston Street.

Late June (22–27)
Dylan attends one of the Rolling Stones's concerts at Madison Square Garden.

June 25
Dylan makes a surprise appearance at the Bottom Line in Greenwich Village, guesting with Victoria Spivey and Muddy Waters, providing harmonica accompaniment on an unspecified number of songs.

> June 26: *The Basement Tapes* (C2 33682): "Odds and Ends," "Million Dollar Bash," "Goin' to Acapulco," "Lo and Behold," "Clothes Line Saga," "Apple Suckling Tree," "Please Mrs. Henry," "Tears of Rage," "Too Much of Nothing," "Yea Heavy and a Bottle of Bread," "Crash on the Levee," "Tiny Montgomery," "You Ain't Goin' Nowhere," "Nothing Was Delivered," "Open the Door Homer," "This Wheel's on Fire"

June 28
Dylan attends Patti Smith's gig at the Other End. After her performance, Dylan is introduced to her and Dylan insists that they be photographed together. Dylan is impressed by her group and tells her so.

June 30
Dylan is driving around the Village in the afternoon with an old friend, Sheena, when he spies an exotic-looking lady carrying a violin case. The woman is Scarlet Rivera. Dylan invites her to his Village studio, where she accompanies him on violin on several new songs, including "One More Cup of Coffee." Dylan then takes her with him to the Other End club and onto a jazz club, before arriving at the Bottom Line, where Rivera on violin and Dylan on harmonica make a (second) surprise guest appearance with Muddy Waters and his band. This time Dylan's surprise appearance is widely reported in the music press. After Muddy Waters's sets, Dylan and Rivera accompany the band to Victoria Spivey's house in Brooklyn, where they spend many more hours jamming, talking to Spivey, and listening to old records.

July 2
Dylan attends a Jack Elliott concert at the Other End, but he does not join Elliott on stage.

July 3
At the Other End, Dylan joins Ramblin' Jack Elliott on stage for a couple of songs. First he backs Elliott on guitar for "Pretty Boy Floyd," then they duet on the old chestnut, "How Long." At this point, Elliott turns the stage over to Dylan for one song, a new composition he has written that week called "Abandoned Love." Fortunately, a member of the audience captures this remarkable performance on tape.

July 4

According to *Rolling Stone,* Dylan again turns up at the Other End on this date joining Bobby Neuwirth on stage during an Independence Day hootenanny, singing harmony on one song.

July 5

The First Annual Village Folk Festival at the Other End. Dylan joins Bobby Neuwirth on stage for one song, and then plays piano as Rob Stoner and Mick Ronson accompany Patti Smith on versions of "Goodnight Irene," "Bank of the Ohio," "Amazing Grace," and "Will the Circle Be Unbroken." Festivities carry on into the wee hours of the morning.

July 9

Dylan spends the night with Madeline Beckman, a young writer, at her Manhattan apartment. He talks to her about his marriage, his kids, and his brother, and plays some Spanish guitar until 4 AM, when he crashes in her bed.

Early to Mid-July

Dylan meets with Jacques Levy again (see Spring 1974). They go up to Levy's Village apartment and work together on a song Dylan has already started called "Isis." Afterward Dylan suggests further collaborations.

• Dylan and Jacques Levy go for dinner at the apartment of Jerry and Marty Orbach. Marty Orbach is working on a book about gangster Joey Gallo. After an evening of stories about Gallo, Levy and Dylan return to Levy's apartment and write "Joey."

• According to Michael Gross, Dylan turned up at the Other End one night during Bobby Neuwirth's residency and performed two new songs, "Joey" and "Isis."

Mid-July

Dylan is in the audience watching Neuwirth and his band, along with Jake and the Family Jewels, sharing a one-week residency at the Other End. After the show, Dylan, Bobby Neuwirth, T-Bone Burnett, and Ramblin' Jack Elliott retire next door, where Dylan performs "Abandoned Love," as well as two songs he has just written with Jacques Levy, "Isis" and "Joey." The version of "Isis" may have been quite different from the released version. A report of the gig refers to "a refrain that changed one word each verse." It is unclear what backing, if any, Dylan was provided with. Afterward, Neuwirth, Elliott, and Burnett sang some songs "while Dylan played rhythm and harmonized."

> *T-Bone Burnett is a singer/songwriter who, at this time, was deep into a born-again Christian phase. He would join with many of the others on Dylan's Rolling Thunder tour.*

July 14

Dylan records two songs, apparently with Dave Mason's band, augmented by some women singers and violinist Scarlet Rivera, at Columbia's New York

Studios. The two songs, "Joey" and "Rita Mae," both end up being rerecorded at the *Desire* sessions later in the month.

Mid- to Late July

Dylan and Jacques Levy retire to East Hampton where, according to Levy, they write 14 songs. Just four songs from the Hamptons, though, appear on *Desire*. Dylan also writes one song on his own. They go out most nights to local bars; one night Dylan plays three of the songs he and Levy have written in a bar for light relief. They stay in East Hampton for about 10 days.

July 28

With his largest ever studio band in tow, Dylan enters Columbia Studios in New York. Columbia in-house producer Don Devito sits at the console. Five guitarists Neil Hubbard, Eric Clapton, Hugh McCracken, Vinnie Bell, and slide guitarist Erik Frandsen a saxophonist/trumpeter (Mel Collins), a harmonica player (Sugar Blue), a bassist (Rob Stoner), a violinist (Scarlet Rivera), a mandolin and accordion player (Dom Cortese), a drummer (Terry Stannard), at least two backing singers (Emmylou Harris and Yvonne Elliman, although Elliman seems to have made no real contribution), and Sheena on tambourine, take turns embroidering the songs. Some six songs are definitely cut at this session, although only "Romance in Durango" will appear on *Desire* (and "Catfish" on *The Bootleg Series*). "Money Blues," "One More Cup of Coffee," "Oh Sister," and "Hurricane" will all have to be revamped at a later session minus much of the clutter. According to Larry Sloman, Dylan also attempted a song called "Wiretappin'" although there is no mention of it on the studio sheets.

July 29

Elliman and Clapton have left the sessions. Otherwise Dylan's big band remains intact for the second *Desire* session. "Black Diamond Bay," "Money Blues," "Catfish," "Mozambique," and "Hurricane" are all attempted big band style, "Hurricane" with apparently a semi-disco arrangement. "Oh Sister" is also attempted, with a more stripped-down sound, although like the remainder of today's cuts it ends up being discarded.

July 30

At tonight's session at Columbia Studios it is back to basics with just Rob Stoner on bass, his regular sidekick Howie Wyeth on drums, Scarlet Rivera on violin, Emmylou Harris on backing vocals, and Sheena on "percussion." Dylan contributes the usual guitar and harmonica as the new combo whip through nine songs in a single night, five of which make it to *Desire:* "Oh Sister" (finally), "One More Cup of Coffee," "Mozambique," "Joey," and "Black Diamond Bay." Originally scheduled for *Desire* is the version of "Hurricane" cut tonight, along with "Rita Mae," eventually released on a 1976 single. "Golden Loom" also gets an eventual official release on *The Bootleg Series,* leaving just tonight's "Isis" in the reject pile.

July 31

Dylan has been in court all day appearing as a character witness for the ex-president of the CBS record division, Clive Davies. He arrives at the evening session in the company of his wife, Sara. Emmylou Harris is absent, so backing vocal duties when required, as on "Isis," are undertaken by Rob Stoner. The two key love songs on *Desire* are both recorded at tonight's session, "Isis" and "Sara," as is the key *Desire* outtake, "Abandoned Love," recorded with and without harmonica and later released on *Biograph* (with harmonica). "Money Blues" is also attempted but once again without success. Sara is in attendance throughout the session.

August 1
Dylan, Devito, Stoner, Rivera, and Wyeth assemble at Columbia Studios to go through the master reels and select the relevant songs and takes for Dylan's new album. When they come to "Romance in Durango," Dylan asks whether they should try to record the song with the stripped-down line-up, but Wyeth and Stoner are happy to let the "Big Band" version stand.

August 2
Dylan leaves the studio at 6 AM for Don Devito's West Side apartment, where they discuss the possibility of a tour. He leaves for Minnesota with Sara the same day.

September 1
Dylan attends the marriage of his cousin, Linda Goldfine, at the Temple Israel Camp in Minneapolis, performing at the reception with a handful of local musicians, singing "Forever Young" and Kenny Loggins's "A Love Song."

Early September
While in Minneapolis, Dylan asks his childhood friend Lou Kemp if he would be interested in organizing a tour for the fall.

September 10
Dylan, accompanied by Scarlet Rivera, Rob Stoner, and Howie Wyeth, performs three songs at WTTW-TV studios in Chicago for "The World of John Hammond," a one-hour tribute to John Hammond, Sr. "Hurricane" is performed twice, the broadcast version being an edit of the pair. The other songs are "Oh Sister," receiving its first public performance and dedicated to "someone watching tonight," and a rewritten version of "Simple Twist of Fate," concentrating more on the narrative and clearly influenced by his collaborations with Jacques Levy.

September 11
After finishing recording the TV special at 2 AM, Dylan walks around Chicago with bassist Rob Stoner before flying directly to Los Angeles.

Mid- to Late September to Early October
Dylan and Sara attend the wedding of Jonathan Taplin and Rosana DeSoto in California.

October 1
Over dinner at Dylan's house in Malibu, plans are finalized for a film of *Lily,*

Rosemary and the Jack of Hearts, to be produced by Jonathan Taplin and John Ptak, and directed by Phil Kaufman, with a screenplay to be written by John Kaye. The project is never realized.

October

Dylan records a new version of "Buckets of Rain" as a duet with Bette Midler at New York's Secret Sound Studios. They lay down two takes of the song, with much lighthearted ad-libbing at the end of each take. The second take is later included on Midler's *Songs for the New Depression* as well as being released as a single.

October 19

Dylan visits the Other End but, when questioned about plans to tour remains evasive. He meets with Roger McGuinn there and they head over to the Kettle of Fish with David Blue, Jacques Levy, and Lou Kemp.

Mid- to Late October (19–26?)

Dylan moves into the Gramercy Park Hotel in New York while the recently assembled Rolling Thunder Revue rehearses at Studio Instrument Rentals (S.I.R.), first at their midtown location and then on West 25th St. Rehearsals last about a week and probably start on or around the 20th. In the words of new recruit Mick Ronson, "There were tape machines and everything getting set up and Dylan starts singing all these songs. He must've played about three hundred songs one after the other." Clearly all the rehearsals were taped, although none of the musical soundtrack for *Renaldo and Clara* derives from these sessions. According to Rob Stoner, "We had no idea what the purpose for these jams was . . . it turns out what we're really doing is rehearsing."

Mid- to Late October (20?)

Dylan meets Joan Baez at a New York hotel hoping to enlist her for the Rolling Thunder Revue. She attempts a spontaneous rehearsal, but Dylan is clearly not interested. Despite this, Baez agrees to join the Revue.

October 22

Dylan turns up at David Blue's concert at the Other End on this date in the company of Bobby Neuwirth. Neuwirth introduces Dylan to singer/songwriter/actress Ronee Blakely, who is also in the audience. After Blue's set, Dylan, Neuwirth, and Blakely stay behind. Dylan gets up on stage and begins singing and playing piano. Blakely joins him as he plays songs from the recently recorded *Desire.* Afterward, Dylan invites Blakely to join the Revue he is putting together and, although she initially refuses because of other commitments, accepts his offer in time for her to sing backing vocals on the rerecording of "Hurricane" on the 24th.

October 23

Dylan and the Rolling Thunder troupe turn up at Gerdes Folk City for Mike Porco's birthday party. The party is filmed by Dylan's film crew, who are pretending to shoot a documentary on Gerdes. After a communal "Happy

Birthday," Dylan takes to the stage with Joan Baez for the first time in 10 years to duet on a version of "One Too Many Mornings." Footage from this show, featuring the Masked Tortilla and Allen Ginsberg, is included in *Renaldo and Clara*, but no Dylan.

October 24

Dylan returns to Columbia's Studio 1 with Don Devito, Rob Stoner, Scarlet Rivera, and Howie Wyeth to rerecord "Hurricane," with slightly rewritten words. Emmylou Harris is unavailable, so Ronee Blakley provides the backing vocals, while Stephen Soles plays guitar and Luther Rix is on congas. Arriving at 10:30 PM, Dylan warms up with renditions of "Jimmy Brown the Newsboy," "Sitting on Top of the World," "That's Alright Ma," and Kinky Friedman's "Ride 'Em Jewboy." The session is a long one, with 11 takes of "Hurricane" recorded, all of variable worth. Dylan intersperses the takes with versions of "I'm Thinking Tonight of My Blue Eyes" and "I Still Miss Someone," as well as a rewritten version of "Simple Twist of Fate," which he plays at the piano for the benefit of journalist Larry Sloman. He is clearly unhappy with the results achieved on "Hurricane," although equally keen to get the single out. So Devito is left with the task of editing the two most satisfactory takes (six and seven) together, as Dylan and the band stagger out into the streets at 5 AM.

October 25

During a break from the New York tour rehearsals, Jim Jerome interviews Dylan for a profile in *People Weekly*. Although there is little apparent empathy between reporter and subject, it is a good interview, with Dylan delighting in his usual word games. Here is a man just about to embark on making a four-hour film about myths who proclaims: "I didn't consciously pursue the Bob Dylan myth." Dylan, Ronee Blakley, and Roger McGuinn join David Blue onstage at the Other End. After the club closes, Dylan jams with McGuinn and Allen Ginsberg.

October 25 or 26

Sam Shepard has his first meeting with Dylan during rehearsals at S.I.R. Shepard has been recruited to work up some written scenes for the movie Dylan is intending to make while on the road. His first meeting with Dylan is suitably oblique, Dylan inquiring whether he is conversant with the films *Children of Paradise* and *Shoot the Piano Player*. A scene featuring Dylan and Louis Kemp discussing the release of "Hurricane" with Walter Yetnikoff in Yetnikoff's office is filmed for *Renaldo and Clara* on one of these two days.

October 26

Larry Sloman, the unofficial chronicler of the Rolling Thunder Revue, conducts his first Dylan interview of the tour. From this point, Sloman is the only reporter who succeeds in getting to Dylan. Even old friend Nat Hentoff has to resort to second-hand accounts for his *Rolling Stone* feature on the tour. This first interview covers Dylan's meeting with Rubin Carter, offers brief thoughts about the tour and the film, and finishes with a discussion about the critical response to Dylan's recent work.

Sloman witnesses part of the Revue rehearsals at Studio Instruments Rental. Dylan and Baez are clearly working on their set together, trying out songs later featured on the tour, such as "Never Let Me Go," "Oh Sister," "The Times They Are a-Changin'," and "The Lonesome Death of Hattie Carroll." They also work on several songs not included in the tour set: "Tears of Rage," "Tomorrow Is a Long Time," and "This Wheel's on Fire." Dylan also performs a rewritten "If You See Her, Say Hello," following it with band versions of "Isis," "When I Paint My Masterpiece," a fast "She Belongs to Me," and "A Hard Rain's a-Gonna Fall." After rehearsals Dylan attends a party at MacDougal Mike's, which is filmed by Dylan's film crew. In the evening, Dylan and the Revue indulge in another informal session at Gerdes Folk City.

October 27
The Rolling Thunder Revue sets out for the Seacrest Motel in North Falmouth for final tour rehearsals.

October 27–28
Dylan and the Revue rehearse at the Seacrest Motel. This may be one of the sources for the non-concert musical soundtrack for *Renaldo and Clara.* Many of the songs in the movie consist of Dylan playing the piano with minimal (or no) backing.

October 29
Rehearsals at the Seacrest Motel, which start at 3 PM, comprise one complete run-through of the show. With the entire show running in excess of four-and-a-half hours, cuts need to be made, and an electric "Tears of Rage" is one of the casualties. In the evening, the Revue performs in the main lounge of the hotel to a bemused bevy of middle-aged Jewish ladies, there to play Mah Jong. The show opens with Ginsberg reading "Kaddish." Various Revue members then take to the stage, the cameras filming the whole performance. Parts of Ginsberg's and Ramblin' Jack Elliott's sets are included in *Renaldo and Clara;* as well as footage of some woman belly dancing, and the awful emcee Merlin Wild introducing the show with a dire rendition of "Wilkommen." When Dylan takes to the stage, he opens with "Simple Twist of Fate" at the piano. No other details are known of his own performance.
  • Dylan and Ginsberg indulge in an extended conversation about the meaning of pleasure at tonight's party.

October 30, War Memorial Auditorium, Plymouth, MA
Dylan and the Rolling Thunder Revue open their bicentennial tour in Plymouth, MA, at the War Memorial Auditorium. Leaving the hotel at 1 PM, the troupe soundcheck at 2 PM. At 8:20 PM the show starts, Bobby Neuwirth taking the first vocal of the evening, followed by T-Bone Burnett, Rob Stoner, Stephen Soles, Mick Ronson, Ronee Blakely, and Jack Elliott for four songs. Finally Dylan hits the stage for a duet with Neuwirth on "When I Paint My Masterpiece." Then it's a countrified "It Ain't Me, Babe," and Dylan's first electric version of "A Hard Rain's a-Gonna Fall." At its conclu-

sion, Dylan introduces violinist Scarlet Rivera for two songs from his forth-coming album: "Romance in Durango" and "Isis." They conclude the first half of the show. When the curtain rises on the second half, Dylan and Baez are together at the microphone singing "The Times They Are a-Changin'," followed by Johnny Ace's "Never Let Me Go" and a one-off "The Lonesome Death of Hattie Carroll." Their joint set finishes with "I Shall Be Released." After Joan Baez's own set, and one song by Roger McGuinn, Dylan returns solo for "Mr. Tambourine Man" before the band rejoins him for a closing set that features four songs from the forthcoming album: "Oh Sister," "Hurri-cane," "One More Cup of Coffee," and "Sara." They finish with "Just Like a Woman" and a grand finale of "This Land Is Your Land" with the whole Re-vue crowded on stage. John Rockwell of *The New York Times* writes an en-thusiastic review of the show, in which he notes that Dylan's singing is "as forceful as the last tour but with a newfound mellowness too."

October 31, War Memorial Auditorium, Plymouth

The film crew is operating at this show. Dylan opens his set wearing a Richard Nixon mask while dueting with Neuwirth on "When I Paint My Masterpiece." This version is later used for the titles sequence in *Renaldo and Clara.* Halfway through "It Ain't Me, Babe," Dylan discards the mask. Af-ter a standard opening set, Dylan and Baez replace "The Lonesome Death of Hattie Carroll" with "Mama, You Been on My Mind." The solo acoustic song is "I Don't Believe You." The closing set with the band is unchanged. This is also the probable date for the filming of a scene featuring the Masked Tor-tilla at the Pilgrim's Party in Plymouth.

> November: "Hurricane Part I"/"Part II" (3-10245)

November 1

Dylan plays an alchemist and Allen Ginsberg plays the emperor of a bank-rupt empire in a scene shot in a diner in Falmouth, MA.

November 1, South Eastern MA University, North Dartmouth, MA

There is a soundcheck at 6:30 PM.

November 2, Lowell Technical University, Lowell, MA

This concert is again filmed for *Renaldo and Clara.* It includes the first Re-vue version of "Knockin' on Heaven's Door," as the final song of the main set. In the afternoon, there is filming at Nicky's Bar in Lowell.

November 3

The filming of a scene with Ginsberg at Jack Kerouac's grave in Lowell, MA. Dylan and Ginsberg sit at the grave, while Dylan plays guitar. Dylan and Ginsberg are also filmed at the Catholic church and grotto in Lowell, walk-ing along the Stations of the Cross. They then arrive at a schoolyard, where they question children about their views on God. Parts of all these sequences are included in *Renaldo and Clara.*

November 4

Dylan and the Revue perform a sunrise ceremony with the Cherokee medicine man, Rolling Thunder. It is filmed.

November 4, Providence Civic Center, Providence, RI

Afternoon and evening shows. Although the Dylan/band sets remain constant, the Dylan/Baez segment and the solo segments continue to be subject to change. At the afternoon show "Blowin' in the Wind" and "The Water Is Wide" are the first and third songs of the Dylan/Baez set. The solo performance is "With God on Our Side," sung live for the first time in 11 years. At the evening show, "I Dreamed I Saw St. Augustine" replaces "The Water Is Wide," and "The Times They Are a-Changin'" supplants "Blowin' in the Wind," while in the acoustic spot Dylan performs the only 1975 "It's Alright, Ma." After all the advance publicity about playing only small venues, Dylan is attacked by the press for playing large venues like the Civic Center. This is to become a constant feature of reports on the tour. After the concert, the Revue heads for Stockbridge, MA, staying at the Red Lion Inn.

November 6, Civic Center, Springfield, MA

Afternoon and evening shows. At the afternoon show, a full electric version of "The Lonesome Death of Hattie Carroll" is performed in place of "A Hard Rain's a-Gonna Fall." The evening show is shot by the film crew.

November 7

A wealth of footage is filmed at Mama's Dreamaway Lounge. Parts of several scenes are used in *Renaldo and Clara,* including one scene with Baez and Dylan in the bar; one of Ronee Blakley and Dylan in the bar; a scene with Mama singing to Baez, who is dressed in Mama's wedding gown; and a scene with Mama massaging Ginsberg's head and then trying, unsuccessfully, to read his palm.

November 8, University of Vermont, Burlington, VT

In the afternoon, Dylan shoots a scene with Bobby Neuwirth at the Curio Lounge in Burlington. The scene is not included in *Renaldo and Clara.*

 • The evening's show is at the Patrick Gymnasium, University of Vermont, Burlington, VT. Dylan's acoustic song is "Simple Twist of Fate," which becomes a regular feature on the tour.

November 9, University of New Hampshire, Durham, NH

November 9 or 10

Dylan and Sam Shepard discuss a possible scene for *Renaldo and Clara* involving Jack Elliott as the captain of a lobster boat at York Harbor, ME. Also the probable date(s) for the composition of Dylan's sleeve notes to *Desire.*

Playwright Sam Shepard began his career as an experimental writer/musician in New York's Greenwich Village, playing drums for a while with the folk-rock band The Holy Modal Rounders.

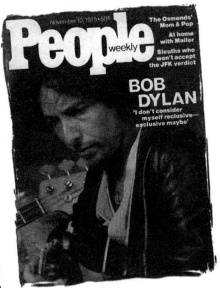

November 11, Palace Theatre, Waterbury, CT

The Dylan/Baez set is extended to five songs. Tonight's set includes the version of "The Water Is Wide" used as background in the "Renaldo, Clara, and the Woman in White" scene. The concert is filmed for *Renaldo and Clara*. However, no footage is used, probably because Dylan uses no white face makeup, for the only time on the tour.

November 13, Veterans Memorial Coliseum, New Haven, CT

Afternoon and evening shows. The afternoon show features two additions to the set: Merle Travis's "Dark as a Dungeon," sung by Dylan and Baez, and a solo "Tangled Up in Blue." The evening show features a two-song solo set, "I Don't Believe You" and "Simple Twist of Fate." Bruce Springsteen, Patti Smith, and Al Grossman are all in attendance at the evening show.

November 14 (and 16th?)

The probable recording date(s) for (the majority of) the nonconcert musical soundtrack for *Renaldo and Clara*. The songs that all appear to be from one session (at Dylan's hotel in Niagara Falls?), just Dylan at a piano, shuffling through song after song, are "Kaw-Liga," "What Will You Do When Jesus Comes?," "Little Moses," "If You See Her, Say Hello," "One Too Many Mornings," "She Belongs to Me" and "Patty's Gone to Laredo." Two other nonconcert performances appear in the film, "People Get Ready" and "I Want You," which clearly sound like they come from different sessions, possibly on the 28th and 16th of November respectively.

November 15, Niagara Falls Convention Center, Niagara Falls, NY

In the morning, a scene is filmed at Niagara Falls of Sara Dylan as a witch-goddess setting Dylan/Renaldo various tasks to prove his worth. It is not included in the film. Another scene filmed at Niagara Falls features Dylan and Ronee Blakley in black oil clothcoats. Sloman conducts a phone interview with Dylan regarding allegations that the tour is not playing small venues and is making too much money. Dylan is clearly tired, and Sloman finds it difficult to keep the conversation going. Later the Revue continues on to the Niagara Falls Convention Center for afternoon and evening shows. At the afternoon show, Dylan replaces "Knockin' on Heaven's Door" with "Like a Rolling Stone," the only time it is performed on the tour. At the evening show, "It Takes a Lot to Laugh" is included for the first time on this tour, extending the first electric set to six songs. Dylan again performs two solo songs, adding the first 1975 performance of "Love Minus Zero."

November 16
Filming for *Renaldo and Clara* continues at the Tuscarora Indian Reservation in New York state. Dylan arrives at about 5 PM and strolls among the crowd at the reservation's Community House. He later plays guitar and sings to the fortunate few. The Revue also indulges in a session of song-swapping with the Tuscarora.

November 17
Ginsberg plays the "Teacher" in a scene for *Renaldo and Clara* at the Niagara Hilton Hotel, required to outshout drunken playwrights and actors. The scene does not appear in the final film.

November 17, War Memorial Coliseum, Rochester, NY
Afternoon and evening shows. At the evening show, the Dylan/Baez set becomes six songs, and includes a beautiful "Wild Mountain Thyme."

November 19, Memorial Auditorium, Worcester, MA
This concert is filmed for *Renaldo and Clara.* A mobile recording studio is also brought in to record the show for a possible live album. The opening scene of *Renaldo and Clara* is filmed in the hotel lobby after the Worcester concert, as Larry Sloman takes Dylan to task over his inaccessibility. This is followed by a scene in the lobby featuring Roger McGuinn, Sloman (as a hotel clerk), and Joni Mitchell, but it is not included in the film.

November 20, Harvard Square Theatre, Cambridge, MA
Once again, this concert is filmed, with three songs appearing in *Renaldo and Clara:* "It Ain't Me, Babe," which appears on the promotional EP as well, "Just Like a Woman," and "Knockin' on Heaven's Door." It is a relatively intimate venue with just 1,850 capacity; and the whole Revue responds with a particularly fine show. Before the concert, a scene is filmed of Sara Dylan as a hitchhiker being picked up in a Rolls Royce. Again, this is not included in the film.

November 21, Boston Music Hall, Boston, MA
Afternoon and evening shows. At the afternoon show, "Mr. Tambourine Man" is the one solo song. For the evening show, there are two solo songs, one of which, "Tangled Up in Blue," is included in *Renaldo and Clara,* as is the electric version of "It Takes a Lot to Laugh."

November 22, Shapiro Gymnasium, Brandeis University, Waltham, MA
The fourth song of the opening set tonight is a dramatic new version of "Tonight I'll Be Staying Here with You."

November 23, The Revue travels to Enfield, CT

November 24, Civic Center Arena, Hartford, CT
The opening set stretches to seven songs as "Tonight I'll Be Staying Here with You" remains in the set, whereas "A Hard Rain's a-Gonna Fall" is rein-

troduced (alternating with "It Takes a Lot to Laugh" for the remainder of the tour).

November 26
Early in the morning, Dylan, Sara, and Sam Shepard shoot a scene at a gas station in Fenway, ME, but the scene fizzles out unresolved.

November 26, Civic Centre Arena, Augusta, ME
Dylan's solo set includes a breathtaking one-off performance of "Fourth Time Around," a marked contrast to its 1974 counterpart.

November 27, Municipal Auditorium, Bangor, ME
During the day, filming takes place at an old farmhouse and involves both Dylan and Scarlet Rivera.

November 28
The crew films Dylan, Rob Stoner, and others singing "House of the Rising Sun" in Larry Sloman's Quebec hotel room. It comes to a halt when the hotel manager threatens to kick them out of the room. The bordello scenes are filmed on the same evening at the same Quebec hotel. In *Renaldo and Clara,* Joan Baez and Sara Dylan discuss an imaginary affair, while Allen Ginsberg brings his supposed son, David Mansfield, to the brothel to be introduced to the pleasures of the flesh.

November 29, Quebec Coliseum, Quebec City, Quebec
At this point, actor Harry Dean Stanton, who had worked with Dylan on *Pat Garrett & Billy the Kid,* and actress Helena Kallianiotes join the tour to help with some additional scenes for *Renaldo and Clara.* This afternoon, they film a scene at the Chant Auteuil in Quebec. Andre Bernard Tremblay, as Maurice, is telling "Renaldo" how difficult love is. The conversation is difficult to follow because of the sheer volume coming from the restaurant/bar.

November 30
The Revue flies to Toronto in the morning where they stay at the Harbour Castle Hotel. In the evening, the crew films Dylan and Gordon Lightfoot playing some folk songs at a party at Lightfoot's Toronto home. This is presumably the source for a version of "Ballad in Plain D" (sung by Lightfoot) used as background music for one scene in *Renaldo and Clara.*

December 1, Maple Leaf Gardens, Toronto, Ontario
During the day, work continues apace on *Renaldo and Clara.* There is a half-hour chase sequence filmed on the streets of Toronto, involving Dylan, although only a small part is subsequently included in the film. There is also a sequence where Helena Kallianiotes and Sara Dylan escape from reform school, and run down to a restaurant where a truck driver tries to pick them up. Part of the scene with the truck driver is included in the film. After Helena Kallianiotes leaves with the trucker, Sara picks up a rose and leaves on her own. Finally, after the evening show, the camera crew catches a very humorous scene where a CBC reporter interviews first Larry Sloman and then Ronnie Hawkins under the impression that they are Bob Dylan.

• The evening show is at Toronto's Maple Leaf Gardens. In a terrific 22-song set, Dylan does a three-song solo spot that includes the first 1975 version of "It's All Over Now, Baby Blue." Dylan's mother, Beatty, joins her son on stage for the encore.

December 1–2

Dylan films a scene between Ronnie Hawkins and Ruth Tyrangiel during which Hawkins tries to cajole her into joining him on the road. The scene is included in *Renaldo and Clara.* Also filmed is a scene with "Renaldo" and the Woman in White walking around Ian Tyson's snow-covered farm north of Toronto.

December 2, Maple Leaf Gardens, Toronto

Another fine show, which is filmed for *Renaldo and Clara,* although none of the footage is used. The set includes a rare solo performance of "Mr. Tambourine Man."

Early December

According to Ronee Blakley, there was a scene shot for *Renaldo and Clara* in which Blakley picks up this vagrant (Dylan), who she then introduces to the whole group, including Joan Baez, (dressed up as Renaldo). The vagrant supposedly sits down and played a solo "Like a Rolling Stone" on the guitar.

December 3

The entire Revue travels to Montreal by train. Presumably, this is when the scene in *Renaldo and Clara* featuring the Masked Tortilla, Renaldo, and a bearded man (Howard Alk) stalking each other on a train is shot. Also filmed on this day is a scene at the Montreal railway station with Renaldo, the Masked Tortilla, and Helena Kallianiotes, who once again accepts a ride with a total stranger, this time on a train.

December 4, Montreal Forum, Montreal, Quebec

Dylan gives one of the finest shows of his career, as well as the longest of the 1975 concerts. A 23-song set (the opening Rolling Thunder show had just 16 Dylan songs) includes a six-song Dylan/Baez set and a three-song solo spot. Although the full concert is never released officially, "Isis" and "Romance in Durango" are both later included on the *Biograph* set. Songs from this show also make up the bulk of the live footage in *Renaldo and Clara,* with Montreal versions of "A Hard Rain's a-Gonna Fall," "Romance in Durango," "Isis," "Never Let Me Go," "One More Cup of Coffee," and "Sara" all featured in the film. After the show, there is a party at the Chateau Frontenac Hotel with a guest-list that includes Jerry Rubin, Emmett Grogan, and Leonard Cohen.

December 4–5

A scene is filmed in which Sara leaves a church in the Chateau Champlin area of Montreal. She hands a rope to Bobby Neuwirth, who proceeds to throw it over a prison wall. Harry Dean Stanton climbs over the wall, the men shake hands, and hurry off in opposite directions.

December 6

Dylan shoots footage at Emmett Grogan's house on his last day in Montreal. Possibly this is where the key scene with Renaldo, Clara, and the Woman in White is filmed.

December 7, Clinton Correctional Institution for Women

As part of the campaign for Hurricane Carter's release, the Revue plays a concert for the inmates of this institution, before a press conference is given by "Hurricane" Carter. The show receives good coverage the day before the benefit show at Madison Square Garden, including a couple of brief features on local TV news programs. The truncated Dylan set consists of "When I Paint My Masterpiece," "The Lonesome Death of Hattie Carroll," "A Hard Rain's a-Gonna Fall," "Blowin' in the Wind," and "I Shall Be Released" (the latter two with Joan Baez). "Hurricane" and "Knockin' on Heaven's Door" conclude the show. Part of the final song appears in *Renaldo and Clara,* as does part of Carter's press conference.

December 8, Madison Square Garden, NY

Tonight is billed as "The Night of the Hurricane," and Dylan is in a good mood, dedicating one song to Al Grossman, who is in the audience and "is not running for President" (a dig at Muhammad Ali's attempts to turn the benefit into a political rally). Baez hams it up during her set with Dylan, and Robbie Robertson joins the Revue for a great "It Takes a Lot to Laugh." Although not as inspired a performance as Montreal, the concert ends the tour on a high note. The traditional end-of-tour party is at the Felt Forum after the show. The partying continues at a restaurant near the Westbury Hotel.

Mid-December (14 and 15?)

Dylan attends a party at Norman Mailer's apartment in Brooklyn Heights, as well as a party at cameraman Mel Howard's Manhattan loft.

Mid-December

Sloman conducts a final telephone interview with Dylan a few days after the conclusion of the 1975 tour. In this interview, Sloman and Dylan cover a lot of bases, although (needless to say) it is mostly about Dylan's impressions of the tour. Interestingly, Dylan states that he had already decided to tour before meeting "Hurricane" Carter. He also discusses his feelings about the 1974 tour for the first time, admitting how little he enjoyed it.

Rock Superstar, 1975

1976

Early Winter

Dylan's lawyer, Michael Perlstein, approaches the US State Department for endorsement of a possible Russian tour.

> January 16: *Desire* (PC 33893): "Hurricane," "Isis," "Mozambique," "One More Cup of Coffee," "Oh Sister," "Joey," "Romance in Durango," "Black Diamond Bay," "Sara"

January 22

Dylan and the Revue rehearse at Studio Instrument Rentals on Santa Monica Boulevard, Los Angeles in preparation for a "Night of the Hurricane II" in Houston, TX. Among the songs rehearsed today are "One More Cup of Coffee," "Oh Sister," "Sara," "Mozambique," and "You Ain't Going Nowhere," a song never performed live on the Rolling Thunder tours.

January 23

The rehearsals continue at Studio Instrument Rentals. Aside from Rick Danko rehearsing "It Makes No Difference" and T-Bone Burnett, "Silver Mantis," the day is taken up with running down versions of "Just Like a Woman," "When I Paint My Masterpiece," "Maggie's Farm," "One Too Many Mornings," "Romance in Durango," "Isis," "Positively Fourth Street," "Oh Sister," "One More Cup of Coffee," "Sara," "Lay, Lady, Lay," "Just Like a Woman" (again), and, inevitably, "Hurricane."

• Dylan and the Revue, minus Baez and Jack Elliott, turn up for the encores at a Roger Miller/Larry Gatlin concert at the Troubador in Los Angeles. Dylan gets up and performs versions of "Lay, Lady, Lay" and "Romance in Durango."

January 24

Dylan and the Revue fly to Houston for "Night of the Hurricane II."

January 25, Houston Astrodome, Houston, TX

After multiple legal wrangles and a last-minute switch from the Louisiana Superdome to the Houston Astrodome, the Rolling Thunder Revue reassembles for "Night of the Hurricane II," hoping to raise more money to cover the legal costs of Carter's retrial. What with the large traveling costs, the cost of hiring the Astrodome, and a disappointing turnout, the benefit is almost a financial disaster. According to a UPI report, the $500,000 gross netted down eventually to a mere $50,000 for the defense fund. Nevertheless, Stevie Wonder is there to help out and plays a well-received 90-minute set before Dylan's appearance. Dylan's own set mixes 1975 Rolling Thunder Revue songs with additions to the repertoire. There is one unique item, the first live performance of "Positively Fourth Street" in 10 years. From the previous year's set comes, "When I Paint My Masterpiece," "Romance in Durango," "Isis," "It's All Over Now, Baby Blue," "Oh Sister," "One More Cup of Coffee," "Just Like a Woman," and the last live performances of both "Sara" and "Hurricane." Also performed are new arrangements of "Maggie's Farm," "One Too Many Mornings," "I Threw It All Away," and "Lay, Lady, Lay." The show is unique among Revue shows in another respect: It does not feature Joan Baez.

January 28
Dylan makes a surprise guest appearance at Joni Mitchell's concert in Austin, TX, where he duets with Mitchell on "Both Sides Now" and performs "Girl from the North Country" himself.

Late January
Dylan reportedly recorded with Doug Sahm in Texas in 1976. Since he spent several days in Houston and Austin after "Night of the Hurricane II," this is the most likely period for any such session.

March
Dylan visits England, presumably to discuss the possibility of a British Rolling Thunder tour.

March 17
Rubin "Hurricane" Carter is granted a retrial.

Late March
Dylan records "Sign Language" with Eric Clapton, a composition he had first played to Clapton back in July 1975. The recording is part of sessions at Shangri-La Studios in Malibu for Clapton's *No Reason to Cry*. Dylan also donates a new song entitled "Seven Days" to Ron Wood, part of the ever-expanding collection of musicians used on the sessions. Dylan sleeps out in a tent on the grounds of Shangri-La for a couple of nights.

March 30
Eric Clapton celebrates his birthday at Shangri-La Studios in Malibu. Dylan attends and the whole thing is recorded. A partial tape of Dylan, Clapton, and Ron Wood making unfocused attempts at "Spanish Is the Loving Tongue," "Adelita," "The Water Is Wide," three "Idiot Wind"s (all in different keys), and "Big River" circulates among collectors.

April 8–10
Dylan reassembles the Revue, minus Ronee Blakley and Luther Rix, to begin rehearsals for a Gulf Coast tour at the Bellevue Biltmore Hotel in Clear-

water, FL. The rehearsals last just 10 days. Rehearsals start in the pool house because the ballroom is not available. These Pool Studio sessions last until the 10th.

> *April 9: Phil Ochs is found dead by his sister. He had hung himself after a severe bout of depression. After hearing of Ochs's death, Dylan temporarily absents himself from rehearsals.*

April 11
Rehearsals begin in the Starlight Room of the Bellevue Biltmore Hotel, although Dylan seems to have been absent on the 11th and even the 12th. At one of these early rehearsals, Dylan and the Revue work on electric versions of "I'll Be Your Baby Tonight," "Where Did Vincent Van Gogh?," "I Pity the Poor Immigrant," and "Blowin' in the Wind."

April 14
Among the songs they rehearse today are versions of "I'll Be Your Baby Tonight," "Where Did Vincent Van Gogh?," and "Weary Blues from Waiting."

April 15
One of the most impromptu rehearsals at Clearwater's Bellevue Biltmore Hotel includes some interesting songs not performed on the tour. According to Stoner, Dylan called the rehearsal in the evening, requesting just the nucleus of the Revue: Stoner, Wyeth, and Rivera. The rehearsal starts with two versions of "Just Like Tom Thumb's Blues," followed by an old Elmore James number, "The Sun Is Shining." The now revamped "Lay, Lady, Lay" precedes an atonal arrangement of "One More Cup of Coffee," a song only performed infrequently in 1976. "It Takes a Lot to Laugh" comes next, followed by a unique version of "Ballad of Hollis Brown" and a traditional blues, "Hold Me in Your Arms." After this the songs become more predictable: "Mozambique," "Idiot Wind," a further "One More Cup of Coffee," a "Shelter from the Storm" almost unrecognizable from its 1976 tour arrangement, "Just Like Tom Thumb's Blues" again, "Isis," "Rita Mae," and "I Threw It All Away."

Also rehearsed on the 15th, presumably during the afternoon, are versions of "Knockin' on Heaven's Door" and "Gotta Travel On."

April 16
Along with standard Rolling Thunder fare like "Mozambique," "Lay, Lady, Lay" and "Idiot Wind," Dylan rehearses what sounds like an old blues tune called "Riding Down the Highway."

April 17
Dylan and the Revue stage a full dress rehearsal of the 1976 show for the 150 employees of the Bellevue Biltmore Hotel. The set starts with Dylan singing a solo "Visions of Johanna," followed by band versions of "Vincent Van Gogh" (a duet with Bobby Neuwirth), "I'll Be Your Baby Tonight,"

"Maggie's Farm," "One Too Many Mornings," and "Seven Days." (This version is later lodged with Special Rider as a publishing demo, thus affirming that this "dress rehearsal" was taped officially.)

After interludes by Roger McGuinn and Joan Baez, Dylan joins Baez for acoustic versions of "Railroad Boy" and "Wild Mountain Thyme" and a very hesitant, electric "I Pity the Poor Immigrant." "Shelter from the Storm" wanders all over the place, "Isis" is stretched out on the first verse, and "I Threw It All Away" features Dylan playing the same white National guitar as on "Shelter from the Storm." "Leopard-Skin Pill-Box Hat, "Mozambique," "Lay, Lady, Lay," "Idiot Wind," "Knockin' on Heaven's Door," and at least three attempts at "Gotta Travel On" (which keeps breaking down) conclude the dress rehearsal. However, after the lucky employees of the Biltmore have returned to their daily tasks, Dylan decides to carry on rehearsing. So a weary band are required to rerun "I Threw It All Away," make three attempts at "Going Going Gone," and have two more "Cups of Coffee." Then, out of nowhere, not previously rehearsed, not down on the master list of tour songs, Dylan and the band work up a tremendous "Tomorrow Is a Long Time." "Mozambique" gets two work outs, "Lay, Lady, Lay" and "Idiot Wind" one each, "I'll Be Your Baby Tonight" has a couple of breakdowns. But Dylan is now really warming up and out come fine versions of "Maggie's Farm," "One Too Many Mornings," "Seven Days," "Going Going Gone" again, "Sara" (destined to be the last-ever version), "Just Like Tom Thumb's Blues," and "It Takes a Lot to Laugh." Dylan wraps up an exhausting day with the first-ever attempt at "You Angel You" outside an LA studio.

April 18, Civic Center Arena, Lakeland, FL

Dylan opens the second leg of the Rolling Thunder Revue with a most unusual set. The opening two songs are solo, an intense "Visions of Johanna" and a rewritten (and rather nasty) "If You See Her, Say Hello." Dylan then duets with Bobby Neuwirth on Robert Friemark's "Vincent Van Gogh," which they follow with a ragged version of Hank Williams's "Weary Blues from Waitin'." The Revue then joins Dylan onstage for four songs, starting with the first version of "I'll Be Your Baby Tonight" Dylan has performed live since 1969. After "Maggie's Farm" and "One Too Many Mornings," a la the second Hurricane Carter benefit, comes "Seven Days," which Dylan is clearly still working on.

This ends Dylan's first set. When he returns, it is with Baez. They perform the traditional "Railroad Boy" and "Wild Mountain Thyme," and the semi-traditional "Blowin' in the Wind." The band returns for "I Pity the Poor Immigrant," on which Baez bravely attempts to harmonize with Dylan. Dylan then rips into "Shelter from the Storm," leading the way on slide guitar, followed by "I Threw It All Away," "Just Like Tom Thumb's Blues," "Mozambique," a rewritten "Going, Going, Gone," and a bawdy "Lay, Lady, Lay." At this point Dylan turns the stage over to T-Bone Burnett for a one-song respite, before finishing the show with an "Idiot Wind" searching for the vicious, "Knockin' on Heaven's Door," and finally an ensemble encore of Paul Clayton's "Gotta Travel On." According to one review, "The crowd seemed relatively unimpressed and bored with the entire evening," despite the quality of Dylan's performance. Indeed the whole 1976 leg of the Rolling Thunder Revue meets with much apathy from crowds and critics alike, although it remains one of Dylan's finest tours.

April 20, Bayfront Civic Center Auditorium, St. Petersburg, FL

For the second gig of the Gulf Coast tour, Dylan changes the opening couplet to "Mr. Tambourine Man," which is the opening song for the remainder of the tour, and "It's Alright, Ma." In the final set, Dylan inserts three songs between "I Threw It All Away" and "Mozambique," all throwbacks to the previous year: "Tonight I'll Be Staying Here with You," "Just Like a Woman," and "It Takes a Lot to Laugh."

April 21, Curtis Hixon Convention Center, Tampa, FL

The second solo song tonight is "Tangled Up in Blue." "Isis" and "Romance in Durango" reemerge in the closing set. Tonight's show is recorded, presumably in preparation for the following day's proceedings, and "Seven Days" is included on *The Bootleg Series*.

April 22, Bellevue Biltmore Hotel, Clearwater, FL

Dylan and the Revue film a projected TV special for NBC. There are two shows, in front of invited audiences of two hundred, tickets being distributed to a fortunate few among those attending the early shows. The two sets are held in the hotel's main ballroom, one in the afternoon and one in the evening.

The afternoon show is primarily acoustic, with five songs selected for the TV special (four of which are acoustic), "Mr. Tambourine Man" and "The Times They Are a-Changin'" feature Dylan solo; two duets with Joan Baez, "Blowin' in the Wind" and "I Dreamed I Saw St. Augustine." After Baez has sung "Diamonds and Rust," Dylan and Neuwirth are joined by the Revue band for "When I Paint My Masterpiece."

In fact Dylan had performed seven songs acoustic at the outset of filming, of which "Times" and "Tambourine Man"—the first two songs—represent a very poor sample. He proceeds to perform a very fine "It's Allright Ma." "Girl from the North Country" and "Don't Think Twice," both with harmonica, unfortunately have Dylan stumbling over words. But then he delivers a quite riveting "Visions of Johanna," seemingly perfect in every way. Dylan, though, is unconvinced and performs the song a second time, this time with a stacatto vocal of absolute precision. Breathtaking stuff. He finishes the solo section with a marvelous "Tangled Up in Blue" with some extravagant harmonica work. When Baez joins Dylan, aside from "I Dreamed I Saw St. Augustine" and "Blowin' in the Wind," they are scheduled to do "Mama, You Been on My Mind" but Dylan switches it to "I Shall Be Released," slow, drawn-out, and acoustic. An electric duet on "I Pity the Poor Immigrant" collapses at the end, convincing Dylan that another take is required. Dylan is then joined by Bobby Neuwirth and the band and they attempt two takes of Neuwirth's most famous songwriting credit, "Mercedes-Benz," before "When I Paint My Masterpiece" concludes the first show.

From the evening show, five more songs are selected for the special, an exhilarating "Like a Rolling Stone," "Isis," "Lay, Lady, Lay," "Just Like a Woman," and "Knockin' on Heaven's Door." However, again some far more interesting choices are omitted from the special, including a lengthy flamenco-style "One More Cup of Coffee" with just Dylan on guitar and Scarlet Rivera on violin. There is also a raunchy "Leopard-Skin Pill-Box Hat," a quirky 1976 arrangement of "It Ain't Me, Babe" with full band backing; the rewritten "Tonight I'll Be Staying Here with You," and the only known Revue version of "Most Likely You Go Your Way." Other omissions include the predictable "Oh Sister," "A Hard Rain's a-Gonna Fall" (whose only other 1976 appearance is as second encore at the Fort Collins show), and fine 1976 arrangements of "You're Gonna Make Me Lonesome When You Go" and "Romance in Durango." In fact, despite a quality performance from Dylan and the band, the finished TV special is very poorly filmed, failing to convey anything of the Rolling Thunder Revue in full flight. Dylan is clearly disappointed and wisely aborts the whole project. He decides to hire his own film crew and shoot a concert at Fort Collins later in the tour. Two songs listed as "possibles" for this second show are not in fact attempted: "Ballad of a Thin Man" and "I Don't Believe You." Presumably both songs were rehearsed, although they do not appear on any of the extant Clearwater tapes.

April 23, Sports Stadium, Orlando, FL
Includes "Seven Days" as well as two songs performed at Clearwater the previous day, "Romance in Durango" and "You're Gonna Make Me Lonesome When You Go."

April 25, University of Florida, Gainesville, FL
"Simple Twist of Fate" is the second solo song. Dylan and Baez also disinter the traditional "Dink's Song." During the final set, "Just Like Tom Thumb's Blues" is given its second and final airing of 1976, along with a rare "One More Cup of Coffee."

April 27, Tully Gymnasium, Florida State University, Tallahassee, FL
The second acoustic song is the rewritten version of "If You See Her, Say Hello."

April 28, University of West Florida, Pensacola, FL
The second solo song is a most unusual rendition of "Just Like a Woman." Dylan also performs the last "One More Cup of Coffee" of 1976, plus a first-ever live version of "Stuck Inside of Mobile," presumably in preparation for the two Mobile concerts the following day. A rehearsal tape of repeated workouts of "Stuck Inside of Mobile" exists. It may well date from some post-Lakeland rehearsal.

April 29, Municipal Auditorium, Mobile, AL
Afternoon and evening shows. At the afternoon show, the second acoustic song is "Simple Twist of Fate," at the evening show it is "It's Alright, Ma."

Naturally "Stuck Inside of Mobile" is also performed. "You're Gonna Make Me Lonesome When You Go" also becomes a regular feature of the tour set.

May 1, Reid Green Coliseum, Hattiesburg, MS
Includes a solo "Simple Twist of Fate" and a particularly exquisite live debut for "You're a Big Girl Now."

May 3, The Warehouse, New Orleans, LA
Afternoon and evening shows. At the afternoon show, Dylan unveils an electric arrangement of "Tangled Up in Blue." At the evening show, the second solo song is "Love Minus Zero." Dylan also performs the only known live version of "Rita Mae."

May 4, Assembly Arena, Louisiana State University, Baton Rouge, LA
Includes the first 1976 tour version of "Oh Sister."

May 6
A show scheduled for Lake Charles is canceled because of poor ticket sales.

May 8, Hofheinz Pavilion, Houston, TX
On his second visit in five months to Houston, Dylan again performs a solo "It's All Over Now, Baby Blue." Even though Willie Nelson is added to the concert bill owing to poor ticket sales, the 11,000 seat venue still remains only three-quarters full. It does mean a second encore, however, with Willie Nelson joining Dylan and the Revue for a version of "Will the Circle Be Unbroken."

May 9
A second show in Houston is canceled.

May 10, Memorial Coliseum, Corpus Christi, TX
Tonight's show includes several unusual performances. Dylan opens with a solo "A Hard Rain's a-Gonna Fall," and during the Dylan/Baez set they once again revive "Wild Mountain Thyme." Finally, during the second electric set, Dylan pulls out the first-ever confirmed live performance of "One of Us Must Know," a song that has been on the master set list since Clearwater.

May 11, Municipal Auditorium, San Antonio, TX
The San Antonio show is switched from the Hemisfair Arena to the smaller Municipal Auditorium because of poor ticket sales. Dylan introduces three songs to the set: "I Want You," Woody Guthrie's "Deportees" (a duet with Joan Baez), and during his opening solo slot, he conjures up a fine "Spanish Is the Loving Tongue," a song he seems only able to perform brilliantly (basements, *New Morning*) or embarrassingly (*Dylan,* "Friends of Chile," Shangri-La session).

May 12, Municipal Auditorium, Austin, TX
Originally both an afternoon and an evening show were booked for this venue, but poor sales again lead to the cancellation of one of the shows. Also,

reserved seats become general admission, much to the chagrin of ticket holders, and there is inevitable chaos on the day of the concert.

May 15
The Rolling Thunder Revue perform a free concert at the Gatesville State School for Boys after a show in Dallas is canceled.

May 16, Tarrant County Convention Center Arena, Fort Worth, TX
This concert is recorded for a possible live album. Four songs are included on *Hard Rain:* "I Threw It All Away," "Stuck Inside of Mobile," "Oh Sister," and "Lay, Lady, Lay." The second solo song at tonight's show is "It Ain't Me, Babe."

May 18, State Fair Arena, Oklahoma City, OK
The second solo song is "Simple Twist of Fate." The show also features "Leopard-Skin Pill-Box Hat."

May 19, Hemy Levitt Arena, Wichita, KS
Includes the second and last "One of Us Must Know" of 1976.

May 20–23
While the Revue prepares for the penultimate Rolling Thunder show at Fort Collins, which is being filmed for the NBC-TV special, they are put up in a well-appointed hotel in the Colorado mountains, where they can relax and prepare for this important show. Unfortunately it rains all weekend, and Dylan's own weekend is somewhat ruined when his wife surprisingly turns up with his mother and his children. Dylan, who has been guilty of a fair share of infidelities on this tour, is understandably perturbed. A pre-Fort Collins rehearsal tape, presumably from the hotel, features Dylan and the Revue working up new electric arrangements of "Just Like a Woman" and "Tangled Up in Blue."

May 23, Colorado State University, Fort Collins, CO
In pouring rain, Dylan plays the open air Hughes Stadium at Colorado State University in Fort Collins. He has elected to film this show to replace the aborted TV special from Clearwater. In the longest set of the tour, there are several highlights, not all appearing in the TV special. Omissions include a fine "It Ain't Me, Babe," a lengthy rocked-up version of "Tangled Up in Blue," and the uptempo country arrangement of "I Want You." Also absent from the TV special but included on *Hard Rain* is "You're a Big Girl Now." Included in the TV special, although in a most peculiar order, are second encore "A Hard Rain's a-Gonna Fall," the entire Dylan/Baez set ("Blowin' in the Wind," "Railroad Boy," "Deportees," and "I Pity the Poor Immigrant"); three songs from the first set ("Maggie's Farm," "One Too Many Mornings," and "Mozambique"); and three from the last set (two tremendously powerful readings of songs from *Blood on the Tracks,* "Idiot Wind" and "Shelter from the Storm" and a faded "Knockin' on Heaven's Door"). Despite the storm clouds raging, the crowd appears to be very enthusiastic, even singing "Happy Birthday" for Dylan before the second encore.

May 25, Salt Palace, Salt Lake City, UT

For the last Rolling Thunder concert, Dylan plays an interesting set, despite playing to a half-capacity crowd at this 17,000 seat venue. The first surprise is the second solo song, Dylan's first Revue version of "Gates of Eden." The first electric set includes a full-band version of "Just Like a Woman." The real surprise, however, is in the Dylan/Baez set, which consists of "Blowin' in the Wind," "I Shall Be Released," and a unique live performance of "Lily, Rosemary and the Jack of Hearts," Dylan and Baez trading verses. The final electric set is a lengthy one and includes the new arrangement of "Tangled Up in Blue." According to one reviewer, "Black Diamond Bay" was also played, although "Romance in Durango" seems the more likely. The full show lasts four-and-a-half hours.

Summer

Dylan attends a Bob Marley and the Wailers concert at the Roxy in Los Angeles.

• Dylan attends a party at Kinky Friedman's house, where he sits in the back room and performs acoustic versions of "Long Black Veil" and "Lay, Lady, Lay."

August

Dylan is interviewed by Neil Hickey for a *TV Guide* cover story to promote the broadcast of the *Hard Rain* TV special. Dylan seems reasonably helpful, though, when asked how he imagines God, replies, "How come nobody ever asks Kris Kristofferson questions like that?"

September 10: *Hard Rain* (PC 34349): "Maggies Farm," "One Too Many Mornings," "Stuck Inside of Mobile," "Oh Sister," "Lay, Lady, Lay," "Shelter from the Storm," "You're a Big Girl Now," "I Threw It All Away," "Idiot Wind"

Late November (23 or 24?)

Dylan and the Band rehearse for an afternoon in the banquet room at the Miyako Hotel in San Francisco. Neil Young is in attendance.

November 25, Winterland, San Francisco, CA

The Band plays its farewell concert at the first venue they ever played as The Band. After a Thanksgiving dinner, the audience is treated to various special guests, backed by the Band, as well as a set by the Band alone. Inevitably, the last special guest of the evening is Dylan, with whom they play a tight set, running the numbers into each other: "Baby Let Me Follow You Down," "Hazel," "I Don't Believe You," "Forever Young," and a return to "Baby Let Me Follow You Down" constituting their 20-minute set. Dylan and the Band are then joined by the other special guests for an ensemble version of "I Shall Be Released," Dylan singing lead vocals on the first and last verses, and Richard Manuel singing the middle verse. It is a euphoric end to a special night and a fine band's career. The concert is recorded and eventually appears as a three-album set; the bulk of Dylan's set (minus "Hazel," for some reason), taking up side five. The concert is also filmed by Martin Scorsese, and *The Last Waltz* features the second part of Dylan's set, from "Forever Young" onward. It is to be Dylan's last concert appearance for 15 months, and when he returns he is a very different performer.

December
Dylan attends a performance by Eric Clapton at the Forum in Inglewood.

1977

Throughout most of 1977, Dylan and Howard Alk work at editing *Renaldo and Clara,* condensing 80 hours of footage into a three-hour-and-fifty-two minute movie. According to Ginsberg, all the footage had been indexed according to themes, characters, dominant colors, and common symbols. It was composed "thematically, weaving in and out of . . . specific compositional references."

Early February
Rubin "Hurricane" Carter is found guilty of multiple murders for a second time.

February 10
Dylan attends the opening of the Pompidou Center of Art in Paris with American painter Robert Rauschenburg and Dotson Rader. While in Paris, he is also spotted at the Hotel Crillon with then-vice president Walter Mondale and poet Rod McKuen.

February 13
According to a statement by Sara Dylan's lawyer, Marvin Mitchelson, in March 1977, it was on the above date that, "she came down to breakfast and found Dylan, the children, and a woman named Malka at the breakfast table . . . Dylan struck her on the face and ordered her to leave."

Late February to Early March
Dylan, Allen Ginsberg, and Bill Diez provide backing vocals on one song for Leonard Cohen's *Death of a Ladies Man:* "Don't Go Home with Your Hard-On," which is recorded at Gold Star Studios in Los Angeles, and produced by Phil Spector, a longstanding admirer of Dylan's work. Ginsberg is staying with Dylan for a few days on his way to Hawaii.

March 1
Sara Dylan files for divorce.

Early March
Dylan attends Ronee Blakley's concert at the Roxy in Los Angeles. A long-haired, not to say unkempt, Dylan is photographed with Blakley, actress Sally Kirkland, and David Blue after the show, and appears to be in reasonable humor despite the impending prospect of an expensive divorce settlement.

March 15

Proceedings commence in the divorce case Sara has filed against Dylan.

Spring

In May of 1978, Dylan talked to Robert Hilburn about songs he wrote just after his divorce the previous spring: "I had some songs last year I didn't record. They dealt with that period as I was going through it. For relief, I wrote the tunes. I thought they were great. Some people around town heard them. I played them for some friends." Although no firm documentation relating to these songs has ever appeared, according to Steven Soles, Dylan came over to his apartment one afternoon in 1977 and played him and T-Bone Burnett, "ten, twelve songs . . . to get our take on it. It was very dark, very intense—none of those songs were ever recorded." The only title Soles recalls is "I'm Cold."

Early May

Jerry Weintraub announces that Bob Dylan has signed with his company for personal legal representation.

June 29

The divorce case concludes. The commissioner is "retaining jurisdiction of (Dylan and Sara's) communal property for future determination."

June 30 to July 1

The art teacher for Dylan's children, Faridi McFree, calls Dylan to ask if he is okay after the trauma of the divorce case. Dylan invites her over and they talk until 5 AM. McFree stays the night, and in the morning Dylan asks her to move in with him. McFree, though, returns to Sara's house, which she is looking after while Sara is in Hawaii, returning to Dylan's house the same evening. They are invited to a party at Linda Ronstadt's, but end up at Sara's house looking at all the art McFree has produced with his children.

July to August

Dylan stays on his farm in Minnesota with Faridi McFree and his children. While there he begins to write the songs that will constitute *Street-Legal,* sharing the songs with McFree as they are written.

August 16: Elvis Presley is pronounced dead at Baptist Memorial Hospital, Memphis. When Dylan hears the news he becomes morose and goes off on his own for a couple of days. As he would later say, "If it wasn't for Elvis . . . I couldn't be doing what I do today."

September

Dylan takes a five-year lease on a Santa Monica rehearsal studio which he subsequently christens Rundown Studio. The studio is to play an important role for both his recorded work and rehearsals.

September 2

Sara Dylan's lawyer asks the court "for permission to move the children to Hawaii to live there with Sara."

September 6

Dylan requests, through his attorney Robert S. Kaufman, that the Santa Monica Superior Court grant him sole custody of their children, because Sara Dylan has violated a court order by taking their four children to Hawaii without his permission. A hearing is set for September 13, and then for October 4, after neither party shows up in court.

Late October

Allen Ginsberg spends a week with Dylan, discussing the finished *Renaldo and Clara* with him. He convinces Dylan that the film does make some kind of sense. Discussing the film shortly afterward on a US radio show, Ginsberg suggests that he is intending to publish a lengthy analysis of *Renaldo and Clara.* He interviews Dylan extensively but Dylan feels his responses are too personal, and so Ginsberg undertakes to interview him again.

October 30th (possibly the 28th)

After Dylan's rejection of the first interviews, Ginsberg tapes at least two further interviews, the first of which may have been on the 28th. The interviews themselves are wholly remarkable, nay unique. For once Dylan is open about his art. In fact, at one point he says, "Is this too intellectual, Allen?" He is happy throughout to refer to other artists, primarily painters. Bosch, Dali, DaVinci, Van Gogh, Cezanne, Modigliani, and Soutine all crop up in the conversations. Perhaps the most revealing aspect of these interviews is the way Dylan explains the role of the film's major characters. So the Woman in White "is the ghost of Death, Death's ghost. Renaldo rids himself of death when she leaves." He even explains the dreamlike quality of the movie: "The man on the floor, who's obviously dreaming, no one asks him anything. But the whole movie was his dream . . . Renaldo lives in a tomb, his only way out is to dream." As for that man who keeps getting up on stage and singing: "The man who puts the white paint on his face obviously becomes the chorus of the movie. He has no name." Two other interviews (or two parts of the same interview) are conducted on the 30th, the interviewers being listed as Pierre Cotrell and Marie. Ginsberg is in attendance at both these interviews. They take place at 10:20 AM and 2:30 PM but are substantially less revealing than the conversations with Ginsberg alone. However, they are still very worthwhile, with Dylan happy to discuss all aspects of the film: "It has the feeling of being improvised [but] once you get it in your head it's a poem, drama."

October 31

Allen Ginsberg continues his conversations with Dylan, interviewing him in his car on the way into Los Angeles, and at his chiropodist in Santa Monica. This interview is just as important as the previous day's, and includes a very interesting commentary on the Hurricane Carter sequences in the film: "Clara will do what Renaldo will only dream about . . . getting a man out of jail. Renaldo may be thinking about it, singing about it, but Clara does it." Of the bordello scenes Dylan comments: "The girls . . . are locked into Diamond Hell and are not giving pleasure to anyone." In the evening, Dylan, Allen Ginsberg, and Howard Alk put on masks and go out onto the streets of Malibu, singing and playing guitars for Halloween.

November 1

Dylan and Howard Alk are in a "sound mixing" studio, working on *Renaldo and Clara.*

November 3

Dylan is instructed by Santa Monica Superior Court Commissioner John R. Alexander to return his children to Sara. Dylan had taken physical custody in September while Sara was in Hawaii trying to set up home there. In a declaration to the court, Sara accuses Dylan and Faridi McFree, one-time art teacher for the children, of "attempting to brainwash the minor children."

November 25

Dylan attends a hearing in Santa Monica, wearing a decidedly ill-fitting three-piece suit. He is ordered to return his 11-year-old son Jesse to Sara.

Late November

During the final stages of the editing of *Renaldo and Clara,* Ron Rosenbaum interviews Dylan 11 years after the original *Playboy* interview. The discussions are conducted over 11 days, and the result is a very extensive, thorough interview extending to 15 pages. Perhaps the most quoted line from the feature is Dylan's description of the *Blonde on Blonde* sound: "It's that thin, that wild mercury sound. It's metallic and bright gold." An important interview.

Early December

Sara Dylan faces battery charges after invading a school classroom and "punching and choking a teacher," Rex Burke, when he asks to see the court order allowing her custody of the children. Flanked by three private detectives, she chases the children through the school: Jesse, Anna, Samuel, and Jakob having "apparently resisted going with Mrs. Dylan."

• Dylan attends a concert by Lainie Kazan at the Playboy Club in Century City, CA.

• Dylan is interviewed by Jonathan Cott for *Rolling Stone.* Unlike the *Playboy* interview, Cott's concentrates almost exclusively on ideas explored in *Renaldo and Clara.* It is a dense interview, although Dylan is happy to have the film treated seriously.

December

Dylan drops in on r&b singer Etta James at Cherokee Studios in Los Angeles. Jerry Wexler is producing the session, and Dylan takes the opportunity to play some new tunes at the piano. One eyewitness at the session recalled that the material played to Wexler had a very high religious content. Also strongly rumored at the time was the possibility of Jerry Wexler producing Dylan's next album.

• Dylan visits the Staple Singers at a Los Angeles studio to offer them a couple of songs.

December 10

After putting the finishing touches to *Renaldo and Clara* at Goldwyn Studios in Hollywood, Dylan and some friends visit a local restaurant to invite customers to a screening of the picture. Opinion afterward is divided as to its merits.

Mid-December to January 1978

Rehearsals begin at Rundown Studios in Santa Monica for Dylan's first world tour in 12 years. Dylan asks Rob Stoner to bring Howie Wyeth and a couple of other people to Los Angeles. Stoner arrives with Wyeth, pianist Walter Davis, Jr., and percussionist Otis Smith. Dylan has also recruited Stephen Soles and David Mansfield from the Rolling Thunder Revue band. Dylan's other problems keep him away from rehearsals for the first week, but he soon starts turning up with assorted female vocalists he wishes to audition.

Initially, the band works with actress Katie Segal, Frannie Eisenberg, and assorted actress-cum-singers. Meanwhile, Howie Wyeth is reluctant to tour Japan for personal reasons and informs Dylan of his decision, flying back to New York around Chistmas. He is replaced by ex-Wings drummer Denny Siewell, who works out very well. Unfortunately, because of his prior association with Wings, Siewell has problems getting a visa for Japan and has to be replaced. The search for a drummer becomes a major problem. Both Bruce Gary and Jim Gordon (previously in the Jack Bruce band and Derek and the Dominoes, respectively) are auditioned. Dylan even considers Mickey Jones, the drummer on that momentous 1966 world tour. The final choice proves to be ex-King Crimson drummer Ian Wallace. After the rapid departure of Walter Davis and Otis Smith, Dylan drafts in Alan Pasqua on organ, although not before attempting to enlist Barry Goldberg and Al Kooper. Andy Stein plays saxophone at the early rehearsals but also proves unsatisfactory. Several guitarists are also auditioned, including Frank Rechard who later recalls Dylan asking him to play "Like a Rolling Stone" as if it was "La Bamba." From the very start Dylan evidently has a large band in mind. All the rehearsals are taped at Dylan's behest so that he can hear how the arrangements are developing and which versions seem most appropriate.

December 26

On the day after Christmas, Dylan is rehearsing with his touring band. The rehearsal includes a fast r&b style "Tangled Up in Blue," "I Shall Be Released" with pedal-steel, a medium-paced "Girl from the North Country" with mandolin, "Most Likely You Go Your Way" with violin, and "Just Like a Woman," also with violin and Dylan on electric guitar. As the session is winding down, Dylan goes to the piano and plays "Just Like a Woman" (with no vocal). Shortly afterward, with just Stephen Soles, Rob Stoner, and guitar-tech Joel Bernstein in attendance, Dylan begins a unique preview of the *Street-Legal* material at the piano. Warming up with a Mexican-style instrumental, he proceeds to perform incomplete yet riveting renditions of "Is

Your Love in Vain?," "Senor," "No Time to Think" (which breaks down fairly quickly), "True Love Tends to Forget," "We'd Better Talk This Over," something that is probably the long-rumored "First to Say Goodbye" (it features the opening line "just be kind to me and say goodbye"), and "Where Are You Tonight." At various points Stoner attempts to pick up the basic riffs on his bass but it is remains largely a solo tour de force that concludes with Dylan asking the assembled few, "[So] what's your favorite song?"

December 30

An early tour rehearsal features embryonic versions of "It's All Over Now, Baby Blue," "Blowin' in the Wind," "Maggie's Farm," "Like a Rolling Stone," "The Man in Me," "To Ramona," "Most Likely You Go Your Way," "Simple Twist of Fate," "Leopard-Skin Pill-Box Hat," "If Not for You," "I Threw It All Away," and "I'll Be Your Baby Tonight." "Most Likely You Go Your Way," "Leopard-Skin Pill-Box Hat," and "If Not for You" are never featured on the '78 tour. The arrangements at this point are only rudimentary, and Dylan is clearly required to direct the band as he feels his way through the songs. The band at this point includes Denny Siewell on drums, Jesse Ed Davis on guitar, and actress Katie Segal and Debbie Dye Gibson on backing vocals.

1978

Early January
Dylan is interviewed by John Rockwell of *The New York Times* as he embarks on an unprecedented bout of interviews, designed to publicize *Renaldo and Clara* at minimal cost. Openly discussing ideas in the film he says, "I've learned as much from Cezanne as I have from Woody Guthrie."

• Gregg Kilday of the *Los Angeles Times* interviews Dylan, who has clearly specified that *Renaldo and Clara* is to be the topic of conversation. However, if sentences like, "You see the truth behind the idle truth, a kind of resurrection of the common man" are meant to clarify the film's themes, they do not.

• Rehearsals continue at Rundown Studios. An extant rehearsal tape features versions of "Simple Twist of Fate" and "Going, Going, Gone" both with reasonably worked out arrangements, and a nice version of "You're Gonna Make Me Lonesome When You Go," with the female vocalists for once complementing Dylan's own singing. Sadly the song is not featured on the 1978 tour. The drummer on this session is ex-Jack Bruce beatmaster, Bruce Gary.

January
Dylan is interviewed by John Austin as part of the bout of promotional interviews for *Renaldo and Clara.*

Mid-January
Joel Kotkin interviews Dylan at Rundown Studios. Parts of the interview are syndicated through the *Washington Post,* and a separate section appears in *New Times.* It is a very bad-tempered affair, however, with Kotkin determined to get Dylan to admit that all these interviews are just a ruse to get free publicity. Dylan starts by defending his motives and finally gives up, suggesting to Kotkin that smoking dope from the age of 13 has addled his mind.

January 24
Dylan gives two press conferences at Rundown Studios in Santa Monica, the first arranged for Australian journalists but also attended by the likes of Robert Hilburn of the *Los Angeles Times.* A second one is organized because of the sheer number of Japanese journalists that have turned up, and is held exclusively for their benefit.

January 25: Renaldo and Clara *opens in New York and Los Angeles.*

Late January
Dylan is interviewed by Jon Bream of the *Minneapolis Star* at Rundown Studios. Bream is one of the more sympathetic journalists who interviews Dylan about *Renaldo and Clara,* and he obtains a second interview eight years later at a time when Dylan is granting very few such requests.

January 26
Among the songs rehearsed at Rundown is a new arrangement of "You're a Big Girl Now."

January 27
With Billy Cross on guitar, Steve Douglas on horns, Bobbye Hall on percussion, and Helena Springs, Jo Ann Harris, and Debbie Dye on backup vocals, the now finalized 1978 tour band rehearses at Rundown Studios with a new urgency. On this day they perform "All I Really Want to Do," "Absolutely Sweet Marie," "Tomorrow Is a Long Time" (which they are clearly still working on), "Oh Sister," "The Times They Are a-Changin,'" "My Babe" (?), "Shelter from the Storm," "Don't Think Twice, It's All Right," "Like a Rolling Stone," and "I Shall Be Released."

Late January (26–31?)
Dylan is interviewed for *Photoplay* magazine. The interview comes after the critical battering *Renaldo and Clara* has received at its New York premiere and is the first of many defenses Dylan has to make of the movie.

Late January to Early February

An early rehearsal(s) with the new female vocalists Dylan has drafted in at very short notice, Helena Springs and Jo Ann Harris (to replace Segal and Eisenberg), features: "I Threw It all Away," "Love Minus Zero/No Limit," "Maggie's Farm," "Ballad of a Thin Man," "Simple Twist of Fate," "To Ramona," "If You See Her, Say Hello," "I Don't Believe You," "My Babe," "Like a Rolling Stone" (attempted a couple of times), "Just Like a Woman" (ditto), "Blowin' in the Wind" (attempted first in reggae form, Dylan then asks the girls to do it church-choir-style; it is this version that is adopted on the tour), "I'll Be Your Baby Tonight," "The Man in Me," and "Don't Think Twice, It's All Right."

Late January to Early February

Barbara Kerr of the *Chicago Daily News* interviews Dylan on two or three occasions over a three-week period for a syndicated four-part profile of the man. It is the best of all the interviews conducted before the 1978 World tour. Starting with Dylan's days in Hibbing, Minneapolis, and then Denver and Chicago, they discuss his early days in New York, the divorce, the 1974 tour, and, of course, the film. A most important interview.

January 30

This session at Rundown Studios features finished arrangements of many of the songs performed at the opening shows. Although only a rehearsal, both Dylan and the band give some great performances, with final workouts for: "I'll Be Your Baby Tonight," "The Times They Are a-Changin'," a waltz arrangement of "If You See Her, Say Hello" (with new lyrics), a rewritten "The Man in Me," "I Don't Believe You," "Tomorrow Is a Long Time," "You're a Big Girl Now," "Knockin' on Heaven's Door," "It's Alright, Ma," and "Forever Young."

January 31

Rehearsals at Rundown today include an ambitious arrangement of "Just Like a Woman" with some extended harmonica work from Dylan (sadly not retained for the tour itself). "Tomorrow Is a Long Time" is also given one more outing.

February 1

Again the material rehearsed at Rundown Studios is fully arranged and well-performed. Indeed, this take of "One of Us Must Know" is not matched by any of the 55 versions performed on the tour. "Repossession Blues" will be featured only briefly in concert, but is delightful in rehearsal. "Girl from the North Country" is also sensitively performed. "Ballad of a Thin Man" corresponds to the tour arrangement. On the basis of these later rehearsals, Dylan must be pleased with how the new arrangements are working out.

February 2

Today's rehearsal at Rundown, which includes a spirited performance of "It's Alright Ma," may well have been the final Rundown run-through before Japan.

Early February

Journalist Harvey Kubernik, reporting on rehearsals at Rundown Studios, refers to some 17 songs, including the likes of "If Not for You," "Winterlude," an old blues song called "Sixty-Four Dollar Question," and one called "First to Say Goodbye."

• Philip Fleishman of *Macleans* interviews Dylan and, getting straight to the point, declares his dislike of *Renaldo and Clara,* which Dylan is understandably keen to defend. The interview does not, however, sink to the level of Kotkin's. Fleishman asks some penetrating questions, which Dylan does his best to answer. In response to a question about the money spent on the film, Dylan dismisses the idea of profit or loss as unimportant: "If the film medium is a true canvas then the film has been worthwhile."

• An interview by Julia Orange, conducted shortly before Dylan's departure from Los Angeles, is subsequently broadcast on Australian radio. It is also published in *Women's Day* magazine. Orange seems obsessed with obtaining Dylan's views on romance. Not a major interview.

• Dylan is interviewed by Mary Campbell, apparently in New York, for syndication through Associated Press. At this point Dylan is still talking about making another film.

• Dylan is interviewed by Randy Anderson for *The Minnesota Daily.* Not surprisingly, given its publication in his home state, the interviewer attempts to question Dylan on his early days in Minnesota.

February 17

Arriving in Tokyo, Dylan is subjected to his first foreign-language press conference in 12 years at Haneda International Airport. With the language difficulties, the conference quickly deteriorates into total chaos.

February 17 to March 6

During Dylan's stay in Japan, he visits the Golden Pavilion and the Ryoan Temple rock gardens in Kyoto, watches a Kabuki play, and attends a concert by the Electric Light Orchestra (presumably during his first week in Japan). The band also jams on "Heartbreak Hotel" in a country and western club, presumably without Dylan.

February 20, Nippon Budokan, Tokyo, Japan

Dylan opens his first-ever Japanese concert with an old blues standard, "Lonesome Bedroom Blues." The comprehensive cross-section of his career begins with "Mr. Tambourine Man," a slightly rewritten "I Threw It all Away," "Love Minus Zero" in its first electric guise, the waltz "If You See Her, Say Hello," a melodramatic "Ballad of a Thin Man," "Girl from the North Country" as torch ballad, and the one and only post-'74 performance of "Something There Is About You." "Maggie's Farm" remains, "Don't Think Twice, It's All Right" returns, now reggaefied, while "To Ramona" gets it's first full-band arrangement. Two anthems, "Like a Rolling Stone" and "I Shall Be Released," and a rewritten "Going, Going, Gone" bring to an end the first set. Dylan has been on stage more than an hour already.

The second half opens with "One of Us Must Know" and a gospelish "Blowin' in the Wind." "Just Like a Woman" gets the full treatment, women

1978

and all, before "Oh Sister" cops a new riff from "Gimme Some Lovin'." "You're a Big Girl Now" is followed by "All Along the Watchtower." Then come three songs given new sets of lyrics: "Simple Twist of Fate," "All I Really Want to Do," and "The Man in Me." A fine "Tomorrow Is a Long Time"; a reggaefied "Knockin' on Heaven's Door," a version of "It's Alright, Ma," that rocks out in furious style in its first (and last) electric arrangement, and "Forever Young" close the second set. "The Times They Are a-Changin'" is the only encore, ending a 28-song marathon, far and away Dylan's longest concert to date and one that shows his new eight-piece band and three female vocalists to be an effective enough unit.

Three alternates are listed on the set list for this first show: "I Want You," "If Not for You," and "I'll Be Your Baby Tonight."

February 21, Nippon Budokan, Tokyo, Japan
"I Want You" and "Shelter from the Storm" replace "Girl from the North Country" and "Something There Is About You."

February 23, Nippon Budokan, Tokyo, Japan
Includes a last performance of "Lonesome Bedroom Blues" and the first 1978 version of "I Don't Believe You."

February 24
Dylan and the band travel on the bullet train from Tokyo to Osaka.

February 24, Matsushita Denki Taiikuhan, Osaka, Japan
Dylan opens with "Repossession Blues" and includes the last 1978 performance of "If You See Her, Say Hello."

February 25, Matsushita Denki Taiikuhan, Osaka
On the first night, Dylan includes an impromptu version of "One Too Many Mornings," supposedly a request from the audience although the song had been rehearsed.

February 26, Matsushita Denki Taiikuhan, Osaka
Includes 1978 debuts for "One More Cup of Coffee," "I'll Be Your Baby Tonight," and a new opener, Tampa Red's "Love Her with a Feeling."

February 28, Nippon Budokan, Tokyo
Includes a final version of "Repossession Blues" and the first performance of a brand-new Dylan composition, "Is Your Love in Vain," introduced with a unique harmonica break. The show is recorded for a possible live album. Seven songs eventually appear on *At Budokan:* "Shelter from the Storm," "Love Minus Zero," "Simple Twist of Fate," "Don't Think Twice, It's All

Right," "It's Alright, Ma," "Forever Young," and "The Times They Are a-Changin'.."

March 1, Nippon Budokan, Tokyo

Again tonight's show is recorded for a possible live album. The show opens with "Love Her with a Feeling" which remains the regular opener until late June. Fifteen songs from this set appear on *At Budokan:* "Mr. Tambourine Man," "Ballad of a Thin Man," "Maggie's Farm," "One More Cup of Coffee," "Like a Rolling Stone," "I Shall Be Released," "Is Your Love in Vain?," "Going, Going, Gone," "Blowin' in the Wind," "Just Like a Woman," "Oh Sister," "All Along the Watchtower," "I Want You," "All I Really Want to Do," and "Knockin' on Heaven's Door."

March 2–3, Nippon Budokan, Tokyo

March 4, Nippon Budokan, Tokyo

Dylan performs the final "Is Your Love in Vain?" on the Far East leg of the world tour.

March 6

Dylan arrives at Auckland International Airport, New Zealand. He proceeds to occupy the entire 14th floor of the Hotel Intercontinental in Auckland.

March 7

Dylan tours Auckland alone in a rental car. There are rehearsals at the hotel.

March 8

Dylan is sighted jogging in Albert Park at the unearthly hour of 5 AM. He meets Maori princess Ra Aranga in the hotel foyer.

March 9

Dylan and the band soundcheck for three hours in the afternoon. Tonight's concert, at Auckland's Western Springs Stadium, is his first in New Zealand.

March 10

Dylan arrives at Kingsford Smith Airport, Sydney, at midday, and is besieged by waiting members of the press. He heads straight for Brisbane on a domestic flight.

March 12–15, Festival Hall, Brisbane, Australia

Having befriended Dylan on his 1966 tour, Craig McGregor is given the opportunity to interview him on the day of his first Australian show in 12 years. The interview spans two hours, interspersed between the soundcheck and the show. Dylan appears relaxed in McGregor's company and they discuss the commercial failure of *Renaldo and Clara,* new songs Dylan has written (he mentions two, "Changing of the Guards" and "Her Version of Jealousy" [?]), and even his marriage.

March 14, Festival Hall, Brisbane, Australia

"Knockin' on Heaven's Door" starts to appear as a second encore.

• Helen Thomas of *The Age* interviews Dylan at the Crest International Hotel, although he only opens up when discussing the commercial failure of his film. When asked about the critical reviews, he launches into a lengthy tirade, lambasting "all those critics" who in 10 years "will be dead and gone."

Mid-March
According to Helena Springs, it was in a hotel room in Brisbane that Dylan first offered to work on some songs with her. Their first evening of song-writing results in "If I Don't Be There by Morning" and "Walk Out in the Rain."

March 18, Westlake Stadium, Adelaide

March 19
Dylan and the band take a morning flight to Melbourne.

Mid- to Late March (19–23)
One night in Melbourne, Dylan attends a nightclub with George Benson. A photograph of the pair by Joel Bernstein appears on the inner sleeve of *Street-Legal*.

March 20–22, Myer Music Bowl, Melbourne
Dylan opens the last show with a one-off live rendition of Robert Johnson's "Steady Rollin' Man."

March 25, 27–28, Entertainment Centre, Perth
Dylan allegedly performed "If Not for You" at one of the 1978 Perth concerts.

April 1
Running into Dylan on the day of the Adelaide show, Karen Hughes, a budding young journalist, asks him for an interview. She is promised one in Sydney, and duly interviews him in his suite at the Boulevard Hotel. It is an extensive interview, lasting 45 minutes, and includes a lengthy discourse on the nature of touring, something Dylan is clearly committed to at this point.

April 1, Sydney Sportsground, Sydney
For the final concert of the Far East tour, Dylan performs a 29-song set, with three encores, the final one being "I'll Be Your Baby Tonight."

April 2
Dylan slips back to Christchurch, New Zealand for a private visit, arriving at 7:10 PM.

April 2–5
Dylan spends three days in Christchurch and Canterbury, New Zealand with Ra Aranga, whom he had met before the show in Auckland in March.

Early April
With Rob Stoner leaving the band after the Far East leg of the 1978 tour, Dylan recruits ex-Presley bassist Jerry Scheff. One session with Scheff at

Rundown Studios features "I Threw It all Away," a one-verse "Coming from the Heart," a fragment of a clearly unfinished "We'd Better Talk This Over," "Love Minus Zero," "Maggie's Farm," an atmospheric "Ballad of a Thin Man," "Simple Twist of Fate," "To Ramona," "If You See Her, Say Hello" (which has been long dropped from the live set), and "I Don't Believe You." Despite his unfamiliarity with both band and material, Scheff will be involved in the *Street-Legal* recording sessions just a couple of days later.

The Last Waltz concert album is released, including six songs by Dylan and the Band.

April 10 (–14?)

Dylan records his new album, *Street-Legal,* at his own studio in Santa Monica, using a mobile truck from Wally Heider's. According to engineer Arthur Rosato, the sessions only lasted five days and only the nine tracks on *Street-Legal* were attempted, although obviously there were multiple takes. The "New Pony" that appears on *Street-Legal* has had a verse edited out.

May 2

Dylan and the band record a new Dylan/Springs composition called "Stop Now" at Rundown. Also recorded around the same time, and possibly on the same day, are three more Dylan/Springs songs, "Coming from the Heart," "If I Don't Be There by Morning," and "Walk Out in the Rain." All four songs are given to Eric Clapton, who records three of them for his *Backless* album.

May 22

Dylan is interviewed by Robert Hilburn of the *Los Angeles Times* to publicize seven nights at the Universal Amphitheatre in Hollywood. As with his interviews in Australia, he does not hide his anger at the attacks on *Renaldo and Clara:* "The reviews weren't about the movie. They were just an excuse to get at me." But when playing his new album, he is happy to talk about sources of inspiration, if equally keen to disassociate his new material from his divorce.

May 23–26

Dylan is present at the Cannes Film Festival during "Director's Fortnight," at which time *Renaldo and Clara* is screened. The film is well received by European critics.

Late May

Rehearsals for the European leg of the world tour take place at Rundown Studios in Santa Monica. Aside from the *Street-Legal* songs, two new arrangements are worked on: "Tangled Up in Blue" and "Masters of War."

June 1

Dylan prepares for his first European tour in 12 years with the first of seven dates at the Universal Amphitheatre. Dylan introduces two songs from his forthcoming album, "Baby Stop Crying" replacing "I Threw It all Away," and "Senor" replacing "Don't Think Twice, It's Alright, Ma" Also introduced are the two arrangements that come in for such critical praise on his European visit, the torch ballad version of "Tangled Up in Blue" with just guitar, saxophone, and keyboard; and the hard-rock version of "Masters of War," the fury of the backing for once matching the venom of the words. "Tangled Up in Blue" replaces a similar arrangement of "Girl from the North Country," "Masters of War" replaces "Oh Sister." The set's finale is condensed down to: "The Man in Me," "It's Alright, Ma," "Forever Young," and a single encore, "The Times They Are a-Changin'."

June 2–3, Universal Amphitheatre, Los Angeles
The set's finale becomes "Just Like a Woman," "To Ramona," "All Along the Watchtower," "All I Really Want to Do," "It's Alright, Ma," "Forever Young," and "The Times They Are a-Changin'" (first encore). This structure remains throughout the European tour, with nightly variations after "Just Like a Woman."

June 4, Universal Amphitheatre, Los Angeles
"Don't Think Twice, It's Alright," is in the "variation slot," and, for the last time on the 1978 tour, there is a second encore of "Knockin' on Heaven's Door."

June 5, Universal Amphitheatre, Los Angeles
"Don't Think Twice, It's Alright, Ma" remains after "Just Like a Woman." After "It's Alright, Ma," however, Dylan responds to an audience request by leading the band through an electric version of "It Ain't Me, Babe."

June 6, Universal Amphitheatre, Los Angeles
"To Ramona" is included in the "variation slot." "Is Your Love in Vain?" also makes a reappearance, after "All Along the Watchtower."

June 7, Universal Amphitheatre, Los Angeles
In the "variation slot," Dylan tries out three songs, presumably in preparation for the European shows: "Don't Think Twice, It's Alright," "Simple Twist of Fate," and "Oh Sister."

June 8
Dylan and the band record a funkier version of "Stop Now" at Rundown in Santa Monica. Possibly he is considering introducing the song into the live set, although it never actually makes a live appearance on the '78 tour.

June 13
Dylan flies into London in the morning. He spends the two days before opening his European tour shopping and surveying the London music scene. This first day he sees the film *The American Friend* and buys presents for his kids. In the evening, he visits the 100 Club on Oxford Street to see the reggae band Merger, and is impressed enough to invite them to open the bill at Blackbushe. He then moves on to Camden's Dingwalls to watch George Thorogood and the Destroyers.

June 13–20

Dylan stays at the Royal Garden Hotel, Kensington, visiting a pool in North London each morning. On the 19th, George Harrison spends time with Dylan after the Earl's Court concert.

June 14

A soundcheck at Earl's Court is scheduled for the afternoon. In the evening, Dylan attends a CBS party in his honor at Covent Garden's Place Next Door, before heading down to Brixton's Clouds' Club, only to discover it is shut. He then travels on to Dalston's Four Aces club, and then to the Music Machine to catch Robert Gordon, whose band now features Rob Stoner and famous guitar-twanger Link Wray. He concludes the evening at the 100 Club, where he catches the set of another reggae band.

June 15–20, Earls Court, London

On the 15th, Dylan plays his first London concert in 12 years, enough of an event to warrant TV coverage on both the ITN and BBC News. He plays a standard set, with "Don't Think Twice, It's All Right" in the "variation slot." The reviews, though, are anything but standard. The *Daily Mail* headline says "The Greatest Concert I Have Ever Seen," the London *Times* reviewer writes, "One of the best [concerts] to happen in London for years," and even *The Sun* admits, "Dylan lives up to his legend." In its next edition, *Melody Maker* includes an eight-page pull-out special comprising four reviews of the show.

> June 15: *Street-Legal* (JC 35453): "Changing of the Guards," "New Pony," "No Time to Think," "Baby Stop Crying," "Is Your Love in Vain?," "Senor," "True Love Tends to Forget," "We Better Talk This Over," "Where Are You Tonight?"

June 16, Earls Court, London

"Oh Sister" is included in the "variation slot." During the day, Philippe Adler of the French *L'Express* magazine interviews Dylan for a cover story, to be published the week of the Paris shows. The interview is designed to cover a lot of basic background for French readers, so the questions are very standard (e.g., Who influenced you?; Why did you change your name?), but there are some good comments from Dylan. On two occasions he refers to his retreat after the motorcycle accident as "the amnesia."

June 17, Earls Court, London

Includes "Simple Twist of Fate."

L'Express, 1978

June 18, Earls Court, London
Includes "Oh Sister."

June 19, Earls Court, London
Includes "To Ramona."

June 20, Earls Court, London
Includes "Don't Think Twice, It's Alright." A bootleg of ten songs from this show, entitled simply *Earls Court,* is available within three weeks of the show and receives considerable publicity from the British music press (much to Dylan's annoyance). Robert Shelton interviews Dylan after this final London show. Despite Shelton's familiarity with his subject, the interview is not a revealing one. Shelton asks many obvious questions already asked by several interviewers earlier in the year. When asked about *Renaldo and Clara,* Dylan responds, "I talked too much about that film already."

June 22
Dylan visits Anne Frank's house and the Rembrandt museum in Rotterdam. A soundcheck at the Feyenoord Stadium is scheduled for this afternoon.

June 23, Feyenoord Stadium, Rotterdam, Netherlands
Includes "Don't Think Twice, It's Alright," and an extra encore of "I'll Be Your Baby Tonight." The audience for Dylan's first Dutch concert is an appreciative crowd of 55,000. After the show, Dylan attends an Elvis Costello concert in Den Haag at the Congresgebouw.

June 25
Dylan travels by train from Amsterdam to Essen. In Essen, Dylan stays for four days at the Hotel Broadway.

June 26, Westphalia Hall, Dortmund, W. Germany
"Love Her with a Feeling" is replaced by another Tampa Red composition, "She's Love Crazy," which stays as the opener for the remaining continental concerts. Two encores becomes the norm for the remaining European shows.

June 27, Westphalia Hall, Dortmund, W. Germany
Includes "Oh Sister." Dylan drops "Going, Going, Gone" for the only time on the European tour.

June 29, Deutschlandhalle, Berlin, W. Germany
Includes "Don't Think Twice, It's Alright." "Love Minus Zero" is replaced with a new arrangement of "It's All Over Now, Baby Blue," Dylan playing harmonica.

June 30
Dylan travels to Nuremburg by train, a journey lasting approximately seven hours.

July 1, Zeppelinfeld, Nuremburg, W. Germany
Dylan returns to the site of Hitler's infamous Nuremburg rallies to perform to

an estimated 80,000 people, including a small number of neo-Nazis who throw things at the stage throughout the show. After "Going, Going, Gone," Carolyn Dennis, Helena Springs, and Steven Soles each get to sing a song before Dylan returns for an acoustic "A Hard Rain's a-Gonna Fall." This solo spot remains for the rest of the 1978 tour. For the two encores, Eric Clapton guests on guitar. After the show, Dylan and Clapton jam in Dylan's hotel room.

July 3
Dylan takes the train from Nuremburg to Paris. At breakfast in the dining car, Morgan Renard takes a series of photographs.

July 3, Pavilion, Paris, France
Dylan returns to Paris 12 years after his legendary Olympia concert, and this time no guitars are out of tune! At the soundcheck, Dylan and the band run through "Something There Is about You," "True Love Tends to Forget," "Knockin' on Heaven's Door," an old blues tune (probably called "Fix It Ma"), and "To Ramona." For the show, Dylan replaces the two opening songs of the second half ("One of Us Must Know" and "You're a Big Girl Now") with "True Love Tends to Forget" and the rewrite of "The Man in Me" performed on the Far East leg. Between these comes an acoustic song, "It Ain't Me, Babe." As with the English press, the reception by the French media is enthusiastic.

July 4, Pavilion, Paris, France
The "variation slot" tonight is filled by the first live performance of "We'd Better Talk This Over." Robbie Robertson and Martin Scorsese visit Dylan backstage.

July 5, Pavilion, Paris, France
At the soundcheck, Dylan tries out three *Street-Legal* songs, the yet-to-be-performed "Changing of the Guards," "New Pony" (which features the extra verse omitted from the officially released version), and "Is Your Love in Vain?" He also rehearses "I'll Be Your Baby Tonight." At the evening show, "Gates of Eden" replaces "It Ain't Me, Babe" in the solo spot, remaining there for the rest of the European tour. Dylan also replaces (second encore) "I'll Be Your Baby Tonight" with "Changing of the Guards."

July 6, Pavilion, Paris, France
At the soundcheck, Dylan tries out a third Tampa Red composition, "But I Forgive Her," as well as "Love Her with a Feeling," "Mr. Tambourine Man," and "Knockin' on Heaven's Door." Tonight's show, though, repeats the set of the previous night.

July 8, Pavilion, Paris, France
The afternoon soundcheck features an unknown blues and an attempt at the yet-to-be-performed "Where Are You Tonight," along with such staples as "One More Cup of Coffee," "To Ramona," and "Mr. Tambourine Man." For this evening's show Dylan reintroduces "Love Minus Zero" and "To Ramona."

July 11

Dylan is interviewed twice on his arrival at Landvetter Airport in Gothenburg, Sweden. The first interview is by Danish TV reporter Mette Fugl, and it lasts only five minutes. This is followed by an even briefer interview with a Swedish TV reporter, who starts off the interview by calling Dylan "the symbol of the sixties." After this, he is clearly not in a mood to talk.

July 11–12, Scandinavian Stadium, Gothenburg, Sweden

The highly praised arrangement of "Tangled Up in Blue" is inexplicably replaced on the 11th with "Girl from the North Country," while "Is Your Love in Vain?" is slotted in between "I Shall Be Released" and "Going, Going, Gone."

On the 12th, Dylan performs a far more intriguing set at the soundcheck than at the concert. The soundcheck includes "Love Her with a Feeling," due for a recall, the now-dropped "Tomorrow Is a Long Time," and "Oh Sister." Dylan also attempts "No Time to Think" (one of two *Street-Legal* songs never performed live) and "We'd Better Talk This Over." "Just Like Tom Thumb's Blues" is then tried out in preparation for a live outing, before the ubiquitous "Mr. Tambourine Man" and an unknown blues conclude the soundcheck. At the concert, Dylan reintroduces "Love Her with a Feeling" and "Simple Twist of Fate."

July 14

Dylan and the band are scheduled to soundcheck in the afternoon for their show at the Blackbushe Aerodrome. He now has a mammoth repertoire to draw upon for his biggest concert since the Isle of Wight.

July 15, Blackbushe Aerodome, Camberley, Surrey

With at least 200,000 people in attendance, Dylan closes his triumphant European tour at the Blackbushe Aerodrome, in Camberley, Surrey. Twenty-five days after the last Earls Court show, Dylan brings a very different set back, performing 10 songs not performed at his previous show in England: "Just Like Tom Thumb's Blues," "It's All Over Now, Baby Blue," "Girl from the North Country," "Is Your Love in Vain?," a tentative "Where Are You Tonight?," an acoustic "Gates of Eden," "True Love Tends to Forget," and a first encore of "Changing of the Guards" with Eric Clapton on guitar. Also performed are "Simple Twist of Fate" and "To Ramona," both performed only one night at Earls Court. Surprisingly, though, Dylan omits "She's Love Crazy," "The Man in Me," and "I'll Be Your Baby Tonight," all performed regularly on the mainland European dates. Nevertheless, few in the massive crowd notice such omissions, as Dylan proves his pulling power is undiminished by his years away, attracting the largest crowd for a pop festival in Britain since the Isle of Wight nine years earlier. Dylan's 1978 tour is by no means over, though. Sixty-five dates in the United States have been lined up to take the band through the fall.

Early to Mid-September

Rehearsals for the American leg of the world tour take place at Rundown

Studios, Santa Monica. By the end of the rehearsals the provisional repertoire for the US leg is established.

Set one: "My Back Pages" (instrumental); "I'm Ready" or "Love Crazy"; "Is Your Love in Vain?" or "Mr. Tambourine Man"; "Shelter from the Storm"; "It's All Over Now, Baby Blue" or "Love Minus Zero"; "Tangled Up in Blue" or "Girl from the North Country"; "Ballad of a Thin Man"; "Maggie's Farm" or "Angel, What'd I Do"; "I Don't Believe You"; "Like a Rolling Stone"; "I Shall Be Released"; "More Than Flesh and Blood" or "Going, Going, Gone" or "Senor."

Set two: "Rainy Day Women" (instrumental); "True Love Tends to Forget" or "One of Us Must Know" or "The Times They Are a-Changin'"; "Gates of Eden" or "It Ain't Me, Babe"; "Stepchild"; "One More Cup of Coffee"; "Blowin' in the Wind"; "I Want You" or "Girl from the North Country"; "Senor" or "Where Are You Tonight"; "Masters of War"; "Just Like a Woman"; "Baby Stop Crying" or "To Ramona" or "Don't Think Twice"; "All Along the Watchtower"; "All I Really Wanna Do"; "It's Alright, Ma"; "Forever Young"; "Changing of the Guards"; or "The Times They Are a-Changin'."

September 15

In Augusta's Senator Motel, Dylan is interviewed by Matt Damsker. The half-hour interview is later broadcast on American radio as well as published in *Circus Weekly*. Dylan seems happy to talk, admitting that he considers *Sgt. Pepper's Lonely Hearts Club Band* "a very indulgent album," and that on *Blood on the Tracks* he was "fighting sentimentality all the way down the line."

September 15, Civic Center, Augusta, ME

After a two-month lay off, Dylan and the band open a massive American tour. This time around Dylan opens with Willie Dixon's classic blues "I'm Ready," moving "Baby Stop Crying" after "Just Like a Woman," and performing "Is Your Love in Vain?" second. "Love Minus Zero" and "Tangled Up in Blue" are reinstated to the set. The second half opens with "True Love Tends to Forget," followed by a solo "It Ain't Me, Babe" and a new Dylan composition, "(You Treat Me Like a) Stepchild." "The Times They Are a-Changin'" is dropped as second encore. "Changing of the Guards" now closes the show. An excerpt of the Augusta encore is included on US television, part of a brief profile of Dylan's career by ABC News.

September 16, Cumberland Civic Center, Portland, ME

A new arrangement of "I Threw It All Away" replaces "True Love Tends to Forget" as opening song in the second set.

September 17

Jonathan Cott conducts his second major interview with Dylan in less than a year. The interview takes place on both bus and plane, and in the dressing room before the New Haven show. Cott concentrates on asking Dylan about themes in the *Street-Legal* songs, although even Cott can't resist asking him about the commercial failure of *Renaldo and Clara*.

September 17, Veterans Memorial Coliseum, New Haven, CT

Dylan continues to experiment at sound checks. At this venue he rehearses at least three new songs, with titles like "You'd Love Me to Go," "This Way, That Way," and "I Must Love You Too Much." "Love Her with a Feeling" is also given the once over, along with "Maggie's Farm" and an attempted 1978 arrangement of "Hazel." At the evening concert, "The Man in Me" is a one-off replacement for "Baby Stop Crying."

September 19, Montreal Forum, Montreal, Quebec

In 1984 Dylan would comment, "there's only been one time when I've wanted to replay a show, that was in Montreal. We played a show in 1978, I had a temperature of 104, couldn't even stand up." Includes the return of "One of Us Must Know" as the opening song of the second half, Dylan also replaces "Love Minus Zero" with "It's All Over Now, Baby Blue."

September 20, Boston Gardens, Boston, MA

"Girl from the North Country" replaces "Tangled Up in Blue."

September 22, War Memorial Auditorium, Syracuse, NY

At the soundcheck, Dylan resurrects one of the songs from the Paris soundchecks, Tampa Red's "But I Forgive You." He also tries out "Where Are You Tonight?" and "Reconsider Baby," a song generally associated with Elvis Presley. After the female vocalists perform their own rendition of "Stepchild," Dylan concludes the soundcheck with "True Love Tends to Forget." At the show, Dylan replaces "It Ain't Me, Babe" for the only time on the American leg; preferring an unimpressive "Fourth Time Around."

September 23, War Memorial Coliseum, Rochester, NY

Marc Rowland interviews Dylan in Rochester, their recorded conversation lasting 45 minutes. The interview once again concentrates on US critical reaction both to *Renaldo and Clara* and to the current American tour, which has already been widely attacked, critics making various unfavorable remarks at Dylan's so-called "Vegas" sound.

September 24, Broome County Veterans Memorial Arena, Binghamton, NY

Dylan performs a new composition at this show, "I Must Love You Too Much." Also featured tonight are "It's All Over Now, Baby Blue" and "Girl from the North Country," replacing "Love Minus Zero" and "Tangled Up in Blue."

September 25

Dylan attends a show by electric blues guitarist Robert " Junior" Lockwood at the Red Creek Inn, Rochester.

September 26, Civic Center, Springfield, MA

"True Love Tends to Forget" opens the second half. "Don't Think Twice, It's Alright" makes a rare appearance in the "variation slot."

September 27, Veterans Memorial Coliseum, Nassau County, NY
Includes "Just Like Tom Thumb's Blues."

September 29, Madison Square Garden, NY
The first night is Dylan's first New York concert in nearly three years. "Just Like Tom Thumb's Blues" and "I Must Love You Too Much" make their second and final live appearances. "One of Us Must Know" returns as the second-half opener. "Baby Stop Crying" continues to be a regular choice in the "variation slot."

September 30, Madison Square Garden, NY

September 29 or 30
Peter Goddard of the *Toronto Sun* obtains a brief interview with Dylan backstage at Madison Square Garden. The interview largely centers on the critical reaction stateside to everything Dylan has done in 1978.

October 3, Scope Arena, Norfolk, VA
"The Man in Me" is in the "variation slot."

October 4, Civic Center, Baltimore, MD
"It's All Over Now, Baby Blue" is now preferred over "Love Minus Zero."

October 5
Dylan is briefly interviewed on the telephone by Pam Coyle for the *Hibbing High Times.* The highlight of the article is when she reports that Dylan is performing a couple of Guthrie songs on the tour: "Passion of Plenty" ["Pastures of Plenty"] and "Ballad of Tom Jones" ["Tom Joad"]. Must have been a real bad connection!

October 5, Capitol Center, Washington, DC
Includes "Don't Think Twice, It's All Right" and a second encore of "The Times They Are a-Changin'." "Girl from the North Country" replaces "I Want You" from this point on the tour.

October 6, The Spectrum, Philadelphia, PA
"Where Are You Tonight" opens the second half. "It Takes a Lot to Laugh" makes its only 1978 tour appearance (in place of "Stepchild"), and "Simple Twist of Fate" makes a rare appearance in the "variation slot."

October 7, Civic Center, Providence, RI

October 9, Memorial Auditorium, Buffalo, NY
"Where Are You Tonight?" becomes a regular feature of the set.

October 12, Maple Leaf Gardens, Toronto, Ontario

October 13, Olympia Stadium, Detroit, MI
At the soundcheck, Dylan performs a new composition called "Legionnaire's Disease."

October 14, Hulman Center, Terre Haute, IN

October 15, Riverfront Stadium, Cincinnati, OH
Includes "Simple Twist of Fate."

October 17–18, Chicago Stadium, Chicago, IL
"Stepchild" is temporarily dropped from the set after the first show. On the 18th, "Is Your Love in Vain?" is dropped from the set, replaced by a new arrangement of "Mr. Tambourine Man." "One of Us Must Know" is also dropped as second-half opener, replaced by a new arrangement of "The Times They Are a-Changin'."

October 20, Richffeld Coliseum, Cleveland, OH
Robert Lockwood visits Dylan backstage.

October 21, Centennial Arena, Toledo, OH
"I'm Ready" is dropped from the set, to be replaced by "She's Love Crazy." "Don't Think Twice, It's All Right" also makes a rare reappearance in the "variation slot."

October 22, University of Dayton Arena, Dayton, OH
"Baby Stop Crying" closes the first half.

October 24, Freedom Hall, Louisville, KY

October 25, Market Square Arena, Indianapolis, IN
"Is Your Love in Vain?" closes the first half.

October 27, Wings Stadium, Kalamazoo, MI
"Baby Stop Crying" closes the first half. "Simple Twist of Fate" makes a rare appearance.

October 28, Illinois State University Arena, Carbondale, IL
At the soundcheck, Dylan tries out "One More Cup of Coffee," "I Must Love You Too Much," and the old Shel Silverstein song, "Carry Me, Carrie," along with a couple of new compositions with titles like "Take It or Leave It" and "One More Time." At the evening show, "Senor" closes the first half, which includes a most unusual yet effective version of "Tangled Up in Blue" in which Dylan's voice gets increasingly histrionic.

October 29, Checkerdome, St. Louis, MO
The soundcheck includes an instrumental run through of "St. Louis Blues," "I Must Love You Too Much," and two great Dylan vocals on Shel Silverstein songs, "Daddy's Little Girl" and "Carry Me, Carrie." At the show, "Don't Think Twice, It's Alright" makes its final 1978 appearance, "True Love Tends to Forget" closes the first half, and "Stepchild" returns to the set.

October 31, Civic Center, St. Paul, MN
Dylan closes the first half of the show with a unique live performance of the Dylan-Helena Springs composition, "Coming from the Heart." Dylan

clearly enjoys playing in his home state and concludes the show with a second encore, "I'll Be Your Baby Tonight."

November 1
Dylan is given the key to the city of Madison, WI by one of his fans, Mayor Paul Soglin. Radio station WISM proclaims it "Dylan day" in Madison.

November 1, Dane County Coliseum, Madison
"Senor" now closes the first half.

November 3, Kemper Arena, Kansas City, MO
Robert Hilburn interviews Dylan for the second time in six months, in a coffee shop in Kansas. It is a brief interview that again concentrates on the critical flak the American leg of his world tour has received.

November 4, Civic Auditorium, Omaha, NE
At the soundcheck, Dylan continues to work on a new composition with the probable title "One More Year," and another song possibly called "Rockin' Chair." Also attempted is "Watching the River Flow."

November 6
In the afternoon, Dylan is interviewed in his hotel suite by John Mankiewicz for West Coast music paper, *Sound.* Pete Oppel joins the tour for a few days to prepare a series of reports for the *Dallas Morning News.* He interviews Dylan after the show.

November 6, McNichols Arena, Denver, CO
"Tangled Up in Blue" is introduced as a song, "I wrote three years ago about three people in love with each other all at the same time." "Simple Twist of Fate" makes its final 1978 appearance.

November 9, Memorial Coliseum, Portland, OR
At the soundcheck, Dylan again tries out "Knockin' on Heaven's Door," plus a couple of new compositions. Pete Oppel again talks to Dylan after the show.

November 10, Hec Edmundson Pavilion, Seattle, WA
Pete Oppel interviews Dylan before the show. The second half opens with the female vocalists performing "Rainy Day Women."

November 11, Pacific Coliseum, Vancouver, BC
Pete Oppel again interviews Dylan before the show. At this show, "Where Are You Tonight?" is replaced by "We'd Better Talk This Over," an occasional alternate for the remainder of the tour.

November 13, Alameda County Coliseum, Oakland, CA

November 14, Alameda County Coliseum, Oakland, CA
The show includes the last "Baby Stop Crying." Pete Oppel continues his conversations with Dylan before the show.

November 15, The Forum, Inglewood, Los Angeles

Pete Oppel concludes his extensive profile of Dylan with one final interview.

November 17, Sports Arena, San Diego, CA

The female vocalists' rendition of "Rainy Day Women" comes after "The Times They Are a-Changin'." At this show, someone throws a little silver cross onto the stage. Dylan picks it up and places it in his pocket.

November 18, Arizona State University Activities Center, Tempe, AZ

At the soundcheck, Dylan performs two songs from the European set, "Oh Sister" and "You're a Big Girl Now." The show includes the last live version of "True Love Tends to Forget."

November 19, McKale Memorial Center, Tucson, AZ

November 21, Special Events Arena, El Paso, TX

Includes the first live version of "Watching the River Flow."

> November 22: *Bob Dylan at Budokan* (PC2 36067) is released in Japan: "Mr. Tambourine Man," "Shelter from the Storm," "Love Minus Zero/No Limit," "Ballad of a Thin Man," "Don't Think Twice It's Alright," "Maggie's Farm," "One More Cup of Coffee," "Like a Rolling Stone," "I Shall Be Released," "Is Your Love in Vain?," "Going, Going, Gone," "Blowin' in the Wind," "Just Like a Woman," "Oh Sister," "Simple Twist of Fate," "All Along the Watchtower," "I Want You," "All I Really Want to Do," "Knockin' on Heaven's Door," "It's Alright, Ma," "Forever Young," "The Times They Are a-Changin'." US and world release occurs on April 23, 1979.

November 23, Lloyd Noble Center Arena, Norman, OK

"Watching the River Flow" makes its second and last 1978 appearance.

November 24, Tarrant County Convention Center Arena, Fort Worth, TX

Dylan is wearing a metal cross around his neck at this concert.

November 25, Special Events Center, Austin, TX

November 26, The Summit, Houston, TX

Tonight the woman in the topless bar in "Tangled Up in Blue" quotes from "the gospel according to Matthew" rather than "some Italian poet from the thirteenth century."

November 28, Coliseum, Jackson, MS

November 29, Louisiana State University Assembly Arena, Baton Rouge, LA

December 1, Mid-South Coliseum, Memphis, TN

After a fine show, Dylan plays a second encore, "I'll Be Your Baby Tonight."

December 2, Municipal Auditorium, Nashville, TN

At the soundcheck, Dylan performs a new song called "Slow Train," although clearly the words are not worked out. Also performed is a song dating all the way back to the New Haven soundcheck, "This Way, That Way." Dylan is also interviewed backstage by an unknown journalist. Although he seems a little defensive at times, Dylan admits that, on *Street-Legal,* "what they were doing in the [mobile] truck wasn't what was happening in the room."

At the concert, there is a film crew shooting and three songs are broadcast in 1979 on Italian TV. They are "Mr. Tambourine Man," "Masters of War," and "Changing of the Guard." All three songs display an impassioned Dylan, even if the length of the tour is starting to wear on his vocal chords.

December 3, Jefferson Civic Center, Birmingham, AL

December 5, Municipal Auditorium, Mobile, AL

"Love Minus Zero" is reintroduced into the set. "One of Us Must Know" makes a one-off appearance as the second half opener.

December 7, War Memorial Coliseum, Greensboro, NC

December 8, Civic Center Arena, Savannah

"Is Your Love in Vain?" replaces "Where Are You Tonight?"

December 9, Carolina Coliseum, Columbia, SC

Includes the last live version of "Where Are You Tonight?"

December 10, Charlotte Coliseum, Charlotte, NC

December 12, OMNI Coliseum, Atlanta, GA

Dylan is interviewed by Lynne Allen backstage at the OMNI. It is not a revealing interview, considering the changes he is going through, although it is later published in *Trouser Press* under the rather ironic title, "Interview with an Icon."

December 13, Jacksonville Coliseum, Jacksonville, FL

Includes "It's All Over Now, Baby Blue."

December 15, Civic Center Arena, Lakeland, FL

December 16, Hollywood Sportatorium, Miami, FL

Dylan finishes his most grueling tour ever with a 29-song set that includes a brand-new song. This debut performance of "Do Right to Me Baby (Do Unto Others)" is lyrically different from the take issued on *Slow Train Coming.* He also plays a final second encore, ending show *and* tour with "I'll Be Your Baby Tonight."

1979

January

One of Dylan's girlfriends, Mary Alice Artes, asks two pastors of the Vineyard Fellowship in West Los Angeles to come and talk to him about Christ. On meeting the pastors, he admits he wants Christ in his life and "prayed that day and received the Lord."

Winter

Dylan attends a three-month course at the School of Discipleship in a back room above a realtor's office in Reseda, Southern California. The course involves "studying about the life of Jesus; principles of discipleship . . . what it is to be a believer; how to grow; how to share." The classes begin at 8:30 AM and continue until noon, four days a week.

January 26

Dylan forms his own record company, Accomplice Records.

February

The *New York Post* publishes a report that Dylan has been baptized into the Christian faith in Pat Boone's swimming pool. According to Ken Gulliksen, Dylan's pastor at the time, "He was baptized at the home of Bill Dwyer." According to Larry Myers, also a pastor at the Vineyard Fellowship, he was indeed baptized, but not at Dwyer's, but he refuses to say where Dylan *was* baptized.

Late Winter

According to Dylan, he originally intended to release the *Slow Train Coming* songs performed by Carolyn Dennis. He would just produce the album. Possibly this was the reason for setting up a record label in January. There are no details as to what material, if any, was recorded by Dennis.

March 29

Dylan attends a Dire Straits concert at the Roxy in Los Angeles. Later, at On the Rox, Dylan asks guitarist Mark Knopfler and drummer Pick Withers to play on the sessions for his forthcoming album.

April

At Rundown Studios in Santa Monica, Dylan runs through the songs he intends to record for *Slow Train Coming,* so that guitarist Mark Knopfler can familiarize himself with the material and suggest suitable arrangements.

Bob Dylan at Budokan released worldwide (see November 22, 1978)

April 30
Dylan arrives at Muscle Shoals Sound Studio in Sheffield, AL to begin recording his first-ever gospel statement, *Slow Train Coming.* He has brought with him Pick Withers and Mark Knopfler from Dire Straits, and Carolyn Dennis, Helena Springs, and Regina Havis, three female backing singers. Along with bassist Tim Drummond, keyboardist Barry Beckett, percussionist Mickey Buckins, and the Muscle Shoals Horns, Dylan will cut the album in five days. Also on hand, and a key element in recreating that authentic Muscle Shoals groove, is legendary Atlantic producer Jerry Wexler, who becomes Dylan's first-ever "name" producer. The first session is spent working on a typically dark slice of blues, "Trouble in Mind," which subsequently appears (minus one verse) on the b-side of the album's first single, "Gotta Serve Somebody."

May 1
Dylan continues work at Muscle Shoals. Again the day is spent working largely on one song, the title of which remains unknown (although at least eight takes are attempted). Also recorded on the 30th or the 1st is one of three known outtakes from the album, "No Man Righteous (No Not One)." Originally scheduled for inclusion on *The Bootleg Series,* this track remains unreleased.

May 2
Once again, Dylan begins the day working on a song not destined to make *Slow Train Coming.* "Ye Shall Be Changed," according to the studio reels, is cut in a single take. It subsequently appears on *The Bootleg Series.* Then it is time for the Muscle Shoals Horns to be brought in for an evangelical call-to-arms, "Gonna Change My Way of Thinking." Also probably cut at this session are the album versions of "Precious Angel" and "When You Gonna Wake Up," both of which utilize the horns.

May 3
The recording of *Slow Train Coming* continues at Muscle Shoals. Dylan cuts two more unequivocal expressions of faith, "I Believe in You" and "Slow Train."

May 4
At what appears to have been the final session for *Slow Train Coming,* Dylan cuts four tracks. "Gotta Serve Somebody" requires four takes, beginning life with Dylan on the piano. "Do Right to Me Baby" starts out with a simple acoustic guitar/piano arrangement, also requiring four takes to reach resolution. "When He Returns" reverses the process, beginning with a full-band

arrangement and ending up with Dylan singing over Barry Beckett's stark piano accompaniment. The final song of the session(s) is somewhat anticlimactic, the trite "Man Gave Name to All the Animals," the fake ending of which causes its fair share of problems.

May 22
While in court defending himself against a defamation-of-character suit by Patty Valentine, Dylan is questioned about his property. He replies: "You mean my treasure here on earth?"

Early August: "Gotta Serve Somebody"/"Trouble in Mind" (1-11072).

August 18: *Slow Train Coming* (FC 36120): "Gotta Serve Somebody," "Precious Angel," "I Believe in You," "Slow Train," "Gonna Change My Way of Thinking," "Do Right to Me Baby," "When You Gonna Wake Up," "Man Gave Names to All the Animals," "When He Returns"

August or Early September
Dylan is on his farm in Minnesota. Sara apparently visits him.

September to October
Dylan returns to Rundown Studios to rehearse for his forthcoming tour. Early rehearsals feature several new Dylan songs including a very simplistic number called "Stand by Faith," and his own arrangement of the traditional, "Blessed Is the Name of the Lord." His new band features several pedigree session musicians: Jim Keltner on drums, Fred Tackett on guitar, Tim Drummond on bass, Spooner Oldham and Terry Young on keyboards, and three female singers, Mona Lisa Young, Regina Havis, and Helena Springs. Early rehearsals feature a horn section. However, Dylan decides he cannot afford such a large band.

October
A whole series of Dylan-Springs compositions are copyrighted presumably from demos recorded at the time (i.e., in August or early September). The songs are "More Than Flesh and Blood," "Responsibility," "Someone Else's Arms," "Tell Me the Truth One Time," "The Wandering Kind," "What's the Matter," and Without You." Possibly the demos lodged with Special Rider are solo Springs performances. Also probably demoed at the time, though, is a new Dylan original, "Saving Grace That's over Me."

October 18
Dylan and his band fly from Los Angeles to New York to appear on "Saturday Night Live," arriving at JFK airport around 6 PM.

October 19
A rehearsal for "Saturday Night Live" is scheduled for 11 AM at NBC Studios.

October 20

Dylan appears on "Saturday Night Live," recorded at NBC Studios in New York. He performs three songs, "Gotta Serve Somebody," "I Believe in You," and "When You Gonna Wake Up" with his new touring band. The host for the show, Eric Idle, is evidently delighted with Dylan's appearance. However, there's precious little humor in his performance.

October 31

Dylan and his new band soundcheck at the Fox Warfield Theater in San Francisco.

November 1–4, 6–11, 13–16, Fox Warfield Theater, San Francisco

Dylan plays a two-week residency in this intimate venue.

November 1, Fox Warfield Theater, San Francisco

An understandably nervous Dylan starts his most controversial tour since 1966 in the sedate surroundings of this 2,000-seat theater. However, his intentions are made clear when the female vocalists open the show with six gospel songs. They conclude with Guthrie's "This Train (Is Bound for Glory)." When Dylan takes the stage, he launches straight into "Gotta Serve Somebody," "I Believe in You," and "When You Gonna Wake Up." A subdued yet powerful "When He Returns," features just Dylan on guitar and Willie Smith on piano. Dylan continues premiering *Slow Train Coming,* with "Man Gave Name to All the Animals," "Precious Angel," and "Slow Train" in rapid succession, before a gorgeous new work called "Covenant Woman" closes the first half of the show.

After one more song by one of the female singers, Dylan performs two more songs from *Slow Train Coming,* "Gonna Change My Way of Thinking" and "Do Right to Me Baby." Dylan then introduces five new songs, all reaffirming his new-found faith, the first of which he introduces by its full title, "Hanging on to a Solid Rock Made Before the Foundation of the World." It is succeeded by "Saving Grace," "Saved," and "What Can I Do for You?" (which includes two lengthy harmonica breaks by Dylan) and finally a majestic "In the Garden." This is not Forest Hills, however, and the crowd demands Dylan's return, being rewarded with two encores. The first is "Blessed Is the Name of the Lord." The second, "Pressing On," features Dylan at the piano for the first verse. He then walks to the front of the stage, no guitar. The first couple of nights Dylan sings a third verse to the song.

When Dylan leaves the stage tonight, he has performed for 95 minutes, singing no song more than a year old. He has included seven unreleased Dylan compositions, two or three of which rank among his finest work. In normal circumstances, this would be a Dylan fan's dream. On this occasion, however, the critics furiously attack the show, calling it, sin-of-sins, evangelical. The *San Francisco Examiner* describes the show as "a pretty grueling experience," whereas the *San Francisco Chronicle* considers the material "banal, uninspired and inventionless." The most objective report is in *Rolling Stone,* whose reviewer admits, "The music was top-notch," although he con-

fesses he does not share the sentiments of the songs. Dylan is clearly upset by all the criticism. However, he remains convinced of the merits of the show and, unrepentant, continues with the same set night after night.

November 2–3
Each morning Dylan sits in a cafe next to the Fox Warfield Theater and reads the (generally unfavorable) reviews of his new show.

November 5
Dylan visits Maria Muldaur at her home in Marin County, and preaches to her about the literal truth of the Bible.

Maria Muldaur was originally one of many New York-based folksingers. She performed in Jim Kweskin's Jug Band in the '60s, and then, briefly, had a successful solo career in the early '70s with her hit "Midnight at the Oasis." In the early '80s, she was "born again."

November 16, Fox Warfield Theater, San Francisco

One of Dylan's finest shows ends a two-week engagement in San Francisco. The shows have been well received by the majority of people attending. Both Dylan's and the band's performances have improved every night. This last night, Dylan includes an extra song at the end of the first half, a terrific version of the *Slow Train Coming* outtake, "No Man Righteous (No Not One)." In the second half, the new songs take on a life of their own. The crowd seems to be enthralled by the virtuosity of the band and the versatility in Dylan's voice. They are not even taken aback when Dylan starts preaching that, "Christ will [indeed] set up his kingdom in Jerusalem for a thousand years, where the lion will lie down with the lamb." Dylan is in a most talkative mood throughout tonight's show.

November 18, Civic Auditorium, Santa Monica

The first of four benefit shows to aid World Vision International, a nondenominational Christian charity organization. Dylan has not played at the Civic Auditorium in 14 years. The audiences at these shows are particularly enthusiastic, and Dylan preaches extensively.

November 19, Civic Auditorium, Santa Monica

November 20, Civic Auditorium, Santa Monica

November 21, Civic Auditorium, Santa Monica

A delighted Dylan plays to a very sympathetic audience and is keen to talk to the audience throughout the show. He introduces Mona Lisa Young singing "God Uses Ordinary People" with a particularly long rap about the origins of the Passover.

November 25–26, Gammage Center, Tempe, AZ

The two Tempe audiences are almost certainly the ones Dylan had in mind when he talks in the *Biograph* booklet of "College kids show(ing) the most disrespect" at the evangelical shows. On both nights, Dylan is clearly in an angry mood. On the first night, Dylan responds to some heckling by declaiming, "Don't you walk out before you hear the message through."

• On the second night, he refers to the crowd as a "pretty rude bunch," and throughout the show mercilessly berates them to repent their evil ways. Indeed, before "When You Gonna Wake Up," he informs the audience that "there is only two kinds of people: there's saved people and there's lost people," preaching for a full five minutes, concluding with "Jesus is Lord and every race shall bow to him!" An even lengthier rap precedes "Solid Rock." Dylan proclaims, "You may have your college education to hang on to now, but you're gonna need something very solid to hang on to when these [end] days come."

November 27–28, Golden Hall, San Diego, CA

In an extraordinary rap on the first night, Dylan talks about playing San Diego in 1978 (November 17). Someone threw a cross on stage that he picked up during that performance. The following night he told himself: "'I need something tonight that I didn't have before,' and I looked in my pocket and I had this cross. So if that person is here tonight, I just wanna thank you for that cross."

November 30 to December 2
Dylan was originally booked to play three nights at the Fine Arts Centre in Salt Lake City. However, the shows are canceled at the last minute, for reasons unknown, leaving a five-day gap in the touring schedule. Presumably, Dylan and the band returned to Los Angeles at this point.

December 4–5, Convention Center, Albuquerque, NM
On the second night, Dylan is again in a very preachy mood, and in one of his more unequivocal speeches announces: "I'm telling you now Jesus is coming back and He is! And there is no other way of salvation."

December 7
Dylan is briefly interviewed over the telephone by Bruce Heiman for Tucson local radio station KMGX. In his only interview from this important year. Dylan responds to a question about the threat of a protest by the American Atheists Association at his Tucson concerts by saying, "Christ is no religion. . . . (He) is the way, the truth and the life . . . religion is another form of bondage which man invents to get himself to God." Dylan also admits that he doesn't "sing any song which hasn't been given to me by the Lord to sing."

December 8–9, Community Center, Tucson, AZ

Mid- to Late December
Dylan visits his mother in St Paul, MN

1980

January 10
The scheduled show for the Paramount Theater in Portland is "snowed out," rescheduled for the 16th. Carolyn Dennis replaces Helena Springs on backing vocals from this point on the tour.

January 11–12, Paramount Theater, Portland, OR

January 13–15, Paramount Theater, Seattle, WA
While in Seattle, Dylan apparently visits jewelers Friedlander and Son, where he purchases a $30,000 diamond engagement ring.

January 16, Paramount Theater, Portland, OR
Rescheduled from the 10th.

January 17–18, Riverpark Center Opera House, Spokane, WA

January 21–23, Rainbow Music Hall, Denver, CO
Allen Ginsberg attends the first night's show, and goes backstage after the concert. Although Ginsberg talks to him of a God of forgiveness, Dylan retorts, "Yes, but he also comes to judge."

January 25–26, Orpheum Theater, Omaha, NE

January 27–29, Uptown Theater, Kansas City, MO

January 31 to February 1, Orpheum Theater, Memphis, TN

February 2–3, Jefferson Civic Center, Birmingham, AL

February 5–6, Civic Auditorium, Knoxville, TN

February 8, Municipal Auditorium, Charleston, SC
Dylan plays a new composition, "Are You Ready?," as the first encore, with "Blessed Is the Name of the Lord" making its last regular live appearance as the second encore.

February 9, Municipal Auditorium, Charleston
This last concert on this leg of the evangelical tour features "Are You Ready?" as first encore and "Pressing On" as the second encore.

February 11
Dylan returns to Muscle Shoals Sound Studio in Sheffield, AL to begin work on the follow up to *Slow Train Coming*. This time, though, he has brought his touring band with him. With Jerry Wexler and Barry Beckett again producing, the first session is taken up with cutting nine takes of "Covenant Woman," none of which makes it to the album (although take seven is pulled to the master reel).

February 12
A far more productive session at Muscle Shoals yields three cuts on *Saved,* including the seemingly improvised opener, "Satisfied Mind," which is cut in a single take, as is "Saved" (although according to Wexler this was one of two songs recut on the 15th). "Solid Rock" is cut in three takes, "What Can I Do for You?" in one, although that Muscle Shoals groove is sadly lacking on both.

February 13
The bulk of today's Muscle Shoals session is taken up with working out a "studio" arrangement for "Pressing On" that conveys the same rollercoaster feel as the live encore. The "Pressing On" they secure in five takes is one of the highlights on *Saved*. Before "Pressing On," Dylan and the band have already laid down "Saving Grace" (in two takes). Finally Dylan begins work on the central song of the live set, "In the Garden," although he abandons it after a single take.

February 14
Dylan returns to "In the Garden," cutting two more complete takes and a new piano introduction. (It is not clear from the studio sheets if this was then grafted onto the album take.) He then records his newest testimony to Armageddon, "Are You Ready?," in just two takes.

February 15
Reviewing the tapes of the previous four days, Wexler and Dylan decide that two songs need to be recut. According to Wexler, versions of "Saved" and "Covenant Woman" were cut on the 15th and appear on the album.

February 26
Between 11:15 AM and 12:30 PM, Dylan and his band perform "Gotta Serve Somebody" at the Shrine Auditorium in Los Angeles as the initial run through for the Grammy Awards.

February 27
At 2 PM, there is a full dress rehearsal of the Grammy Awards. Dylan and his band are again scheduled to run through "Gotta Serve Somebody." Dylan is nominated for a Grammy Award for "Best Male Rock Vocal Performance of 1979" for his "Gotta Serve Somebody" single. At 6 PM, he performs the song dressed in full evening attire, to a very appreciative audience. It is a great performance, ironically far surpassing his vocal on the actual record. He even plays some demon harmonica. With typical perver-

sity, he also changes the words, and the entire performance clocks in at over six minutes. Not surprisingly, Dylan wins his first Grammy Award, thanking in his acceptance speech "The Lord, Jerry Wexler, and Barry Beckett . . . who believed." The award ceremony takes place at the Shrine Auditorium in Los Angeles and receives the usual extensive television coverage. After the show, there is a buffet dinner laid on at the Biltmore Hotel.

Late February to March
Dylan invites Maria Muldaur over to his apartment in Brentwood, Los Angeles to hear *Saved,* which he has just finished recording.

March
Dylan plays harmonica on "Pledge My Head to Heaven," a song on Keith Green's *So You Wanna Go Back to Egypt* album. The harmonica playing on the track is very reminiscent of that on "What Can I Do for You?" The session is held at Mama Jo's in the San Fernando Valley.

Early April
Dylan meets with artist Tony Wright, who is designing the sleeve for *Saved,* at Rundown Studios. They discuss Wright's idea for a hand coming down and other hands stretching out to meet it. Dylan requests a little bit of blood on the hand. The sleeve they design comes in for considerable flak on the album's release and becomes the only Dylan front cover to be replaced.

Mid-April
Rehearsals are held at Rundown Studios, Santa Monica, in preparation for leg three of the so-called gospel tour. Clydie King, Gwen Evans, Mary Elizabeth Bridget, and Regina Peeples (nee Havis) are the female vocalists on this leg.

April 16
Dylan and his band fly from LA to Toronto at 12:50 PM, arriving shortly after 8 AM.

April 17, Massey Hall, Toronto, Ontario
At the soundcheck, Dylan and the band work on three new compositions, "Ain't Gonna Go to Hell," "Coverdown, Breakthrough," and "I Will Love Him." There is also a run through of "Pressing On." At the show, Dylan unveils a slightly changed set. After the opening three numbers, which remain, "Gotta Serve Somebody," "I Believe in You," and "When You Gonna Wake Up," he introduces two new songs, "Ain't Gonna Go to Hell" and "Coverdown, Breakthrough"; followed by four more songs from *Slow Train Coming.* ("Gonna Change My Way of Thinking" is dropped.) Five songs from *Saved* conclude the main set: "Solid Rock," "Saving Grace," "Saved," "What Can I Do for You?," and "In the Garden." "Are You Ready?" is now the first encore. "Pressing On" concludes the show.

April 19, Massey Hall, Toronto, Ontario
This show is filmed at Dylan's request, although the footage has never been utilized. Tonight "Covenant Woman" replaces "I Believe in You" and in-

stead of "Pressing On," the lucky audience hears the one-and-only live performance of a new Dylan song, "I Will Love Him." The show is recorded by a 24-track mobile truck for a possible live album. The album was scheduled to feature seven tracks in all: "Gotta Serve Somebody," "Covenant Woman," "When You Gonna Wake Up," "Precious Angel," "Slow Train," "Solid Rock," and "In the Garden." However, the project is scrapped, apparently at CBS's behest.

April 20, Massey Hall, Toronto, Ontario
This show is also filmed and recorded on 24-track. "When He Returns" makes a rare reappearance in place of "When You Gonna Wake Up." Before "Solid Rock," Dylan gives his longest rap since the Tempe shows, relating how the Tempe audience had booed when he started to preach about the Book of Revelation. Ronnie Hawkins attends tonight's show and meets Dylan backstage. He is unimpressed by Dylan's Christian stance, later saying, "He had this black chick following him everywhere carrying a Bible and praising the Lord."

April 22, Theatre St-Denis, Montreal, Quebec
At the soundcheck, Dylan continues to work on "I Will Love Him," "Ain't Gonna Go to Hell," and "Coverdown, Breakthrough." The female vocalists also try out a gospel song called "I Will Sing."

April 25, Theatre St-Denis, Montreal, Quebec
After Dylan's departure from Montreal, the *Montreal Gazette* reports that Dylan had returned a cartoon published in the Gazette welcoming Dylan to Montreal. The cartoon had been inscribed: "The law was given to Moses. But grace and truth through Jesus Christ (Book of John). Love Bob Dylan."

April 27–28, Palace Theater, Albany, NY

April 30 to May 1, Kleinham's Music Hall, Buffalo, NY

May 2–3, Memorial Auditorium, Worcester, MA

May 4–5, Landmark Theater, Syracuse, NY
From Albany onward, Dylan preaches with as much intensity as he had on the later 1979 shows. At the second Syracuse show, he talks about Springsteen: "You know Bruce, he was born to run. . . . But you can't run and you can't hide. . . . "

May 7, Bushnell Memorial Auditorium, Hartford, CT
Dylan performs "No Man Righteous (No Not One)" as a duet with Regina Peebles at the start of the second half. At both Hartford shows, Dylan preaches extensively. This first night, before "Solid Rock," he proclaims: "Walking with Jesus is no easy trip, but it's the only trip." After the show, Dylan talks to Australian journalist Karen Hughes. Although Hughes claims they talked for three hours in Dylan's hotel room, it is clearly more a conversation than an interview, and in subsequent articles Hughes reveals little of what was said. One comment Dylan makes is quoted, "It would

have been easier if I'd become a junkie, or a Buddhist, or a Scientologist." Hughes obtains a full interview later in the tour.

May 8, Bushnell Memorial Auditorium, Hartford

Again, Dylan is very talkative during the show, this time leading from an explanation of the origins of the word hypocrite into a five-minute attack on "homosexual politics" in San Francisco: "It's a growing place for homosexuals. I mean they have homosexual politics. It's a political party . . . well I guess the iniquity is not yet full."

May 9–10, City Hall, Portland, ME

May 11–12, Ocean State Performing Arts Center, Providence, RI

On the first night, before "Slow Train," Dylan gives one of his more eloquent evangelical raps, an updated version of the parable of the seeds, implying that for some of his audience "those riches and those cares (of this world) are gonna choke the Word." A version of this rap becomes a regular feature of the remaining shows on the tour.

May 14, Stanley Theater, Pittsburgh, PA

May 15, Stanley Theater, Pittsburgh, PA

Pat Crosby obtains a brief interview with Dylan at the Hilton Hotel. Lasting just three minutes, the interview is broadcast on KDKA-TV the same day. When asked about his old songs, Dylan retorts, "the old stuff's not going to save [my audience]."

May 16, Stanley Theater, Pittsburgh, PA

May 17–18, Civic Theater, Akron, OH

Dylan is well received in Akron, and on both nights he performs three encores. On this first night, the third encore is "Blessed Is the Name of the Lord." Dylan comments on the friendly reception before "Coverdown, Breakthrough": "What a friendly crowd! I'm not used to friendly crowds. We're used to the devil's working all kinds of mischief in the crowds we've faced." On the second night, "When He Returns" is performed in place of "Do Right to Me Baby." The third encore is a one-off live performance of "I Will Sing."

May 20, Franklin County Veterans Memorial Auditorium, Columbus, OH

May 21, Memorial Hall, Dayton, OH

This is the last of the gospel shows. A second Dayton show was planned but had to be canceled as a result of poor ticket sales. After the show, Karen Hughes interviews Dylan, eliciting the only worthwhile exposition given to the press at this time. Although Hughes's feature is not widely circulated, Dylan makes it clear what his faith means to him: "You're not talking about some dead man who had a bunch of good ideas and was nailed to a tree."

June 20: *Saved* (FC 36553): "A Satisfied Mind," "Saved," "Covenant Woman," "What Can I Do for You?," "Solid Rock," "Pressing On," "In the Garden," "Saving Grace," "Are You Ready?"

September (23)

Dylan records some songs he has written in Minnesota during the summer at Rundown in Santa Monica. Possibly these songs include a composition called "Her Memory," cowritten with Helena Springs and Ken Moore and copyrighted at this time. Definitely recorded with just piano, guitar accompaniment (by Fred Tackett), and backup vocals (by Jennifer Warnes) is a sublime new work called "Every Grain of Sand." Dylan sends a copy of the demo to Nana Mouskouri, who records it the following year. This version is later released on *The Bootleg Series*. Another version of "Every Grain of Sand," with full band backing, is also cut on the same day.

Late September to Early November

The rehearsals conducted at Rundown Studio, Santa Monica in the weeks leading up to the briefest of fall tours represent perhaps the most intriguing repertoire of Dylan's career. The songs rehearsed include some eight brand-new Dylan compositions, five of which are copyrighted from tapes made at Rundown at this time. All five copyrighted songs are of a very high caliber: "Yonder Comes Sin," "Let's Keep It Between Us," "The Groom's Still Waiting at the Altar," "Every Grain of Sand," and "Caribbean Wind." The other three new songs are "She's Not for You," which Dylan plays to Mark Knopfler in an LA hotel room, "City of Gold," which is subsequently copyrighted from a live tape, and a song called "Makin' a Liar," about which nothing else is known.

The remainder of the songs rehearsed for the tour are divided into three categories: the "religious" songs, "covers," and Dylan oldies. The 14 Dylan oldies rehearsed include five songs not performed at the Warfield shows: "Fourth Time Around" (presumably intended to be acoustic), "Tangled Up in Blue," "Maggie's Farm," "Is Your Love in Vain?," and "Lay, Lady, Lay." Of the other nine songs, the snatch of a rehearsal version of "Mr. Tambourine Man" played in the background to a radio ad for the Warfield shows sounds very different to the single performance at the Warfield. "Don't Think Twice" may have also been planned as an electric performance (although it only appears in acoustic form). "Simple Twist of Fate," "Blowin' in the Wind," "To Ramona," "Just Like a Woman," "Like a Rolling Stone," "Senor," and "It's All Over Now, Baby Blue" all form part of the core set.

Of the religious songs under consideration for the fall '80 shows, a surprising number never make it to the live set. "Coverdown, Breakthrough," "Saving Grace," "Gonna Change My Way of Thinking," "Blessed Is the Name," "Pressing On," "When He Returns," and "No Man Righteous" are all listed as songs rehearsed, along with "Gotta Serve Somebody," "I Believe in You," "When You Gonna Wake Up," "Ain't Gonna Go to Hell," "Precious Angel," "Man Gave Name to All the Animals" (listed as "Animal

Song"), "Slow Train," "Do Right to Me Baby," "Solid Rock," "What Can I Do for You?," "Saved," "In the Garden," and "Covenant Woman," which are all featured at the Warfield.

By far the most intriguing aspect of the song list for this fall tour is the 21 covers itemized. Even discounting the six songs that appear to be intended for the backing singers—"Saved by the Grace of Your Love," "I Apologize," "Falling in Love," "Backstairs," "What About Me?," and "Going to See the King" and the five covers Dylan does perform at the shows—"Couple More Years," "Fever," "We Just Disagree," "Abraham, Martin and John," and "Mary of the Wild Moor"—there are nine covers rehearsed but not attempted at the shows. The omitted songs span every field of popular music. The soul melt down of "Heatwave" and "You Don't Know Me" certainly seem more suited to this band than MOR stalwarts like "Somewhere over the Rainbow" (really!), "If You Could Read My Mind," or Neil Diamond's "Sweet Caroline." If "Willing" would have to wait 10 more years for its Dylan debut, "Sad Songs and Waltzes," "Rainbow Connection," "Goin' On" (?), and "This Night Won't Last Forever" have never been featured in any documented rehearsal, soundcheck, or show since.

October 29

After attending a Dire Straits concert at the Roxy in Los Angeles, Dylan returns with Mark Knopfler to his hotel suite. There Dylan and Knopfler indulge in a jam session, starting with what journalist Michael Oldfield describes as "maybe an old Buddy Holly song." This is followed by the old Presley nugget, "Baby, What You Want Me to Do." Dylan then sings a duet with Clydie King, who has been with him throughout the evening, before performing "Caribbean Wind" in its entirety and the traditional "Jesus Met a Woman at the Well," which leads into a bluesy instrumental featuring Knopfler on lead guitar. "No Man Righteous (No Not One)," "Fever," "A Couple More Years," and "She's Not for You" are all tried, giving way to fragments of songs and loose instrumentals, until a remarkable jam session eventually fizzles out.

November 9, Fox Warfield Theater, San Francisco

Dylan returns to the Warfield Theater for 12 shows. Advertisements on local radio have promised a retrospective show of both old and new songs. As further evidence of a change in emphasis, there is an extensive Dylan photo retrospective in the lobby of the theater. However, the set on opening night is little changed from the evangelical tour, with 10 of the 17 songs performed having been included on the previous tour. The female vocalists also continue to perform six gospel songs before Dylan appears, and he still opens the show with "Gotta Serve Somebody" and "I Believe in You." Then it is "Like a Rolling Stone," to which the audience reacts enthusiastically. However, the stage is then turned over to Carolyn Dennis for one song, followed by "Man Gave Name to All the Animals" and a sensitive "Precious Angel." "Ain't Gonna Go to Hell" is still in the set, although it has been dramatically rewritten. Then it is a semiacoustic version of "Girl from the North Country," featuring just Willie Smith on piano and Dylan on guitar. "Slow Train" closes the first half.

After Regina Peebles sings a song, Dylan and Clydie King duet at the piano on the old Dion hit, "Abraham, Martin and John." This is followed by a new Dylan song, "Let's Keep It Between Us." "Covenant Woman" returns to the set, followed by a lackluster "Solid Rock." "Just Like a Woman," "When You Gonna Wake Up," a spooky version of "Senor," and "In the Garden" conclude the main set. On this first night there is only one encore, "Blowin' in the Wind," after which Dylan suggests the audience come up on stage and perform themselves. After the show, promoter Bill Graham holds an inquest with some members of the audience clearly dissatisfied with this so-called retrospective. Reviews are predictably unfavorable, the *San Francisco Chronicle* condemning the show as "a bore."

November 10, Fox Warfield Theater, San Francisco

After a disappointing opening show, Dylan gives a far better performance on the second night, even if the actual set is little changed. "Precious Angel" is replaced with "What Can I Do for You?," and a powerful "To Ramona" comes before "Girl from the North Country." However, after the "Blowin' in the Wind" encore, Dylan is coaxed back to sing a new song, "City of Gold," which writer Paul Williams describes as "the first song of his in a long time that has a sense of community, a positive vision." Dylan then picks up his acoustic guitar and plays his first solo "Love Minus Zero" since the days of the Rolling Thunder Revue. This 20-song set becomes the basis for the remaining 17 shows of the fall 1980 tour.

November 11, Fox Warfield Theater, San Francisco

Again the audience receives a three-song encore, including a solo "It's All Over Now, Baby Blue." A rewritten "Simple Twist of Fate" replaces "To Ramona" and "What Can I Do for You?" in the main set.

November 12, Fox Warfield Theater, San Francisco

Dylan tries a different arrangement of "Precious Angel." Also attempted is a traditional song, "Mary from the Wild Moor." After "Just Like a Woman,"

Dylan unveils a major new work, probably his finest song in five years. It is entitled "Caribbean Wind." He prefaces it with a story about Leadbelly writing children's songs when he came out of prison that concludes with the observation, "But he didn't change, he was the same man!" This is met with whoops of delight from the audience. As Paul Williams has said of this performance, "He sang [the song] with tremendous feeling and energy despite frustration at the band's inability to follow him."

November 13, Fox Warfield Theater, San Francisco
The set for this night sticks to the November 10 template, except for the acoustic encore, which is "It Ain't Me, Babe," and Carlos Santana guesting on lead guitar for four songs: "Covenant Woman," "Solid Rock," "What Can I Do for You?," and the bluesy, new "The Groom's Still Waiting at the Altar," which includes some vintage Dylan lines.

Mid-November (14?)
Dylan visits his ex-producer Bob Johnston, Maria Muldaur, and Michael Bloomfield, all of whom are residing in Marin County.

November 15, Fox Warfield Theater, San Francisco
The audience gets a real treat tonight as Dylan brings onstage special guest Michael Bloomfield for an exhilarating version of "Like a Rolling Stone," complete with those memorable guitar runs that graced the original version. After a smoking version of "Senor," Bloomfield returns to play lead guitar on "The Groom's Still Waiting at the Altar," dueling with Dylan's singing to superb effect. Sadly this is Bloomfield's last live performance. "Love Minus Zero" makes its last appearance on this tour.

November 16, Fox Warfield Theater, San Francisco
Jerry Garcia is a surprise guest, playing guitar from "To Ramona" right through to "The Groom's Still Waiting at the Altar." "Mary from the Wild Moor" reappears in the set, after "Let's Keep It Between Us," where it stays for the remainder of the tour.

November 17, Fox Warfield Theater, San Francisco
A most unusual show. "I Believe in You" is replaced by both "Simple Twist of Fate" and the first 1980 version of an under-rehearsed "All Along the Watchtower." Tonight also features four other debuts: Dave Mason's "We Just Disagree," which nicely reinforces the message of the previous song, "To Ramona"; a spirited "Just Like Tom Thumb's Blues" (after "Let's Keep It Between Us"); and the best of the 1980 covers, Shel Silverstein's "A Couple More Years." Finally, the acoustic encore is "Don't Think Twice, It's All Right."

November 18, Fox Warfield Theater, San Francisco
Paul Vincent, from Bay Area radio station KMEL, goes backstage before the show to interview Dylan. It is a good interview, Dylan insisting at one point that, "this is a stage show we're doing, it's not a salvation ceremony." Vincent tries to get him to talk about his new songs and what direction he sees

himself going in. Dylan, though, is reluctant to talk on this subject. "All Along the Watchtower" remains in the set, although placed after "Man Gave Names to All the Animals." The show also features a Dylan/King piano duet on the contemporary Christian ballad, "Rise Again," and the only version of "Do Right to Me Baby" performed on this tour. By this point in his Warfield residency, Dylan has become quite talkative on stage, although he refrains from preaching at the audience. Before "Slow Train," Dylan relates a most peculiar tale about being stranded on a beach during one of his stays with Joan Baez at Carmel in the early '60s, and nearly drowning when he gets stuck in an underwater cave with the tide coming in.

November 19, Fox Warfield Theater, San Francisco

Dylan is interviewed by Robert Hilburn in his hotel room before tonight's concert. The interview is mainly concerned with how Dylan became a born-again Christian. Hilburn is clearly one of the few journalists with whom Dylan is prepared to discuss his conversion. Dylan and the band soundcheck at the Warfield in the afternoon, running through two songs: "Rise Again" and "Saved."

• Again a most unusual set: "We Just Disagree" replaces "Man Gave Names to All the Animals," which in turn supplants "Slow Train." "A Couple More Years" and "Nobody's Fault But Mine," the latter sung by tonight's guest, Maria Muldaur, replace "Abraham, Martin and John" and "Let's Keep It Between Us." At the close of the show, there is a rare performance of "Saved." "Covenant Woman" makes its last appearance on this tour.

November 21, Fox Warfield Theater, San Francisco

Tonight's show includes "Just Like Tom Thumb's Blues." Dylan is interviewed on the telephone by Erneste Bladden for San Diego's KPRI-FM radio station.

November 22, Fox Warfield Theater, San Francisco

Dylan delivers one of his finest shows at the end of an historic Warfield residency, with a 24-song set. Between "Simple Twist of Fate" and "Girl from the North Country" he sings, in Paul Williams's words, "one of the true high points of these shows . . . a knock-'em-dead rendition of Little Willie John's "Fever." The song is prefaced by a rap in which Dylan tells of how he heard the song when he was 12 years old in a bingo parlor in Detroit. After "Abraham, Martin and John," Dylan and Clydie King duet on "Rise Again," now with the backing of the band rather than as the intimate piano duet given on the 18th. This arrangement is retained for the remaining shows.

After "Senor" there is one more surprise guest, Roger McGuinn. As a gesture, the band plays the Byrds's distinctive introduction to "Mr. Tambourine Man" before Dylan and McGuinn trade verses in a one-off version of the song perhaps both men are best remembered for. Dylan and McGuinn then revive the spirit of the Rolling Thunder Revue with the only 1980 version of "Knockin' on Heaven's Door." Dylan closes the set with "In the Garden." For the encores, the acoustic song is "It Ain't Me, Babe." But this time it does not conclude the show. The band rejoins Dylan for the first electric

1980

version of "A Hard Rain's a-Gonna Fall" since the Rolling Thunder Revue, proceeding at a somewhat more stately pace than the manic 1975 arrangement.

November 24, Community Center, Tucson, AZ

November 26, Golden Hall, San Diego, CA

Includes the last live version of "The Groom's Still Waiting at the Altar."

November 29–30, Paramount Northwest Theater, Seattle, WA

The first night includes the second and last "Saved" of the tour. The second night includes "Fever" and "Just Like Tom Thumb's Blues." Instead of an acoustic encore, Dylan and the band perform the new arrangement of "A Hard Rain's a-Gonna Fall."

December 2, The Salem Armory, Salem, OR

"A Hard Rain's a-Gonna Fall" and "Like a Rolling Stone" swap positions in the set.

December 3, Paramount Theater, Portland, OR

A 26-song set includes twelve songs not played on the first night of the tour, including "It's Alright, Ma," a second solo encore, and a lovely "A Couple More Years." "Senor" is dedicated to a lady named Victoria, whom Dylan says he met in Mexico in 1972.

December 4, Paramount Theater, Portland, OR

Dylan concludes one of his finest tours with a 25-song set, which includes "Just Like Tom Thumb's Blues" and a version of "To Ramona" featuring California bluegrasser David Grisman on mandolin. The tour ends with a five-song encore: "Blowin' in the Wind," "City of Gold," "Don't Think Twice, It's All Right," "It's Alright, Ma,"and "A Hard Rain's a-Gonna Fall."

December 8: John Lennon is assassinated by Mark Chapman outside the Dakota building in New York, shortly after midnight, as he returns from a recording session.

1981

January 8

Dylan is sighted on Bleeker Street in New York, possibly after visiting Yoko Ono.

March 11

At some point in March, Dylan begins working on arrangements of his new songs for impending album sessions. Today's session at Rundown involves the usual touring band. Dylan tries out "Shot of Love," which is very rough, with a long workout on the chorus, and "You Changed My Life," which seems more worked out, although initially Dylan sings the song as a duet with one of the female vocalists, before reverting to a solo vocal.

Late March

A session at Rundown finds Dylan running down mostly instrumental versions of new songs like "Heart of Mine," "Every Grain of Sand," "Yes Sir, No Sir," and "Is It Worth It?" Regina Peebles sings a couple of songs, "Please Be Patient with Me" and Dylan's own "No Man Righteous (No Not One)." Dylan and Clydie King also work on an arrangement of "Let's Begin."

• Dylan conducts various sessions at Rundown and assorted small-time LA studios, working on new songs like "Every Grain of Sand," "Need a Woman," "Angelina," "The Groom's Still Waiting at the Altar," and "In the Summertime." Also recorded at this time are several songs later copyrighted but absent from subsequent *Shot of Love* sessions: "Almost Persuaded," something identified simply as "Tune After Almost," "Rockin' Boat," "Borrowed Time," "I Want You to Know I Love You," "Wait and See," and an instrumental called "Gonna Love Her Anyway."

March 31

At what may be considered the first *Shot of Love* session, Dylan and assorted favorites convene at Studio 55 in LA. Dylan's intention is to record "Caribbean Wind" with Jimmy Iovine producing. Aside from his usual band, Dylan has asked the likes of guitarist Steve Ripley, keyboardist Carl Pickhardt, multi-instrumentalists David Mansfield and Stephen Soles from the Rolling Thunder bands, and Bobbye Hall from the 1978 band to attend the session. Despite several takes of "Caribbean Wind," the session does not go well. At one point, Dylan suggests they record "White Christmas."

April 2

Dylan continues to experiment with various studios in Los Angeles. Today's session is at United Western Studio A. There are several attempts at the riff-driven "Ah Ah Ah Ah," the equally oblique "Yes Sir, No Sir," a nice bluesy original called "Fur Slippers," and the Everlys's "Let It Be Me," performed sensitively by Dylan and the band. Also rumored to have been recorded at one of the early April sessions is a song called "The King Is on the Throne."

Early April

Further sessions, possibly at United Western, result in three vocal tracks, "Child to Me," "Wind Blowin' on the Water," and "All the Way Down," and a whole series of instrumentals, copyrighted under the titles: "My Oriental Home," "It's All Dangerous to Me," "More to This than Meets the Eye," "Straw Hat," an instrumental calypso, "Walking on Eggs," "Well Water," and "All the Way."

April 6

Dylan records a version of "Shot of Love," presumably at Rundown Studios.

April 7

Dissatisfied with the results of the March 31 session, Dylan returns to "Caribbean Wind," now on its fourth set of lyrics. This lame version of a once-great song probably derives from Rundown. It appears on the *Biograph* set. Possibly also recorded on the sixth or the seventh are versions of "Let's Keep It Between Us" and "She's Not for You."

April 23

One of the most confusing sessions from this rather bewildering period occurs at Rundown Studio (although *The Bootleg Series* credits this session to Clover). Listed on a Rundown tape box are three songs almost certainly attempted on this date: "Trouble," "Magic," and "Don't Ever Take Yourself Away." Also possibly attempted at this session is a song called "Be Careful." Definitely recorded on this day are an instrumental version of "Heart of Mine," "You Changed My Life" (which appears on *The Bootleg Series*), "Shot of Love," "Mystery Train," "Half as Much," "The Groom's Still Waiting at the Altar," and "Dead Man, Dead Man." None of these versions appear on *Shot of Love*.

Late April

Dylan continues to work on/record songs at Rundown Studio with his regular band. Some of these basic tracks will end up misattributed to Clover Studios. One of the songs cut at Rundown is with legendary rock & roll producer "Bumps" Blackwell, the title track that ends up on *Shot of Love*. Also recorded at Rundown are versions of "Watered Down Love" and "Property of Jesus." Possibly also recorded at these sessions, according to one list made at Rundown, are a whole series of "lost" songs from Dylan's gospel period: "Ain't Gonna Go To Hell," "Blessed Is the Name," "City of Gold," "Ye Shall Be Changed," "I Will Love Him," "Yonder Comes Sin," and "Stand by Faith."

Early to Mid-May (4–11?)

After a month of sporadic work on *Shot of Love,* Dylan finally gets down to the matter at hand at Clover Studios, cutting all but two songs for *Shot of Love* in eight to 10 days, with Chuck Plotkin producing and Toby Scott engineering. Aside from the likes of "Property of Jesus," "Lenny Bruce," "Watered Down Love" (listed on the reels as "Pure Love") from which a verse has been cut on the official version, "Dead Man, Dead Man," "In the Summertime" (an extended harmonica break has been faded 40 seconds too soon on the album), "Trouble," and the sublime "Every Grain of Sand," there are at least six other songs cut at Clover. Two are covers recut at these sessions, "Let It Be Me" and "Mystery Train." Although neither seems to have been short-listed for the album, this slightly off-key "Let It Be Me" appears as a European b-side to "Heart of Mine." The version of "Heart of Mine" recorded at Clover was on a test sequence for the album and has much to recommend it. Also under serious consideration was a stomping version of "The Groom's Still Waiting at the Altar" that would finally appear as the US b-side to "Heart of Mine" (US airplay would eventually lead to its inclusion on the reissued *Shot of Love*). The epic "Angelina" is attempted as both a full-blooded band performance and in a more muted, stately guise. The latter arrangement appears on *The Bootleg Series,* along with the inconsequential "Need a Woman," originally recorded with at least two different sets of lyrics.

Late May

Although Plotkin and Scott are in the throes of mixing and sequencing *Shot of Love,* Dylan cannot resist recutting one track with his old friends Ringo Starr and Ron Wood (presumably at Rundown). A makeshift band comprising Keltner, Clydie King on second vocal, Donald "Duck" Dunn on bass, and Willie Smith on organ help to make proceedings a tad less ramshackle, although the resultant version of "Heart of Mine" still sounds a mess o' the blues.

Late May to Early June

Rehearsals for a major European tour take place at Rundown Studios. Dylan and the musicians now know each other so well that the band is game for pretty much anything Dylan wishes to try. Evidence of this can be found in the list of provisional songs for the tour that divides the shows into five sections: first main set; Dylan/King duet(s); second main set; acoustic encore; band encore(s). The first main set contains little in the way of surprises except for something called "I Don't Care," "Saving Grace" (which never appears in 1981), and "It's Allright Ma," which only ever appears in acoustic guise. The other songs in this set are "Man Gave Name to All the Animals," "Mr. Jones" (i.e., "Ballad of a Thin Man"), "City of Gold," "We Just Disagree," "Just Like a Woman," "Senor," "Like a Rolling Stone," "What Can I Do for You?," "When You Gonna Wake Up," "Shot of Love," "Heart of Mine," "All Along the Watchtower," "Solid Rock," "I Believe in You," "To Ramona," and "I Don't Believe You."

Not surprisingly, the options listed for the Dylan/Clydie King slot are considerably more intriguing. Only one of the 11 "alternates" ever appears in the 1981 set, and "Let It Be Me" hardly qualifies as a perennial. The other 10 are "Leaving It All Up to You," "Dearest," "Cheating Heart," "Big River," "Voyez Con Dios" (surely not), "Guess Things Happen That Way," "Mansion Builder," "I Ain't Never," "Slowly" (?), and "Smoke Gets in Your Eyes."

The selection for the second main set, although not quite as startling, does contain two remarkable suggestions, "Seven Days" (!) and Woody Guthrie's "Pastures of Plenty." "Trouble" also fails to appear in the 1981 repertoire. One of the songs is listed as "instrumental D" (presumably the key), although whether this is the instrumental performed in Basle (see July 23) is not known. The other songs—"Gotta Serve Somebody," "Rise Again," "In the Garden," "Lenny Bruce," "Simple Twist of Fate," "Masters of War," and "I'll Be Your Baby Tonight"—all make at least one live appearance in 1981.

The five acoustic encores contain just one surprise, "Song to Woody," although "Girl from the North Country" is only performed in the same piano/guitar arrangement as the late '80 shows. "Love Minus Zero/No Limit," "It's All Over Now, Baby Blue," and "It Ain't Me Babe" all appear acoustically on a regular basis in 1981.

Of the seven electric encore selections, only two appear in this slot, "Knockin' on Heaven's Door" and "Blowin' in the Wind," although "Mr. Tambourine Man," "All Along the Watchtower," "Just Like a Woman," "A Hard Rain's a-Gonna Fall," and "Forever Young" all appear with full electric arrangements in the main set(s).

Although the 1981 rehearsals do not match the mouth-watering prospect of (taped) fall 1980 rehearsals, a tape of the '81 Dylan/King duets would certainly be a welcome addition to the man's circulating work. Given the sheer number of songs rehearsed, it is a disappointment that the sets soon settle into a rigid formation in Europe.

June 10, Poplar Creek Music Theater, Chicago, IL

Dylan starts his first European tour in three years with four warm-up shows in the United States. He opens with the same four songs that opened the late 1980 shows, "Gotta Serve Somebody," "I Believe in You," "Like a Rolling Stone," and "Man Gave Names to All the Animals." Then it's a raucous "Maggie's Farm," the lovely fall 1980 arrangement of "Simple Twist of Fate," and an atmospheric "Ballad of a Thin Man," Dylan singing the first verse with just piano backing, before the whole band crash in. The 1980 arrangement of "Girl from the North Country" is retained, followed by a new song, "Dead Man, Dead Man." After one song by Carolyn Dennis, Dylan and Clydie King duet on "Abraham, Martin and John." Dylan introduces another new song, a eulogy for "Lenny Bruce." "Covenant Woman" makes a rare 1981 appearance, followed by "Solid Rock" and "Just Like a Woman." The third song from *Shot of Love* is an uptempo "Watered Down Love," featuring the verse omitted from the album. The last four songs of the main set include

"Forever Young," augmented by an effective harmonica solo, along with "What Can I Do for You?" (minus harmonica), "When You Gonna Wake Up," and "In the Garden." "City of Gold" has been dropped from the set, so the encore comprises just "Blowin' in the Wind" and one solo song, on this occasion "It's All Over Now, Baby Blue."

June 11, Pine Knob Music Theater, Clarkston, MI
Three songs are added to the set. After "Dead Man, Dead Man," Dylan interpolates "We Just Disagree" and "Slow Train," and then, before "In the Garden," a rocked-up "Masters of War," a la 1978, is born again. "It Ain't Me, Babe" is the solo encore.

June 12
Before his third warm-up show in the States, Dylan gives three telephone interviews to publicize concerts on his European tour. Two are for English radio: one with Paul Gambicinni for BBC Radio One, the other with Tim Blackmore for London's Capital Radio. The third is with Yves Bigot for France's "Europe #1" radio station. The interviews are all fairly similar in content, with questions about Dylan's band, his choice of material for the forthcoming tour, and his new album, *Shot of Love.*

June 12, Pine Knob Music Theater, Clarkston
Two remnants from the late 1980 shows make their only 1981 appearances: "Fever" and "Rise Again." "Mary from the Wild Moor" is performed in place of "Abraham, Martin and John." "Don't Think Twice, It's All Right" is the solo encore.

June 14, Merriweather Post Pavilion, Columbia, MD
Includes "Just Like Tom Thumb's Blues."

June 20
A soundcheck at the Stade Municipal Des Minimes in Tolouse is scheduled for 7 PM.

June 21, Stade Municipal Des Minimes, Tolouse, France
"Knockin' on Heaven's Door" makes its first appearance on the tour, before "Slow Train." Also introduced into the set is "Mr. Tambourine Man," slotted in after "Lenny Bruce." Clydie King is not at this concert, so there is no Dylan/King duet at the beginning of the second half. French TV station Antenne II broadcasts clips of "Just Like a Woman," "Watered Down Love," and "Solid Rock" from the show.

June 23, Stade Yves-du-Mano, Colombes, France
While riot police engage with bottle-throwing youths outside the stadium, Dylan is singing an impassioned "I Believe in You." Clydie King has rejoined the band, dueting with Dylan on "Let It Be Me." The London *Times* reviewer writes that Dylan's performance "reached rare heights of power and authority."

June 24
Dylan and his band arrive in London, staying at the White House Hotel in Regent's Park.

June 25
Dylan and the band are scheduled to soundcheck at Earl's Court at 7 PM.

June 26, Earls Court, London
Dylan returns to the scene of his great triumph three years earlier. The opening night contains few real surprises, although Dylan does lead the band through a full electric arrangement of the English folk standard "Barbara Allen" after "Abraham, Martin and John." However, the remainder of the second half is very lackluster. Not surprisingly, the reviews on opening night are mixed: Philip Norman in the *Sunday Times* compares Dylan's show unfavorably with the limp Bruce Springsteen Wembley show the previous month, which Mr. Norman informs us "altered forever the principles of rock performance." The *New Musical Express* headline, "Bored Again," disguises a sensible review, whereas *Sounds* reviewer Hugh Fielder admits that "Dylan's voice was in great shape." In *Melody Maker,* Patrick Humphries feels uncomfortable, but can't tell us why.

June 27, Earls Court, London
Dylan takes to the stage in a much better mood. He stalks the front of the stage while the band plays the introduction to "Gotta Serve Somebody." During "Ballad of a Thin Man," he repeatedly punches the air as if directing some great parade. He also plays a one-off version of "I Don't Believe You," which starts off effectively but runs out of steam halfway through. At the beginning of the second half, Dylan and Clydie King sing the old Jimmy Webb song, "Let's Begin," which becomes their regular '81 duet. At the end of the show, after a marvelous "It's All Over Now, Baby Blue," the crowd will not allow Dylan to leave, and he calls the band back for a spirited version of "Knockin' on Heaven's Door," which remains as final encore for the remainder of 1981.

June 28, Earls Court, London
After a standard first half, Dylan and Clydie King open the second half with the last live performance of "Mary from the Wild Moor," followed by the first "All Along the Watchtower" of 1981 and "In the Summertime," a song from the new album that works particularly well in concert. The acoustic encore is "It's Alright, Ma."

June 29, Earls Court, London
Includes the only performance of "Love Minus Zero" on the 1981 European tour.

June 30, Earls Court, London
Includes a final "Abraham, Martin and John" and a rare performance of "Just Like

Tom Thumb's Blues." Throughout the show, Dylan and the band are clearly having difficulty with the stage monitors.

July 1, Earls Court, London
One of Dylan's greatest performances, this 26-song set includes live debuts for "Shot of Love" and "Heart of Mine," the latter with Dylan on organ. He also attempts "Here Comes the Sun," but abandons it when he realizes he knows few of the words, seguing into "Girl from the North Country." The solo encore is once again "It's Alright, Ma."

July 2
Dave Herman interviews Dylan for New York's WNEW radio station. The interview lasts 45 minutes, with Dylan doodling on the guitar throughout. CBS subsequently issues the interview as a promotional album, titled *The London Interview,* ostensibly to promote *Shot of Love.*

• A report in the *New York Post* says Albert Grossman is suing Dylan for more than a million dollars. Dylan has 30 days to answer the suit, which presumably explains his haste to return to the States at the end of the European tour.

July 3
Dylan leaves London by bus at 3 PM, arriving at Penns Hall Hotel in Walmley, Sutton Coldfield, by early evening. Dylan's bus may have stopped in Stratford-upon-Avon for a couple of hours on the way to Birmingham. A third show in Birmingham on the third had originally been penciled in but there is not sufficient demand and so Dylan gets a two-day break between shows.

July 4, National Exhibition Centre, Birmingham, England
The first show offers a surprise: for the first time in three years (and over a hundred shows), Dylan does not open tonight's concert with "Gotta Serve Somebody," preferring to announce himself with "Saved." "Barbara Allen" is included for the second and last time.

July 5, National Exhibition Centre, Birmingham, England
At the soundcheck for the second show, Dylan and the female vocalists try out a version of the Everly Brothers's "Bye Bye Love." At the concert, Dylan's voice is clearly in bad shape, reflected in the set being four songs shorter than the previous night. It does, however, include the only 1981 version of "City of Gold," in place of "Blowin' in the Wind."

July 6
Dylan and the band leave the Penns Hall Hotel at noon.

July 7
Arriving at Stockholm Airport at 11:35 PM on the sixth, Dylan checks into the Hotel Sheraton, Stockholm in the early hours of the seventh. On the evening of the seventh, between 9:30 and 10:30 PM, a Swedish TV station broadcasts a program on Dylan that includes Michael Wicke performing "It's

All Over Now, Baby Blue" in Swedish. Dylan refers to this rendition at the following night's show, saying he hopes he can do the song as well.

July 8, Johanneshovs Isstadion, Stockholm, Sweden
Dylan opens his set with two solo songs, the first live "She Belongs to Me" since 1974 and an acoustic "The Times They Are a-Changin'."

July 9–10, Drammenhalle, Drammen, Norway
On the first night, Dylan includes "The Times They Are a-Changin'," this time with full band backing, before "Slow Train." Also featured is a new song Dylan has written during his stay in Oslo, "Jesus Is the One."

Dylan opens the second show with "The Times They Are a-Changin'," the band joining in part way through. "Jesus Is the One" is again included, as is "It Ain't Me, Babe," which now becomes the regular solo encore.

July 12, Brondbyhallen, Copenhagen, Denmark
For the last time, Dylan opens with a solo song. This time it is "Blowin' in the Wind," which he also performs as a first encore with the band.

July 13
Having seen a fabricated interview in a Danish paper, Dylan calls a press conference with just four hours notice at the Kurhaus Hotel in Travemunde. The conference starts at 11 PM. Dylan seems prepared to discuss most subjects, confessing that *Self Portrait* "was a joke"; and that he "got a kick out of . . . play(ing) nothing but new songs" at the Warfield in 1979.

July 14, Freilichttheater, Bad Segeberg, W. Germany
On the morning of the 14th, Dylan and members of the band visit Bad Segeburg's famous stalactite caves.
• "Saved" now replaces "Gotta Serve Somebody" as the opening song. An acoustic "The Times They Are a-Changin'" opens the second half.

July 15, Freilichttheater, Bad Segeberg, W. Germany
An electric "The Times They Are a-Changin'" opens the show.

July 17, Freilichtbuhne Goarhausen, Loreley, W. Germany
The band version of "The Times They Are a-Changin'" opens the second half of the show.

July 18, Eisstadion, Mannheim, W. Germany
"It's All Over Now, Baby Blue" makes its last appearance on the European tour, as does "Dead Man, Dead Man." Dylan plays to an extremely enthusiastic crowd on one of his favorite nights of the tour.

July 19–20, Olympiahalle, Munich, W. Germany
"Shot of Love" becomes a regular feature of the set, the penultimate song in the first half of the show. Neil Spencer, editor of *New Musical Express,* having interviewed Dylan briefly backstage before his first Munich show, obtains a full interview on the second night. It takes place in Dylan's fourth-floor hotel suite. Spencer's interview technique is very good. He gets Dylan

to talk about "the politics of sin," two unreleased songs ("Angelina" and "Caribbean Wind"), and even the Second Coming. Sadly, the interview, although worthwhile, is not as extensive as one would have liked.

July 21, Stadthalle, Vienna, Austria
The opening song is a unique medley of "Saved" and "Gotta Serve Somebody."

July 22
Dylan is briefly interviewed while he is signing autographs outside his hotel in Vienna. This largely inconsequential interview is later included in an Austrian TV special on Dylan, *Die Zeit Vergeht.*

July 23, Jacobshalle, Basel, Switzerland
Between "Mr. Tambourine Man" and "Solid Rock," Dylan and the band play an unidentifiable instrumental. Dylan says hello to Bridgette Bardot during the concert, which has led to the suggestion that it is a Bardot movie theme that they are playing. It may also be the "instrumental D" listed in the tour rehearsals (see Late May to Early June 1981).

July 25, Parc des Sports, Avignon, France
As Dylan concludes his moderately successful European tour, tragedy strikes with two deaths in the crowd. "Saved" is seconds old when the stage is shrouded in darkness as a member of the crowd falls onto the electrical cables. In the confusion a girl falls from a wall. Dylan and the band are forced to improvise some acoustic rhythms on stage until power is finally restored, after which Dylan performs a 25-song set to an enthusiastic crowd. The set includes five songs from *Shot of Love:* "In the Summertime," "Shot of Love," "Lenny Bruce," "Watered Down Love," and "Heart of Mine."

July 26
Dylan returns to the States, flying from Paris's Charles de Gaulle Airport.

August
Dylan is on his farm in Laredo, MN, where he is allegedly writing new songs.

> August 12: *Shot of Love* (TC 37496): "Shot of Love," "Heart of Mine," "Property of Jesus," "Lenny Bruce," "Watered Down Love," "Dead Man, Dead Man," "In the Summertime," "Trouble," "Every Grain of Sand"

Late August to Early September
Dylan is rumored to have recorded at United Western Studios in Los Angeles at around this time. Since no details have emerged regarding what material may have been taped, this source may well have misattributed the date of the April sessions.

Early October
Rehearsals start at Rundown Studios for the American leg of the 1981 tour.

Carolyn Dennis has left the tour band, as has Willie Smith. Drafted in on keyboards is Al Kooper. Dylan also decides to experiment with a second drummer and so technician Arthur Rosato is assigned the task of embellishing Keltner on certain songs.

• Having attended a party for the Rolling Stones at the China Club in Los Angeles, Dylan allegedly cuts some songs in Malibu with Ron Wood and Keith Richards during the West Coast leg of the Stones's 1981 tour.

October 15
Dylan, the band, and crew fly from Los Angeles to Milwaukee on United Airlines, leaving LA at 12:15 PM and arriving in Milwaukee shortly after 5 PM.

October 16–17, Mecca Auditorium, Milwaukee, WI
As Dylan takes to the road for the American leg of his 1981 tour, "Gotta Serve Somebody" has returned to the set as its regular opener. There are few surprises in the set, and Dylan's voice is in far worse shape than during the European shows. The only real surprise on this first night is the replacement of Carolyn Dennis's solo spot, after "Like a Rolling Stone," with a nice version of "I Want You." The only female vocalist's spot comes after "Just Like a Woman" and is followed by "A Hard Rain's a-Gonna Fall," "Watered Down Love," and "Senor." "Let's Begin" makes one of only two appearances on this leg of the tour, as does a solo encore of "It's All Over Now, Baby Blue." A new, slowed-down version of "Solid Rock" makes for one of Dylan's worst ever rearrangements, yet remains a regular feature of the tour. The one unique performance at this show is "Blowin' in the Wind," on which Dylan sings the whole song, rather than having the female vocalists sing the first verse before he takes over.

• The second night is a more representative set than the one given on the first night. The second half opens with "The Times They Are a-Changin'," followed by "A Hard Rain's a-Gonna Fall" and "Slow Train." Dylan and Clydie King duet on a ragged version of "It's All in the Game." After "Just Like a Woman," Dylan seems to respond to a request in the audience, launching into an old Roscoe Gordon song, "Just Want a Little Bit." "Senor" follows, in the same position as the late 1980 shows. "It Ain't Me, Babe" is the solo encore, and remains the regular choice throughout this leg of the tour. Dylan is briefly interviewed after the show in his Wisconsin hotel by Divina Infusino of the *Milwaukee Journal.* He has little to say and, in fact, does not grant any more interviews for the remainder of the tour. It is July 1983 before he speaks to the press again.

October 18, Dane County Coliseum, Madison, WI
Includes "Simple Twist of Fate," which features yet another new set of lyrics.

October 19, Holiday Star Theater, Merriville, IN
Includes the only "We Just Disagree" of the American leg. For the last encore, "Knockin' on Heaven's Door" is replaced by Chuck Berry's "No Money Down," sung by Dylan's wheelchair-bound friend Larry Kegan. Dylan plays saxophone alongside Kegan.

October 21, Orpheum Theater, Boston, MA

Again Dylan plays sax while Larry Kegan sings "No Money Down" as the final encore.

October 23, The Spectrum, Philadelphia, PA

"Senor" makes its last regular appearance on the tour.

October 24, Penn State University Recreation Hall, University Park, PA

"In the Summertime," "Slow Train," and "It's All in the Game" all make their last regular appearances on the fall US tour.

October 25, Stabler Hall, Lehigh University, Bethlehem, PA

A delightful honky-tonk version of "I'll Be Your Baby Tonight" is introduced into the set in place of "In the Summertime." "Watered Down Love" replaces "Slow Train." "It's Allright, Ma" becomes a regular solo encore. Before "Knockin' on Heaven's Door," Dylan and the female vocalists sing "Happy Birthday" for photographer and filmmaker Howard Alk, who has been with the crew throughout, filming the shows and certain off-stage scenes.

October 27, Brendan T. Byrne Sports Arena, East Rutherford, NJ

"Let's Begin" makes its last live appearance. "Dead Man, Dead Man" is reintroduced into the set. *The New York Times* review of this show refers to Dylan as "alternately thrilling, exasperating and impenetrable," concluding that it was "a fascinating performance by a magnetic renegade."

October 29, Maple Leaf Gardens, Toronto, Ontario

Includes a Dylan/King duet on "Let It Be Me."

October 30, Montreal Forum, Montreal, Quebec

Dylan again includes "Let It Be Me." From this point in the tour, Dylan starts to perform two solo encores, which tend to be "It Ain't Me, Babe" and "It's Alright, Ma."

October 31, Kitchener Arena, Kitchener, Ontario

In a five-song encore, "Blowin' in the Wind" is followed by a one-off "Don't Think Twice, It's All Right" and "It's Alright, Ma," before the band returns for the only 1981 performance of "Are You Ready?"

November 2, Civic Center, Ottawa, Ontario

"Saved" makes its only appearance on the North American tour, in place of "Gotta Serve Somebody." On the encore, Dylan is about to play a second solo song when he stops, calls the band back onstage, and plays "Jesus Is the One," concluding the show with the ubiquitous "Knockin' on Heaven's Door."

November 4–5, Music Hall, Cincinnati, OH

On the first night, "Senor" and "It's All in the Game" reappear, along with the now-forsaken "When He Returns." The second night brings "It's All Over Now, Baby Blue" as the first solo encore. "Shot of Love" is reintroduced into the set, after "Watered Down Love."

November 6, Elliot Hall of Music, Purdue University, West Lafayette, IN

November 7–8, Hill Auditorium, Ann Arbor, MI
On the 8th, "In the Summertime" and "Senor" are performed for the last time in 1981.

November 10, Saenger Theater, New Orleans, LA
The "Heart of Mine" recorded at the first show is subsequently issued on *Biograph.* The last "Dead Man, Dead Man" of 1981 is performed, and is also belatedly released, as a b-side to the 1989 "Everything Is Broken" single. The entire first show is recorded for a possible official live album, although the bulk of the concert remains unreleased, even a new song, given its only live performance at this show, "Thief on the Cross." From this show until the Sunrise concert, the second drummer is Bruce Gary, who has recently left the Knack.

November 11, Saenger Theater, New Orleans, LA
"Mr. Tambourine Man" makes its last 1981 appearance. During their two days in New Orleans, Dylan and Alk film the tour musicians playing in the streets of the town.

November 12, The Summit, Houston, TX
"The Lonesome Death of Hattie Carroll" replaces "I Want You" in the set. "Simple Twist of Fate" includes a rare harmonica solo, blasting over the top of Kooper's organ arpeggio. It is this song that prompted the reviewer for the *Fort Worth Star* to credit Dylan with, "the phrasing mastery of a jazz singer."

November 14, Municipal Auditorium, Nashville, TN

November 15, Fox Theatre, Atlanta, GA
"Girl from the North Country" features some more of Dylan's harmonica work.

November 16, Fox Theatre, Atlanta, GA
The second night includes the last performance of "It's All in the Game."

November 19–20, Sunrise Musical Theater, Sunrise, FL
On the 20th, after "Girl from the North Country," the only "Just Like Tom Thumb's Blues" of the American tour is played. This is Bruce Gary's last show.

November 21, Civic Center Theatre, Lakeland, FL
The original intention had been to finish the tour in Tallahassee on the 22nd. However, poor ticket sales again lead to a change of plans and makes this

the last show. This is one of Dylan's longest concerts, a 28-song set that includes a six-song encore. The first surprise is a unique harmonica solo introduced into "I Believe in You." "The Lonesome Death of Hattie Carroll" is replaced by "Simple Twist of Fate." After "Ballad of a Thin Man," Dylan sings the long-awaited live debut of "Every Grain of Sand." Although a pleasant-enough rendition, it is sadly lacking the two lovely harmonica solos that are so effective on the official release. After a straightforward second half and the statutory "Blowin' in the Wind" encore, Dylan plays three solo encores: "Love Minus Zero," "It's Alright Ma," and "It Ain't Me, Babe." The band then returns for a second US performance of "Jesus Is the One," before "Knockin' on Heaven's Door" concludes a tour that has delivered little of the promise of the late 1980 shows, or indeed the first few European concerts. Often during the American shows, Dylan's delivery is little more than perfunctory, possibly suggesting that he can no longer push his voice through two-hour shows on lengthy tours. After four years of continuous touring, this is to be Dylan's last concert for three years, except for two brief guest appearances.

Early December
Dylan records some new songs at Rundown Studios, with Bruce Gary on drums. According to Gary, one of the songs is a primitive version of "Jokerman." There is speculation in the press during the winter of 1982 that Dylan has been recording with Bruce Gary and Al Kooper, but this is Gary's only studio recording with Dylan.

December 8
Dylan is working at Rundown Studios in Santa Monica on the first anniversary of John Lennon's death.

1982

January 1
Howard Alk, a longstanding collaborator and friend of Dylan's, is found dead at Rundown Studios in Santa Monica. He had apparently taken his own life.

February
At Rundown Studios, Allen Ginsberg records two songs, with Dylan on bass, Jim Keltner on drums, Steven Taylor on guitar, and an unknown organist. The tracks are "Do the Meditation," of which at least two takes are recorded, and "Airplane Blues."

Early March
Dylan and Allen Ginsberg work on some song lyrics together at Dylan's house in Malibu.

March 15
Dylan is inducted into the Songwriters Hall of Fame at its annual dinner at the Hilton Hotel in New York. In his brief acceptance speech he professes, "I think this is pretty amazing really, because I can't read or write a note of music." Later, when briefly interviewed by Jane Hansen for NBC News, he claims to only know three chords. His one request is to be photographed with Dinah Shore, there to receive a Lifetime Achievement Award.

March 20
Dylan is in California for the bar mitzvah of one of his sons, presumably Samuel.

Winter to Spring
Dylan is rumored to have recorded some material at this time with Mick Taylor and Jack Bruce. Bruce, though, denies working with Dylan. Possibly some demos may have been recorded with Taylor alone.

May 10
Dylan attends a memorial service for founder of Buddha Records, Neil Bogart, at the Hillside Memorial Chapel in Los Angeles.

June 6, Rose Bowl, Pasadena, CA
Eighty-five thousand people have gathered for a concert and rally in support of the United Nations Special Session on Nuclear Disarmament. The con-

cert is named "Peace Sunday: We Have a Dream." Dylan is a surprise guest during Joan Baez's set, joining her for "With God on Our Side," an old Jimmy Buffet song entitled "Pirate Looks at Forty," and a disastrous "Blowin' in the Wind" in which Baez has to tolerate not only Dylan's idiosyncratic singing but also the fact that he can't remember the words. The performance is professionally filmed in its entirety, but has not been broadcast. After his appearance, Dylan avoids both the reception tent and the performers' area, taking off immediately in a van.

June
Dylan attends one of the Clash's five Hollywood Palladium shows. He is accompanied by T-Bone Burnett. One report suggests that Dylan said he was due to go into the recording studio the following morning.

Summer
Dylan produces at least four songs for Clydie King at Gold Star Studios in Los Angeles. He implies, in an interview with Mikal Gilmore in 1985, that an entire album was recorded: "I've also got a record of just me and Clydie King singing together and it's great, but it doesn't fall into any category that the record company knows how to deal with."

• Dylan visits the small Caribbean island of Anguilla on his boat. During his stay he befriends a local musician, Bankie Banx, and they apparently record a song together called "It's Right." Dylan plays keyboards. The session is at Banx's own home studio.

• During a relaxing summer in Minneapolis, Dylan attends a series of concerts, several with his eldest son, Jesse. They see such acts as the Alley Cats, X Big Joe Turner, the Stray Cats, Kris Kristofferson, Squeeze, Trashmen, Willie and the Bees, and the T.C. (Twin Cities) Jammers.

• Dylan attends at least one session at the Record Plant in Sausalito, CA, during the recording of Van Morrison's *Beautiful Vision* album.

July 28
Keith Green, with whom Dylan recorded in 1980, is killed in a plane crash near Lindale, TX.

August
Elliott Roberts officially becomes Dylan's manager.

August 7
Dylan attends Elvis Costello's post-gig party in Minneapolis, arriving with his sons Jesse and Samuel, plus Larry Kegan and Clydie King.

December 22
Dylan arrives at the home of Frank Zappa and plays him a dozen new songs. He has in mind to ask him to produce his new album.

1983

Mid- to Late January (17–23)
Dylan turns up at the Power Station, where Dire Straits are recording, to ask Mark Knopfler if he would like to produce his new album. Knopfler accepts, and Dylan starts calling round at Knopfler's house to run through some of the material already composed.

January 29
Melody Maker reports that Costello may produce the new Dylan album. However, Costello has already turned the job down because of tour commitments.

Early February
The London *Evening Standard* (February 6) reports that Dylan and Mark Knopfler are in New York choosing musicians to work on Dylan's new album. Musician rehearsals for *Infidels* apparently take place at the Palladium in New York and last a couple of days.

February 16
Dylan attends Bonnie Koloc's set at the Other End in New York then heads across town to the Lone Star Cafe where he joins Levon Helm and Rick Danko on stage during their scheduled set, providing backup vocals and guitar on "Your Cheatin' Heart," "Willie and the Hand Jive," "Blues Stay Away from Me," "Ain't No More Cane," and "Going Down." The whole performance is ragged, reflecting the impromptu nature of Dylan's appearance.

Late February
Dylan sails to Barbados in his boat.

Late Winter
Dylan gives Mark Knopfler some demos, presumably to help him become familiar with some of the songs he intends to record at the *Infidels* sessions. These may well have included a song called "Prison Guard"; Knopfler later told music journalist Bill Flanagan that Dylan had given him a song of that title at this time.

March 17
Dylan attends a concert by Three O'Clock and Peter Case at the Music Machine in Los Angeles.

March 30

The London *Evening Standard* reports that CBS is intending to issue a "five album retrospective" of Dylan's work with "at least ninety minutes of rare and unreleased material." It will be over two-and-a-half years before *Biograph* is finally released.

Spring: *First Blues* by Allen Ginsberg is released, featuring three songs from the 1971 Dylan/Ginsberg session (see November 9, 1971).

April 3

Dylan flies from New York to Los Angeles International Airport, where he allegedly assaults a photographer attempting to take his picture in the arrivals area.

Mid-April

Dylan and Mick Taylor are spotted at Matt Umanov's guitar shop on Bleeker Street. Dylan buys an acoustic guitar.

April 11 to May 8

For the first time in his career, Dylan books a month of sessions to record an album. The sessions will take place at the Power Station in New York, across the way from Sony Studios. Dylan coproduces the album with Mark Knopfler. The band they have devised for the sessions ranks as one of his most inspired gatherings. The rhythm section is Sly Dunbar and Robbie Shakespeare. The two-pronged guitar attack is to be provided by Knopfler and ex-Stones axeman Mick Taylor. Keyboardist Alan Clark has been enlisted from Knopfler's band. The sessions result in 16 original new songs, 14 cover versions, and a couple of instrumentals (copyrighted under the titles, "Dark Groove" and "Don't Fly Unless It's Safe"). The titles of all 14 covers are not known, although apparently they include a perfectly straight version of "Green, Green Grass of Home" and a less-serious rendition of Dire Straits's first hit, "Sultans of Swing." Also recorded are versions of Willie Nelson's "Angel Flying too Close to the Ground," b-side to "Sweetheart Like You," and (two takes of) the MOR standard, "This Was My Love." If such covers offered some light relief from the daily routine, Dylan seems to have applied himself with surprising discipline when cutting the new songs. A tape of Dylan working with the band on "Sweetheart Like You" shows that he is no longer relying on serendipity to get a worthwhile result; the song ends up being recorded by Dylan at least three times. Indeed the *Infidels* sessions have spawned some of Dylan's most important outtakes. Of the eight cuts on the album, "Sweetheart Like You," "Don't Fall Apart on Me Tonight," "Jokerman," and "Union Sundown" all exist in radically different form on Power Station tapes. In the case of "Union Sundown," there is both a prototype for the basic track, with only a dummy vocal, as well as what sounds like a piano demo of the original song, which varies considerably from the released take. Of the eight tracks excluded from the album, five—

"Tell Me," "Someone's Got a Hold of My Heart," "Foot of Pride," "Blind Willie McTell," and "Lord Protect My Child"—appear on *The Bootleg Series,* although alternate versions for three of the five circulate among collectors and, in the case of "Blind Willie McTell" and "Someone's Got a Hold of My Heart," in decidedly superior form. "Foot of Pride" was also apparently attempted with a bossa nova arrangement. "Lord Protect My Child" is identified as take four on the tape. One other *Infidels* outtake has also been released: "Death Is Not the End" appears on *Down in the Groove.* "Julius and Ethel" and "Clean-Cut Kid" both remain unreleased, although Dylan would return to the latter on his next album. At the end of the sessions, Dylan and Knopfler have a falling out about song selection and mixing, resulting in Dylan mixing and sequencing the album himself—with disastrous results.

May
Dylan visits Jacques Levy at his house in New York. He has just completed the sessions for *Infidels* and seems dissatisfied with the results, telling Levy, "If I knew it was going to sound like that, I would have sung it different."

May 19
Dylan appears at the Los Angeles city attorney's office for a hearing concerning the alleged assault of a photographer on April 3.

June
Dylan attends his stepdaughter Maria's college graduation ceremony with Sara in St. Paul, MN.

June 6
New York magazine reports that Dylan has been spending time with a Jewish Hasidic sect known as the Lubavitchers. According to one rabbi, he had been studying at the Lubavitchers' center in Brooklyn. It was widely reported in the summer of 1983 that Dylan had recorded an album of Hasidic songs that was to be released on the Mitzvah record label to raise funds for the Lubavitchers. No evidence has ever been forthcoming.

Early June to July 5
After a short break, Dylan returns to the Power Station to mix *Infidels.* As Knopfler has stated, "He went on and overdubbed certain things, he resang certain things." Full Force, recording with Kurtis Blow at the time, are used on backing vocals on a couple of songs, appearing on the released "Death Is Not the End." "Union Sundown," "Sweetheart Like You," "Don't Fall Apart on Me Tonight," and "Jokerman" all have new Dylan vocals overdubbed. In the case of "Jokerman," the overdubbed vocal contains a whole new set of lyrics. Also given instrumental touchups at these sessions are "Angel Flying Too Close to the Ground," still apparently under consideration for the album, and "I and I." Dylan works very hard with engineer Ian Taylor, trying to come to terms with the technology available. He had, after all, used very few overdubs in his career up to this point.

July 3

As Dylan concludes the mixing of *Infidels,* he is interviewed by Martin Keller for the *Minneapolis City Pages.* The interview is very widely syndicated. After the long period of silence, it is an important article. To his credit, Keller gives Dylan a chance to talk at length; the reporter asks about his Jewish roots, political songs, even reincarnation. At one point, Dylan launches into a long speech about "the purpose of music," and how product is subverting good intentions.

July 6

Infidels is finally mastered, after much mixing and redubbing by Dylan.

July 7

Dylan attends a concert by Stevie Ray Vaughan's band, Double Trouble, at the Manhattan club, First City.

August 26

A report in the English newspaper, *The Sun,* says that Dylan and Sara have been seeing a lot of each other and "that a remarriage is in the cards." It is also reported at the time that Dylan and Sara may be renting an apartment together.

September 19

Dylan is in Jerusalem for the bar mitzvah of his eldest son, Jesse. Photographs of Dylan at the bar mitzvah are widely syndicated. A photograph taken by Sara of him on the hills above Jerusalem later appears as the inner sleeve for *Infidels.*

Early October

In the continuing case with Al Grossman, not only does Dylan provide the usual refutation of charges but also a confused eight-page narrative protesting his innocence. "I didn't do it," he says.

October

Although clearly not intent on an extensive bout of promotional interviews for his most commercial album in four years, Dylan decides to give his second and last interview of 1983 to Robert Hilburn of the *Los Angeles Times.* In it he declares, "I'm not going to release a record until I feel it is worked on properly," an indication of a major change in attitude.

• Dylan films the "Sweetheart Like You" video in Los Angeles, with Carla Olsen from the Textones, Charlie Quintana from the Plugz, Greg Kuenn from Cathedral of Tears, and Clydie King, all miming with the best.

November

Dylan attends a Big Country concert in Los Angeles.

November 1: *Infidels* (QC 38819): "Jokerman," "Sweetheart Like You," "Neighborhood Bully," "License to Kill," "Man of Peace," "Union Sundown," "I and I," "Don't Fall Apart on Me Tonight"

Fall 1983 to Winter 1984

Charlie Quintana of the Los Angeles post-punk band The Plugz travels to Dylan's Malibu home to jam with him for two or three days a week. A report in the English music paper *Sounds* in November 1983 refers to Dylan working with the Plugz. Although bassist Tony Marisco and guitarist Steve Hufsteter both play on some of the sessions, the leader of the Plugz, Tito Larriva, does not attend any of them. Other musicians who briefly participate include bassists Jeff Eyrich and Greg Sutton, and guitarist Mick Taylor, who had made such a sterling contribution on *Infidels*. Charlie Sexton also plays on some sessions at this time. Some demos featuring Sexton and Quintana were played to Jules Shear of Jules and the Polar Bears in the fall of 1984.

J. J. Holliday, then going under the name Justin Justing, finally is drafted in on guitar, and they get down to some regular rehearsals. Clydie King would also join Dylan on a regular basis. There is a break for Christmas, but sessions resume in January. An extant recording of one of the rehearsals, probably from early March 1984, features Dylan showing them the Inkspots's "We Three" on guitar, talking about recording "Heart of Mine," and running down "Don't Start Me Talkin'," "Lost on the River," "We Three," "Jokerman," an instrumental called "Just One Look," "Back in My Arms Again," "Johnny Too Bad," "Saved," and "A Woman Will Give You the Blues." Clydie King also joins them for half-a-dozen songs including "Who Loves You More," "Lonely Dreamer," and "My Guy."

1984

Winter
Dylan offers half-a-dozen unfinished songs to Dave Edmunds for the Everly Brothers's reunion album, which Edmunds is producing.

February 28
Dylan and Stevie Wonder present an award at the Grammy Awards ceremony in Los Angeles.

March (14)–20
Dylan asks Charlie Quintana of the Plugz to put a band together for an as-yet-unspecified purpose. After initially talking about playing Hawaii, it turns out Dylan wants a band to play David Letterman's TV show.

March 21
Dylan and his new band rehearse in New York for their TV appearance the following night. According to Quintana, they ran "through fifty fucking songs we didn't know," without any endings to the songs being finalized.

March 22
Dylan performs on the popular talk show "Late Night with David Letterman," with a band composed of Justin Jesting, Charlie Quintana, and Tony Marisco on bass. At a final rehearsal in the afternoon, they run through seven songs, including Roy Head's "Treat Her Right," a song called "I Once Knew a Man," an instrumental blues, a slow "License to Kill," a three-verse "Jokerman," and, apparently, "Sweetheart Like You" (which Dylan initially considered for inclusion). They record their set at 6 PM. Despite the ragged sound, the band plays with considerable fire and Dylan's own performance really is quite startling. Clean shaven (unlike the appalling "Sweetheart Like You" video), Dylan gives an exuberant vocal performance. He also provides some fine harmonica work on both "License to Kill" and "Jokerman" that, as in rehearsal, is abbreviated to three verses, although it features an extended instrumental break at the end while someone tries to find Dylan the correct harmonica for his harp break. The opening song of the three-song set is a great Sonny Boy Williamson blues called "Don't Start Me Talking," which also sets the tempo for the remaining two songs. Sadly, the promise of this exhilarating performance is not realized two months later on the 1984 tour. One person certainly impressed by the performance is David Letterman, who jokingly asks Dylan if he and the band could possibly make it

every Thursday. After the show, Dylan attends a Boston Celtics basketball game at Madison Square Garden.

Late March

Dylan records his segments for the "Jokerman" video, which has been put together by two old friends from the Rolling Thunder period, George Lois and Larry Sloman. The actual video is one of the more innovative from the video age. A series of images drawn from paintings and photographs illustrate the words of the verses, whereas the lyrics are featured at the bottom of the frame, and Dylan is only shown on the chorus. Dylan gives his first *Rolling Stone* interview in six years at a Greek cafe on Third Avenue, during a break from filming "Jokerman." Although seemingly willing to discuss most subjects, the interview does not start auspiciously, interviewer Kurt Loder questioning Dylan about his "spiritual stance." Matters soon improve, although asking the man his opinion on vasectomy does not qualify as the most penetrating question ever asked Dylan.

• While in New York, Dylan attends gigs by Al Kooper and Peter Wolf, and hangs out with Keith Richards and Ron Wood.

April

Dylan visits Hibbing for one day, presumably while staying on his farm in Minnesota.

• Dylan and photographer Ken Regan arrange a photographic session to provide some contemporary publicity shots. One of the photos is used as the cover for Dylan's 1984 *Rolling Stone* interview. He has been photographed by Regan on several occasions; indeed, Regan was the only official photographer on the Rolling Thunder Revue.

April 28

Dylan officially signs with promoter Bill Graham in San Francisco for a joint European tour with Santana.

Late April to Mid-May

Dylan rehearses with various musicians at his home in Malibu, preparing for a tour of Europe. The lineup remains fluid throughout rehearsals, but at various stages it features Charlie Quintana and Ian Wallace on drums; Greg Sutton, Tony Marisco, and Jeff Eyrich on bass; Ira Ingber and Mick Taylor on guitar; and Nicky Hopkins, Benmont Tench, and possibly Vince Melamed on keyboards. At one point, Mick Taylor is uncertain whether he wants to tour. Benmont Tench does in fact turn down the tour because of other commitments.

May (22–24)

Dylan rehearses with his finalized band: Mick Taylor on guitar, Greg Sutton on bass, Ian MacLagan on keyboards, and Colin Allen on drums, at the Beverly Theater in Los Angeles. The sessions last only three or four days, clearly not long enough to fully work on the material. Even in rehearsal the group sounds lifeless and lacking in invention. According to Greg Sutton, although rehearsals at Malibu lasted several weeks, the lineup for the band was only decided upon in late May. Sutton himself is not offered the gig until a week before flying out, having auditioned for the tour at the start of the Malibu rehearsals. Likewise, MacLagan is a last-minute replacement for Benmont Tench. A list handed out at the Verona press conference details the set intended for the tour, presumably resulting from these rehearsals. Aside from seven acoustic songs, including "Desolation Row," the list contains three new songs: "Dirty Lie," "Enough Is Enough," and "Angel of Rain." It also includes five "changeables": "Tombstone Blues," "Leopard-Skin Pill-Box Hat," "Blowin' in the Wind," "It's All Over Now, Baby Blue," and "To Ramona" (not in fact performed with the band on the 1984 tour). In the main sets, the songs listed include all those played at the first show in Verona plus "Simple Twist of Fate," "I Don't Believe You" (listed as "Never Did Meet"), and "Watered Down Love." Also listed as a "possibly" was "Tangled Up in Blue," although it is unclear if any rehearsed version was augmented by the band. Since Dylan has claimed that the 1984 rewrite of this song took place in Rotterdam, presumably a rehearsal version featured the original lyrics. Among the songs rehearsed over the three or four days, according to Sutton, was a version of "Positively Fourth Street." Carlos Santana joins the band for at least one rehearsal session.

Certainly 21 songs are rehearsed on May 23: "Maggie's Farm," "All Along the Watchtower," "Just Like a Woman," "When You Gonna Wake Up" (which includes most of the original lyrics), "Shelter from the Storm," "Watered Down Love," "Masters of War," "Jokerman," "Simple Twist of Fate" (which only partially corresponds with the new lyrics sung on the tour), "Man of Peace," "I and I," "Heart of Mine," "Ballad of a Thin Man," "Highway 61 Revisited," a fragment of a song with a title like "Round and Round," "Leopard-Skin Pill-Box Hat," "It's All Over Now, Baby Blue," "Every Grain of Sand," "Girl from the North Country," another fragment of a song with lines about "the dawn is gonna shine" (a considerably more finished version of this song is rehearsed in Verona four days later, now with the audible refrain "Almost Done"), and the Tin Pan Alley standard "You're Always on My Mind," which Dylan attempts twice, first with harmonica, then without.

May 27–28

Dylan rehearses with his new band in Verona, Italy, presumably at the Arena di Verona, scheduled to be the venue for his first show in two years. A recording from the first day of these rehearsals seems to suggest that Dylan did precious little work on the songs he intended to perform in Verona, spending most of the time working on new songs, trying a couple of covers, and jamming on some instrumentals. He earnestly works on several versions of a new song he has nearly finished, seemingly titled "Almost Done." The song's lovely, lilting melody is clearly in place, but the words are not (it seems likely that this is the fabled "Angel of Rain," although the lyrics do not feature those words). It is a shame this song does not appear in concert. The other two new songs mentioned in the list of rehearsal songs, "Enough Is Enough" and "Dirty Lie," are both attempted on the 27th, as are Willie Nelson's "Why Do I Have to Choose?" and the Inkspots's "To Each His Own." The afternoon of the first show, Dylan and the band at last apply themselves to working on the songs they intend to play, running through all nine songs scheduled for the first band set. They also work on band arrangements of "Girl from the North Country" and "To Ramona," although they will only appear on the tour in an acoustic guise.

May 28, Arena di Verona, Verona, Italy

Dylan returns to touring after a 30-month respite, although perhaps he should have stayed in the rehearsal hall. Backed by a clearly under-rehearsed band, Dylan gives one of his most untogether performances. Fortunately the Italian Dylan fans, who have waited some 20-odd years to catch him, have no real parameters with which to measure tonight's show and react enthusiastically. As per usual with Dylan, the choice of material at the first show on a tour is most unusual. He opens with the inspired choice of "Jokerman," but it fails to match the official version, and follows it with meandering versions of "All Along the Watchtower" and "Just Like a Woman," both unduly extended by no one being sure when to end the song. Indeed, Colin Allen has stated that the band did not really rehearse the beginnings and endings of songs. A swaggering "Highway 61 Revisited" restores spirits, followed by a commendable "I and I." "Shelter from the Storm" disturbs the flow, holding the dubious honor of being the first poor live arrangement of a *Blood on the Tracks* song. "License to Kill" is the third selection from *Infidels*. "Ballad of a Thin Man" is a hollow version, lacking any sense of theater; while a rewritten "When You Gonna Wake Up" lacks the power of the original, and is a poor choice to close the first half of the show.

After one song by Greg Sutton, Dylan returns carrying just an acoustic guitar and, with no band to hold him back, sings four songs with conviction: "It's Allright Ma," "Girl from the North Country," "Don't Think Twice, It's All Right," and "The Times They Are a-Changin'." The band returns at this point, having brushed up on the remainder of the set. Straight away there is an effective version of "Masters of War" with new lyrics. "Maggie's Farm" has little to recommend it, but is followed by an "Every Grain of Sand" that starts hesitantly but works far better than the more arranged versions performed later in the tour. On this night, the organ shares some of the limelight, and Dylan even attempts a harmonica break between the second and third verses, though quickly changes his mind. Taylor's guitar comes to the fore on a "Man of Peace" straight off *Exile on Main Street,* although the song does not become a regular feature of the tour. "Heart of Mine" makes six out of 18 songs drawn from the last two albums, a nice average, albeit not one maintained at later shows. A butchered "Like a Rolling Stone" ends the set, but the crowd cries for more, so Dylan returns for a solo rendition of "The Lonesome Death of Hattie Carroll." Carlos Santana then joins him on stage for a surprisingly sensitive "Blowin' in the Wind," Santana's guitar flourishes for once enhancing the mood of the song. The band joins Santana and Dylan for a romp through one of Dylan's wittier songs, "Tombstone Blues," though the arrangement obscures the song's lyrics. All in all, a very disappointing beginning to a Dylan tour.

May 29, Arena di Verona, Verona, Italy

On the afternoon of his second show in Verona, Dylan conducts a press conference at the Villa Cortine Palace Hotel, Sirmione. Most of his answers are brief and seem to infuriate some of the journalists present, one hack exclaiming, "What do you want us to know?" Dylan replies, "Nothing, I'm here to play the show!"

"Highway 61 Revisited" is promoted to opening song that evening. The first section with the band is cut to seven songs, with "Leopard-Skin Pill-Box Hat" slotted in before "I and I." "Ballad of a Thin Man" and "When You Gonna Wake Up" are transplanted to the second set. "Man of Peace," "Shelter from the Storm," and "Heart of Mine" all disappear from the set. The acoustic set is also reduced to three songs: "It Ain't Me, Babe," "It's Alright, Ma," and "Don't Think Twice, It's Alright." The solo encore is "The Times They Are a-Changin.'" The changes make for a better-paced but less adventurous show than the previous night.

May 31, Saint Pauli Stadium, Hamburg, W. Germany

In the clubhouse at the Saint Pauli Stadium, Dylan conducts his second and last press conference of the 1984 European tour. If Dylan's answers were brief in Verona, they are positively terse in Hamburg. Halfway through the conference, Joan Baez joins Dylan and Carlos Santana, which Dylan takes as a cue to exit the press conference. At the show, Dylan gets his guitars confused and ends up playing electric on "Just Like a Woman," and acoustic on "All Along the Watchtower" and "I and I." "Maggie's Farm" replaces "Leopard-Skin Pill-Box Hat." This is to be the format for the first half throughout the remainder of the tour. After the solo set, Dylan starts "It's All Over Now, Baby Blue," seemingly acoustic, before the band joins in, albeit with a proper sense of the understated. After a solo encore of "The Lonesome Death of Hattie Carroll," there is the inevitable Dylan/Baez duet (Baez is sharing the bill with Dylan and Santana for this show), on the equally inevitable "Blowin' in the Wind."

June 2, Jakobshalle, Basel, Switzerland

A five-song encore features solo versions of "To Ramona" and "Girl from the North Country" before Dylan is joined by the band (plus Carlos Santana) for "Tombstone Blues," Willie Nelson's "Why Do I Have to Choose?," and an electric version of "Blowin' in the Wind."

June 3, Olympiahalle, Munich, W. Germany

A seven-song encore opens with solo versions of "Girl from the North Country" and "The Lonesome Death of Hattie Carroll." Joan Baez and Carlos Santana then join Dylan for versions of "Blowin' in the Wind" and "I Shall Be Released," Dylan looking visibly uncomfortable until Baez departs, leaving Dylan and Santana to do one of the better 1984 versions of "Tombstone Blues," "Why Do I Have to Choose?," and a rare 1984 "Forever Young."

June 4, 6, Ahoy Sportpaleis, Rotterdam, Netherlands
The first of two nights in the smallest venue of the tour, the Ahoy having a capacity of just 8,000. Dylan responds to the relative intimacy, despite the poor sound at the concert. In the solo set, "Don't Think Twice, It's All Right" is replaced by a stunning new version of "Tangled Up in Blue." On the first night, his delivery is tentative as he struggles to recall the new words, but over the next couple of shows his performance goes from strength to strength. "When You Gonna Wake Up" is replaced by "Man of Peace," while the four-song encore, minus Santana, includes a second and last "Forever Young."

   • The second night is another fine show in which "Tangled Up in Blue" becomes the first of two solo encores, replaced by "A Hard Rain's a-Gonna Fall" in the solo set. Another rewrite of a *Blood on the Tracks* song, "Simple Twist of Fate," is added to the set. It is even blessed with a sympathetic performance from the band. After the two solo encores, Dylan introduces a "Love Minus Zero" that, like "It's All Over Now, Baby Blue," has the band joining in after the first verse. Carlos Santana joins them for "Blowin' in the Wind."

June 7, Schaerbeek Stadium, Brussels, Belgium
"Man of Peace" is dropped from the set and "Mr. Tambourine Man" replaces "A Hard Rain's a-Gonna Fall" in the acoustic set. A five-song encore features the finest "Tangled Up in Blue" of the tour, complemented by "Girl from the North Country" and "Love Minus Zero." "Tombstone Blues" and "Why Do I Have to Choose?" conclude a show played to an audience caked in mud, the result of persistent rain throughout the day. One unimpressed critic devotes the center pages of the English *Daily Express* to reviewing "the least inspired rock concert it has been my misfortune to attend."

June 9, Ullevi Lordagen, Gothenburg, Sweden
Includes "When You Gonna Wake Up." The six-song encore includes four songs with the band: "Blowin' in the Wind," "Tombstone Blues," "Love Minus Zero," and the first band version of "The Times They Are a-Changin'" on this tour.

June 10, Idraets Parken, Copenhagen, Denmark
A seven-song encore includes "Why Do I Have to Choose?"

June 11, Offenbach, W. Germany
Includes "Man of Peace" and a seven-song encore that concludes with Santana and his percussion section joining Dylan and his band for a second "All Along the Watchtower."

June 13, West Berlin, Germany
Dylan is interviewed by Robert Hilburn of the *Los Angeles Times,* the fifth Dylan/Hilburn interview in six years. Dylan seems at ease, even claiming,

"I don't think I'll be perceived properly till 100 years after I'm gone." Includes "Man of Peace" and a solo encore of "Girl from the North Country," but with Dylan playing electric guitar.

June 14, Stadthalle, Vienna, Austria
An interesting show. "A Hard Rain's a-Gonna Fall" concludes the solo set, followed by "Shelter from the Storm." "When You Gonna Wake Up" replaces "Man of Peace." On the encores, Santana and his percussion section again join Dylan and his band, this time contributing to "Heart of Mine," "Tombstone Blues," and "Blowin' in the Wind."

June 16, Mungersdorfer Stadthalle, Cologne, W. Germany
"Love Minus Zero" comes immediately after the acoustic set. "Simple Twist of Fate" replaces "When You Gonna Wake Up." A seven-song encore includes five songs with the band: "Leopard-Skin Pill-Box Hat," "Tombstone Blues," "Blowin' in the Wind," a one-off "Just Like Tom Thumb's Blues," and "Why Do I Have to Choose?"

June 17, Stade de l'Ouest, Nice, France
Backstage at the Stade de l'Ouest, Dylan gives his first bona-fide TV interview in 19 years. To publicize the three remaining French shows, Dylan has agreed to be interviewed by Antoine De Caunes for "Antenne 2." However, he appears impatient and nervous throughout the interview. De Caunes tries to get him to talk about the influence of the surrealists on his art, and about videos, a medium Dylan is obviously unhappy with. He says, "You look real sanitized on the video. In reality it's never that way." At the show, "Simple Twist of Fate" replaces "Love Minus Zero."

June 19, Palaeur, Rome, Italy
The first show includes "When You Gonna Wake Up" and "I Shall Be Released," part of a six-song encore.

June 20, Palaeur, Rome, Italy
A seven-song encore includes a solo "To Ramona."

June 21, Palaeur, Rome, Italy
On the final night, Dylan introduces a couple of nice surprises, singing a quite passable "Desolation Row" during the acoustic set. Then, in place of "When You Gonna Wake Up," he introduces the brand-new "Enough Is Enough," which remains in the set until the end of the tour. A seven-song encore again includes "I Shall Be Released."

June 24, San Siro Stadium, Milan, Italy
An eight-song encore includes the last live version of "Why Do I Have to Choose?" and the first "Knockin' on Heaven's Door" of the tour.

June 26, Estadio del Rayo Vallecano, Madrid, Spain

June 27, Madrid, Spain
Mick Brown of the London *Sunday Times* interviews Dylan in a cafe in

Madrid, obtaining the best of the 1984 tour interviews. Dylan paints himself as a man repeatedly misunderstood, although he admits to a continuing interest in the prophecies of the Book of Revelation.

June 28, Minestadio C. F. Barcelonon, Barcelona, Spain

Probably Dylan's finest concert since the last night at Earl's Court three years earlier. The band is now accustomed to Dylan but not jaundiced by endless performances, while Dylan is in excellent voice throughout. At the end of the main set, he is not at all anxious to leave the stage. After a powerful "Every Grain of Sand," he launches into an impromptu "Lay, Lady, Lay," which the band struggles through. Pointing to somebody in the audience he then announces, "That was for you!"

The eight-song encore starts with three acoustic songs: a strident "Mr. Tambourine Man" and "Don't Think Twice, It's All Right," both broadcast by Spanish TV, and "Girl from the North Country." Then it's an extended "Knockin' on Heaven's Door" with both Dylan and Santana in fine fettle, followed by "Senor," a last-minute suggestion of Dylan's. The band protests that the song has not even been rehearsed. Nevertheless, the crowd roars its recognition, and their response does not lessen for "The Times They Are a-Changin'" or "Tombstone Blues." Finally there is "Blowin' in the Wind," again broadcast on Spanish TV and one of the most exciting performances by Dylan ever filmed. After 22 years, Dylan rediscovers a song that has rarely been effective in concert. A clearly surprised Dylan reacts to the Spanish crowd's harmony vocals on the first chorus with a barely audible "oh awright!" before delivering an astonishing vocal performance, which concludes with him cajoling the audience into a series of choruses, "once more," and then, "just once more," clearly wishing to play on and on. But it is 4 AM.

June 30, Stade Marcel Daupin, Nantes, France

The seven-song encore includes the only 1984 version of "It Takes a Lot to Laugh," the seventh song from *Highway 61 Revisited* performed on this tour.

July 1

Dylan is briefly interviewed by Pamela Andriotakis for *People* magazine. The headline for the feature reads, "The Times May Be Changin' But Mr. Tambourine Man Shows He'll Always Have Paris."

July 1, Parc de Sceaux, Paris, France

The eight-song encore includes a semi-French version of "The Times They Are a-Changin'" sung with old friend, French folksinger Hughes Aufray, and a ragged "It's All Over Now, Baby Blue" with Van Morrison, a late replacement for Joan Baez on the bill. The show is recorded by the Rolling Stones's mobile truck for a possible live album, and is also filmed by Dylan's own film crew. The audience is the largest of the tour, with close to 100,000 fans in attendance.

July 3, Grenoble, France

Includes "When You Gonna Wake Up," as well as "Senor," part of a six-song encore. The concert is recorded for a possible live album.

July 5, St. James Park, Newcastle, England

Playing his first show in Newcastle in 18 years, and to an English-speaking audience for the first time on this tour, Dylan clearly enjoys the experience. One highlight is a lengthy "Knockin' on Heaven's Door," Dylan's harmonica dueling with Santana's guitar. The next day the *Newcastle Evening Chronicle* proclaims that, "Dylan the magician had breathed the kiss of life all over his work." The concert is recorded officially, and "License to Kill" and "Tombstone Blues" both feature on *Real Live*.

July 6

Dylan is seen on Chelsea's Kings Road buying clothes. He is staying at the Hilton.

July 7, Wembley Stadium, London, England

Seventy-two thousand turn up at Wembley on the hottest day of the year to see UB40, Santana, and, primarily, Dylan, who is interviewed backstage at Wembley by Martha Quinn for MTV. The interview lasts over half an hour. Dylan is extremely talkative, discussing such matters as his early days at the Cafe Wha, the recording of *Infidels,* and his attitude toward videos. MTV broadcasts very little of the interview. At the end of the interview, Dylan tells Quinn that she asked some really good questions.

After a very standard main set, Dylan plays a ten-song encore that lasts nearly an hour, starting with three solo songs: "Mr. Tambourine Man," "Girl from the North Country," and "It Ain't Me, Babe." For "Leopard-Skin Pill-Box Hat" and for the remainder of the concert, Dylan fronts a band with three guitarists: Mick Taylor, Carlos Santana, and Eric Clapton. Chrissie Hynde even gets in on the act on backing vocals, but forgets her lyric sheet. Van Morrison also joins Dylan for one song, "It's All Over Now, Baby Blue," which is followed by "Tombstone Blues," "Senor" (after a brief interruption while Dylan teaches Clapton the chords), and the inevitable "The Times They Are a-Changin'," "Blowin' in the Wind," and "Knockin' on Heaven's Door" (with Hynde back on stage again). The concert is recorded for a live album. Indeed the majority of the rather mediocre *Real Live* is culled from this show: "Highway 61 Revisited," "Maggie's Farm," "It Ain't Me, Babe," a very disappointing "Tangled Up in Blue," "Masters of War," and "Ballad of a Thin Man" are all wretched choices from a concert that never reaches the heights of Paris or Newcastle, let alone Barcelona. Reviews vary from *Sounds*'s highly original "Boring Bob" to *Rolling Stone*'s over-the-top headline "Bob Dylan back in peak form." The encores are filmed by MTV. After the show, Dylan travels to Stansted Airport to catch a private jet to Dublin.

July 8, Slane Castle, near Dublin, Ireland

Davy Hammond interviews Dylan back-stage at Slane for a documentary on the Clancy Brothers. Dylan has agreed to the interview in advance, and seems happy to talk about those almost idyllic times of the early '60s. Meanwhile, the Irish music paper *Hot Press* has managed to arrange an exclusive interview between Bono Vox of U2 and Dylan. Bono clearly is not used to being the interviewer, and it comes across as more of a conversation than an interview. At least Bono does not ask the usual questions, "What's your main message?; Are you still born again?" and so on. Dylan also gets to meet folksinger Paul Brady backstage and asks him to teach him his arrangement of "The Lakes of Pontchartrain," which he later incorporates into his live sets.

The day starts ominously with reports of rioting fans arriving early for the show and, clearly the worse for drink, smashing windows and overturning two cars and a police van. Nevertheless, the show goes on, Dylan delivering a 27-song set that is recorded for a live album and filmed for MTV, although the only song from this show included on *Real Live* is an antiseptic "I and I." The acoustic set concludes with "To Ramona," followed by a rare version of "Shelter from the Storm." Dylan also plays another 10-song encore, which includes a solo "With God on Our Side," Van Morrison (in theory) sharing lead vocals on both "It's All Over Now, Baby Blue," and "Tupelo Honey," and "Blowin' in the Wind," on which Bono Vox improvises a ludicrously ill-conceived verse of his own.

July 9
Dylan and his son Jesse board a flight from Dublin to Shannon, for a connecting flight to New York.

Mid-July
Dylan and Ron Wood record with the Al Green band at Intergalactic Studios in New York. The engineer is Joe Blaney. According to Ron Wood, "We did six or seven brand-new songs." However, the only two songs that are known from this session are the old 50s doo-wop classic, "Mountain of Love," and an uptempo r&b song called "Honey Wait," which may be a cover as well.

Mid- to Late July
Dylan spends one or more days recording at Delta Studios in New York, on or around July 24. The basic lineup comprises Anton Fig, John Paris, and Ron Wood (on drums, bass, and guitar, respectively). Also a participant is Benmont Tench, from Tom Petty's Heartbreakers, who contributes keyboards. Recorded at these sessions is the *Empire Burlesque* version of "Clean Cut Kid" and the basic track for the *Knocked Out Loaded* take of "Driftin' Too Far from Shore," although the vocal track (indeed the words) and possibly the drum track are the product of the *Knocked Out Loaded* sessions. Another version of "Clean Cut Kid" is recorded with slightly different words, and a less worked-out version of "Driftin' Too Far from Shore," complete with handclaps. (Dylan refers to recording a song with handclaps during the "Westwood One" interview—see July 30).

Also recorded at these sessions is a publisher's demo, "Go 'Way Little Boy," which Dylan's girlfriend, Carole Childs, convinces him to donate to Los Angeles cow-punk outfit, Lone Justice. The demo only features a desultory guide-vocal from Dylan himself. Three outtakes remain unreleased, including two instrumentals (copyrighted as "Groovin' at the Delta" and "Wolf"). Surprisingly, though, no version of "Enough Is Enough" is attempted at these sessions. It is copyrighted from a live take from the European tour.

Late July
Dylan attends a Eurythmics concert in New York.

July 30
Dylan gives a major interview for "Westwood One" as part of a three-hour radio special called *Dylan on Dylan,* where it is interspersed with a battery of Dylan songs. The interview is conducted at the Ritz-Carlton Hotel in New York by Bert Kleinman and Dylan's old friend Artie Mogul and covers a lot of basic ground, Dylan talking at length about the early days and new recording technology. Clearly he is not impressed by any possibilities the new technology might afford! At the end of the interview, he once again emphasizes the importance to him of playing live: "If I went out to play and nobody showed up that would be the end of me. . . . I only make records because people see me live."

Late July to August
Dylan attends foreign-language classes.

August 30
Rolling Stone reports that Dylan has been writing songs with songwriter Ellie Greenwich, famed for girl-group hits of the early '60s.

September 14
The *New York Post* reports that Al Grossman has requested a third redraft from Dylan in defense of charges made by Grossman relating to outstanding fees. The second draft had proved to be as incomprehensible as the first (see October 1983).

September to Early October
Dylan is rumored to be recording in Nashville with Jamaican rhythm-duo Sly Dunbar and Robbie Shakespeare.

September
Dylan and Ron Wood attend a Lone Justice recording session at Record Plant studios in New York. The band is recording Dylan's "Go 'Way Little Boy." According to singer Maria McKee, both Dylan and Wood played on the song, which was subsequently issued on the 12-inch single of "Sweet, Sweet Baby (I'm Falling)." If Dylan does contribute to the released take, then it is presumably his demon harmonica-work on the track.

Fall
The Cruzadoes record their debut album for EMI in Los Angeles, and drummer Charlie Quintana phones Dylan to ask him if he would play harmonica on one of the songs. Dylan duly obliges, playing on "Rising Sun," but EMI scrap the album before it can be released. Although the Cruzadoes secure another record deal, they end up rerecording the album and this version of the song is never released.

• Dylan rehearses at his Malibu home with Vince Melamed, Ira Ingber, Don Heffington, and Carl Sealove, before sessions at Cherokee studios, in Los Angeles (see Late November/Early December).

Late October (25) to Early November (4)

Dylan attends one of Bruce Springsteen's shows at the Los Angeles Sports Arena. After the show, they spend some time in conversation backstage.

November 18

Dylan watches a taping for U.S. television of Lou Reed, Lone Justice, and the Textones at the Palace, Los Angeles.

(Late?) November

Dylan spends one of his more bizarre days in the studio recording two covers and half a dozen instrumentals at Oceanway Studios. The two covers are Mungo Jerry's "In the Summertime" that, despite four takes, is ghastly beyond words, and Allen Toussaint's "Freedom for the Stallion," which is a whole lot better. The remainder of the session is devoted to what sound like little more than a series of instrumental jams.

Late November to December

Dylan records several new songs at Cherokee studios, Los Angeles. The musician lineup for the session comprises Don Heffington on drums, Carl Sealove on bass, Ira Ingber on guitar, and Vince Melamed on synthesizer. Dylan records "Something's Burning Baby." When Dylan and the band first attempt the song, they are dissatisfied with the results. While Dylan takes a break, the band records the backing track, and when he returns Dylan adds a new vocal track. The second part of the song is later rewritten, and a new vocal is added to the original backing track. Ira Ingber also returns to the studio to add some extra guitar a couple of weeks after the original recording. On second vocals is Madelyn Quebec.

With the same lineup, Dylan records a major 12-minute composition called "New Danville Girl," which he has cowritten with playwright Sam Shepard. A 17-verse opus, the song also features Dylan on harmonica at the conclusion of each chorus. He clearly wishes to work on the song further, so the finest song of these sessions is not included on *Empire Burlesque*. A substantially rewritten version is released on *Knocked Out Loaded* with a new vocal, saxophone, and trumpet dubbed onto the Cherokee basic track. On the basis of the copyright dates "New Danville Girl" was probably recorded before "Something's Burning Baby," probably in late November.

December 3: *Real Live* (FC 39944): "Highway 61 Revisited," "Maggie's Farm," "I and I," "License to Kill," "It Ain't Me, Babe," "Tangled Up in Blue," "Masters of War," "Ballad of a Thin Man," "Girl of the North Country," "Tombstone Blues"

1985

January
Dylan visits Jerusalem to discuss a plan for an open-air concert there.

Late January
Further sessions at Cherokee studios yield two of Dylan's most mawkish ballads, "I'll Remember You" and "Emotionally Yours," backed by Heartbreakers Mike Campbell on guitar, Howie Epstein on bass, and Benmont Tench on organ (for "Emotionally Yours"), Jim Keltner on drums, and Madelyn Quebec on second vocals (on "I'll Remember You"). However, the talents of such stellar musicians are not pushed to the limits. Also recorded at the same sessions are the more worthwhile "Trust Yourself" and the raunchy "Seeing the Real You at Last," with Campbell and Tench augmented by Don Heffington on drums and Bob Glaub on bass. There are two known versions of this song, the copyrighted take featuring an alternate verse. Also recorded at the same session/s is the basic track for "Maybe Someday," subsequently released on *Knocked Out Loaded,* featuring a lineup of Mike Campbell, Howie Epstein, and Don Heffington. One night Dylan disappears from the studio around 10 PM. It turns out he has gone over to A&M studios.

January 28–29
Dylan is part of the "We Are the World" recording session at A&M recording studios in Los Angeles. Arriving about 10 PM, he maintains a low profile throughout an evening of mutual backslapping. At 5:30 AM, Dylan records his solo vocal all four lines of it. He is nervous and uncertain until Stevie Wonder provides some voice-coaching and a piano backing, helping to set Dylan at ease. This moment is immortalized on the official *We Are the World* video.

February 19
As part of the final set of sessions for *Empire Burlesque* in New York, Dylan records at Power Station studios with E Street Band guitarist Steve Van Zandt and keyboard-player Roy Bittan. Sly Dunbar and Robbie Shakespeare are the requisite rhythm section. Although some 12 songs are apparently attempted at the session, only six are ever finished, and only one, a cathartic "When the Night Comes Falling from the Sky," is ever released, some six years later on *The Bootleg Series.*

Mid-February

At the Power Station in New York, Dylan finishes the *Empire Burlesque* album. With Sly Dunbar and Robbie Shakespeare retained on rhythm, he rerecords the album's "magnum opus," "When the Night Comes Falling from the Sky," supported by Al Kooper and Stuart Kimball on guitars, and with Madelyn Quebec providing second vocals. Also recorded is "Never Gonna Be the Same Again," with Alan Clark laying down the synthesizer track between work on Dire Straits's *Brothers in Arms* album. On this song, Sly & Robbie are augmented by Syd McGuinness on guitar, while Carolyn Dennis provides second vocal. Also presumably recorded at this set of sessions are three songs not included on *Empire Burlesque*: the reggaefied "Waiting to Get Beat," "The Very Thought of You," and Dylan's high-school prom song, "Straight As in Love." This is also the most likely location for "Tight Connection to My Heart," which is loosely based on *Infidels* outtake, "Someone's Got a Hold of My Heart." This song is recorded with Sly and Robbie and Mick Taylor and Ted Perlman on guitars.

Early March

Dylan plays harmonica on Sly Dunbar and Robbie Shakespeare's "No Name on the Bullet," recorded for the *Language Barrier* album at RPM Recording Studios in New York, presumably as a thank you for their work on *Empire Burlesque* and *Infidels*.

March

After producing all the *Empire Burlesque* sessions himself, Dylan lets another producer mix the album for him. After one unnamed producer proved too meticulous, Arthur Baker is selected for the task. Meanwhile, Dylan records the final song for the album solo at the Power Station, a lilting little ditty called "Dark Eyes." Some of the mixing also takes place at the Power Station, with Baker drafting in Richard Scher on synthesizer, Bashiri Johnson on percussion, and the Urban Blight Horns. Much of this overdubbing probably took place at Right Track or Shakedown Sound studios (the latter studio being owned by Baker). The Queens of Rhythm also provide some unnecessary backing vocals. During the mixing process, Dylan is briefly interviewed by Kurt Loder for an article about the album in *Rolling Stone*. Loder witnesses Dylan and two of the backing singers performing "We Three (My Echo, My Shadow and Me)," "My Guy," and "Somewhere Over the Rainbow." Unfortunately, Baker can't resist whomping drums and synthesizers, and his remixing detracts from the original feel of some of the songs.

In a break from mixing *Empire Burlesque* at the Record Plant, Dylan talks to Bill Flanagan, editor of *Musician,* who is compiling a book of interviews with current songwriters about the art of songwriting (later published as *Written in My Soul*). Dylan is very happy to discuss his craft, and the interview lasts nearly two hours. As an interview specifically concerned with his songwriting it is unique, with discussions of songs like "Don't Fall Apart on Me Tonight," "Every Grain of Sand," "Brownsville Girl," "Mr. Tambourine Man," "Tangled Up in Blue," "Idiot Wind," and even "Ballad in Plain D."

March 25
The *New York Post* reports that Dylan recently dropped in on rehearsals for a production of *Big River* at the Eugene O'Neill Theater. Dylan says hello to Carolyn Dennis and songwriter Roger Miller.

Mid-April
Dylan visits Allen Ginsberg at his E. 12th St. apartment, playing him his new album, *Empire Burlesque.* They discuss the choice of title. Dylan is still uncertain, but decides to stay with it.

Late April
Dylan flies to Tokyo to film a video for "Tight Connection to My Heart," directed by film director Paul Schrader. The filming spans a couple of days, although both Dylan and Schrader disparage the results. However, Schrader's own schedule does not allow any further work on it.

> June 8: *Empire Burlesque* (FC 40110): "Tight Connection to My Heart," "Seeing the Real You at Last," "I'll Remember You," "Clean-Cut Kid," "Never Gonna Be the Same Again," "Trust Yourself," "Emotionally Yours," "When the Night Comes Falling from the Sky," "Something's Burning Baby," "Dark Eyes"

June 9, Los Angeles
Dylan attends a Leonard Cohen concert at the Wilton Theater. After the show, he goes backstage.

June 17
For the first time in 19 years, Dylan appears on a phone-in radio show, "Rockline," a syndicated show, recorded in Hollywood and hosted by Bob Coburn. The whole affair is fairly miserable, the questions mostly dumb, and the answers brief.

June to Early July
Dylan visits Dennis Hopper at his home in Venice Beach, CA, to discuss the possibility of making a video with him. The project does not come to pass.

July 10–11
Dylan rehearses with Ron Wood and Keith Richards for his "Live Aid" appearance. Aside from "Ballad of Hollis Brown" and "Blowin' in the Wind," they consider performing "Trouble," but no full version is actually attempted. They do, however, rehearse "Girl from the North Country," apparently a personal favorite of "Keef's."

July 12
Dylan turns up at the Lone Star Cafe in the company of Ron Wood, Keith Richards, and Mick Jagger to see Lonnie Mack perform. A syndicated report erroneously suggests that he jammed on stage with Mr. Jagger.

July 13, JFK Stadium, Philadelphia, PA

With a worldwide audience exceeding one billion, the typically perverse Dylan delivers one of his worst-ever performances. Backed by two badly worn Stones, Keith Richards and Ron Wood, and with the stage monitors behind the curtains, Dylan is clearly having difficulties hearing himself. All of which is compounded by a large gathering of people behind said curtains who are not remotely interested in Dylan's performance, but who are busily remembering aloud the words to "We Are the World." Dylan opens with "Ballad of Hollis Brown." After the song, he delivers a brief speech requesting the audience to remember the needy at home, the American farmers, as much as the starving in Ethiopia. (His comments inspire Willie Nelson and Neil Young to arrange "Farm Aid"; see September 22, 1985.) Then he plays the first live version of "When the Ship Comes In" in 22 years. Dylan, though, is finding it increasingly difficult to pitch his voice. A disastrous "Blowin' in the Wind," with Richards playing some long-lost Chuck Berry riff for most of it, concludes Dylan's set. As the ensemble behind the curtain organizes a bit of community singing, Dylan takes the opportunity to exit stage right.

July 23

Dylan arrives in Moscow for the Twelfth World Festival of Youth and Students.

July 25, Lenin Stadium, Luzhniki Sports Complex, Moscow, USSR

Dylan sings to six thousand Russians at a major Russian poetry festival, having been invited by Russian poet Yevgeny Yevtushenko. He sings three songs: "Blowin' in the Wind," "A Hard Rain's a-Gonna Fall," and probably "The Times They Are a-Changin'." He is not announced in advance, appearing as a surprise guest.

July 26

Dylan leaves Moscow after the poetry festival, traveling to Odessa, the homeland of some of his ancestors. He does not return to the States until the second week of August (around the 16th).

August 20

Dylan has dinner with Dave Stewart at the Talesai Restaurant on Sunset Boulevard to discuss the forthcoming video shoot for "When the Night Comes Falling from the Sky."

August 21

Dylan arrives at the First United Methodist Church on Sunset Boulevard late in the afternoon for a rehearsal before two days of filming. Dylan brings two women to audition for the female voice in the video of "When the Night Comes Falling from the Sky." The final selection is made by directors Eddie Arno and Markus Innocenti. The afternoon is spent getting playback levels correct and checking camera angles.

August 22

Dylan and the various musicians assemble for the video shoot, including Dave Stewart, Steve Scales, Clem Burke, and Hunt Sales. They film a scene in the morning in an old school bus; this scene opens the video for "When the Night Comes Falling from the Sky." On the way to the church, though, the bus breaks down and Dylan decides to walk the rest of the way, along Sunset Boulevard, followed by anxious security and film crew. After lunch, they film the live sequence of the video in front of an invited audience. Having insisted that all the musical equipment be playable, he jams extensively with the band. The day's filming concludes around 8 PM.

August 23

Dylan is not required to attend the shoot in the morning as the directors are filming inserts for the video of "When the Night Comes Falling from the Sky." In the afternoon, Dylan and actress Jill Hollier shoot the "Emotionally Yours" video, starting with the exterior scene where Dylan is meant to be recalling informing his ex-lover that their affair must end. Around 5 AM, the filming moves inside the church to shoot the interior scene, where Dylan sits alone playing guitar, remembering the lady in question. Michael Campbell makes a cameo appearance on the song's guitar solo. The cover photograph for *Down in the Groove* is one of a series taken during this part of the filming.

August to September

Scott Cohen of *Spin* magazine spends several days with Dylan at his home in California, interviewing him for a major cover story. Dylan and Cohen stay in touch over the next two weeks as the interview is put together. The result is an interview of major importance, with Dylan talking at length about subjects ranging from who he would have liked to interview (which includes the likes of John Wilkes Booth), to something called "the messianic complex." The feature also includes some remarkable photos taken at his home, including one of him in his studio, surrounded by his own charcoal drawings on the wall. Aside from this detailed feature Scott Cohen also succeeds in getting him to answer his first questionnaire in 20 years, requiring of Dylan lists like "A Dozen Influential Records," "Five Bands I Wish I Had Been In," "Three Authors I'd Read Anything By," "Some Great Minor Masterpieces," and even "A Couple of Actors I'd Like to Play Me in My Life Story" (one is black, the other is Mickey Rooney). The questionnaire is later published in Andy Warhol's *Interview* magazine.

• Another major series of interviews is conducted by Cameron Crowe, who incorporates the material he obtains into a 36-page book on Dylan's career included with the *Biograph* five-album set. He also gets Dylan to talk about the songs included in the set for sleeve notes along the lines of Neil Young's *Decade* set. Even more exhaustive than Cohen's *Spin* interview, Crowe clearly is anxious to cover as many aspects of Dylan's career as possible. Another valuable conversation that sees Dylan reviewing his own past.

September (15?)–19

Rehearsals for "Farm Aid" are held at Soundstage 41, Universal Studios, with Tom Petty and the Heartbreakers and the Queens of Rhythm. The rehearsals feature various Motown and Hank Williams's songs and even "I Second that Emotion," as well as originals like "The Lonesome Death of Hattie Carroll." On the final day of the rehearsals (the 19th), ABC cameras are invited onto the set to film some material for a profile of Dylan for the *20/20* program. A version of "Forever Young," backed by just the Queens of Rhythm and Benmont Tench (on organ), is included in the broadcast. Also filmed are performances of "What'd I Say," "Baby What You Want Me to Do," "I'll Remember You," "Then He Kissed Me," "Alabama Bound," "Trust Yourself," "Louie, Louie," and a heart-tugging rendition of "That Lucky Ol' Sun."

September 19

Bob Brown interviews Dylan for *20/20*. Although a brief interview, Brown asks some excellent questions, to which Dylan seems prepared to give full answers. He admits that he wasn't very convinced by the message of "We Are the World."

Mid-September (20?)

Charles Young interviews Dylan briefly for MTV. In it, Dylan mentions his collaboration with Dave Stewart, and how he'd be touring next year, giving "sixty to one hundred shows."

September 21

At about 10 PM, Dylan and the Heartbreakers soundcheck at the Memorial Stadium, Champaign, IL, hoping to ensure that there is no repetition of the "Live Aid" debacle. They run through "Shake," "Trust Yourself," "That Lucky Ol' Sun," "Maggie's Farm," and a cover of Chris Kenner's "I Like It Like That."

September 22, Memorial Stadium, Champaign, IL

At about 9:35 P.M., near the conclusion of "Farm Aid," an all-day benefit for American farmers (originally inspired by his comments at "Live Aid"), Dylan joins Tom Petty and the Heartbreakers (who have just concluded their own set) on stage. Together they launch straight into "Clean-Cut Kid" followed by a blues song called "Shake," seemingly a Dylan lyric set to the tune of Roy Head's "Treat Her Right." Then comes the live debuts of two *Empire Burlesque* songs, "I'll Remember You" and "Trust Yourself," both of which have Dylan dueting with Madelyn Quebec, who is clearly struggling to keep up with his idiosyncratic phrasing. A searing version of "That Lucky Ol' Sun" follows, before Willie Nelson joins them on guitar for a romp through the highly appropriate "Maggie's Farm." Although the American TV broadcast, courtesy of the Nashville Network, manages to omit the first and fifth songs and cut the second, the excitement of the performance comes across, reaffirming Dylan's power in concert after the very public disaster at "Live Aid." The buzz from the concert is enough for him to suggest a more long-term collaboration with the Heartbreakers.

Tom and Bob, Farm Aid, 1985

Late September

Dylan is interviewed by Mikal Gilmore for the *Los Angeles Herald-Examiner* at Gilmore's house in Hollywood. Although ostensibly the first of several interviews to promote *Biograph,* Dylan is not the greatest salesman; he dismisses the project (except for "Cameron's book"). He also considers the money donated from the recent benefit concerts to be "almost guilt money."

Fall

Dylan is interviewed by Charles Kaiser for *The Boston Review.* The interview takes place in a Manhattan hotel room, and is a most peculiar affair, Dylan claiming at one point that he remarried in 1980. The interview is not published until April 1986.

October

David Fricke interviews Dylan for *Rolling Stone.* Although not a major interview, there are a few good quotes. Referring to Crowe's booklet in the *Biograph* set, Dylan says: "I had a chance to clarify a lot of wrong things said about me. It was a chance to set a few things straight."

October 12–13

The "Sun City" video is filmed in Los Angeles. Dylan makes a brief appearance alongside Jackson Browne.

October

Dylan attends a Tom Petty recording session in Los Angeles. The producer is Dave Stewart.

October 28: *Biograph* (C5X 38830): "Lay Lady Lay," "Baby Let Me Follow You Down," "If Not for You," "I'll Be Your Baby Tonight," "I'll Keep It with Mine," "The Times They Are a-Changin'," "Blowin' in the Wind," "Masters of War," "Lonesome Death of Hattie Carroll," "Percy's Song," "Mixed-Up Confusion," "Tombstone Blues," "Groom's Still Waiting at the Altar," "Most Likely You Go Your Way," "Like a Rolling Stone," "Jet Pilot," "Lay Down Your Weary Tune," "Subterranean Homesick Blues," "I Don't Believe You," "Visions of Johanna," "Every Grain of Sand," "Quinn the Eskimo," "Mr. Tambourine Man," "Dear Landlord," "It Ain't Me, Babe," "You Angel You," "Million Dollar Bash," "To Ramona," "You're a Big Girl Now," "Abandoned Love," "Tangled Up in Blue," "It's All Over Now Baby Blue," "Can You Please Crawl Out Your Window," "Positively 4th Street," "Isis," "Caribbean Wind," "Up to Me," "Baby I'm in the Mood for You," "I Wanna Be Your Lover," "I Want You," "Heart of Mine," "On a Night Like This," "Just Like a Woman," "Romance in Durango," "Senor," "Gotta Serve Somebody," "I Believe in You," "Time Passes Slowly," "I Shall Be Released," "Knockin' on Heaven's Door," "All along the Watchtower," "Solid Rock," "Forever Young"

Early November

Denise Worrell of *Time* magazine interviews Dylan in a small cabin on his Malibu estate for an article on *Biograph* and his new edition of *Lyrics.* Dylan again talks little about *Biograph,* but rather about making records, writing, and "keeping on." A considerably longer version of the interview is published in a 1989 collection of Worrell's interviews, *Icons.*

• Robert Hilburn interviews Dylan for a sixth time, supposedly to discuss the *Biograph* set. However, Dylan is more than willing to talk about other things, such as how he'd like to write about his own religious stance, or about a book of character sketches he'd like to publish. So in the space of just over a month, both the *Los Angeles Herald-Examiner* and the *Los Angeles Times* have carried (and syndicated) interviews with Dylan.

Lyrics 1962–1985, a revision of the earlier Writings and Drawings *(see July 1973), is published.*

November 8

Rubin "Hurricane" Carter is finally released from Rahway State Prison.

November 13

A tribute to Dylan arranged by Walter Yetnikoff (then-president of CBS Records) is held at the Whitney Museum in New York. The tribute includes an award for the sale of 35 million records. Stars attending include David

Bowie, Billy Joel, Neil Young, Pete Townshend, and Dave Stewart. The function receives wide news coverage in the US.

November (16)
The *New York Daily News* reports that Dylan, upset at a premature report of a Far East tour in a Hollywood paper, has temporarily stopped rehearsals with the Heartbreakers. More likely, rehearsals were put on hold so that Dylan could travel to New York for the Whitney tribute (see November 13, 1995), before traveling on to London to record with Dave Stewart. However, the report confirms that rehearsals were taking place as early as the beginning of November.

November 18
Dylan attends a secret gig by ex-Undertones frontman Feargal Sharkey at the Greyhound in Fulham, London, before heading up to Dingwalls, in Camden Town, to see South African trumpeter Hugh Masekela.

November 19–22
Dylan records at the Church Studios in Crouch End, London. According to Andy Kershaw, who interviews Dylan at the sessions, some 20 songs are recorded (more accurately, this would be 20 basic tracks, i.e., without vocals or with dummy vocals only). The only backing-track that ends up utilized is "Under Your Spell," the last track on *Knocked Out Loaded.* Dylan and Dave Stewart are on guitars, Clem Burke is on drums, Patrick Seymour is on keyboards, and John McKenzie is bassist. Annie Lenox apparently sits in on piano on the 21st, but does not appear on "Under Your Spell." On one of the days, the band is joined by Mike Scott and Steve Wickham of the Waterboys, and they attempt a version of Mike Scott's "We Will Not Be Lovers," although, as with all the material, Dylan refrains from doing a vocal, insisting that the vocal tracks would be added in New York.

November 22
Dylan is briefly (and unrevealingly) interviewed by Andy Kershaw for BBC's "The Whistle Test" program. The show features one of the basic tracks recorded on the 19th–22nd.

Early to Mid-December
Dylan and the Heartbreakers start rehearsing in earnest at Universal Studios's Soundstage 41 for a Far East tour. Early rehearsals include versions of "Union Sundown" and "In the Garden."

> "Sun City" issued with cameo appearance by Dylan.

Late December
As usual, Dylan is with his family on his farm in Minnesota for Christmas.

1986

Early January

Don McLeese of the *Chicago Sun-Times* interviews both Dylan and Tom Petty during rehearsals for the "True Confessions" tour. Although not a major interview, McLeese does provide an interesting behind-the-scenes report on the rehearsals.

• Toby Creswell of Australian *Rolling Stone* conducts a telephone interview with Dylan, concentrating on Dylan's most recent album and his collaboration with the Heartbreakers.

January

Rehearsals continue at Soundstage 41. According to Petty, the band rehearses 60 songs, among which are "Gotta Serve Somebody," "Man of Peace," "All My Tomorrows Belong to You," and "This Was My Love."

January 20, The Kennedy Center for Performing Arts, Washington, DC

Dylan maintains his recent high profile on American TV, appearing at the Martin Luther King benefit organized by, among others, Stevie Wonder. Dylan performs one song with Wonder, "Let the Bells of Freedom Ring" (which is not broadcast). He also sings a rewritten "I Shall Be Released," backed by his own singers and Wonder's band, and the inevitable "Blowin' in the Wind," with Stevie Wonder, and Peter, Paul, and Mary. He looks suitably uncomfortable during a communal finale of Wonder's own tribute to Martin Luther King, "Happy Birthday."

> *January 25: Albert Grossman dies of a heart attack on a flight to London.*

January 29

A charcoal drawing by Dylan bearing this date is later sold at an auction for the Live Aid Foundation.

Late January

George Neegus visits Dylan at his Malibu home and interviews him for the Australian current affairs program, "60 Minutes." Dylan, though, seems reluctant to open up to Neegus, and throughout the interview he comes across as bored.

February 3
Dylan flies from Los Angeles to Auckland, then to Wellington, after a delay at Auckland in the afternoon. He finally arrives at 6 PM, attending a party at Wellington's Ohariu Club at around 11 PM.

February 4
Between 7 PM and 10:15 PM Dylan and the Heartbreakers soundcheck at the Athletic Park, playing so loud that the neighbors' protests almost result in the cancellation of the following day's concert. Much of the soundcheck is spent practicing a mixture of old Everly Brothers and Buddy Holly songs.

February 5, Athletic Park, Wellington, New Zealand.
Despite some of Dylan's most extensive rehearsals, Dylan and the Heartbreakers on the opening night of the "True Confessions" tour sound surprisingly under-rehearsed. They open with a bluesy instrumental that segues straight into "Like a Rolling Stone," followed by a reworked version of "Shake," "I'll Remember You," and "Trust Yourself." A Ry Cooder/John Hiatt song, "Across the Borderline," and "Masters of War" (receiving it's statutory hard rock arrangement) close Dylan's first set. After two songs by the Heartbreakers, Dylan comes back solo with "It's Allright, Ma" and "It Ain't Me, Babe." This is followed by Petty and Dylan raggedly dueting on "I Forgot More (Than You'll Ever Know)." The Heartbreakers rejoin Dylan for a very standard arrangement of "Just Like a Woman," Hank Snow's "I'm Moving On," a surprisingly impressive "Lenny Bruce," an abbreviated "When the Night Comes Falling from the Sky," Rick Nelson's old chestnut "Lonesome Town," and a good "Seeing the Real You at Last," with the spotlight turned on the audience for the title line. "Ballad of a Thin Man" closes Dylan's second set. After two more songs by Petty, Dylan and the Heartbreakers revamp five songs from the early '80s: "Shot of Love," "I and I," "Gotta Serve Somebody," "In the Garden," and "Heart of Mine," closing the main set with another Dylan/Petty duet on "Blowin' in the Wind." The two encores are "Rainy Day Women" and "Knockin' on Heaven's Door."

The sound at the show is poor, and the crowd remains muted throughout, perhaps because Dylan's choice of songs is fairly ambitious, with only nine of the 25 songs drawn from his '60s "heyday." Reviews are mixed: The *Church Star* refers to "a revitalized Bob Dylan," although another reviewer concludes that, "Dylan has become too much of nothing." After the show, Dylan returns to the Hotel Royal where he joins the female vocalists and assorted members of the entourage in a midnight singalong at the piano. The songs that feature Dylan are largely '50s covers like "Blue Moon," Buddy Holly's "Every Day," Presley's "Trying to Get to You," "Sincerely," "Daddy's Home," and the Coasters's "Poison Ivy."

February 6
Dylan leaves for Auckland around 4 PM.

February 7, Mount Smart Stadium, Auckland, New Zealand

After the instrumental opener, Dylan performs his first "Positively Fourth Street" in 10 years, followed by "Clean-Cut Kid." "Across the Borderline" is dropped from the first set. In the acoustic set, "The Times They Are a-Changin'" replaces "It Ain't Me, Babe." The final set is substantially altered. "Heart of Mine" is dropped, "Rainy Day Women" is now first, and "In the Garden" last. "Blowin' in the Wind" becomes the first encore, followed by "Gotta Serve Somebody" and "Knockin' on Heaven's Door." The *Auckland Star* enthuses "All Hail, Saint Dylan."

February 8

In the early hours of the morning, Dylan is interviewed by Stuart Coupe for *The Age* at the Regent Hotel in Auckland. Elliot Roberts, Dylan's manager, remains with Dylan and Coupe throughout the interview, which clearly unnerves Coupe, who does his best to probe. Dylan does not respond enthusiastically.

February 8–9

Flying into Australia on the morning of the 8th, Dylan and the Heartbreakers ensconce themselves at the Festival Recording Studio in Sydney to record a new Dylan composition, Tom Petty acting as producer. The song is the title track of a film called *Band of the Hand,* although its subtitle, "(It's Helltime, Man)," describes its contents better. Several other unknown songs are attempted.

February 10

Dylan gives his first Sydney press conference in 20 years at artist Brett Whitley's studio in Surry Hills, Sydney. As one critic wrote of the conference: "Dylan . . . interspersed . . . one liners with the occasional two or even three sentences when he was asked a question that he felt deserved more than cursory dismissal." A couple of excerpts from the conference are shown on breakfast TV the following day.

February 10, Entertainment Centre, Sydney, Australia

On opening night, "That Lucky Ol' Sun" comes after "Trust Yourself." In Dylan's final set, "Across the Borderline" is added after "Shot of Love," and "Like a Rolling Stone" is reinstated before "In the Garden." "Gotta Serve Somebody" is replaced by an oldie, "Cross on Over and Rock 'Em Dead." The three-song encore features Mark Knopfler, who is touring Australia with Dire Straits. Australian reviews are more favorable than in New Zealand, one headline proclaiming, "simply rapture for today's dapper Dylan." Another reviewer extols the "energy and warmth" in his performance.

February 11, Entertainment Centre, Sydney, Australia

On the second night, "Shake" is dropped from the set, while "Emotionally Yours" receives its first live performance, replacing "I'll Remember You." The acoustic set now features "A Hard Rain's a-Gonna Fall," "Girl from the North Country," and "It's Alright, Ma." In his second set with the Heartbreakers, Dylan performs his first electric version of "House of the Rising Sun," in place of "I'm Moving On" and "Lenny Bruce." "Shot of Love" is dropped from the set, although an extra encore is added, another cover, "Baby Don't You Go," a one-off performance. After the show, Dylan goes to a party at the Seebel Country Club with Lauren Bacall.

February 12, Entertainment Centre, Sydney, Australia
On the third night, the instrumental opener now has lyrics, the refrain of which appears to be "On the Train." In the acoustic set, between "It Ain't Me, Babe" and "A Hard Rain's a-Gonna Fall," Dylan leads the audience through "Happy Birthday" for backup singer, Queen Esther Marrow. But the real surprise is a performance of "License to Kill" in place of "Across the Borderline." It is introduced as "a song about the space program." He then refers to "America's tragedy," a reference to the seven people who had been killed in the space shuttle disaster, suggesting that, "they had no business being up there in the first place . . . as if we haven't got enough problems down here on earth." For the final encore, Fleetwood Mac singer Stevie Nicks joins them on "Knockin' on Heaven's Door," which gets her in trouble with the Australian authorities because she does not have a work permit.

February 13
Dylan attends the matinee performance of *Sweet Bird of Youth,* starring Lauren Bacall.

February 13, Entertainment Centre, Sydney, Australia
The final night includes a solo "Don't Think Twice, It's All Right."

February 14
Dylan arrives at Adelaide airport in the evening. All attempts by reporters to question him are met with a brusque stare.

February 15, Memorial Drive, Adelaide, Australia
"Girl from the North Country" becomes a regular feature of the acoustic set.

February 16
Dylan arrives at Perth airport, wholly ignoring questions from both press and public.

February 17–18, Entertainment Centre, Perth, Australia
According to one eyewitness, Dylan performed "Every Grain of Sand" at one of the Perth shows. The *West Australian* enthusiastically reviews the first night's show, proclaiming: "Dylan knocked the wind from absent critics with a performance of polish, poise and humor."

February 19
Dylan returns Knopfler's favor, joining Dire Straits on stage at the Melbourne Sports and Entertainment Center for four songs: "All Along the Watchtower," "Knockin' on Heaven's Door," "License to Kill" and "Leopard-Skin Pill-Box Hat."

February 20, Kooyong Stadium, Melbourne, Australia
The first show includes a solo version of "To Ramona."

1986

February 21, Kooyong Stadium, Melbourne, Australia

Dylan includes the only 1986 performance of "Never Gonna Be the Same Again," in place of "I and I."

February 22

Unhappy at the way he came across in the George Neegus interview, Dylan agrees to another television interview, this time with Maurice Parker for Channel 7's "State Affair." He seems in good humor, although the interview is brief. It takes place in Dylan's hotel room in Melbourne during the afternoon. In the evening, Dylan plays the last of three shows at Kooyong Stadium. The four-song acoustic set includes "To Ramona." After the concert, Dylan goes to Middle Park Hotel, Melbourne, to see Vanetta Fielos.

February 24–25, Entertainment Centre, Sydney

The first night features a 26-song set. By this point, the opening blues song has lyrics about someone called "Justine." The second night's performance runs to 27 songs, including a failed attempt at "Dark Eyes."

These last two Sydney concerts are filmed by Gillian Armstrong for a TV special to be broadcast in the States (HBO had reportedly paid $500,000 for the rights). The one-hour special is subsequently issued officially as "Hard to Handle." From the first night, "Ballad of a Thin Man," "When the Night Comes Falling from the Sky," "Girl from the North Country," "I'll Remember You," "In the Garden," and "Just Like a Woman" are used by HBO; "I'll Remember You" and "Just Like a Woman" also are part of a "Westwood One" radio broadcast in the "Superstars in Concert" series, as are versions of "Positively Fourth Street," "That Lucky Ol' Sun," "Masters of War," and "I Forgot More (Than You'll Ever Know)." HBO drew from the second night the spoken introduction to "In the Garden," "Like a Rolling Stone," "It's Alright, Ma," "Lenny Bruce," and "Knockin' on Heaven's Door." Two of these songs are also used by "Westwood One," as is a rendition of "Blowin' in the Wind."

February 28

Dylan arrives in Brisbane.

March 1, Lang Park Brisbane, Australia

March 2

Dylan flies to Tokyo.

March 3–4

The two days preceding the Japanese concerts are set aside for rehearsals.

March 4: Richard Manuel of The Band hangs himself in a motel room in Winter Park, FL, during a reunion tour.

March 5, Budokan Hall, Tokyo, Japan

March 6, Castle Hall, Osaka, Japan

Dylan includes the old 1963 instrumental "Sukiyaki," before "Knockin' on Heaven's Door." It is retained for all of the Japanese shows.

March 8, Gymnasium, Nagoya, Japan

Includes "Just Like Tom Thumb's Blues" after "Across the Borderline." "Lenny Bruce" is introduced by Dylan with a quote from Tennessee Williams: "I don't ask for your pity, just your understanding. Not even that, but just your recognition of me in you; and Time, the enemy in us all." Dylan is quite talkative at the later shows on this tour, introducing "In the Garden" as "a song about my hero," and "Ballad of a Thin Man" as written "in response to people who ask me questions all the time."

March 10, Nippon Budokan, Tokyo

Dylan includes a version of the Inkspots's "We Three (My Echo, My Shadow and Me)," performed in response to a request from "a very special person." "Mr. Tambourine Man" also receives its first 1986 outing as part of the four-song acoustic set. The concert is the longest of the tour, with 29 songs. The performances have improved throughout the tour, and, although not visually stunning, the last few Australian shows and the Japanese shows confirm that all the promise of "Farm Aid" has not yet dissipated. After the final Japanese show, Dylan is briefly interviewed for MTV. Only a couple of snippets from the six-minute interview are subsequently shown. The interview is about Dylan's impressions of the Far East tour. Tom Petty is also interviewed, and parts of tonight's show are filmed.

March 31

Dylan continues to receive awards: he is presented with a Founders Award from ASCAP (American Society of Composers, Authors and Publishers) at Chasen's Restaurant in Beverly Hills.

Spring

Dylan raps a verse on Kurtis Blow's "Street Rock," returning the favor for Blow lending him some backup singers at the time of *Infidels*. Blow is later quoted as saying, "He raps, he really raps." The song is featured on *Kingdom Blow*.

April 6

Dylan leaves New York for an unknown destination, presumably Los Angeles.

April 10

Dylan and Tom Petty conduct a joint press conference, announcing the American leg of the "True Confessions" tour, featuring Dylan, Petty, and the Heartbreakers. The press conference takes place at the Los Angeles offices of "Westwood One," who are sponsoring the tour. The full itinerary is not actually announced at this point. Indeed, quite a few shows are later added to the tour, causing a slight delay in the filming of *Hearts of Fire* (see mid-

April 1986). After the "Westwood One" press conference, Dylan attends a concert by Mink DeVille at the Palace in Hollywood.

Mid-April (12–14)
Dylan flies from Los Angeles to New York with Julian Lennon.

Mid-April
Dylan undergoes a screen test for the part of Billy Parker in *Hearts of Fire,* having met previously with director Richard Marquand at his home in Malibu to discuss the project.

April 15
The *New York Daily News* reports that Dylan is considering relocating back to Manhattan.

Late April to Early May
Booked for a month of sessions at Skyline Studios in beautiful Topanga Canyon, Dylan records "well over 20 songs, including r&b, Chicago-steeped blues, rambunctious gospel and raw-toned hillbilly forms." This material consists almost exclusively of covers, three of which appear on *Knocked Out Loaded:* "You Wanna Ramble," "They Killed Him," and "Precious Memories." Also attempted is a version of Ray Charles's "Come Rain or Come Shine," arranged by Ira Ingber at Dylan's request. The musicians for these sessions include Al Kooper on keyboards, Raymond Lee Pounds on drums, and James Jamerson, Jr., on bass. ("They Killed Him" features Vito San Flippo on bass.) On "Precious Memories" Larry Meyers plays mandolin, Al Perkins steel guitar, and Milton Gabriel, Mike Berment, and Brian Parris are on steel drums, all presumably overdubbed onto a basic track. Also playing guitar on some of the tracks is T-Bone Burnett ("You Wanna Ramble"), Jack Sherman ("They Killed Him"), Cesar Rosas of Los Lobos, and Ira Ingber, neither of whom appear on any of the released cuts. Saxophonist Steve Douglas is also in attendance at some sessions.

Mid-May
Dylan and the Heartbreakers record a Dylan/Petty composition, "Got My Mind Made Up," at Sound City Studios in Van Nuys, CA. The original intention had been to record several songs, possibly even a Dylan/Heartbreakers album, but, according to Petty, "Bob [just] wasn't ready," i.e., he did not have enough material to record such an album. However, Petty and Dylan do cowrite another song together, called "Jammin' Me." Mike Campbell later adapts the tune and it appears on the Heartbreakers's *Let Me Up (I've Had Enough).* By this point, Dylan has decided to discard most of the rock & roll tracks he has been working on in Topanga and compile his next album from various session tapes accumulated over the last couple of years. He admits to Mikail Gilmore of *Rolling Stone* that the album "doesn't really have a theme or a purpose."

Mid- to Late May
Dylan returns to Skyline Studios in Topanga Canyon to put together *Knocked Out Loaded.* With Steve Douglas on saxophone, Steve Madaio on trumpet,

and the Queens of Rhythm on backing vocals, Dylan mixes and overdubs five songs: "They Killed Him," one of the tracks recorded at The Church in London called "Under Your Spell," and three songs whose basic tracks were recorded at the *Empire Burlesque* sessions: "Maybe Someday," "Driftin' Too Far from Shore," and "Brownsville Girl."

May

Dylan and the Heartbreakers rehearse at Zoetrope Studios in Hollywood for Dylan's first American tour in five years. The songs rehearsed include "License to Kill" and "I Dreamed I Saw St. Augustine."

May 15

Lorimar Productions announces Dylan is to star in a film called *Hearts of Fire*, budgeted at $12–13 million, to be shot at Lee Studios in England, starting on the 11th of August. Filming is scheduled for seven weeks in London and a further four weeks in the States. Dylan is expected to write six songs for the film.

May 21

Dylan is interviewed by phone from Topanga Canyon during the *Knocked Out Loaded* sessions by Bob Fass as part of a 45-hour radio special on WBAI commemorating his 45th birthday.

June 6

Dylan and the Heartbreakers warm up for their American tour by performing three songs at an Amnesty International benefit at the Inglewood Forum in Los Angeles: the new single, "Band of the Hand," "License to Kill" which gets its last 1986 outing, and the oldie, "Shake A Hand." The brief set is well-received by the audience, having been filmed in its entirety.

June 8

Dylan arrives in San Diego in the early afternoon and checks into the Sheraton Harbor Hotel. From 7:30 PM until midnight, Dylan and the Heartbreakers soundcheck at the Sports Arena.

June 9, Sports Arena, San Diego, CA

Dylan opens his first American tour in five years with a swaggering r&b tune, "So Long, Good Luck and Goodbye." Proof that this is the second leg of the "True Confessions" tour comes with "Positively Fourth Street," "Clean-Cut Kid," and "I'll Remember You." "Shot of Love" then returns to the set, followed by "That Lucky Ol' Sun" and "Masters of War." For the American tour the Heartbreakers get to perform two four-song sets of their own, a reflection of their greater status in their homeland. After their first set, Dylan returns solo for "To Ramona," "One Too Many Mornings," which he concludes with, "Someone bet me a dollar I couldn't remember it all," and "It Ain't Me, Babe." A more convincing "I Forgot More (Than You'll Ever Know)" is retained from March, as is "Just Like a Woman." Ray

Charles's "Unchain My Heart" is introduced. "When the Night Comes Falling from the Sky" receives a new arrangement, the first verse sung slowly, with each word stretched out, the song building in intensity. "Lonesome Town" and "Ballad of a Thin Man" conclude the middle set. The remainder of the show duplicates the Japanese shows, with "Seeing the Real You at Last" coming after "Rainy Day Women." The lucky first-night crowd, however, get an extra song after "Blowin' in the Wind": the only live performance of "Got My Mind Made Up." The concert gets extensive media coverage, with items on "Entertainment Tonight" and three local TV stations.

June 11, Lawlor Events Center, Reno, NV
This is a quite different set from the opening night. "Emotionally Yours" makes one of its sporadic appearances in place of "I'll Remember You," "Trust Yourself" replaces "Shot of Love," and the tearjerker "We Had It All" takes the place of "That Lucky Ol' Sun." "A Hard Rain's a-Gonna Fall" and a rare performance of "Song to Woody" are featured in the acoustic set. "Let the Good Times Roll" replaces "Unchain My Heart," while "Band of the Hand" becomes the first encore. Up to half-a-dozen covers per concert are to be a regular feature of the US shows. In fact, these generally prove to be the songs Dylan brings the greatest vocal commitment to, as if uninterested by his own material.

June 12, Cal Expo Amphitheatre, Sacramento, CA
"Lenny Bruce" makes a rare appearance in place of "Just Like a Woman," while "I'm Moving On" replaces "Let the Good Times Roll." "Rock with Me Baby" replaces "Cross on Over, Rock 'Em Dead" as one of the encores.

June 13, Greek Theater, Berkeley, CA
Includes an acoustic "The Lonesome Death of Hattie Carroll." "Unchain My Heart" replaces "Rock with Me Baby."

June 13 (14?)
Dylan is interviewed by Jon Bream of the *Minneapolis Star and Tribune*, publicizing Dylan's first concert in Minneapolis in 20 years.

June 14, Greek Theater, Berkeley
Includes "Don't Think Twice, It's All Right" and "Girl from the North Country" in the solo set. "Band of the Hand" and "Just Like a Woman" replace "Lenny Bruce." The encore includes "Rock with Me Baby."

June 16–17, Pacific Amphitheatre, Costa Mesa, CA
The first night's set includes "Girl from the North Country"; on the second night, Dylan performs the second and last "Song to Woody" of the US tour.

June 18, Veterans Memorial Coliseum, Phoenix, AZ
"Shake a Hand" opens this show.

June 19
Dylan arrives in Houston, staying at the Lancaster Hotel.

June 20, The Summit, Houston, TX

Includes a rewritten, if unintelligible, "Union Sundown" in place of "Masters of War," and "So Long, Good Luck and Goodbye" as an encore.

June 21, Frank Erwin Center, Austin, TX

Before the concert, Dylan goes shopping for clothes at Electric Ladyland.

"Hard to Handle," a one-hour concert film of Dylan and the Heartbreakers filmed in Sydney, premieres on HBO.

June 22, Reunion Arena, Dallas, TX

Includes "Union Sundown," "The Lonesome Death of Hattie Carroll," and "One Too Many Mornings," the last of which becomes a regular feature of the set.

June 23

Dylan drives to Memphis on a day off, staying at the Peabody Hotel.

June 24, Market Square Arena, Indianapolis, IN

June 26

Dylan gives an interview to Bob Aschenmacher of the *Duluth News-Tribune and Herald* before his concert at the Metrodome. Not surprisingly, it concentrates on his youth in Hibbing.

June 26, Hubert H. Humphrey Metrodome, Minneapolis, MN

Includes "Just Like a Woman" (in place of "Band of the Hand"), and "Let the Good Times Roll" as an encore.

June 27, Alpine Valley Music Theater, East Troy, WI

Includes the Sun classic "Red Cadillac and a Black Mustache" in place of "Across the Borderline," and "Let the Good Times Roll" as an encore.

June 28

Dylan, Petty, and assorted Heartbreakers visit the Kingston Mines Blues Club in Chicago.

June 29, Poplar Creek Music Theater, Hoffman Estates, IL

Includes "Red Cadillac and a Black Mustache."

June 30, Pine Knob Music Theater, Clarkston, MI

After "Rainy Day Women," Dylan does a ragged version of "All My Tomorrows Belong to You" especially for his "dresser," Suzy Pullen during the first show; Dylan then leads the crowd through "Happy Birthday."

July 1, Pine Knob Music Theater, Clarkston, MI

Includes the first US 1986 version of "The Times They Are a-Changin'," as well as the last "Lenny Bruce." The only "I Still Miss Someone" of the tour is a welcome respite from "I Forgot More (Than You'll Ever Know)." "Rock with Me Baby" is an encore.

July 2, Rubber Bowl, Akron, OH

Includes the last performance of "Red Cadillac and a Black Mustache." Dylan then joins the Grateful Dead, whose idea of rock music has infiltrated this show. He jams on "Little Red Rooster," then sings lead on a surprisingly pleasant "Don't Think Twice, It's Alright." All plus points are lost, however, when the Dead and Dylan conspire to massacre "It's All Over Now, Baby Blue."

July 4, Rich Stadium, Buffalo, NY

Includes a final version of "Rock with Me Baby." Three songs are broadcast by satellite on American TV as part of "Farm Aid II." If "Rainy Day Women" is a throwaway, "Across the Borderline" and "Seeing the Real You at Last" are both intense enough. None of the songs duplicates choices for the HBO special, "Hard to Handle," broadcast two weeks earlier.

July 5

In the afternoon, Dylan attends the Smithsonian Folklife Festival on the Mall in Washington, DC. He then travels to the American Legion Hall in Bethesda to see the Vibrato Brothers and the Original Sun Rhythm Band.

July 6, Robert F. Kennedy Memorial Stadium, Washington, DC

July 7, Robert F. Kennedy Memorial Stadium, Washington, DC

"I'm Moving On" is included (for the last time) before "Band of the Hand." "Just Like a Woman" also receives its last performance of 1986. During "Like a Rolling Stone," Dylan is doubled over with laughter, presumably at the mess he is making of his best-known song. Not content with his previous guest appearance with the Dead, Dylan again insists on wreaking havoc on "It's All Over Now, Baby Blue," which pales alongside what Dylan and Bobby Weir then do to "Desolation Row."

July 9, Great Woods Center for the Performing Arts, Mansfield, MA

In the early hours of the morning, a lucky group of fellow guests at the Marriott Hotel in Mansfield witness Dylan performing four songs "You Win Again," "I'm a King Bee," "Let the Good Times Roll," and the old Penguins's hit "Earth Angel" backed by the Queens of Rhythm and a local bar band.

July 11, Civic Center, Hartford, CT

Includes a one-off encore of "Lay, Lady, Lay."

July 13, Performing Arts Center, Saratoga, NY

Includes "Union Sundown" in place of "Band of the Hand," an acoustic "Mr. Tambourine Man," and an electric "House of the Rising Sun" as one of the encores. Lena Spenser, ex-owner of Saratoga's Cafe Lena, visits Dylan backstage after the show.

July 14

Dylan attends the Fabulous Thunderbirds's show at New York's Felt Forum, visiting backstage afterward.

July 15, Madison Square Garden, NY
Ron Wood plays guitar during part of all three New York shows but to no discernible effect. On the first night, "Unchain My Heart" is performed instead of "We Had It All."

July 16, Madison Square Garden, NY
During the second concert, "All Along the Watchtower" is introduced into the set, replacing "Positively Fourth Street."

July 17, Madison Square Garden, NY
At the third show, "I'll Remember You" is replaced by the only US performance of "We Three (My Echo, My Shadow and Me)." It also includes a nice solo "Mr. Tambourine Man," the only "I Want You" of 1986, and "Union Sundown." The encore features "Blowin' in the Wind," "Shake a Hand," and a fiery version of "House of the Rising Sun." It is one of the best shows on the tour.

   The New York reviews of the three shows generally are positive, with headlines like "Like a Rolling Dylan, Ragged But Intense" and "Still Rocking After All These Years." David Hepworth interviews Dylan backstage before the final Madison Square Garden concert for a new UK monthly music magazine Q. Dylan has little to say and apparently complains afterward that, "The guy keeps asking me questions."

July 19, The Spectrum, Philadelphia, PA
The first show includes a real surprise after "Rainy Day Women," "I Dreamed I Saw St. Augustine," the female vocalists "oohing" away in the background. "Let the Good Times Roll" is one of the encores.

July 20, The Spectrum, Philadelphia, PA
The second night offers the last "Emotionally Yours" of 1986, another "I Dreamed I Saw St. Augustine," and an encore that comprises "Blowin' in the Wind," "Cross on Over and Rock 'Em Dead," and "Let the Good Times Roll." It is one of the more interesting sets from the latter part of the "True Confessions" tour.

July 21, Brendan Byrne Arena, East Rutherford, NJ
Dylan gets downright talkative at this show, joking about New Jersey being, "the land of the Boss." He ends "Like a Rolling Stone" with what sounds like a parody of the stop-start ending to Springsteen's "Born in the USA." He responds to a request for "Hurricane" with, "Don't talk to me about 'Hurricane.' Y'know what this state did to him." The show also includes the last 1986 version of "I Dreamed I Saw St. Augustine." Before the encore, a guitar-shaped birthday cake is carted onstage for Howie Epstein, while everyone sings "Happy Birthday," including Al Kooper, sitting in on piano during the latter part of the show. The encore includes "Union Sundown."

July 22, Great Woods Center, Performing Arts, Mansfield, MA
Includes the last 1986 "Girl from the North Country," and "Union Sundown."

July 24, Sandstone Amphitheater, Bonner Springs, KS

Dylan opens the show with "Kansas City," and then remarks, "That's the first time I've ever played that song. Anyway I know where I am." After "I and I," he performs the only US 1986 "Leopard-Skin Pill-Box Hat."

July 26, Red Rocks Amphitheater, Denver, CO

On the first night, before "Ballad of a Thin Man," Dylan refers to the time he played "a stripjoint called the Gilded Garter in Central City because the folk club across the street wouldn't let me play."

July 27, Red Rocks Amphitheater, Denver, CO

The second show includes the final 1986 version of "The Times They Are a-Changin'."

July 29, Memorial Coliseum, Portland, OR

Although the city noise control officer threatens to cancel the concert, it goes ahead, in front of an enthusiastic crowd of 18,000. Includes a rare "Trust Yourself."

July 31, Tacoma Dome, Tacoma, WA

Before "I and I," Dylan performs a version of "Gotta Serve Somebody" with another new set of words, in response to a request from the front row. The song is retained for the remainder of the tour. Tonight's version of "All Along the Watchtower" is used in "Westwood One's Superstars in Concert" broadcast. A Japanese version of the same broadcast also includes tonight's "It Ain't Me, Babe."

August 1, The BC Place, Vancouver, BC

Dylan half-fills a venue of eighty thousand for the only Canadian show of the tour. The concert opens with Petty singing "Bye Bye Johnny" backed by the Heartbreakers, with Dylan on guitar. "That Lucky Ol' Sun" makes a rare appearance.

August 3, The Forum, Inglewood, CA

Two months on, Dylan returns to the Inglewood Forum at the end of a 41-date tour. "Shake a Hand" is now the regular opener. Dave Stewart is a surprise guest.

August 5, Shoreline Amphitheater, Mountain View, CA

After "I and I," Dylan invites a special guest, John Lee Hooker, onstage to perform "Rock Me All Night Long." Dylan records a terrific version of Hank Williams's "Thank God" with the Heartbreakers at the soundcheck for tonight's show. This is subsequently broadcast on the Lubavitcher's Chabad telethon.

August 6, Mid-State Fairground, Paso Robles, CA

As the *San Francisco Examiner* reports, "They were winding up the evening-gown competition for the Maid of San Luis Obispo County as Bob Dylan, on the other side of the fairgrounds, started on 'One Too Many Mornings'." It is a last-minute decision that the successful 1986 US tour should conclude in such a strange place. With just nine thousand inhabitants, Paso Robles's main claim to fame is that James Dean died nearby. At the soundcheck, Dylan and the female vocalists work on the chorus to "Brownsville Girl," and sure enough Dylan includes just the same fragment at the evening show, a snippet of which is shown on "Entertainment Tonight" the following day.

> August 8: *Knocked Out Loaded* (OC 40439): "You Wanna Ramble," "They Killed Him," "Driftin' Too Far from Shore," "Precious Memories," "Maybe Someday," "Brownsville Girl," "Got My Mind Made Up," "Under Your Spell"

Early to Mid-August
Sam Shepard conducts a quasi-interview with Dylan one afternoon. It is subsequently published as "a one-act play" in *Esquire* magazine, coming across as a typically surreal conversation between two renowned play-actors. Although difficult to consider as more than a conversation, it provides some interesting insights.

August 17
Dylan arrives in England to start work on *Hearts of Fire*. A press conference is held at the National Film Theater in London to publicize the making of the film. The majority of media attention focuses on Dylan, and the conference receives wide national coverage, including excerpts on breakfast TV the following day.

August 19–24
Some final camera tests and rehearsal scenes occupy six days before the filming of *Hearts of Fire* begins in earnest.

August 25 to Mid-September
Filming for *Hearts of Fire* commences at Shepperton Studios, where it occupies two to three weeks. Scenes shot here include two scenes with Bones (Ian Dury) and Molly (Fiona), one in the hotel, one in a pub, the latter of which is not included in the film; a scene in a hotel with Molly in the morning; scenes in a recording studio/s with James Colt (Rupert Everett) and Molly; being served lunch by the butler Albert; and sequences playing pool and watching *The Concert for Bangladesh* in Colt's house; plus possibly a scene in which the publicist tries to sign Molly up.

August 27–28
Dylan spends two days at the popular London Townhouse studio trying to find the slightest shard of inspiration, recording the musical soundtrack for *Hearts of Fire*. Backed by the familiar faces of Ron Wood and Eric Clapton, (on bass and guitar) and the less-familiar bassist Kip Winger, drummer Henry Spinetti, and keyboardist Beau Hills, Dylan cuts a whole series of versions of John Hiatt's "The Usual" (later overdubbed with the New West Horns) and the dire "Had a Dream About You Baby," an appropriate song for *Hearts of Fire*. Also recorded over the two days are "Night After Night,"

two semi-improvised ditties, probably called "Ride This Train" and "To Fall in Love With You," and a Billy Joe Shaver song called "Old Five and Dimer Like Me," which is recorded both solo and with the band. One other song appears in the film, Shel Silverstein's "A Couple More Years," but it probably dates from a later session.

September
Dylan is briefly interviewed by Donald Chase for an article in the *San Francisco Chronicle* on the making of *Hearts of Fire*. He also talks about related matters like *Pat Garrett & Billy the Kid*.

Mid-September (13–16)
One sequence for *Hearts of Fire* is filmed at Heaven, the alternative club in London, with an audience of extras made up of two-hundred punks. Presumably this is the sequence where Molly sings at the New Cavern Club. "Billy Parker" (Dylan) plays in the band.
 • One of the scenes for *Hearts of Fire* is filmed at Fairoaks Airport in Surrey. The scene features Parker, Molly, and Colt in a helicopter.

September 15
Robert Shelton visits Dylan on the film set.

September 18, Colston Hall, Bristol
They film a scene with Parker, Bones, and Molly packing equipment. A press conference is probably also filmed here, in which "Parker" is required to be his usual sarcastic self.

September 19
Filming takes place at Bristol's Colston Hall with nearly one thousand paid extras as an audience. Dylan lipsynchs to a tape of "Had a Dream About You Baby" five times. The final take is at 3:35 PM.

September 20
Filming continues at Bristol's Colston Hall with further attempts at "Had a Dream About You Baby." Dylan also performs a brief instrumental with the band, which comprises Ron Wood, Clem Clemmons, and Terry Williams. During a break from filming, Dylan is briefly questioned by Christopher Sykes, who is working on an "Omnibus" special on Dylan. Also due to be filmed on this day are two other scenes: "Parker recruiting band. All bad. Molly storms off," and, "Jack Rosner asks Parker to sing at his club. Molly does the deal. Check signed." The latter scene constitutes part of the post-concert party and is presumably completed the following day.

September 21
Filming continues at Colston Hall, minus most of the extras. The sequence filmed features a post-concert party. This had in fact been scheduled to be a rest day. Presumably the crew travels to Swansea at the end of the day's shooting, although Dylan may have returned to London, not being needed until the 24th.

September 24

Filming takes place at Rhoose Airport in Cardiff (renamed Gatwick for the day). "Parker is met by man. He does not recognize London . . . Parker and Molly in corridor." On the roads near Cardiff airport: "Parker and Molly are driven from Gatwick to London. Parker hates all things English." Although part of the filming is shown in the "Omnibus" special, neither of these scenes are included in the finished film.

September 25

Parker, Molly, and Colt are filmed near Dunraven Beach, Southerndown, Bridgend, South Wales: "Parker watches Molly and Colt on the beach . . . Parker and Molly by bonfire. Parker wants to go home."

September 26

Filming continues at Dunraven Beach. The whole crew travels to London.

September 28

Shooting for *Hearts of Fire* continues on L Stage at Shepperton Studios: "Parker packs up, then smashes up hotel room."

September 29

On L Stage at Shepperton Studios, a scene featuring Parker, Molly, and Colt in a Liverpool hotel corridor is filmed: "Parker tells Molly he wants to go home. He hits Colt."

September 30

Dylan is filmed at the Electric Ballroom in Camden Town, London, playing to an audience of two to three hundred punks, who are shouting "off! off!" and flicking cigarettes at him. He dives into the audience. Molly proceeds to show Parker how it is done (cough). This is also probably the date of a brief interview used on the "Film '86" program.

October 1

Further filming at the Electric Ballroom. "Parker leaves with Hot Blonde." Both his departure with the blonde and a conversation with Molly about the experience are excised from the film. Later in the day, they film the exterior scene following Parker's trashing of his hotel room: "TV crashes down at commissionaire's feet. Parker and Molly pass debris looking for taxi. Parker leaves in taxi." This scene is filmed at Plantation House, London. Dylan is not involved in subsequent filming in England, which continues through October 3.

October 3

Dylan flies from Heathrow to Los Angeles unaccompanied.

October 5

Dylan and Fiona Flanagan arrive in Toronto to begin filming the second part of *Hearts of Fire.*

October 7

The first day of shooting in Hamilton, Ontario. Sherman Avenue is closed to the public, while an auto body shop is converted into "Woody's Bar." The sign outside reads Lonesome Don and the Red Hot Lovers. The cinema opposite is now showing *Pat Garrett & Billy the Kid.* Shooting starts at 7 PM and continues until 4 AM. Dylan arrives about 9 PM, and they attempt to shoot a scene with Fiona jumping out in front of Dylan's brown pickup truck. This is probably also the day when they film the scene inside "Woody's Bar" when Parker sings "The Usual."

October 8

Filming continues in Hamilton, with Molly walking out of Woody's Bar and meeting Parker on the street. They buy frozen custard and talk. Again the filming is at night time.

October 9

Tonight's filming is at the northwest end of Hamilton. Parker and Molly are in the pickup truck. Parker has just robbed the Burger King restaurant.

October 10

Tonight's filming is at the Canadian General Electric warehouse in Toronto. On a makeshift grandstand, Parker and Colt join Molly onstage to sing the song, "Hearts of Fire." This is the intended climax of the film.

Mid-October (11–17?)

The probable dates for several scenes set on Parker's farm (including Molly's first visit where Parker's chickens attack her, which is cut from the film); Molly waking Parker up to drop off a tape of her songs; Molly on Parker's sofa the morning of her big homecoming gig, with Parker cooking breakfast (cut from the film); a scene where she returns to Parker's farm to reclaim the money he had stolen from the box office (also cut from the film), and a scene "the morning after" where Parker plays "A Couple More Years" to her as she wakes up in his barn.

October 17

An ever-cautious Dylan agrees to a "dry-run" interview with the BBC's Christopher Sykes before formally deciding to allow an on-camera interview. The 40-minute conversation is hardly probing, although Sykes seems to succeed in putting Dylan at ease.

October 18

Dylan finally agrees to an on-camera interview with Christopher Sykes, who is filming an "Omnibus" special on the making of *Hearts of Fire,* "with especial emphasis upon Bob Dylan." During a fascinating 25-minute interview in Dylan's trailer, Dylan talks while sketching Sykes. It is a conversation that reveals a most inscrutable side to Dylan, who pronounces at the beginning, "If you're looking for revelation it's just not gonna happen." Nevertheless, something is revealed.

• Today's filming in Hamilton takes place outside the Kenilworth Tavern, starting at 7:30 AM. The scene consists of Parker boarding a bus to take him to the airport on his way to England. As it drives off, Molly jumps in front of the bus and proceeds to board it, although only after Parker has convinced the bus driver to stop the bus with his harmonica, which the driver believes is a gun. Most of the subsequent filming does not involve Dylan.

October 25
Dylan visits a Toronto bar called Mr. Lees, where he watches a band called V.I.C.

November 1
Dylan appears at the Nag's Head in Markham, a town just north of Toronto, and plays guitar with the Paul James Band. He remains onstage for about 90 minutes.

November 8
The last day of filming for *Hearts of Fire.*

November 10
Dylan inducts Gordon Lightfoot into the Juno Hall of Fame at the annual Canadian Academy of Recordings Arts and Science dinner at the Harbor Castle Convention Center in Toronto. He describes Lightfoot as a "rare talent." Afterward, Dylan spends about 90 minutes at a WEA party in a Toronto hotel with Lightfoot, Ronnie Hawkins, and Matt Dillon.

November 13
Dylan attends Tanya Tucker's concert at the Royal York Hotel in Toronto. He has problems getting admitted, because of his appearance.

Late November to December
Dylan unexpectedly calls at Artie Traum's home in Woodstock, NY, hopeful of a nostalgic singalong. Artie calls up brother Happy Traum and ex-Greenbriar Boy John Herald. The evening is spent at John Herald's cabin singing Guthrie songs and traditional fare like "Barbara Allen."

Hearts of Fire poster

1987

January
Dylan has dinner at Mary Lou's in Greenwich Village with actresses Patti D'Arbanville and Ellen Barkin.

• Dylan meets the Grateful Dead at the Marin County Veterans Memorial Auditorium, where they are recording an album.

Late January
Dylan records for two days with the Grateful Dead at San Rafael Stadium. Versions of "She Loves You," "Nowhere Man," and "Maggie's Farm" apparently are attempted (this conflicts with the previous entry, suggesting someone has got their wires crossed).

Late Winter
Dylan guests on harmonica for Warren Zevon on "The Factory," recorded for Zevon's *Sentimental Hygiene* album.

February 19
At the Palamino Club in North Hollywood, Dylan, George Harrison, and John Fogerty join the Grafitti Band, which features Jesse Ed Davis and Taj Mahal, for a 90-minute onstage jam session. Dylan is not tempted to sing lead vocals but is happy to play guitar throughout. Songs performed include "Matchbox," "Gone, Gone, Gone," "Lucille," "Crosscut Saw," "Bacon Fat," "Knock on Wood," "In the Midnight Hour," "Honey Don't," "Blue Suede Shoes," "Watching the River Flow," "Proud Mary," "Roll Over Beethoven," "Johnny B. Goode," "Willie and the Hand Jive," "Peggy Sue," "Dizzy Miss Lizzy," and "Twist and Shout." On the last four songs, Dylan provides some half-hearted backing vocals.

March 2
Dylan is one of the guests at Elizabeth Taylor's 55th birthday party, held at Burt Bacharach's Los Angeles home. Apparently he even sings a duet with Michael Jackson, and a birthday song with Stevie Wonder, Dionne Warwick, and Gladys Knight.

March 10
Dylan joins the Grateful Dead before their concert in Oakland for a pre-tour publicity photo.

March 11

At the Brooklyn Academy of Music, Dylan sings one song at a gala tribute to George Gershwin held on the 50th anniversary of his death. He performs a solo version of "Soon" from the 1930 film *Strike Up the Band.* There is an afternoon rehearsal. Dylan's performance is subsequently broadcast on TV.

(Winter to Spring)

Several quotes by Dylan are included in a four-part BBC Radio Two special on Woody Guthrie broadcast at the end of 1987. Presumably he was interviewed at some point early in the year.

April 3

One of the early *Down in the Groove* sessions results in five songs, none of which would have been out of place on *Self Portrait.* In the mawkish stakes "Just When I Needed You Most" barely wins out over "Important Words" and "When Did You Leave Heaven?" "Willie and the Hand Jive," and "Twist and Shout" have even less to recommend them. The session is presumably at Sunset Sound Studios in Los Angeles.

April

One session at Sunset Sound features Dave Alvin of the Blasters on guitar, Steve Douglas on sax, and James Jamerson, Jr., on bass, as well as the ubiquitous Queens of Rhythm. Alvin recollects four songs being recorded, "Look on Yonder Wall," "Rollin' and Tumblin,'" "Red Cadillac and a Black Mustache," and "Rock With Me Baby," which is first attempted without the gaggle of female vocalists. Dylan just can't resist recutting it, girls and all. None of the cuts end up on *Down in the Groove.* Other sessions at this time involve the likes of Randy Jackson on bass, Steve Jordan on drums, and Danny Kortchmar on guitar, and bassist Nathan East, drummer Mike Baird, and keyboardist Stephen Shelton. Carolyn Dennis and Madelyn Quebec are utilized throughout these sessions, which result in the likes of "Got Love If You Want It," "Important Words," "Let's Stick Together," "Ugliest Girl in the World," "Silvio," "Shenandoah," "When Did You Leave Heaven?," "Ninety Miles an Hour," and "Rank Strangers to Me," all of which will be on the original test sequence for *Down in the Groove.* "Got Love If You Want It" and "Important Words" will be cut from the album at the last minute, though "Got Love If You Want It" will appear on the Argentinian version of *Down in the Groove* by mistake.

Mid-April

In Los Angeles, Dylan attends the soundcheck for Al Kooper's gig at the Roxy. However, he does not appear for the actual show.

April 14

Dylan travels to Memphis to play harmonica at a session with Ringo Starr at Chips Moman's Three Alarm Studios. The song they record is entitled "Wish I Know Now What I Knew Then." The sessions apparently last from the 14th to the 17th, although whether Dylan attended more than the first session is not known. Starr subsequently refuses to allow any of these sessions to be released, claiming he was "under the influence" when they were made.

• Dylan decides to visit Graceland while in Memphis, where he is given a VIP tour. Also possibly dating from this trip to Memphis is a recording session with U2 on which he contributes backup vocals for a Dylan/Bono composition released on *Rattle & Hum* as "Love Rescue Me."

April 20, Los Angeles Sports Arena

U2's encore features a very special guest. After Bono sings the first verse of "I Shall Be Released," he introduces the song's composer, who sings the remainder of the song. They then sing "Knockin' on Heaven's Door," with Bono once again needlessly improvising words far less effective than the original lines.

May

Dylan's cover of "Sally Sue Brown" on *Down in the Groove* presumably dates from a one-off session postdating the (other) Sunset sessions. With ex-Pistol Steve Jones on guitar, ex-Clash Paul Simonon on bass, Myron Grombacher on drums, and Kevin Savigar on keyboards, Dylan cuts the most convincing track on his lamest album. Backing vocalists Willie Green and Bobby King add their own b'rroooms to the song, possibly at a separate session. (They also add harmonies to Dylan's version of Hank Snow's "Ninety Miles An Hour.")

June 1

Dylan flies from Los Angeles to San Francisco to rehearse with the Grateful Dead.

Early June

Dylan rehearses for his forthcoming tour with the Grateful Dead in San Rafael, CA. Tapes of the rehearsals, although they illustrate a commendable willingness on Dylan and the Dead's part to attempt rare or never-performed songs from Dylan's vast repertoire, show a Dylan barely willing to sing a song through, let alone work up an arrangement. This, combined with the lack of imagination shown by his new backing band, make these rehearsals a worrying preview of the forthcoming Dylan/Dead tour. The songs attempted are "The Times They Are a-Changin'," "When I Paint My Masterpiece," "Man of Peace," "I'll Be Your Baby Tonight," folksinger Peter La Farge's "Ballad of Ira Hayes," "I Want You," "Ballad of a Thin Man," "Stuck Inside of Mobile," "Dead Man, Dead Man," "Queen Jane Approximately," Paul Simon's "The Boy in the Bubble" (on which Dylan contributes backing vocals), Ian and Sylvia's "The French Girl," "In the Summertime," "Man of Peace" again, a largely unintelligible "Union Sundown," "It's All Over Now, Baby Blue," "Joey," "If Not for You," "Slow Train," "Tomorrow Is a Long Time," "Ballad of Frankie Lee and Judas Priest," "John Brown," "I'll Be Your Baby Tonight" again, an exuberant performance of the bluesy "Don't Keep Me Waiting Too Long," the traditional "Stealin'," "I Want You," Buddy Holly's "Oh Boy" (on which Dylan plays harmonica), "Tangled Up in Blue," a brave but barely coherent stab at "Walkin' Down the Line,"

"Simple Twist of Fate," "Gotta Serve Somebody," "Gonna Change My Way of Thinking," "Maggie's Farm," "Chimes of Freedom," "All I Really Want to Do," "John Brown" again, "Heart of Mine" twice, an interesting arrangement of "The Wicked Messenger," "Watching the River Flow," "Pledging My Time," and "Senor." The highlights of these rehearsals, though, are the couple of songs (the traditional "Rollin' in My Sweet Baby's Arms" and "John Hardy") on which Dylan sings accompanied by just acoustic guitars, presumably his and Garcia's. Sadly, Dylan attempts no such acoustic respite during the actual shows.

July 3
Dylan and the Grateful Dead make plans to meet the evening before each of the six Dylan/Dead shows to decide the set for the following day. Presumably they also soundcheck at Sullivan Stadium on this day.

July 4, Sullivan Stadium, Foxborough, MA
The first of the Dylan/Dead concerts features a 70-minute Dylan/Dead set. None of the songs sound particularly well worked out and the Dead's playing is uninspired, although the set does feature its share of surprises. Opening with "The Times They Are a-Changin'," "I'll Be Your Baby Tonight," and "Man of Peace," Dylan revives the truly awful "John Brown," followed by a more worthwhile "I Want You" and a lame "Ballad of a Thin Man." Three real surprises follow: the first live version of "Stuck Inside of Mobile" in 11 years, a live debut of "Queen Jane Approximately," and the first "Chimes of Freedom" in 23 years. "Slow Train," a nearly complete "Joey," and "All Along the Watchtower" wrap up the set. The encore is the inevitable "Knockin' on Heaven's Door." "Slow Train" and "Joey" are subsequently included on the *Dylan and the Dead* live album.

July 10, J.F.K Stadium, Philadelphia
Dylan rings the changes, featuring "Tangled Up in Blue" in place of "The Times They Are a-Changin'," "Ballad of Frankie Lee and Judas Priest" rather than "I Want You," "Simple Twist of Fate" instead of "Queen Jane Approximately," and "Gotta Serve Somebody" replacing "Slow Train." There is no Dylan encore.

July 12, Giants Stadium, Meadowlands, NJ
A most unusual quintet of songs opens the third and best Dylan/Dead show, in front of a massive New Jersey crowd: "Slow Train," "Stuck Inside of Mobile," "Tomorrow Is a Long Time," "Highway 61 Revisited," and "It's All Over Now, Baby Blue." Between "John Brown" and "Queen Jane Approximately," Dylan performs his first live version of another *John Wesley Harding* gem, "The Wicked Messenger," the fourth song from that oft-neglected album to be performed with the Dead. The set concludes with "The Times They Are a-Changin'"; although Dylan returns to play guitar on the Dead's own encore, "Touch of Gray," and to sing lead on that perennial favorite "Knockin' on Heaven's Door." No songs from this show appear on the *Dylan and the Dead* album.

July 19, Autzen Stadium, Eugene, OR

Again Dylan performs several songs not previously played on the Dylan/Dead tour. Opening with "Maggie's Farm," "Dead Man, Dead Man," and "Watching the River Flow," he also includes "Heart of Mine" and a hilarious version of "Rainy Day Women," clearly one of the few Dylan songs Dead fans can really relate to. Finishing the set with "Tangled Up in Blue," Dylan again appears on stage for the Dead's encore, "Touch of Gray," before making "All Along the Watchtower" his own encore. Tonight's version of "Queen Jane Approximately" is included on *Dylan and the Dead*.

July 24, Alameda County Coliseum, Oakland, CA

The set has now stabilized and features just one song not previously performed with the Dead, a pleasant enough "Shelter from the Storm." "I Want You" is included on *Dylan and the Dead*.

July 26, Anaheim Stadium, Anaheim, CA

Dylan opens the last of his shows with the Dead with a lamentable version of "Mr. Tambourine Man." Although the show improves after this, it contains no further surprises. "Knockin' on Heaven's Door" concludes a series of shows that must represent one of Dylan's all-time worst career decisions. Although playing to more than a quarter of a million people, the vast majority are Deadheads first and last. The one blessing of Dylan's association with the Dead is that they have clearly encouraged him to perform some of the less-obvious songs from his back catalogue. Tonight's versions of "Gotta Serve Somebody," "All Along the Watchtower," and "Knockin' on Heaven's Door" are included on *Dylan and the Dead*.

September 2

Dylan flies into Cairo with the Heartbreakers and two of his sons, Jesse and Samuel.

September 3–4

Booked for rehearsals in Tel Aviv, Dylan prefers to stay in Cairo an extra day, arriving in Tel Aviv by bus late on the afternoon of the fourth. During his stay in Tel Aviv, he spends one evening with Israeli singer Uri Zohar.

September 5, Hayarkon Park, Tel Aviv, Israel

Dylan opens a European tour with his first shows in Israel. After his brief flirtation with the Dead, Dylan has returned to playing with a real rock & roll outfit, the Heartbreakers, unfortunately still augmented by the Queens of Rhythm. A last-minute decision is made to cancel one of the two Tel Aviv concerts. The chaos that ensues is an inauspicious start to the tour. Dylan has clearly decided to do shorter sets, a wise decision considering the punishment his voice had taken during the 1986 shows. Fears of a rerun of 1986 are quickly dispelled, Dylan performing a far more audacious cross-section of his songs, possibly a result of his time with the Grateful Dead. After opening with "Maggie's Farm," Dylan introduces faithful versions of "I'll Be Your Baby Tonight" and "Senor." Three uptempo numbers provide ample opportunity for the Heartbreakers to show their pedigree "Highway 61 Revisited,"

"I and I" a la 1986, and a delightful "Watching the River Flow" before a sensitive "Simple Twist of Fate" slows things down, Dylan sticking to the original words and singing with a real warmth. A less effective "Stuck Inside of Mobile" is followed by another staple from the 1986 tour, "In the Garden." "Joey" has survived the Dylan/Dead desecration. "Dead Man, Dead Man" also makes a reappearance, while "I'll Remember You" remains one of the few effective songs from *Empire Burlesque* in live performance. "Tangled Up in Blue" has also returned to the released arrangement and words, but "All Along the Watchtower" represents a definite improvement over the stock arrangement, being a slow brooding version with few signs of the ghost of Jimi Hendrix. The encores of "Knockin' on Heaven's Door" and "Blowin' in the Wind" surprise no one (although Petty is thankfully absent from the latter). The final song is a special performance, the traditional spiritual "Go Down Moses." All in all, a most encouraging start to the tour in front of forty thousand fans.

September 6
Dylan is interviewed in his suite at Tel Aviv's Daniel Hotel by (surprise, surprise) Robert Hilburn. It is a brief affair. In reference to the way he chooses material, Dylan reveals, "I never think about whether a song is a hit. I don't even know what has been a hit in some places. We went to France and they asked why I didn't do 'Man Gave Names to All the Animals' because they said it was Number One there. . . . I didn't even know it was released there."

September 7, Sultans Pool, Jerusalem, Israel
In this relatively intimate nine thousand-seat venue, the second show of the 1987 tour does not duplicate a single song from the previous night. Dylan opens with "The Times They Are a-Changin'" and a most effective "Man of Peace." "Like a Rolling Stone," "Rainy Day Women," "Emotionally Yours," "Shot of Love," and "Ballad of a Thin Man" are all remnants from the 1986 tour, although "Emotionally Yours" has Dylan toying with the words and the arrangement, and "Shot of Love" is a much punchier performance than the previous year. Tonight's most welcome choice, though, is the first live version in nine years of "You're a Big Girl Now." "John Brown" remains from the Dylan/Dead shows and is surprisingly effective. "License to Kill" and "It's All Over Now, Baby Blue" also return, Dylan concluding the main set with a rewritten "Gotta Serve Somebody." The first encore is "Slow Train," which starts slowly and builds in tempo. Halfway through the song, however, there is an electricity failure and the stage is bathed in darkness and silence. Despite attempts to repair the damage, this signals the end of the gig.

• Back at his hotel after the show, Dylan is interviewed by Kurt Loder. The interview is intended for the 20th anniversary issue of *Rolling Stone* and thus is more concerned with Dylan's feelings about events in the past than his current state of mind. The interview is part of a whole series with figures "whose work has stood out and whose voices have often been heard in the pages of *Rolling Stone*."

September 9

Dylan and the Heartbreakers are scheduled to rehearse at the Jakobshalle in Basel, Switzerland on this day. It is not known if rehearsals did take place, but the continuing variations in the set suggests perhaps they did.

September 10, Jakobshalle, Basel, Switzerland

Dylan plays another main set that does not duplicate the previous shows of the tour at all. He opens with "Forever Young," leading into a subdued "Shelter from the Storm." "Seeing the Real You at Last," and "When the Night Comes Falling from the Sky" compete with their 1986 arrangements. Then come three impressive additions to the set, an effective "Queen Jane Approximately" (far superior to the Grateful Dead version), "When I Paint My Masterpiece," making a welcome return to performance, and the recently resurrected "Ballad of Frankie Lee and Judas Priest." "Clean-Cut Kid" is still featured, before a romping "I Want You." "Masters of War" is a less-welcome remnant from previous tours. "I Shall Be Released" reappears, with the odd line from the Martin Luther King benefit rewrite. "Trust Yourself" concludes the main set. The two encores are "In the Garden" and "Like a Rolling Stone."

September 12, Autodromo, Modena, Italy

Dylan gives a terrific performance on his return to Italian shores as if to make up for the lackluster shows three years earlier. Only one song not previously featured on the tour appears tonight, but it is a song Dylan has never performed live, "Pledging My Time." The show also features rare 1987 versions of "Stuck Inside of Mobile," "All Along the Watchtower," and a particularly impressive "Joey." After the show, Dylan participates in an impromptu hotel lounge singalong, performing, among others, "(I Left My Heart In) San Francisco," "Sittin' on the Dock of the Bay," and "You've Got a Friend."

September 13, Palasport, Turin, Italy

Another great show features major changes in the set. Opening with "Positively Fourth Street" (a la 1986), Dylan also includes particularly fine versions of "The Wicked Messenger" and "Heart of Mine" as well as two songs performed sporadically in 1986, "Lenny Bruce" and "License to Kill," both prefaced with lengthy harmonica solos by Dylan.

September 15, Westfalenhalle, Dortmund, W. Germany

Includes a rollicking "Watching the River Flow."

September 16, Frankenhalle, Nuremburg, W. Germany

September 17, Treptower Festwiese, East Berlin, E. Germany

Although originally booked for a show in West Berlin, Dylan and the Heartbreakers switch their show to this massive venue in East Berlin. Owing to the scarcity of name acts in the country, something like a hundred thousand fans attend the show, which is marred by running battles between fans and security. Some 130 fans are injured. Dylan's set is less than an hour long, although it does feature a new arrangement of "I Dreamed I Saw St. Augustine."

September 19, Sportpaleis Ahoy, Rotterdam, Netherlands

Three years on, Dylan returns to this relatively intimate venue, and, although the acoustics remain poor, he presents a high-energy show. After concluding the main set with a version of "Slow Train," he returns with the Heartbreakers and Roger McGuinn (who has opened all the shows) for a fine version of "Chimes of Freedom," Dylan singing the first and last verses, and Mr. McGuinn the second. The second encore is "Gotta Serve Somebody."

September 20, Halle 20, International Trade Center, Hanover, W. Germany

Includes a final version of "Slow Train."

September 21, Valbyhallen, Copenhagen, Denmark

Includes a second "When I Paint My Masterpiece," which is not as impressive as at Basel, and an electric arrangement of "Desolation Row," which is surprisingly effective, primarily because of some fine playing by Mike Campbell, whose guitar work throughout the tour is something of a revelation.

September 23, Isshallen, Helsinki, Finland

This is Dylan's first show in Finland. Three songs receive their final 1987 outings: "Highway 61 Revisited," "Stuck Inside of Mobile," and "It's All Over Now, Baby Blue."

September 25, Scandinavium, Gothenburg, Sweden

Includes a second "Trust Yourself." Dylan also introduces a new slot halfway through the set where he sings a song backed by Mike Campbell on guitar and Benmont Tench on piano. On this occasion, Dylan sings a beautiful version of "Tomorrow Is a Long Time."

September 26, Johanneshovs Isstadion, Stockholm, Sweden

September 28, Festhalle, Frankfurt, W. Germany

September 29, Martin Schleyerhalle, Stuttgart, W. Germany

Includes "Positively Fourth Street" and a fine "Don't Think Twice, It's All Right," accompanied by just Campbell and Tench.

September 30, Olympiahalle, Munich, W. Germany

Includes "I Dreamed I Saw St. Augustine."

October 1, Arena di Verona, Verona, Italy

Returning to the venue where he had opened the 1984 tour, Dylan gives a somewhat more together performance, opening with "When the Night Comes Falling from the Sky" and featuring a version of "I'll Be Your Baby Tonight" with some fine harmonica.

October 3, The Paleur, Rome, Italy

Includes "Heart of Mine" and "The Wicked Messenger."

October 4, Arena Civica di Milano, Milan, Italy

October 5, Piazza Grande, Locarno, Switzerland
Includes "Ballad of Frankie Lee and Judas Priest."

October 7, P.O.P.B. Bercy, Paris, France
Despite failing to sell enough tickets to justify a second Paris show, Dylan gives a great performance. Opening with "Man Gave Names to All the Animals," the main set also includes a "Forever Young" with extended harmonica intro. This remains the standard arrangement for the remainder of the tour. After a 12-song main set, the Parisian audience is treated to a four-song encore, including the only "House of the Rising Sun" of 1987. Dylan finishes with "Shot of Love."

October 8, Forest National Stadium, Brussels, Belgium
Another 16-song set opens with "Desolation Row," an ambitious choice, and includes two songs with just Campbell and Tench, "Don't Think Twice, It's Alright," and almost-effective version of "The Lonesome Death of Hattie Carroll." "Man Gave Names to All the Animals" is one of the encores.

October 9: UK release of the film Hearts of Fire; *the soundtrack album followed on the 13th.*

October 10, National Exhibition Centre, Birmingham, England
Returning to the N.E.C after six years, Dylan is slow to warm up, but after a lackluster "Senor," he whips out the ol' harmonica and plays the introduction to "I Want You." After a powerful version of the song, he launches into "Pledging My Time," and the rest of the show maintains the momentum.

October 11, National Exhibition Centre, Birmingham, England
The second night features a 15-song set, including "I Dreamed I Saw St. Augustine" as first encore, with some resplendent guitar work from Mike Campbell.

October 12, National Exhibition Centre, Birmingham, England
On the final night, Dylan is clearly in a good mood, despite a particularly good Heartbreakers's set, performing a 17-song set. Both "License to Kill" and "Joey" receive their final 1987 outings, and the three-song encore includes a final "Positively Fourth Street." Dylan heads for London after this show, staying at the Mayfair Hotel.

October 13
Dylan and a lady friend go to see the film *Rita,*

Sue and Bob Too at the Leicester Square Empire before partaking of a three-hour meal at Romeo and Juliet's restaurant.

October 14, Wembley Arena, London
Dylan concludes his European tour with four nights at the smallest English venue he has played in 21 years. The first night's 15-song set includes a particularly worthwhile "Ballad of Frankie Lee and Judas Priest," and a fine "Man of Peace" with harmonica introduction. The scheduled setlist for this show apparently includes "Folsom Prison Blues" and "Every Grain of Sand" as alternates, although neither are performed. Throughout the tour, Dylan has frequently departed from the agreed setlist.

October 15, Wembley Arena, London
On the second night, Dylan performs another 15-song set, including "I'll Remember You" with harmonica introduction.

October 16, Wembley Arena, London
The third night, despite being the shortest of the London shows, is the most impressive. Highlights include a one-off performance of "To Ramona," as one of the two Dylan-Campbell-Tench songs, a good "Shelter from the Storm" with a harmonica introduction, and an exuberant "Rainy Day Women" as second and final encore.

October 17, Wembley Arena, London
Although not as consistent or impressive as on the previous night, Dylan pulls out all the stops for his final London show, playing the longest show of the tour (20 songs compared to a norm of 14). The opening song, "The Times They Are a-Changin'," features a lengthy harmonica introduction. The set then includes a cross-section of some of the most effective songs from the tour set: "Dead Man, Dead Man," "I Dreamed I Saw St. Augustine," "I'll Be Your Baby Tonight," "Gotta Serve Somebody," and "Man of Peace," Dylan seemingly finishing the set with "In the Garden." The lights go down, but his scarf has caught in his guitar strings. As he wrenches it free, he launches into "Knockin' on Heaven's Door," while the Heartbreakers hastily return to the stage. Then, after a first encore of "Chimes of Freedom," surprise guest George Harrison joins Dylan for "Rainy Day Women." Again the lights go down, but Dylan stays onstage, bringing the tour full circle by launching into an impressive version of "Go Down Moses." He leaves the stage having closed his best tour in six years in fine style, thanks in no small part to the Heartbreakers, who have rediscovered something lacking in 1986. After the show, the C.B.S. Managing Director (UK), Paul Russell, presents Dylan with a platinum disc to mark UK sales in excess of five million.

October 18
Dylan visits George Harrison at his home in Henley-on-Thames.

October 22
Dylan turns up at the Empress of Russia folk club in Islington to see the Campbell Family perform.

October 31
Dylan calls at Barry White's house in Los Angeles.

November
There are reports of a fire in one of the garage/huts on Dylan's Malibu estate. No one is reported injured, but the fire causes considerable damage.

November 22
Dylan rehearses with then-"Saturday Night Live" bandleader G. E. Smith and other, unknown musicians. Among the songs they run through are an unknown instrumental, "Dancing in the Dark," "Six Days on the Road," "Carrying My Cross," two versions of "Susie Q," "You're a Big Girl Now," "All I Really Wanna Do," "Leopard-Skin Pill-Box Hat," "Dead Man, Dead Man" (three takes), "Everbody's Movin'," "It's So Easy," a version of "Trail of the Buffalo" with accordion, "Heart of Mine," two attempts at "Joey," "I'll Be Your Baby Tonight," "(I Heard That) Lonesome Whistle," and "Shelter from the Storm."

(Date Unknown)
Dylan records a version of "Pretty Boy Floyd," which is subsequently released on *Folkways: A Vision Shared,* a tribute album to Woody Guthrie and Leadbelly to benefit the Smithsonian/Folkways archives.

1988

Date Unknown

Dylan provides Alan Douglas, the ostensible overseer of the Hendrix estate, with a 500-word tribute to Jimi Hendrix for an exhibition that Douglas is planning to celebrate the art of Hendrix. The text Dylan provides is actually remarkably confessional in that he talks about other people covering his songs and how much more difficult it is to do one of his songs compared with, say, the Beatles or Chuck Berry, that with his work one needs to get "somewhat inside and behind them." Dylan proceeds to pay tribute to Hendrix's covers of his own songs, but concludes that "he paid a price he didn't have to pay."

January 20, Rock & Roll Hall of Fame

Dylan is inducted into the Rock & Roll Hall of Fame at its second annual ceremony, held at the Waldorf Astoria Hotel in New York. After accepting his award from Bruce Springsteen, Dylan participates in a shambolic jam session backed by David Letterman's band. He sings lead on "Like a Rolling Stone," and shares lead with George Harrison on "All Along the Watchtower."

January 28

Dylan attends a party at the Los Angeles Museum of Contemporary Art premiering the spring collection of designer Giorgio Armani. In his own concession to radical chic, Dylan wears an Angora knit hat.

Late Winter

Dylan contributes to at least one song for a forthcoming U2 album as the band winds up recording in Los Angeles. He plays Hammond organ on "Hawkmoon 269." He also provides backing vocals on a song he has cowritten with Bono, "Love Rescue Me," recorded at Sun Studios in Memphis (the latter song may date from an April 1987 session in Memphis).

March

Dylan is reportedly back at Sunset Sound, remixing *Down in the Groove*. Yet only "Had a Dream about You Baby" features a mix discernibly different from the prerelease tapes; Mitchell Froom's keyboards are added to the *Hearts of Fire* version, and the drums are whomped up in the mix.

Spring

Dylan plays a small acting role as an artist protecting murder witness Jodie

Foster in a film entitled *Backtrack.* The involvement of Neil Young in a similar cameo role on the same production suggests that filming took place
shortly before the 1988 tour. Dylan and Young spend some time together
at this juncture.

Early April
Requiring a studio at short notice in order to record an extra song for a European 12-inch single, George Harrison calls Dylan to ask if he can use his
garage studio in Malibu. Jeff Lynne comes along to coproduce, bringing Roy
Orbison, whom he is also currently producing. When they have to call at
Tom Petty's house to pick up a guitar, Petty tags along, and so, with Dylan at home and keen to participate in the revelries, the Traveling Wilburys
are born. The song they come up with on this day is "Handle with Care."
Rather than waste the song on the b-side of a single, however, they decide
to record a Traveling Wilburys album and arrange to reconvene at the beginning of May, when all five have a gap in their schedules.

April 24
Dylan attends Mick Fleetwood's wedding reception at Fleetwood's Malibu
home.

Late April
Dylan's first rehearsals for a band to tour through the summer of 1988 ap-
parently feature Steve Jordan on drums, Randy Jackson on bass, and Hiram
Bullock on guitar. These rehearsals do not take place in New York but in
California. Dylan, unhappy with the sound, starts again after the comple-
tion of the Wilburys's album.

Early (7?) to Mid-May
The Traveling Wilburys, augmented by Jim Keltner on drums, reassemble
at Dave Stewart's Los Angeles studio to record the remaining songs for the
Wilburys's *Volume One* in just 10 days. Of the nine songs cut, three are sung
by Dylan: "Dirty World," "Tweeter and the Monkey Man," and "Congratulations." He also sings one verse of "Margerita." According to Harrison, the
epic "Tweeter and the Monkey Man" was composed by Dylan and Tom
Petty, and recorded in just two takes. A rough version of "Dirty World,"
with the lyrics not quite honed and the ending not worked out at all, circulated on a working tape, although none of the other songs on the working tape differ markedly from their official counterparts.

Spring to Summer
Dylan plays Bono Vox of U2 some of the songs that will later appear on *Oh
Mercy.* Bono suggests Daniel Lanois as a suitable producer.

Mid- to Late May
Dylan rehearses for an extensive US tour at S.I.R. Studios, NY. The tour
band initially consists of Marshall Crenshaw on six-string bass, G. E. Smith
on guitar, and Christopher Parker on drums. After three or four days of rehearsals, however, it is apparent that Crenshaw's six-string bass does not fill
the sound out enough, and Dylan decides to recruit a conventional bassist.

Late May to Early June

Kenny Aaronson is assigned the task of fleshing out Dylan's touring band as rehearsals continue at Montana Studios, NY. After a day of playing minus Dylan, Aaronson has just five days to learn the 60 songs that comprise the basic repertoire for a major summer tour.

May 29

Presumably as a break from tour rehearsals, Dylan pops down to New York's Lone Star Cafe, making a brief guest appearance with Levon Helm to sing lead on "Nadine" and "The Weight."

> May 31: *Down in the Groove* (C 40957): "When Did You Leave Heaven?," "Sally Sue Brown," "Death Is Not the End," "Had a Dream about You Baby," "Ugliest Girl in the World," "Silvio," "Ninety Miles an Hour," "Shenandoah," "Rank Strangers to Me"

June 7, Concord Pavilion, Concord, CA

Dylan embarks on his second major US tour in two years, this time with his most stripped-down band: just lead and bass guitar, drums, and some (for once audible) rhythm guitar by Dylan himself. There are no girls, no harmonica, even keyboards are absent. However, as soon as he launches into "Subterranean Homesick Blues," it is clear that this is a tough, punchy, no-frills band. The first show defines the format for the tour, consisting of a six-song electric set followed by a three-song acoustic set (on which Dylan is accompanied by G. E. Smith), before three more electric songs conclude the main set. On this first night there is only a one-song encore, a full-band version of "Maggie's Farm," although the norm for the tour will be two or three songs, the first song usually being acoustic. The main sets lasts approximately one hour, with 10- to 15-minute encores. Although the length of the shows is criticized in some quarters, as in Europe in 1987, a high-energy level is maintained throughout, more than justifying Dylan's decision to play shorter sets. As in 1987, the sets for the first leg of the US tour constantly change and are chock full of unusual arrangements and performances.

The first show of the tour sounds surprisingly polished. There is also a special guest on guitar, one Neil Young. Dylan also performs only four songs featured on his 1986 US tour: "Masters of War," "Gotta Serve Somebody," "In the Garden," and "Like a Rolling Stone." Songs that receive live debuts include "Subterranean Homesick Blues," "Absolutely Sweet Marie," and a remarkably good "Driftin' Too Far from Shore" (all performed with the band). The traditional "Lakes of Pontchartrain" is performed in the acoustic set, along with two golden oldies, both receiving their first airings in 25 years, "Man of Constant Sorrow" and "Boots of Spanish Leather." "Gates of Eden" receives its first electric arrangement as part of the second electric set, and a magnificent rendition it is, Dylan even managing to remember most of the words. Although the show only clocks in at 65 minutes, it is an auspicious start to what soon becomes the "Never Ending Tour."

June 9, Cal Expo, Sacramento, CA

Once again it's all change! Dylan duplicates only the opening and closing songs from Concord. Tonight, however, is a bad-tempered affair. Dylan, apparently disappointed at the turnout (the venue is only half-full, fewer than six thousand fans attending), refuses to return for an encore. Because of this, he receives considerable bad press in the San Francisco area. Tonight's set is far more of a greatest hits package than Concord, with "It's All Over Now, Baby Blue," "I Shall Be Released," "Ballad of a Thin Man," "Girl from the North Country," and "Just Like a Woman" all restored to favor. Far more surprising is the inclusion of an awful "The Man in Me," an exhilarating romp through "Stuck Inside of Mobile" (a regular since the Dylan/Dead shows), and "Had a Dream about You Baby," the first new Dylan song to be sung onstage since "Got My Mind Made Up" at San Diego in June 1986. The acoustic set also includes a couple of real surprises: another selection from Dylan's first album, "Baby, Let Me Follow You Down," and an old Spanish-American war song, "The Two Soldiers."

June 10, Greek Theater, Berkeley, CA

Ever a man of moods, Dylan returns to blazing form with a terrific 95-minute, 17-song set. Again a wealth of songs are introduced, five songs in the electric sets being performed for the first time on the 1988 tour: "Joey," "Watching the River Flow," "Tangled Up in Blue," "It Takes a Lot to Laugh," and Glen Glenn's "Everybody's Movin'." Also introduced into the acoustic set are "San Francisco Bay Blues," which is met with whoops of recognition by the Bay Area audience, "The Times They Are a-Changin'," and a sensitive "Rank Strangers to Me," the second selection from *Down in the Groove.* Neil Young joins the band for the second electric set, staying on stage for the remainder of the show.

June 11, Shoreline Amphitheater, Mountain View, CA

Dylan again rings the changes. A 16-song set includes nine additions to the tour repertoire. If the additions to the acoustic set are not exactly startling ("It Ain't Me, Babe," "Blowin' in the Wind," and "The Lonesome Death of Hattie Carroll"), the same could not be said of the electric additions. Most surprising is the first live performance of "My Back Pages," which works well, even though Dylan has difficulty with the convoluted lyrics. Less surprising, although equally worthwhile, are two *Blood on the Tracks* songs, "Simple Twist of Fate" and "Shelter from the Storm." "I'll Remember You," "I Want You," and "I Dreamed I Saw St. Augustine," although less effective than in 1987, also work well enough. After "I'll Remember You," Dylan, presumably upset by a comment in a review of an earlier show, says, "I don't think that's an obscure song. Do you think that's an obscure song? I don't think so." Neil Young again joins the band during the second electric set. The first four California shows have seen some 40 songs performed by Dylan.

June 13, Park West, Park City, UT

Five more songs make their tour debuts, although four of them hardly qualify as unusual selections for Dylan's '80s tours: "I'll Be Your Baby Tonight," "All Along the Watchtower," an acoustic "A Hard Rain's a-Gonna Fall," and a one-off version of "License to Kill." Dylan also adds another traditional song in the acoustic set. "Barbara Allen" for once retains a traditional melody.

June 15, Fiddler's Green Amphitheater, Denver, CO
Dylan continues to mix up his repertoire, introducing the first live version of "One More Cup of Coffee" in 10 years. "Seeing the Real You at Last," a song obviously suited to this raunchy band, also makes its first 1988 appearance. The acoustic set comprises three additions, "Mama, You Been on My Mind," Irish ballad "Eileen Aroon," and "Don't Think Twice, It's All Right."

June 17, The Muni, St. Louis, MO
Although the acoustic set contains no surprises, Dylan introduces two songs into the electric set. If "Highway 61 Revisited" works well, "I Shall Be Released" (with a verse from the 1986 Martin Luther King version) meanders. Also performed is the turgid "John Brown" and, as one of two electric encores, an enthusiastic "Nadine," a homage to Chuck Berry for Berry's hometown crowd.

June 18, Alpine Valley Music Theater, East Troy, WI
Although the surprises now begin to tail off, Dylan still manages to introduce a one-off acoustic "Ballad of Hollis Brown" and a full-band version of "Ballad of Frankie Lee and Judas Priest," retaining much of its 1987 arrangement.

June 21, Blossom Music Center, Cuyahoga Falls, OH
Tonight's additions include a regular crowd-pleaser in 1988, "Silvio," as well as a cover making its only 1988 appearance, "Across the Borderline."

June 22, Riverbend Music Center, Cincinnati, OH
Includes an electric "Clean-Cut Kid" and an acoustic "Wild Mountain Thyme."

June 24–25, Garden State Arts Center, Holmdel, NJ
On the first night, his 11th show of the tour, Dylan performs no songs new to the 1988 set. Night number 2 brings just one addition, but a particularly fine one it is, a gripping acoustic rendition of "Trail of the Buffalo."

June 26, Saratoga Performing Arts Center, Saratoga Springs, NY
A new arrangement of "Tomorrow Is a Long Time" is a pleasant addition to the electric set.

June 28, Finger Lakes Performing Arts Center, Canandaigua, NY
Dylan excavates another "Sun" classic, Johnny Cash's "Give My Love to Rose," which he slots into the acoustic set.

June 30, Jones Beach, Long Island, NY
Dylan opens his two-night stay with a rare 17-song set that includes a fine band version of "Just Like Tom Thumb's Blues."

July 1, Jones Beach, Long Island, NY

July 2, Great Woods Center, Mansfield, MA
Tonight's electric set includes a rare "Had a Dream about You Baby" and a folk-rock version of "Pretty Peggy-O." "Mr. Tambourine Man" and "Love Minus Zero" make their first 1988 appearances in the acoustic set.

July 3, Old Orchard Beach Ball Park, Portland, ME
"To Ramona" makes its first 1988 appearance during the acoustic set.

July 6, Mann Music Center, Philadelphia, PA

July 8, Montreal Forum, Montreal, Quebec
The fourth song in the first electric set is a Leonard Cohen song, "Hallelujah," presumably intended as another special performance for a home town.

July 9, Civic Center Arena, Ottawa, Ontario
The acoustic "It's Allright, Ma" returns to the live set.

July 11, Copps Coliseum, Hamilton, Ontario

July 13, The Castle, Charlevoix, MI

July 14, Poplar Creek, Hoffman Estates, IL
"Song to Woody" is the first song in the acoustic set, and the fourth song from *Bob Dylan* to be performed this summer.

July 15, The Grandstand, State Fairgrounds, Indianapolis, IN

July 16
After the Indianapolis show, Dylan apparently travels to Fairmount, IN, James Dean's hometown. He arrives about midnight and stays for three hours, visiting Dean's grave and the house where he grew up.

July 17–18, Meadow Brook Music Festival, Oakland University Campus, Rochester Hills, MI.

July 20, Merriweather Post Pavilion, Columbia, MD

Mid- to Late July (20?)
Dylan provides some brief comments to Edna Gundersen for a feature on the 1988 tour in *USA Today*. Gundersen's review of the Maryland show runs alongside the profile.

July 22, Starwood Amphitheater, Nashville, TN
During the day, Dylan visits the Country Music Hall of Fame in Nashville.

July 24–25, Chastain Park Amphitheater, Atlanta, GA
The second night includes debuts for "Forever Young" and "Leopard-Skin Pill-Box Hat."

July 26, Mud Island, Memphis, TN
"Forever Young" is the second encore.

July 28, The Starplex, Dallas, TX
"Every Grain of Sand" receives only its second-ever US performance. Despite the band's inability to handle the song convincingly, Dylan sings it with gusto.

July 30, Mesa Amphitheater, Mesa, Phoenix, AZ
"Forever Young" is performed for the third and last time on the 1988 tour, this time acoustically.

July 31, Pacific Amphitheater, Costa Mesa, CA

> August: *Folkways: A Vision Shared* released with Dylan's performance of "Pretty Boy Floyd"

August 2, Greek Theater, Los Angeles, CA
On the first night, Dylan invites the audience to move down to the front after his acoustic set. With an enthusiastic crowd he can finally see, he responds with an impressive second electric set (and encore), including "Every Grain of Sand," performed for the second time on the tour, and an acoustic "She Belongs to Me," which receives its first live airing in seven years.

August 3, Greek Theater, Los Angeles, CA
The second acoustic encore on the middle night is that crooners' staple, "I'm in the Mood for Love." Possibly it is intended for long-standing girlfriend Carole Childs, who is in the audience.

August 4, Greek Theater, Los Angeles, CA
The final show brings a revival of the Leonard Cohen song Dylan had performed in Montreal, "Hallelujah." During the acoustic set, he breaks two strings on "It Ain't Me, Babe" but manages to finish, seguing into a fifth acoustic song, an old country nugget called "I'll Be Around." The final encore is "Knockin' on Heaven's Door," on which he shares lead vocals with The Alarm's Mike Peters. The rest of The Alarm join Dylan and band on stage for this final encore. The Alarm have been the support act throughout the first leg of the tour, although this is the first time they have joined Dylan.

August 5
Dylan is interviewed by Kathryn Baker at an Italian restaurant in Los Angeles called Un Cielo. The interview is widely syndicated through Associated Press.

August 6, Sammis Pavilion, Batiquitos, Carlsbad, CA

Tonight's show is the first rock gig at an intimate, three thousand-seat, open-air venue, located just outside San Diego. Dylan responds with a particularly fine show that includes two unusual acoustic choices. "Don't Think Twice, It's All Right" segues into a first-ever acoustic "Knockin' on Heaven's Door," while the first acoustic encore is a sensitive "We Three (My Echo, My Shadow and Me)."

August 7, County Bowl, Santa Barbara, CA

For this last show on the first leg of the 1988 tour, Dylan pulls out all the stops. Playing in a natural amphitheater, minus any stage lighting, on a beautiful Sunday afternoon, he performs a 17-song set that includes three songs new to the California audiences (it would have been four if he had included "Queen Jane Approximately," as the set list indicated). "Leopard-Skin Pill-Box Hat" shows G. E. Smith's guitar work in its best light; a tender, acoustic "One Too Many Mornings" is equally gripping; and, as the third song of a four-song encore, he does a rockabilly rendition of "Big River." The final encore is a second version of "Knockin' on Heaven's Door" with the Alarm, making their last appearance on the tour.

• Although Dylan's voice is now showing real signs of wear, he has decided to stay on the road, embarking on a second leg on August 18. However, the song selections from this point on will contain few surprises. If Dylan has not quite sung with the soul he displayed in Europe in 1987, he has nevertheless put considerable energy and thought into the shows, and the acoustic sets, almost without exception, have been delightful. The band has provided a solid bedrock, and although the electric sets have occasionally been a tad unrelenting, the less ambitious songs have usually worked well in this environment. And the US press has responded with something close to unbridled enthusiasm to this new incarnation.

August 8–17

Dylan attends his stepdaughter Maria's wedding to Peter Himmelman in Minnesota. He also enjoys a brief holiday in Sirmione, Italy.

August 18, Civic Auditorium, Portland, OR

August 20, Champs De Brionne Summer Music Theater, George, WA

August 21, Pacific Coliseum, Vancouver, British Columbia

As the second electric encore, Dylan performs "Knockin' on Heaven's Door" with special guest Tracy Chapman.

August 23, Olympic Saddledome, Calgary, Canada

Dylan again performs "Knockin' on Heaven's Door" with Tracy Chapman.

August 24, Northlands Coliseum, Edmonton, Canada
Dylan performs "Knockin' on Heaven's Door" with Tracy Chapman, before bringing Doug Sahm onstage to lead the band through "She's about a Mover."

August 26, Winnipeg Arena, Winnipeg, Manitoba

August 29, CNE Exhibition Stadium Grandstand, Toronto, Ontario

August 31, New York State Fairground, Syracuse, NY

September 2, Orange County Fair, Middletown, NY

September 3, Riverfront Park, Manchester, NH
Dylan performs his first-ever electric "Visions of Johanna." He also re-introduces "Rank Strangers to Me" and "I Don't Believe You" into the acoustic set.

September 4, Festival Park, Bristol, CT
Dylan again performs "I Don't Believe You," but this time with the full band. Also featured tonight are a rare "Just Like Tom Thumb's Blues" and three songs from *Down in the Groove:* "Rank Strangers to Me," "Silvio," and a disastrous "Had a Dream about You Baby." Sixty minutes of tonight's show is subsequently broadcast on a local radio station, apparently without Dylan's permission.

September 7, Champlain Valley Fairgrounds, Essex Junction, Burlington, VT
Includes the second and last "I Don't Believe You" electric.

September 8, Broome County Veterans Memorial Arena, Binghamton, NY
Includes a final version of "Had a Dream about You Baby."

September 10, Waterloo Village, Stanhope, NJ

September 11, Patrick Center, Fairfax, VA

September 13, Civic Arena, Pittsburgh, PA
Includes "It Takes a Lot to Laugh."

September 15, University of NC, Chapel Hill, NC

September 16, Carolina Coliseum, Columbia, SC
Includes a part-acoustic, part-electric version of "Give My Love to Rose."

September 17, The Paladium, Charlotte, NC
Includes "Mama, You Been on My Mind."

September 18, Knoxville, TN

September 19, University Hall, Charlottesville, VA

September 21, University of Southern FL, Sundome, Tampa, FL

September 23, Miami Arena, Miami, FL

September 24, University of FL O'Connell Center, Gainesville, FL

September 25, Audubon Zoo, New Orleans, LA

By this point on the 1988 tour, Dylan's voice is in terrible shape, and he is shouting his way through most of the show. The only surprise tonight is a part-electric version of "Forever Young," the band joining in halfway through the song. During his time in New Orleans, Dylan stops in on the recording sessions for the Neville Brothers's *Yellow Moon,* which is being produced by Canadian Daniel Lanois. The Neville Brothers have recorded two Dylan originals for the album, "Ballad of Hollis Brown" and "With God on Our Side," the latter of which features an extra verse, written by the Neville Brothers themselves, that Dylan now incorporates into his own live version.

October 5

Dylan attends a party in Beverly Hills, CA, to celebrate the conclusion of six sellout shows by George Michael in Los Angeles. He is accompanied by Carole Childs.

Late September to Early October

According to Jackie Leven, ex-singer of British punk band Doll By Doll, he meets Dylan in a bar in Berlin and travels with him by train to St. Petersburg the following day. On the way, Leven reads him a lyric he is writing called "As We Sailed Into Skibereen." Dylan suggests that he set it to the tune of "One Too Many Mornings."

Note: Leven attributes this to October 5, 1988 in an interview in *The Telegraph No. 51.* However, Dylan was in Los Angeles on that date (see the preceding).

October 13–14, Tower Theater, Upper Darby, PA

After a three-week break, Dylan has scheduled four shows in New York with two warmup shows on the outskirts of Philadelphia to conclude his 1988 touring activities. Before the first Philadelphia show, Dylan has an extended soundcheck during which he runs through three country classics with the band: "Give My Love to Rose," "I Don't Hurt Anymore," and "I'm Moving On." The show itself is Dylan's first since 1986 to feature over 20 songs, including a seven-song encore—four acoustic, three electric—concluding with an impressive "Every Grain of Sand." "Bob Dylan's 115th Dream" and "With God on Our Side" are included. The notion of a full-band version of "Bob Dylan's 115th Dream" sounds amazing, but in reality Dylan strips it of all its humor. It is, however, retained for the remaining shows, along with a somber acoustic "With God on Our Side," which includes the verse referring to Vietnam, courtesy of the Neville Brothers.

• The second night, although not such a marathon performance, still clocks in at 17 songs, and features two additions to the acoustic set: "Gates of Eden" and the traditional "Wagoner's Lad." The latter features a particularly beautiful vocal by Dylan. Both are retained for the New York shows.

October 16–19, Radio City Music Hall, NY
Dylan ends his 1988 tour on a low note. His voice is in very poor shape, and he shouts his way through songs, stripping them of nuance and subtlety. Opening night is the briefest of the October shows, featuring a 15-song set. The final night features all three of the regular 1988 electric encores: "Knockin' on Heaven's Door," "All Along the Watchtower," and "Maggie's Farm."

October 18: *Traveling Wilburys: Volume I* (Warners 925796).

Early November
Dylan is in Minnesota, presumably on his farm in Laredo, with Carole Childs.

November
Dylan flies to Las Vegas to watch a Donny Lalonde boxing match, returning to Minneapolis almost immediately after the fight.

December 4, Oakland Coliseum, Oakland, CA
Dylan is part of "an all acoustic evening of music to benefit the Bridge School." It is the second such benefit (the first was in 1986), and Dylan performs six songs, with G. E. Smith accompanying him on second acoustic guitar. The six songs are a cross-section of Dylan's 1988 acoustic material: "San Francisco Bay Blues," drawn from the early shows; "With God on Our Side" and "Gates of Eden" from the October shows; "Girl from the North Country," a popular staple; and only the second acoustic performance of "Forever Young." The set also features a unique outing for "Pretty Boy Floyd."

December 7, 1988: Roy Orbison suffers a fatal heart attack in Nashville.

Late December
Dylan reluctantly joins the surviving Wilburys in Los Angeles to produce a video for their second single, "End of the Line." The video simulates a train trip through the Wild West, and Dylan's role is minimal. However, he still apparently storms off the set with the video unfinished, resulting in some harsh words from George Harrison and Tom Petty.

1989

January (10?)
Dylan attends a party with Carole Childs in Los Angeles, at which he is re-ported to have been flirting with other women, much to Childs's annoyance.

Mid-January, Montana Studios, NY
Dylan is at his favorite New York rehearsal studio, presumably working on some songs with the 1988 touring band.

Late January to Early February
Ever controversial, Dylan manages to upset the chef at R. J. Scottys in New York when he complains about the world-famous linguini with lobster.

February 6: *Dylan and the Dead* (OC 45056): "Slow Train," "I Want You," "Gotta Serve Somebody," "Queen Jane Approxi-mately," "Joey," "All Along the Watchtower," "Knockin' on Heaven's Door"

February 12, The Forum, Inglewood, CA
Dylan makes a surprise appearance at a Grateful Dead show. Although he is onstage for some eight songs, he only contributes vocals on two: "Stuck In-side of Mobile," on which he seems to lose interest halfway through, and a perfunctory encore of "Knockin' on Heaven's Door."

Early March
Dylan begins recording an album of original songs in New Orleans under the supervision of the Canadian production team of Daniel Lanois and Mal-colm Burns. Utilizing their Studio on the Move, a mobile setup, the sessions originate at Emlah Court, although they soon transfer to a house on Soniat Street. Just two songs are cut at Emlah Court, although these may well in-clude "Where Teardrops Fall," on which Dylan and Lanois are augmented by Paul Synegal on guitar, Larry Jolivet on bass, Alton Rubin, Jr., on scrub-board, John Hart on sax, and Rockin' Dopsie on accordion. A piano demo of "Ring Them Bells" may also originate from Emlah Court.

March 7–24
The "official" *Oh Mercy* sessions commence at 1305 Soniat, with producer Daniel Lanois prepared to chip in on lap steel, dobro, guitar, and omnichord,

and engineer Malcolm Burns contributing keyboards, bass, and tambourine. The musical pedigree of producer and engineer means that Dylan is able to get by with a handful of pedigree New Orleans session players. On most of the sessions, Mason Ruffner and Brian Stoltz are the guitarists, Tony Hall plays bass, Cyril Neville and Daryl Johnson contribute some percussion, and Willie Green is drummer. The basic tracks are cut in a couple of weeks, with a minimum of fuss, "Dignity" being cut on March 13, "Broken Days" (later to become "Everything Is Broken") on March 14, "God Knows" on March 9, and "Series of Dreams" on March 23. At least nine other songs are cut during these sessions, including a superb "Born in Time," omitted from the album. Dylan rerecords the vocal for "God Knows" on March 16, and some new guitar and Vox organ parts are added. In most cases, new vocals are recorded for the songs in early April. Exceptions, i.e., songs whose March vocals make it to the album, appear to comprise three: have been "Where Teardrops Fall," "Man in the Long Black Coat," and "Ring Them Bells."

April 3–12

Sessions at 1305 Soniat continue. However, these sessions are intended solely for overdubbing vocals and some instrumentation. On April 3, "Broken Days" is turned into "Everything Is Broken" thanks to two new vocal tracks, with new lyrics and a new harmonica break. "God Knows" is given its second vocal overdub on April 10, but still ends up as an outtake. "Dignity" suffers a similar fate, despite no fewer than three vocal overdubs on April 11. (The song reappears in the Dylan repertoire in his "MTV Unplugged" concert/album/video.) "Political World" is given a new vocal, "Most of the Time" at least two new vocal tracks (from which the released version is compiled), as does "Series of Dreams," although the composite vocal on *The Bootleg Series* manages to mix up the vocal tracks at one point. "What Good Am I?," "Disease of Conceit," and "What Was It You Wanted" are also given new vocals, as is "Shooting Star," which, like "Everything Is Broken," has been largely rewritten in the intervening period. Although Lanois and Burns add some instrumental overdubs in mid- to late April, Dylan has already taken off for New York, only returning to New Orleans to hear the final results.

April 29

Dylan turns up at Madigan's Club in New Orleans to see bluesman John Mooney perform.

Early May

Dylan, Malcolm Burn, and Daniel Lanois complete final mixes for *Oh Mercy,* which is mastered at Sterling Sound Studios in New York.

Mid-May, Montana Studios, NY

Dylan and the band rehearse a whole stack of covers at these 1989 rehearsal sessions, including the Who's "I Can See for Miles," the Supremes's "You Keep Me Hangin' On," Rodgers and Hart's "Where or When," Junior Parker's "Mystery Train," a song called "12 Volt Waltz," Patsy Cline's "Sweet Dreams" and "Waltzing after Midnight," Robert Johnson's "Little Queen of

Spades," the Coasters's "Poison Ivy," the traditional "Hang Me Oh Hang Me," Jerry Lee Lewis's "High School Confidential," Johnny Rivers's "Mountain of Love," Johnny Cash's "Ring of Fire" and "Give My Love to Rose," Buddy Holly's "Love's Made a Fool of You," the Beach Boys's "God Only Knows," and Rick Nelson's "Lonesome Town." Some Dylan songs are also rehearsed. Drummer Christopher Parker specifically mentions rearranging "The Man in Me," "Shot of Love," "Gotta Serve Somebody," "If Not for You," "Man of Peace," "Man Gave Names to All the Animals," "Tears of Rage" (G. E.'s request), and "When I Paint My Masterpiece" (Parker's request).

• At one session, they rehearse "I Shall Be Released," "Making Believe," "Early Morning Rain," three takes of "Shot of Love," "Give My Love to Rose," "Man Gave Name to All the Animals," "(I Heard That) Lonesome Whistle," "Silvio," two more versions of "Shot of Love," an instrumental, "Little Queen of Spades," "I'm Not Supposed to Care," another unidentified instrumental, "Not Fade Away," "Everyday," "When Did You Leave Heaven?," "Everybody's Movin'," "I'll Remember You," "Ballad of a Thin Man," "Peace in the Valley," "Shelter from the Storm," "Most Likely You Go Your Way," "Just Like Tom Thumb's Blues," and "Tomorrow Is a Long Time."

May (25)
Dylan is interviewed for syndication by L.P.I. "hours before he caught the plane that would take him to Europe." According to L.P.I., the interview was conducted in Los Angeles, where Dylan is "getting his next film ready." It is a brief interview and Dylan seems to have little to say, although he admits, "The worst times in my life were when I tried to search for the past."

May 27, Christinehof Slott, Andarum, Sweden
Dylan and his reassembled 1988 band launch their 1989 European tour in the backwaters of Sweden, in a castle some 30 miles from Malmo, as in 1988 opening with "Subterranean Homesick Blues." The second and third songs of the set, however, are new, Eddy Arnold's "You Don't Know Me," and "Most Likely You Go Your Way." Dylan also performs a semielectric version of "Give My Love to Rose," part of a three-song encore. The 15-song set contains one sign of hope for the 1989 tour: it marks the reintroduction of Dylan's harmonica playing in concert. Indeed, at this show and most later shows on the European tour, it proves difficult to stop Dylan from playing the mouth harp, adding a much-needed dimension to the sound of the band. Tonight Dylan and the band show signs of road rust, and Dylan wears an anorak hood over his head throughout the show, most disconcerting to the fans.

May 28, Globen Arena, Stockholm, Sweden
This is a much better show than the previous night. Dylan opens with a ragged "The Times They Are a-Changin'," which proves to be only a passing whim. The second song is even more incongruous. Sounding like a Swiss folk song, it appears to bear the title "My La-La." Dylan decides to grace the rather trite song with some spirited harmonica work. After a disastrous "All Along the Watchtower," Dylan starts to get into the groove, performing

"When Did You Leave Heaven?" with the band, the fourth song from *Down in the Groove* to appear in live performance. Dylan again remains hooded throughout the show.

May 30, Jaahalli, Helsinki, Finland
Although Dylan opens with "Subterranean Homesick Blues," the 1989 shows are at last beginning to display their own identity. Ironically, this year it is the electric sets that are a delight, and the acoustic sets that are often disappointing. His harp playing is erratic but he still has his moments. Dylan is also incorporating a cover into the first set at most shows. Tonight's second song is another '50s cover, "Confidential to Me." The highlight of tonight's show, though, is a gripping electric rendition of "Ballad of Hollis Brown," it's nagging, insistent riff complementing some impressive singing from Dylan.

May 31
Dylan flies to Dublin, where he stays at the Westbury Hotel.

June 1
Dylan's band rehearses with replacement bassist Tony Garnier. Kenny Aaronson is due to return to the US for an operation after the Wembley show. The rehearsals take place at Windmill Studios, but Dylan is not involved.

June 2
On this second day of rehearsals at Windmill Studios, Dylan joins Garnier, and the band and they run through some of the rather daunting set Garnier needs to quickly learn.

June 3, RDS Simmons Court, Dublin, Ireland
Dylan and the band have spent the day rehearsing with new bassist Tony Garnier at the Factory in Ringend. Garnier is the bassist at the first night's show. The set includes an electric version of "Every Grain of Sand," which is finally performed with a harmonica break. Dylan also plays an intense electric rendition of the traditional "The Water Is Wide," before the obligatory "Like a Rolling Stone" finale.

June 4, RDS Simmons Court, Dublin, Ireland
On the second night, Dylan finally abandons the hood, performing for the remainder of 1989 in full view of the paying customer. The show provides few surprises, although Bono insists on joining Dylan for encores of "Knockin' on Heaven's Door" and "Maggie's Farm," much to the delight of the celebrating Irish fans, whose national football team has just recorded a historic World Cup victory the same afternoon. Aaronson temporarily resumes bass duties.

June 5
Dylan travels to Scotland on the Larne-to-Stranraer ferry.

June 6, Scottish Exhibition Centre, Glasgow, Scotland
Dreadful acoustics mar Dylan's first Scottish show in 23 years, although he

does perform the first live version of one of the Traveling Wilburys's songs, "Congratulations," complete with a piercing harmonica introduction.

June 7, National Exhibition Centre, Birmingham, England

Dylan seems to enjoy playing the N.E.C. In good voice and mood, he responds to the enthusiastic crowd with a set that includes a full-band version of "Lonesome Town" (for the first time since 1986); and a second "Congratulations." In the wings tonight are fellow Wilburys Jeff Lynne and George Harrison, but Dylan does not invite them onstage.

June 8, Wembley Arena, London, England

Dylan's only London date of 1989 features "When Did You Leave Heaven?" Tonight is Aaronson's last gig with the band.

June 10, Statenhal, Den Haag, Netherlands

New bassist, Tony Garnier, is thrown into the deep end as Dylan decides to break the routine of opening with "Subterranean Homesick Blues," introducing "Most Likely You Go Your Way," which remains the regular opener until the end of August. Also introduced tonight are "I'll Be Your Baby Tonight," a bizarre stop-start arrangement of "Shelter from the Storm," a superb electric "I Don't Believe You," with a wild harmonica coda, and an astonishing electric "Trail of the Buffalo," which uses an arrangement similar to the band renditions of "John Brown" and "Ballad of Hollis Brown."

June 11, Vorst National, Brussels, Belgium

A less impressive show includes an acoustic "Mama, You Been on My Mind."

June 13, Les Arenes, Frejus, France

A most unusual set. Dylan opens with "My La-La," which still fails to impress, repeats "I Don't Believe You," introduces his first "Lakes of Pontchartrain" of 1989, and as part of a four-song encore performs both his 1979 French hit, "Man Gave Names to All the Animals" and a heartfelt rendition of the Presley staple, "(There'll Be) Peace in the Valley."

June 15, Sportpalace, Madrid, Spain

The surprises come early on the 15th. Song number two is a dead ringer for Hank Williams's "Lost Highway," but is in fact another Williams song, "House of Gold." Next up is a new, fast arrangement of "It Takes a Lot to Laugh," which will come into its own later in the year with a more considered arrangement. Finally, the first acoustic song is "Song to Woody."

June 16, Sportpalace, Madrid, Spain

"Forever Young" provides a little relief from the semielectric "Knockin' on Heaven's Door," opening the second band set on the 16th.

June 17, San Sebastian, Spain

Includes a "Never Ending Tour" debut for "Shot of Love."

Athens, 1989

June 19, Paltrussardi di Milano, Milan, Italy
Tonight's opening song, "Tangled Up in Blue," makes its only appearance of the European tour.

June 20, Gradinate, Rome, Italy
Includes "You Don't Know Me" and "Mama, You Been on My Mind."

June 21, Stadio Lamberti Cava dei Tirreni, Italy
Tonight Dylan includes a fine version of Townes Van Zandt's salutary ballad, "Pancho and Lefty."

June 22, Stadio di Ardenza, Livorno, Italy
"Seeing the Real You at Last," "I Want You," and "The Man in Me" all make 1989 debuts.

June 24, Istanbul, Turkey
Dylan's first show in Turkey is an exclusive affair. Only three thousand people are fortunate enough to get tickets. Dylan responds with a 21-song set, that includes a second and last "The Water Is Wide," a 1989 debut for "Leopard-Skin Pill-Box Hat," and a one-off performance of a country standard, "Making Believe."

Bob Dylan: A Life in Stolen Moments

June 26, National Stadium, Patras, Greece

Includes the first live performance of "Tears of Rage," although little survives of the song's beautiful melody. After his marathon performance in Istanbul, Dylan reverts to a 16-song set. His eccentric behavior also returns. During "Silvio," he asks for the lights to be turned down mid-song, playing the remainder of the show in virtual darkness.

June 27 or 28

Dylan spends time with Van Morrison while a BBC-TV film crew shoot a TV special about Morrison for "Arena." They perform four songs together on a hill overlooking the Acropolis. Three of the songs are included in the March 1991 "Arena" special, Dylan contributing backing vocals on "Crazy Love" and "One Irish Rover" and some sterling harmonica on "Foreign Window." Their duet on "And It Stoned Me" is not, however, broadcast.

June 28, Panathinaika Stadium, Athens, Greece

The final show of Dylan's month-long European sojourn is one of the best shows of the tour. Although the main set is a standard length, Dylan includes a unique acoustic "Every Grain of Sand," and a second and last "House of Gold." The encore is extended to five songs when Van Morrison joins Dylan onstage, performing two of Van the Man's better known songs, "Crazy Love" and "And It Stoned Me." Filmed for the BBC "Arena" special, they end up unused, presumably because Dylan again has the lights way down.

July 1, Civic Center Arena, Peoria, IL

After 21 European shows, Dylan returns to the US for 51 more shows on the same circuit traversed the previous year. If the sound of Dylan's band no longer surprises, the opening songs at this first US gig do. "Pancho and Lefty," a superb version of Van Morrison's "One Irish Rover," and the first live "I Believe in You" in eight years are the opening trio of songs.

July 2, Poplar Creek Music Theater, Hoffman Estates, IL

Dylan continues the surprises, with a "Never Ending Tour" debut for "Pledging My Time," a second stab at "Tears of Rage," and a 1989 debut for "Gotta Serve Somebody," featuring its nth set of words.

July 3, Marcus Amphitheater, Milwaukee, WI

Perhaps the most interesting US show to date includes 1989 debuts for "Driftin' Too Far from Shore," "I Dreamed I Saw St. Augustine," "Early Morning Rain," "Just Like Tom Thumb's Blues," and an acoustic "Black Girl (In the Pines)," Dylan apparently having written the lyrics on his arm.

July 5, Howard C. Baldwin Memorial Pavilion, Rochester, MI

"Lonesome Town" makes a rare appearance on opening night.

July 6, Howard C. Baldwin Memorial Pavilion, Rochester, MI

"I Don't Believe You" and an electric "It's All Over Now, Baby Blue" reappear on the 6th, along with 1989 debuts for "Tomorrow Is a Long Time" and an acoustic "She Belongs to Me." The real surprise, though, comes when

Dylan opens the second band set with his own version of Van Morrison's "And It Stoned Me," rewritten by Dylan and delivered with great panache.

July 8, Deer Creek Pavilion, Noblesville, IN

July 9, Blossum Theater, Cuyahoga Falls, OH
An electric "Forever Young" comes into temporary favor as the second song of the show.

July 11, Skyline Sports Complex, Harrisburg, PA

July 12, Allentown Fairgrounds, Allentown, PA
Includes the first live version of "Rainy Day Women" on the "Never Ending Tour."

July 13, Great Woods Performing Arts Center, Mansfield, MA

July 15, Seashore Performing Arts Center, Old Orchard Beach, ME
"Forever Young" is usurped by a rollicking cover of Steve Earle's "Nothing but You."

July 16, Lake Compounce Park, Bristol, CT

July 17, Waterloo Village, Stanhope, NJ

July 19, Merriweather Post Pavilion, Columbia, MD
Another delightful cover is introduced, Don Gibson's "(I'd Be) a Legend in My Time," a rather ironic choice on Dylan's part.

July 20, Bally's Grand Hotel, Atlantic City, NJ
Dylan temporarily abandons the six electric, three/four acoustic-three/four electric format, favoring a five-three-five split. Tonight's set also includes a one-off performance of "Lenny Bruce" with an extended harmonica introduction.

July 21, Garden State Theater, Holmdel, NJ
Dylan remembers his 80s albums, playing four unusual selections. "Trouble" receives its live debut, opening the show. "Shot of Love" is also part of the opening set. The acoustic set includes a version of "When Did You Leave Heaven?," no more successful than in electric guise. Dylan also revives "I'll Remember You" in the second band set.

July 23, Jones Beach State Park, Long Beach, NY
Kenny Aaronson, who is back to full health, guests on bass during the second band set, which opens with a rare "Pledging My Time."

July 25, Performing Arts Center, Canandaigua, NY
Includes "You Don't Know Me" and "Confidential to Me." "It's All Over Now, Baby Blue" also returns to the set, now in acoustic guise.

**July 26, Saratoga Performing Arts Center,
Saratoga Springs, NY**
Dylan revives the electric arrangement of "Pretty Peggy-O" performed just once in 1988. He also includes a second and last acoustic "When Did You Leave Heaven?"

July 28, Civic Arena, Pittsburgh, PA

July 29, Kingswood Music Theater, Maple, Ontario
"My La-La" makes a fleeting return.

July 30, Civic Center, Ottawa, Ontario
"It Takes a Lot to Laugh" returns to favor, after some considerable doodling while Dylan decides how to finish the first band set.

July 31, L'Amphitheatre, Jolliett, Quebec
Dylan performs another one-off cover, "Don't Pity Me."

August 3, Riverfest, Saint Paul, MN
Dylan performs at the annual fair, playing to fifty thousand fans.

August 4, Dane County Coliseum, Madison, WI
"Nothing but You" makes a welcome return.

August 5, Welsh Auditorium, Grand Rapids, MI
Three regulars from the early part of 1988 return to the set: the acoustic "Man of Constant Sorrow," a still disappointing "The Man in Me," and a bluesy "Watching the River Flow."

August 6, Cooper Stadium, Columbus, OH
Includes "Confidential to Me."

August 8, Savage Hall, Toledo, OH
Dylan plays "I'm in the Mood for Love" as part of tonight's acoustic set.

August 9, The Muny, Saint Louis, MO
Includes electric versions of "I'm in the Mood for Love" and "Heart of Mine," the fifth song from *Shot of Love* to be performed in 1989.

August 10, Riverbend, Cincinnati, OH
The electric "I'm in the Mood for Love" makes a second and last appearance.

August 12, King's Dominion Amusement Park, Doswell, VA
Includes "Tomorrow Is a Long Time."

August 13, Carowinds Amusement Park, Charlotte, NC

August 15, Chastain Memorial Park Amphitheater, Atlanta, GA

August 16, Chastain Memorial Park Amphitheater, Atlanta, GA
Dylan opens with "Trouble" and includes the electric "Trail of the Buffalo" and a slow, methodical arrangement of "Queen Jane Approximately."

August 18, Freedom Hall, Louisville, KY
A semielectric "Rank Strangers to Me" opens the second band set.

August 19, State Fair Grandstand, Springfield, IL
Two songs are added to the set: "Positively Fourth Street," which is retained for the remainder of 1989, and Jimmy Cliff's "The Harder They Come," which lasts just four performances, despite an impassioned delivery by Dylan.

August 20, Starwood Amphitheater, Nashville, TN
Includes "The Harder They Come."

August 22, Sandstone Amphitheater, Bonner Springs, KS
Includes "The Harder They Come" and an acoustic "Trail of the Buffalo."

August 23, Zoo Amphitheater, Oklahoma City, OK
Appropriately enough, Dylan performs "Man Gave Names to All the Animals."

August 24
Dylan and the band arrive in New Orleans, staying at the Maison Dupuy Hotel. At 10 PM, they head for Brightsen's Restaurant.

August 25, Kiefer UNO Lakefront Arena, New Orleans, LA
Dylan reverts to his 1986 repertoire, opening shows with an instrumental, seguing into "Positively Fourth Street." The instrumental is listed on the set list as "E Thang."

August 26, The Summit, Houston, TX
Dylan again opens with "E Thang" and "Positively Fourth Street." The second band set opens with a country blues, "More and More (I'm Forgettin' 'Bout You)."

August 27, Starplex Amphitheater, Dallas, TX
Dylan attempts a variant on "E Thang."

August 29, Pan American Center, Las Cruces, NM
For their first show in New Mexico, Dylan and the band open with an instrumental "El Paso." They conclude the show with the same song.

August 31, Fiddler's Green, Englewood, CO
Tonight's opener returns to a variant of "E Thang."

September 1, Park West, Park City, UT
Dylan continues to open with "E Thang." Tonight's show also includes "Man Gave Names to All the Animals." The length of the US sets has gradually crept up from a norm of 15 songs to 18 or even, as tonight, 19 tunes.

September 3, Greek Theater, Berkeley, CA
Dylan continues opening with an instrumental, tonight's being a version of the 1968 hit, "Man without Love." He also revives "The Harder They Come," and an acoustic "Baby, Let Me Follow You Down."

September 5, County Bowl, Santa Barbara, CA

A show that rarely approaches the heights of the August 1988 show. By now Dylan's voice is showing real signs of wear, and many of the songs meander to an end while Dylan decides whether to play harmonica, sing another verse, or just instruct the band to finish the song.

September 6, Starlight Bowl, San Diego, CA

Dylan finally plays a show entirely composed of songs from the '60s. The instrumental opener has given way to an electric "Visions of Johanna." Of the 16 songs performed tonight, only "Baby, Let Me Follow You Down," "One Too Many Mornings," and "I Shall Be Released" originate outside the 1965–1966 era.

September 8, Pacific Amphitheatre, Costa Mesa, CA

"Most Likely You Go Your Way" opens tonight's show.

September 9, Greek Theater, Los Angeles, CA

"Visions of Johanna" makes its second appearance.

September 10, Greek Theater, Los Angeles, CA

September 13

Dylan gives his first worthwhile interview in three years, to Edna Gundersen of *USA Today* at the Beverly Hills Comstock Hotel in Los Angeles. She had briefly interviewed Dylan in 1988, but this is a far more important affair. According to Gundersen, the conversation lasted some two and a half hours, with Dylan sipping coffee and smoking Marlboros throughout. Dylan talks at length about *Oh Mercy,* and what it is like trying to live down the legend. He even explains why he no longer talks to the audience when he is onstage, a regular bugbear with reviewers: "It just doesn't seem relevant anymore. It's not standup comedy or a stage play. Also it breaks up my concentration to have to think of things to say or to respond to the crowd. The songs themselves do the talking."

Mid- to Late September

Dylan is interviewed by Dan Meer of WNEW for a two-hour syndicated radio special, aimed at promoting *Oh Mercy.* The interview is scheduled to be broadcast the first week in November. A recalcitrant Dylan fails to provide enough material to fill out the program, and WNEW has to intersperse Dylan's comments with interview material from people like Daniel Lanois and Jim Keltner.

September

Allen Ginsberg plays a show at McCabe's Guitar Shop in Santa Monica. According to Ginsberg, Dylan turned up and played bass for him.

September 19

Variety reports that Dylan has left the management of Elliot Roberts, and that Jeff Kramer, previously an employee of Roberts's Lookout Management, will henceforth be Dylan's tour manager.

September 22: *Oh Mercy* (OC 45281): "Political World," "Where Teardrops Fall," "Everything Is Broken," "Ring Them Bells," "Man in a Long Black Coat," "Most of the Time," "What Good Am I?," "Disease of Conceit," "What Was It You Wanted?," "Shooting Star"

September 24

Dylan makes his second appearance on the Chabad telethon, appearing for this annual cable TV event with his son-in-law Peter Himmelman and the actor Harry Dean Stanton. He provides some restrained backup vocals and idiosyncratic recorder playing on three songs, "Einsleipt Mein Kind Dein Eigalach," "Adelita," and "Hava Nagilah." The trio, fronted by Himmelman, is introduced as Chopped Liver.

October 5–6

Dylan apparently travels to Washington to make a video with Tracy Chapman in aid of the homeless. No such video has ever been released.

October 7–9, Montana Studios, NY

Dylan and band rehearse several songs from *Oh Mercy* in preparation for a month of shows beginning with a four-date residency at the Beacon Theater in New York.

October 10, Beacon Theatre, NY

The major question before these New York shows is how many songs might Dylan perform from his newly released *Oh Mercy* album? After opening with an extended "Seeing the Real You at Last," a visibly nervous Dylan tackles one of the more difficult new songs, "What Good Am I," a gutsy performance. Although some songs performed on opening night, notably third song "Dead Man, Dead Man," resurrect the meandering California blues, there are some stunning performances. "Ballad of a Thin Man," with a furious harmonica introduction, is a revelation. Song number six, "Positively Fourth Street," reinterprets the whole song with a stately, mournful arrangement. Again Dylan's harmonica begins and ends the song. Indeed, throughout the entire Beacon residency Dylan will play some very audible rhythm guitar and a lot of harmonica. Tonight's opening band set lasts 50 minutes and includes eight songs, concluding with an extended "Rank Strangers to Me," prefaced by an indeterminate instrumental. After a disappointing acoustic set, the band returns for a slow, bluesy "It Takes a Lot to Laugh." After a false "I Shall Be Released" introduction, Dylan leads the band through another song from *Oh Mercy,* "Everything Is Broken." The final song is, predictably, "Like a Rolling Stone." The arrangement, though, is anything but standard, with Dylan switching to acoustic guitar halfway through (his electric guitar strap snaps). After the final verse, he plays a prolonged harmonica coda, which the band has some difficulty following. The first encore provides the final highlight of the evening, "Most of the Time," complete with some strident rhythm work from Dylan's guitar. "All Along the Watchtower" ends a 95-minute show of highs and lows, hinting that Dylan may have taken on a new lease on touring life.

October 11, Beacon Theatre, NY
Dylan retains the same three songs from *Oh Mercy*. The acoustic set, however, is far more impressive. The electric "My Back Pages" is also resurrected. Tonight's set list includes "Man of Peace," but it is not performed.

October 12, Beacon Theatre, NY
At the afternoon soundcheck for the third night, Dylan and the band attempt a version of "You're Gonna Make Me Lonesome When You Go." The third show is the most energetic of the Beacon performances, Dylan including a bizarre "I Don't Believe You," complete with some outrageous vocal mannerisms, followed by what sounds at first to be "Trust Yourself" but soon resolves into "Man of Peace." The highlight tonight, though, is a superb "Queen Jane Approximately," one of the two or three greatest performances of the "Never Ending Tour."

October 13, Beacon Theatre, NY
Dylan completes his Beacon residency in some style. He has visibly grown in confidence during the shows, and the *Oh Mercy* songs have grown in musical stature. "What Good Am I?" is graced with a harmonica solo, as is a fine "Man of Peace." A lengthy "Precious Memories" becomes only the second "Never Ending Tour" performance of a song from *Knocked Out Loaded*. Dylan responds to a request during the acoustic set, performing an impromptu "Song to Woody." The real surprises, however, are reserved for the encore, which opens with the haunting "Man in the Long Black Coat." Then, during "Leopard-Skin Pill-Box Hat," Dylan unhooks his microphone from the stand and, harmonica in hand, walks to the very lip of the stage, where he plays some knee-bending harp, before jumping into the audience and departing via the fire exit.

October 15, Tower Theater, Upper Darby, PA
The surprises continue as Dylan opens the first show with the first live version of the somewhat obscure "To Be Alone with You." He follows up with "Man in the Long Black Coat," a brief harmonica burst thrown in at the end. "Man of Peace" remains, followed by an extended "Tears of Rage."

October 16, Tower Theater, Upper Darby, PA
The second show includes a rare run-through of "The Man in Me."

October 17, Constitution Hall, Washington, DC
The first show includes the final "Precious Memories" of 1989.

October 18, Constitution Hall, Washington, DC
"I Believe in You" makes a rare appearance during the second night.

October 20, Mid-Hudson Arena, Poughkeepsie, NY

After "Everything Is Broken" tonight, Dylan goes over to the piano, leading the band through "When You Gonna Wake Up" and "Ring Them Bells," the latter apparently a request from tour manager Jeff Kramer. Reverting to guitar, Dylan then sings "Tears of Rage" and "Everybody's Movin'" before the perennial "Like a Rolling Stone" concludes one of Dylan's more remarkable "Never Ending Tour" sets. The final encore is "All Along the Watchtower," but after performing the entire song once, he slows the tempo right down, and proceeds to sing the first two verses again.

October 21

Dylan is interviewed at his hotel in Narrangsett, RI, by Adrian Deevoy of *Q* magazine. Although the interview lasts 40 minutes, Dylan has little to say, and Deevoy does little to extract any worthwhile material from the man's lips.

October 22, University of RI, South Kingston, RI

"Trouble" briefly returns to favor.

October 23–25, Opera House, Boston, MA

"Wagoner's Lad" makes a one-off reappearance during the acoustic set on opening night.

October 27, Palace Theater, Albany, NY

Dylan opens the show with an old favorite, "Gotta Serve Somebody," during which he plays piano standing up. "Lenny Bruce" also makes a surprise return. After a 17-song main set, Dylan seats himself at the piano for the first encore and plays perhaps the weakest song on *Oh Mercy,* "Disease of Conceit." This piano encore is retained for the remaining shows.

October 29, Ithaca College, Ithaca, NY

A 15-song set includes an acoustic "Knockin' on Heaven's Door" and an electric "Lay, Lady, Lay." Dylan also reverts to playing all of the *Oh Mercy* songs in the second half, which now comprises "Everything Is Broken," "What Good Am I?," "Most of the Time," "Man in the Long Black Coat," and "Like a Rolling Stone," with "Disease of Conceit" as the first encore.

October 31, Arie Crown Theater, Chicago, IL

November 1, Hill Auditorium, Ann Arbor, MI

Tonight Dylan opens the show with a one-off electric version of "Don't Think Twice, It's All Right." He also pulls out the first acoustic "Visions of Johanna" in 13 years.

November 2, State Theater, Cleveland, OH

November 4, University of PA, Indiana, PA

November 6, VA Polytechnic Institute, Blacksburg, VA

November 7, Chrysler Hall, Norfolk, VA
The fourth song tonight is a traditional ballad, "When First unto This Country." Despite a more than perfunctory arrangement, this is a one-off performance.

November 8, Duke University, Durham, NC
Dylan revives an old acoustic chestnut from the Rolling Thunder Revue, Merle Travis's "Dark as a Dungeon."

November 10, Fox Theater, Atlanta, GA
Includes a second "Dark as a Dungeon."

November 12, Sunrise Musical Theater, Sunrise, FL
Aside from stumbling and falling over in the middle of "Everything Is Broken," Dylan's return to Florida passes without incident.

November 13, Sunrise Musical Theater, Sunrise, FL
On the second night, Dylan decides to open the acoustic set with "Tangled Up in Blue." During the song, a woman from the audience jumps on stage and proceeds to strip down to her G-string. Dylan, the true professional, carries on, visibly amused.

November 14, Tampa Bay Performing Arts Center, Tampa, FL
Roger McGuinn joins Dylan for the first show's encores, contributing some vocals on "Knockin' on Heaven's Door."

November 15, Tampa Bay Performing Arts Center, Tampa, FL
The second night is the final show of 1989. It ends with Dylan making a brief, unintelligible speech from the stage.

November 20
Dylan records a version of Curtis Mayfield's "People Get Ready" for the soundtrack to Dennis Hopper's new film, *Flashback*. The session is at John Cougar Mellencamp's Bellmont Mall recording studio, in Brown County, just east of Bloomington, IN. The producer is Barry Goldberg.

November 21
Dylan makes his first promotional video in four years (discounting his spartan contributions to the two Wilburys videos). The video of "Political World" is shot in studios five and six of the radio and television building on the Indiana University campus. The video involves Dylan playing the song at a diplomatic ball as the camera cuts to and fro between the masters of war, their lady friends, and Dylan on stage.

1990

January 6

Dylan begins work on *Under the Red Sky* with a solitary session at Oceanway Studios in LA. Don and David Was are the producers this time around and it is down to them to assemble the musicians for today's session. The lineup of David Lindley, Jimmy and Stevie Ray Vaughan on guitars, Jamie Muhoberac on organ, Don Was on bass, and Kenny Aranoff on drums is one of the Was's more inspired combinations. Four songs are recorded, including one leftover from *Oh Mercy,* "God Knows," as well as "10,000 Men," "Handy Dandy," and "Cat's in the Well." A version of "Handy Dandy" with some intense slide work from Stevie Ray Vaughan ends up unused.

January 12, Toad's Place, New Haven, CT

In one of the most remarkable concerts of his career, Dylan performs for over four hours at a club with a seven hundred capacity, as a rehearsal for the brief winter 1990 tour. The show comprises four sets—all electric—the first lasting for 50 minutes, the second 45, and the last two both around the 65–70-minute mark, beginning at approximately 9 PM and ending at well past 2 AM. Dylan performs some 50 songs, of which 18 are covers: "Walk a Mile in My Shoes," "Trouble No More," "Hang Me Oh Hang Me," "Everybody's Movin'," "Telling Lies on Me," "Across the Borderline," "I've Paid the Price," "Help Me Make It Through the Night," "Dancing in the Dark," "(I Heard That) Lonesome Whistle," "Confidential to Me," "So Long, Good Luck and Goodbye," "Pretty Peggy-O," "Key to the Highway," "When Did You Leave Heaven," "Black Girl (in the Pines)," and "Precious Memories." From *Oh Mercy* he includes three songs not yet performed live, "Political World," "Where Teardrops Fall," and "What Was It You Wanted." Perhaps most surprising of all, Dylan does one of only two songs from *Empire Burlesque* not previously performed, "Tight Connection to My Heart." To reinforce the sense that this is a rehearsal, Dylan performs two songs twice, "Hang Me Oh Hang Me" and "Where Teardrops Fall,"and one song three times, "Political World." Although Dylan's voice (and some of the arrangements) sound extremely rough, he remains in a good mood throughout, performing requests like "Congratulations" and "Joey," talking regularly between songs, and introducing "Man of Peace" as a song from his religious period and "Lay, Lady, Lay" as a song from the days when romance was important to him.

January 14, Penn State, State College, PA

Tonight's show follows more conventional lines than Toad's, although the Penn State concert preserves one innovation: no acoustic set. As such, there is only a one-song encore to the 95-minute show. Five of the covers performed at Toads—"(I Heard That) Lonesome Whistle," "Across the Borderline," "Pretty Peggy-O," "Hang Me Oh Hang Me," and "Wiggle Wiggle"—the three songs from *Oh Mercy* debuted at Toad's, as well as "Tight Connection to My Heart," are all retained. Dylan also delivers his first live performance of "You Angel You," apparently in response to a request. Unfortunately, he has not scanned a set of lyrics beforehand.

January 15, McCarter Theatre, Princeton University, Princeton, NJ

The last of three warmup shows features a more orthodox set. A five-song acoustic set ends with a part-electric version of "Forever Young." However, this is no midshow acoustic set, but comes after just one song with the band, a rare "Watching the River Flow." "What Good Am I?" and "Most of the Time" both receive 1990 debuts. There is no encore.

January 16

Dylan flies to Sao Paolo.

January 18, Morumbi Stadium, Sao Paulo, Brazil

Dylan's first South American show is part of a festival that also features the Eurythmics. He plays to 110,000 fans.

January 19

In the evening, after relocating from Sao Paolo to the Rio Palace Hotel in Copacabana, Dylan is interviewed on a somewhat informal basis by Brazilian journalist Eduardo Bueno. Bueno drops a lot of the right names—Matisse, Cezanne, Michelangelo—and one wrong one, Presley, but Dylan has little to say.

January 20

Dylan spends the evening in the bar of the Rio Palace Hotel drinking caipirinha (rum and lemon) with Dave Stewart, discussing the idea of making a film together.

Mid- to Late January

While in Brazil, Dylan apparently goes into a recording studio to cut some material with local musicians.

January 25, Sambodromo, Rio de Janiero, Brazil

Dylan's second Brazilian show again requires him to play in front of a hundred thousand-plus fans, and he responds with an impressive cross section of his work. Although the first electric set sticks fairly doggedly to the '60s, the highlights are a fragile "You're a Big Girl Now," with some nice harmonica, and a down and dirty "Seeing the Real You at Last." Although the acoustic set is culled entirely from his first five albums, the second electric set is exclusively from the '80s except for the statutory "Like a Rolling

Stone." "Tight Connection to My Heart," in particular, is coming into its own live. Five songs from tonight's show are subsequently broadcast on Brazilian TV.

January 29, Grand Rex Theatre, Paris, France
The first night's set features few surprises except for a startling, arrhythmic arrangement of "Don't Think Twice, It's All Right" in the acoustic set, and the statutory French hit, "Man Gave Names to All the Animals."

January 30
In a ceremony at the Ministry of Culture in Paris at 6 PM, Dylan is presented with an award, Commandeur des Artset des Lettres. The presentation and Dylan's brief acceptance speech are both broadcast on French TV.

January 30, Grand Rex Theatre, Paris, France
If the first night was energetic, the second is positively frenetic. The Parisians are rewarded for their enthusiasm with four songs from *Oh Mercy*.

January 31, Grand Rex Theatre, Paris, France
Dylan is at his most outlandish on the third night, wearing a gold suit and white cowboy boots and playing a gold guitar.

February 1, Grand Rex Theatre, Paris, France
Finally, on the fourth night, with G. E. visibly suffering from what appears to be food poisoning, Dylan seeks to compensate with a performance full of that inimitable authority. Highlights include an almost word-perfect acoustic "Visions of Johanna" and effective electric excursions for "Tears of Rage," "Lenny Bruce," and "Man of Peace."
 • Dylan and Leonard Cohen meet in a cafe in the 14th Arrondissment after one of these shows. They talk to each other about songwriting, Dylan claiming that he wrote "I and I" in 15 minutes.

February 3, Hammersmith Odeon, London, England
The highlights of the opening show, enthusiastically received by the English press, include a definitive "Pretty Peggy-O," an increasingly good "Tight Connection to My Heart," and a menacing "Man in the Long Black Coat."

February 4, Hammersmith Odeon, London, England
The second night features "One More Cup of Coffee," "My Back Pages," and a slightly fumbled acoustic "Man of Constant Sorrow."

February 5, Hammersmith Odeon, London, England
The third night is more disappointing. After an exhilarating first electric set that includes the definitive "Tight Connection to My Heart," with a heartstopping harmonica introduction, Dylan slips into "greatest hits" mode after the acoustic set.

February 6, Hammersmith Odeon, London, England
Four gigs into a landmark residency at the Odeon, Dylan finally responds

to the enthusiasm he is receiving. Tonight's audience is the best crowd yet, and Dylan gives them expressive acoustic versions of "Song to Woody" and "Dark as a Dungeon."

February 7, Hammersmith Odeon, London, England

The real surprise on the fifth night is a first performance in 14 years of "Tonight I'll Be Staying Here with You." The band seem genuinely unaware of Dylan's intentions even as he starts playing it.

February 8, Hammersmith Odeon, London, England

Finally, a classic Dylan gig concludes the most exciting leg of the "Never Ending Tour." A 23-song set clocks in at a hundred-plus minutes, and features such welcome rarities as "Pledging My Time," "You Angel You" (Dylan recalling most of the words he had such difficulty with at Penn State), "Every Grain of Sand," and an electric encore of "Hang Me Oh Hang Me." Dylan also gives his one-and-only piano performance of the entire tour, "Disease of Conceit," at the end of the acoustic set.

February 10

Dylan leaves London via Heathrow Airport.

February 24

Dylan makes a surprise appearance at a tribute to Roy Orbison at the Universal Amphitheater, Universal City, Los Angeles, joining three of the original Byrds (David Crosby, Roger McGuinn, and Chris Hillman) on a version of "Mr. Tambourine Man." He remains onstage, playing guitar on "He Was a Friend of Mine," and joining in on an ensemble encore of "Only the Lonely." The version of "Mr. Tambourine Man," on which Dylan competes with McGuinn for the "lead" vocal, subsequently appears in a cable TV special of the benefit, as well as on CBS's four-CD Byrds retrospective, simply titled *The Byrds.*

March 1

Dylan makes his second guest appearance in a week, turning up for the encore at a Tom Petty and the Heartbreakers gig at the Inglewood Forum. After singing "Rainy Day Women," Tom Petty joins him for a duet on "Everybody's Movin'." However, Dylan is not the only surprise guest at the show. The Heartbreakers are then joined by Bruce Springsteen, who insists on singing "Travelin' Band" and "I'm Crying." Dylan is restricted to playing inaudible guitar.

March 2

A Record Plant 24-track mobile truck is set up in Culver City, where Dylan is recording a version of "Most of the Time," intended to be his new promotional video. The new version is filmed by his son Jesse, Dylan being backed by David Lindley on guitar, Randy Jackson on bass, and Kenny Aranoff on drums. The video derives from some seven different takes, one of which is also issued on a Sony promotional CD single.

Mid- to Late March

Dylan records with NRBQ at The Complex, Los Angeles. They record four songs together, ostensibly for *Under the Red Sky,* although nothing ends up being used. According to NRBQ, one of the songs was "Some Enchanted Evening."

Dylan completes *Under the Red Sky* with three sessions at The Complex in Los Angeles. With Don Was and Randy Jackson alternating on bass, Waddy Wachtel and Robben Ford trading guitars, and Kenny Aranoff on drums, plus Al Kooper on keyboards and David Lindley on slide guitar, Dylan records the basic tracks for "Wiggle Wiggle," "Under the Red Sky" (twice), "Born in Time" (twice), "Two by Two" (twice), two radically different versions of "T.V. Talkin' Song'," "Unbelievable," and "Shirley Temple Don't Live Here Anymore."

Late March to Early April

Dylan and the Was Brothers set about adding vocal overdubs to the songs scheduled for *Under the Red Sky* at The Complex and Record Plant in LA, Dylan taking the opportunity to rewrite some of the songs. "T.V. Talkin' Song" undergoes the most dramatic changes, although "Two by Two" and "Unbelievable" are also subject to lyrical tinkering. "Wiggle Wiggle," "Under the Red Sky," and "Born in Time" are also given new vocal tracks. After the vocal overdubs are completed, the Was Brothers bring in luminaries such as Dave Crosby, Elton John, Al Kooper, Slash, and George Harrison to add some embellishments to "Wiggle, Wiggle," "Under the Red Sky," "Born in Time," "Two by Two," "Handy Dandy," and "Cat's in the Well."

Early- to Mid-April

The four-piece Traveling Wilburys rent a palatial Spanish-style ranch house high in the hills of Los Angeles, build a mobile studio in the library, and set about recording their second album (the locale is cryptically referred to as the "Wilbury Mountain Studio" on *Volume Three*). According to Jeff Lynne, the sessions lasted about three weeks. They came up with 14 songs, three of which do not make *Volume Three*— Del Shannon's "Runaway," George Harrison's "Maxine," and Dylan's "Like a Ship."

• Although no further songs will be recorded at the mixing sessions in England in July, Lynne and Harrison will mask a lot of Dylan's vocal contributions at this point. At least one song in its original form is entirely a Dylan vocal. However, "She's My Baby" appears on the album with all four Wilburys singing a verse apiece. Dylan's vocal contributions on "Where Were You Last Night?" and "Seven Deadly Sins" are also abbreviated on the released versions, while a frantic harmonica sawing away in the backgrounds of "Poor House," "Runaway," and an instrumental "New Blue Moon" are all cut from the released versions. Despite such edits, Dylan is by far the most significant Wilbury on *Volume Three,* making the major vocal contributions on "Inside Out," "If You Belonged to Me," "Seven Deadly Sins," and "Where Were You Last Night?," as well as singing a verse apiece on "She's My Baby," "The Devil's Been Busy," "New Blue Moon," and "The Wilbury Twist." The Wilburys also record an extra song at these sessions especially for a Rumanian children's appeal. Rush-released in June, the song is the country standard, "Nobody's Child."

May 1
Dylan goes backstage at an Eric Clapton show at the Forum in Inglewood, CA.

May 21
Allen Ginsberg does a photo shoot with Dylan in Tomkin Square, NY. Dylan, however, is unhappy with the results, presumably because of the unflattering nature of some of the shots. None of the photographs are ever utilized.

May 29, University of Montreal, Montreal, Quebec
A most unusual show opens Dylan's early summer jaunt. Although the set contains just two songs new to the "Never Ending Tour," a semiacoustic "Desolation Row" and a powerful cover of Joel Sonnier's "No More One More Time," there are other surprises. First, Dylan shows a willingness to embellish every other song with harmonica, and his previous, erratic relationship with the instrument is a thing of the past. Second, the acoustic set now features the entire band, with Dylan and Smith on acoustic guitars, Garnier on standup bass, and Parker playing with brushes or simply maintaining a backbeat. A most promising continuation from the heights of Hammersmith.

May 30, Memorial Arena, Kingston, Ontario
Dylan maintains the momentum with a show of consistency and quality. Tonight's one-off performance is a version of "Where Teardrops Fall," Dylan plonking on the piano until the last verse when he walks back to center stage to play a final harmonica solo. The (now semi)acoustic set is considerably more assured than last night's, and the six songs played remain a "Never Ending Tour" record. Four of the titles are drawn from *Bringing It All Back Home*. A fast, countryish "She Belongs to Me" works much better than its solitary acoustic form, and "Ballad of Hollis Brown" retains it's electric arrangement, albeit with acoustic instruments.

Early June
Dylan writes a letter to "Jamie," editor of a feminist fanzine entitled *Sister 2 Sister*. In it he talks about life on the road and the illusion of time: "My soul is unaware of any time, only my mind. My poor mind which is so bombarded with dates, calendars and numbers, has been deceived into believing there is such a thing as time." The letter is published in the July 1990 issue.

June 1, National Arts Centre, Ottawa, Ontario
Opening night is a standard performance except for a simmering version of "Like a Rolling Stone," on which Dylan sings the first verse backed by just guitar, the band kicking in on the first chorus, a piano-less version of "Disease of Conceit," and a first encore of "Mr. Tambourine Man" with a spellbinding harmonica "outro."

June 2, National Arts Centre, Ottawa, Ontario

Dylan is positively verbose on the second night, asking the audience before "Boots of Spanish Leather" whether, in the light of a less-than-complimentary review of the first night's show in the *Ottawa Citizen*, they would mind if he played harmonica. The audience roars their approval. Before "It Ain't Me, Babe" he delivers a monologue about theft, before asking for a stolen guitar to be returned to him. G. E. plays some slide guitar on tonight's "Simple Twist of Fate."

June 4, University of Western Ontario, London, Ontario

June 5, O'Keefe Centre, Toronto, Ontario

The first night's semi-acoustic set features two requests from the eighth row. The first is "Tomorrow Is a Long Time," shouted out as Dylan is about to start "It's All Over Now, Baby Blue." Dylan surprisingly responds, "It sure is. Awfully long," and proceeds to unearth a lovely, subdued version. Two songs later, the same misfit asks for "John Brown," and Dylan duly obliges with his most mannered rendition.

June 6, O'Keefe Centre, Toronto, Ontario

Gordon Lightfoot's "Early Morning Rain" makes its statutory Toronto appearance in the second show. A shade more surprising is the *Nashville Skyline* nugget "One More Night," performed halfway through the second band set, not sung by Dylan but by guest Ronnie Hawkins. A semiacoustic "Hang Me Oh Hang Me" is intense, as is a version of "You're a Big Girl Now," where Dylan discards his guitar and plays a couple of fine harmonica breaks on either side of the final verse.

June 7, O'Keefe Centre, Toronto, Ontario

Finally, on the third night, "Hang Me Oh Hang Me" makes a second semi-acoustic appearance, this time as an encore, complete with harmonica break. On the set list, but absent from the show, is the one *Oh Mercy* song still to be performed in concert, "Shooting Star."

June 9, Alpine Valley Music Theater, East Troy, WI

The first live performance of "Shooting Star" contains a double run-through of the bridge and final verse. "Tight Connection to My Heart" is the only song tonight to benefit from any extended harmonica work.

June 10, Adler Theater, Davenport, IA

"It's All Over Now, Baby Blue" makes it's first appearance in semi-acoustic guise.

June 12, La Crosse Center, La Crosse, WI

June 13, Civic Arena, Sioux Falls, SD

June 14, Civic Center, Fargo, ND

June 15, Civic Center, Bismark, ND

"Political World" makes its first appearance on this leg of the "Never Ending Tour."

June 17–18, Centennial Concert Hall, Winnipeg, Manitoba

A second performance of "No More One More Time" occurs on the opening night.

June 24

Dylan films a video for "Unbelievable" in the Mojave Desert. Starring in the video are Sally Kirkland and Molly Ringwald. Dylan plays a chauffeur who spends his time driving a pig with a ring through its nose around.

June 27, Laugardalsholl, Reykjavik, Iceland

Dylan's first-ever show in Iceland features a "Shooting Star" with an effective harmonica conclusion, and a semi-acoustic "A Hard Rain's a-Gonna Fall." "Don't Think Twice, It's Alright" is prefaced with a rap about Vikings settling in Minnesota, a rather oblique reference to an American football team.

June 29, Roskilde Festival, Denmark

June 30, Oslo, Norway

July 1, Abo Festival, Turkko, Finland

July 3, Stadtpark, Hamburg, Germany

On tonight's set list are four covers, "No More One More Time," Fats Domino's "Blue Monday," "Old Rock and Roller," and "Let's Learn to Live and Love Again." Only the first and third selections are actually performed, and "No More One More Time" is disappointingly insipid. Dylan does introduce "Old Rock and Roller" as an autobiographical song. It paints a picture of a has-been touting hits of yore around the world. This is the best European show on this brief tour.

July 5, ICC, Berlin, Germany

Dylan seems to be rediscovering a little of the fire absent throughout most of June, performing a fine semiacoustic "Song to Woody." Jack Scott's "Let's Learn to Live and Love Again" is also given a respectable arrangement.

July 7, Turhout Festival, Belgium

Playing second on the bill to the Cure, Dylan delivers a 15-song, 70-minute set devoid of subtlety, and featuring exactly one song from his '80's *oeuvre*, the opener, "Silvio."

July 8, Werchter Festival, Belgium

Another support slot to The Cure at a muddy Belgian festival; another 15-song, 70-minute set.

July 9, Casino, Montreux, Switzerland

Although his voice is in bad shape, Dylan discovers enough enthusiasm to conclude a disappointing European stint with an energetic show that is part of the annual Montreux Jazz Festival. A rare "Across the Borderline" features Dylan's best vocal of the European tour and the apposite accompaniment of Ry Cooder's accordion player, Flaco Jimenez.

Summer

The saccharine Michael Bolton is invited to Dylan's house in Malibu to write a song with rock's finest lyricist. Needless to say, the song that results, "Steel Bars," ain't no "Visions of Johanna."

Mid-July

The sessions required to complete the second Wilburys album take place at George Harrison's studio, Friar Park, in Henley-on-Thames. These sessions have been arranged to redub some vocals and embellish some of the songs with extraneous sounds, courtesy of Jeff Lynne. Dylan seems to have had no input at this stage.

July to August

While in New Orleans for a couple of days, Dylan hangs out with guitarist Jimmy Page.

Late July to Early August

Dylan rehearses for the summer 1990 leg of the "Never Ending Tour," presumably at Montana Studios in New York. The band now includes a second guitarist, John De Staley. They work on a wealth of songs not performed on the "Never Ending Tour" to date. Indeed, a list of songs rehearsed, given to De Staley at the time, contains some 160 titles. Divided into four categories—Electric B.D.; electric covers; acoustic B.D.; and acoustic covers—the acoustic covers include "In the Pines" and "Young But Daily Growin'" and the acoustic B.D. includes "With God on Our Side," "Mama, You Been on My Mind," and "Song to Woody." The electric lists are considerably more intriguing. Among the electric covers are some 10 songs never performed on the "Never Ending Tour"—"Old Number Nine," "High School Hop," "Not Supposed to Care," "This Old House," "Family Bible," "Little Queen of Spades," "Wild Wood Flower," "Silver and Gold," "Southern Man," and "Where or When"—as well as the likes of "Key to the Highway," "Give My Love to Rose," and "Hallelujah."

However, the longest list by far, some 86 items, is the one for electric B.D. songs. Although it is mostly songs already performed on the "Never Ending Tour," the list includes "Fourth Time Around," a song called "Shut Your Mouth" (remember this is supposed to be a list of "original" songs), the yet-to-be-released "Under the Red Sky," and "T.V. Talkin' Song" (listed simply as "T.V. Song"), "New Morning," "I Threw It All Away," "Wicked Messenger," "Dear Landlord," "Something's Burning, Baby," "One of Us Must Know," "Spanish Harlem" (presumably "Spanish Harlem Incident"), "Eternal Circle," "On a Night Like This," "Watered Down Love," and "One More Night."

August 12–13, Jubilee Auditorium, Edmonton, Alberta

As with his early summer tour, Dylan's third stint of the year starts in Canada. Rumors abound that G. E. is leaving the band after this leg of the tour. The first show proves to be one of the more interesting sets, featuring a bizarre electric version of "Nowhere Man" and a restrained, semi-acoustic "The Water Is Wide." On the second night, "No More One More Time" makes a rare appearance.

August 15–16, Jubilee Auditorium, Calgary, Alberta

"Early Morning Rain" is performed on the opening night.

August 18, Champs de Brionne Theater, George, WA

Dylan seems a little out of control tonight, manifested most obviously in a brave but disastrous stab at Otis Redding's "Sittin' on the Dock of Bay," some off-key harmonica replacing the more famous whistling on the original.

August 19, Memorial Arena, Victoria, BC

Tonight De Staley's place is taken by Steve Bruton, who last played with Dylan in Mexico City in January 1973.

August 20, Pacific Coliseum, Vancouver, BC

Bruton continues his onstage audition for G. E.'s place.

August 21, Arbne Schnitzer Auditorium, Portland, OR

Bruton plays his part in a very high-energy show, with a rather fine semi-acoustic set, featuring "Lakes of Pontchartrain."

August 24, CO State Fair, Pueblo, CO

August 26, Iowa State Fair, Des Moines, IA

De Staley temporarily returns to the fray as Dylan includes a rare performance of "Let's Learn to Live and Love Again." After the show, Dylan learns of the death of Stevie Ray Vaughan in a helicopter accident leaving Alpine Valley, WI.

August 27, Holiday Star Theater, Merriville, IN

Bruton returns for the two most interesting shows of the late summer tour. On the opening night, "Man of Peace" provides a respite from "Gotta Serve Somebody," concluding the first electric set. Then, after the semi-acoustic set, Dylan dedicates a heartfelt version of "Moon River" to Stevie Ray Vaughan, following it with a rather magnificent cover of a Robert Hunter song, "Friend of the Devil."

August 28, Holiday Star Theater, Merriville, IN

The second night is perhaps the best of the late summer shows, featuring a frenetic "Silvio," with extensive harmonica, and an electric "Hang Me Oh Hang Me," which leads straight into a one-off performance of the gospel standard, "Stand By Me."

August 29, MN State Fair, Saint Paul, MN
Dylan begins opening with a brief instrumental version of "The Battle Hymn of the Republic." "Joey" returns to the set, and "Friend of the Devil" is retained from Merriville.

August 31
Dylan is interviewed for the third time by Edna Gundersen for *USA Today*. However, Dylan has very little to say about his new album.

August 31, Bob Devaney Sports Center, Lincoln, NE
"Tangled Up in Blue" comes after "The Battle Hymn of the Republic."

September 1, Swiss Villa Lampe, MO
Dylan tries out his third potential replacement for G. E., Miles Joseph.

September 2, Riverfront Amphitheater, Hannibal, MO
Tonight's show hints at a return to a more varied approach to the sets, with an electric arrangement of "Tomorrow Is a Long Time," semi-acoustic versions of "Trail of the Buffalo," and "Mama, You Been on My Mind" and— making their first appearances since the London Hammersmith shows— "Pledging My Time" and "Man in the Long Black Coat."

September 4, Riverpark Amphitheater, Tulsa, OK
"Every Grain of Sand" returns.

September 5, The Zoo, Oklahoma City, OK
Dylan opens tonight's show with a brief instrumental version of "Old McDonald Had a Farm."

September 6, Fair Park Music Hall, Dallas, TX
Includes a first live performance of the Lowell George classic, "Willing," and a further "Every Grain of Sand."

September 8, Sunken Garden Theater, San Antonio, TX

September 9, Palmer Auditorium, Austin, TX
Includes a rare "Just Like Tom Thumb's Blues."

September 11, Paolo Solerli Amphitheatre, Santa Fe, NM
Tonight's highlight is a spirited "Friend of the Devil," Dylan incorporating two harmonica breaks.

> *Under the Red Sky* (CK 46794): "Wiggle Wiggle," "Under the Red Sky," "Unbelievable," "Born in Time," "TV Talkin' Song," "10,000 Men," "Two by Two," "God Knows," "Handy Dandy," "Cat's in the Well"

September 12, Amphitheatre, Mesa, AZ
The final show of a disappointing tour features "Watching the River Flow"

and sensitive electric arrangements of "Tomorrow Is a Long Time" and "Willing."

Early October
Dylan and his fellow Wilburys film promotional videos for "She's My Baby" and "Inside Out."

October 8–10
Dylan and his band rehearse at Montana Studios in New York. The rehearsal on the 9th includes "Shelter from the Storm," "Wiggle Wiggle," "10,000 Men," "Under the Red Sky," "Two by Two," "Masters of War," "Man in the Long Black Coat," "The Water Is Wide," "I Shall Be Released," "Unbelievable," "Shooting Star," "Just Like a Woman," "Maggie's Farm," and "Like a Rolling Stone."

October 11, C.W. Post College, Greenvale, NY
With *Under the Red Sky* finally in the shops, Dylan at last introduces some new originals into the set, although fans have to sit through a mundane opening set. G. E. is still leading the band, now accompanied by his long-standing guitar technician, Caesar Diaz, on rhythm guitar. The acoustic set, embellished by Steve Bruton on mandolin, is equally mundane. In the second band set, though, Dylan unveils the title track of *Under the Red Sky* and, more surprisingly, "TV Talkin' Song" as well as a welcome version of "Friend of the Devil."

October 12, Paramount Theater, Springfield, MA
After another acoustic set embellished by Bruton's mandolin, the second electric set again features just two songs from the new album, "Under the Red Sky" and "Wiggle Wiggle," as well as Little Feat's "Willing." The three songs from *Under the Red Sky* performed on these two nights are to be the only new Dylan songs performed on the fall 1990 tour.

October 13, US Military Academy, West Point, NY
Diaz and Smith take all guitar duties tonight. Dylan attracts considerable press simply for playing "Masters of War" at the famous military academy.

October 15, Beacon Theatre, NY
After last year's landmark residency, Dylan returns to the Beacon for five more shows. Despite featuring a good cross section of his work on opening night, he only performs the title track from his new album. "Shelter from the Storm" collapses halfway through as Dylan appears to forget the words.

October 16, Beacon Theatre, NY
G. E. Smith is absent for the first three songs of the second show. After Smith plugs in, Dylan plays three straight songs from *Under the Red Sky*. During the acoustic set, Dylan performs a delicate "One Too Many Mornings" following it up with an equally impressive "Two Soldiers."

October 17, Beacon Theatre, NY
John De Staley returns on night three, appearing during an acoustic set in

which Dylan pulls out a rare "A Hard Rain's a-Gonna Fall." "Willing" is the highlight of the electric sets, which still feature Smith and Diaz.

October 19, Beacon Theatre, NY
The fourth night's show features a slice of Dylan showmanship to compare with his aberration the previous year when he dived into the audience on the final night. This time he shimmys across the entire stage during "Masters of War" as Lenny Kravitz's saxophonist joins his band for two songs (the other being "Gotta Serve Somebody"). The response warrants an encore performance the following night.

October 20, Beacon Theatre, NY
On the last night of a sporadically impressive residency, Dylan again summons Lenny Kravitz's sax player to join him on two songs, "Gotta Serve Somebody" and "All Along the Watchtower." The highlight tonight, however, is a semi-acoustic "Dark as a Dungeon." Diaz and De Staley play the first three songs, an indication of what is in store for the remaining fall 1990 dates; tonight is G. E. Smith's last show. Although Diaz accounts for himself well enough, the band soon lacks the flexibility Smith has been able to bring to most performances in his three years on the road with Dylan. On the encores, Smith sings the final verse of "Highway 61 Revisited," and Lenny Kravitz's band joins Dylan's band onstage for a mass ensemble version of "Maggie's Farm." Wire Train take over the support slot from this point on.

October 21, Richmond Mosque, Richmond, VA

October 22, Syria Mosque, Pittsburgh, PA

October 23, Municipal Auditorium, Charleston, WV

Volume 3 by the Traveling Wilburys (Warners 26324)

October 25, Tad Smith Coliseum, University of MS, University, MS
There are two major surprises tonight. First, Dylan opens with Z Z Top's "My Head's in Mississippi." During the acoustic set Dylan performs the song he wrote about the events at this very university in 1962, "Oxford Town." The audience accord him a standing ovation.

October 26, Coleman Coliseum, University of AL, Tuscaloosa, AL
Dylan opens the show with a perfunctory version of Hank Williams's "Hey Good Lookin'."

October 27, Memorial Gymnasium, Vanderbilt University, Nashville, TN
Dylan revives "My Head's in Mississippi."

October 28, The Institute of GA Coliseum, Athens, GA

October 30, Varsity Gymnasium, Charleston, WV

October 31, Owens Auditorium, Charleston, NC
Dylan and the band opens with an instrumental version of "Dixie."

Early November
Dylan is briefly interviewed by Edna Gundersen for an article on *Hearts of
Fire* in *USA Today,* coinciding with the film's belated release on video in the
US. Dylan suggests he would have preferred the film to be like *Chariots of
Fire.*

November 2, Memorial Coliseum, University of Kentucky,
Lexington, KY

November 3, Southern IL University, Carbondale, IL
Tonight's instrumental opener is "Old MacDonald Had a Farm."

November 4, Fox Theater, St. Louis, MO
Dylan and the band open with an instrumental version of "Shenandoah."

November 6, Chick Evans Fieldhouse, Northern IL University,
Dekalb, IL
Dylan opens with "My Head's in Mississippi." During the semi-acoustic set,
he performs a rather ragged "Visions of Johanna."

November 8, Carver Hockey Arena, University of IA,
Iowa City, IA

November 9, Chicago Theatre, Chicago, IL

November 10, Riverside Theater, Milwaukee, WI

November 12, Wharton Centre, East Lansing, MI
Dylan opens tonight's show with Bobby Bare's "Detroit City."

November 13, U.D. Arena, University of Dayton, Dayton, OH

November 14, Braides Auditorium, IL State University,
Normal, IL

November 16, Palace Theater, Columbus, OH
Includes a rare live version of "Clean-Cut Kid."

November 17, Music Hall, Cleveland, OH

November 18, Fox Theater, Detroit, MI
Tonight's opener is the first live performance of "Buckets of Rain."

December

Dylan contributes some less-than-impressive vocals to a new Brian Wilson ditty, "Spirit of Rock & Roll," at a session in LA. Wilson records various celebrities' takes on this song for his album, *Sweet Insanity,* which subsequently is rejected by his label, Sire, and never released. Bootleg versions featuring Bob's out-of-tune crooning have surfaced.

• Dylan conducts informal auditions at his home in Malibu. John De Staley and Christopher Parker are both due for replacement. Possible recruits for the guitar slot include British guitarist Chris Spedding. For the drummer's seat, Dylan goes through a few options before settling on Ian Wallace, who last played with him on the 1978 world tour (although he had apparently auditioned for the 1984 band).

1991

January

Dylan records a solo version of the nursery rhyme, "This Old Man," for a Disney charity album at his home studio in Malibu.

January 18

Dylan participates in a promotional video for the Traveling Wilburys's "Wilbury Twist" at a mansion in Los Angeles, continuing the innocuous tradition of Wilburys performance videos.

January 21–25

Dylan conducts final rehearsals for a European tour at Montana Studios in New York. The reconstituted "Never Ending Tour" band is now Tony Garnier on bass, Cesar Diaz on rhythm guitar, John Jackson, formerly of Jo-El Sonnier's band, on lead guitar, and Ian Wallace on drums. Supposedly "Handy Dandy" is one of the songs they rehearse for the tour.

January 23

Taking a break from rehearsals, an unkempt Dylan is filmed on the streets of Manhattan for a composite video intended to promote "Series of Dreams" from *The Bootleg Series*. A reporter from the *New York Daily News*, asking whether Dylan was dressed as a homeless person for the film, is informed, "No, he's dressed as Bob Dylan."

January 28, Hallenstadion, Zurich, Switzerland

For the second time, Dylan opens a European tour with a badly under-rehearsed band. The opening song, "Most Likely You Go Your Way," is embarrassing, and although the show improves, the band never attains more than a bare competence. Aside from live debuts for "Bob Dylan's Dream" and "God Knows"—which both become perennials on this European leg—the set is ultra-standard.

January 30, Forest National, Brussels, Belgium

January 31, Muziek-centrum, Utrecht, Netherlands

February 2–3, SECC Hall 3, Glasgow, Scotland

Dylan's second night in Glasgow is the one show on this European tour to deviate markedly from the standard set, featuring the likes of "What Was

It You Wanted," "Watching the River Flow," "Positively Fourth Street" (during which Dylan disappears offstage for four minutes, causing panic in the band), "I'll Be Your Baby Tonight," "Ballad of Hollis Brown," "Just Like a Woman," and "Political World." Dylan even opens the show with an instrumental version of "The Mountains of Mourne."

February 5, The Point Depot, Dublin, Ireland

February 6, Dundonald Ice Bowl, Belfast, Northern Ireland

Van Morrison joins Dylan onstage for the fifth time in seven years, dueting on "Tupelo Honey."

February 8, Hammersmith Odeon, London, England

On opening night, Dylan attempts "What Good Am I?" at the piano but soon abandons it, completing the song center stage.

February 9, Hammersmith Odeon, London, England

After spending two hours in the afternoon playing piano at a soundcheck, Dylan performs an intense "Shooting Star" at the piano during the evening's second electric set.

February 10, Hammersmith Odeon, London, England

February 12, Hammersmith Odeon, London, England

Dylan opens the show by leading the band through a lengthy, harmonica-driven introduction to "Tangled Up in Blue" before singing the entire song, guitarless, at the microphone. Other surprises include a semiacoustic "Tomorrow Is a Long Time" and a complete "What Good Am I?" at the piano.

February 13, Hammersmith Odeon, London, England

Highlights are a semi-acoustic "To Ramona" and "Shooting Star" at the piano.

February 15, Hammersmith Odeon, London, England

He replaces "Shooting Star" with "Under the Red Sky."

February 16, Hammersmith Odeon, London, England

The 16th brings piano versions of the usually mundane "Most Likely You Go Your Way" and "Lay, Lady, Lay." Ron Wood makes his usual, inaudible guest appearance during the second electric set.

February 17, Hammersmith Odeon, London, England

On the final night of Dylan's most disappointing British shows, "Under the Red Sky" receives the piano arrangement.

The lack of variations, the abysmal lighting, the barely competent band, and Dylan's lack of interest ensures that the 1991 Hammersmith residency is not remembered fondly by most English fans.

February 20

Dylan receives a Lifetime Achievement award at the 33rd Grammy Awards ceremony, held at Radio City Music Hall in New York. Introduced by Jack Nicholson, he proceeds to perform, with his motley touring band, an all-but-unintelligible version of "Masters of War," presumably his idea of a comment on America's involvement in Iraq. On accepting the award, he gives the impression of being more than a little the worse for wear. In a brief acceptance speech, he pauses a full 20 seconds while he reads the award before delivering a typically upbeat message about defilement.

February 21, Capital Theatre, Williamsport, PA

Dylan plays electric piano on "Lay, Lady, Lay" and "Under the Red Sky."

February 22, Painters Mill Music Fair, Owing Mills, MD

Dylan plays electric piano on "Most Likely You Go Your Way," "Lay, Lady, Lay," and "Shooting Star."

February 23–24

According to a story in the *Guadalajara Colony Reporter,* Dylan is practicing with his band in Austin, TX in the week preceding his Mexican shows. While there, he answers four questions on the phone from one of the *Reporter*'s reporters.

February 25, 27, Patio Mayor Del Instituto Cultural Cabanas, Guadalajara, Mexico

March 1–2, Palacio de los Deportes, Mexico City, Mexico

Early March

Dylan is interviewed by Elliot Mintz in a hotel bungalow in Los Angeles on the subject of the pending three-CD set, *The Bootleg Series.* His answers make very little sense, suggesting an almost total lack of awareness of the set released in his name.

March 26: The Bootleg Series, Vols. 1–3, Rare and Unreleased 1961–1979 (C3K 47382): "Hard Times in New York Town," "He Was a Friend of Mine," "Man on the Street," "No More Auction Block," "House Carpenter," "Talking Bear Mountain Massacre Blues," "Let Me Die in My Footsteps," "Rambling, Gambling Willie," "Talkin' Hava Nagilah Blues," "Quit Your Low Down Dirty Ways," "Worried Blues," "Kingsport Town," "Walkin' Down the Line," "Walls of Red Wing," "Paths of Victory," "Talkin' John Birch Paranoid Blues," "Who Killed Davey Moore?," "Only a Hobo," "Moonshiner," "When the Ship Comes In," "Times They Are a-Changin'," "The Last Thoughts on Woody Guthrie," "Seven Curses," "Eternal Circle," "Suze (The Cough Song)," "Mama, You Been on My Mind," "Farewell, Angelina," "Subterranean Homesick Blues," "If You Gotta Go, Go Now," "Sitting on a Barbed Wire Fence," "Like a Rolling Stone," "It Takes a Lot to Laugh," "I'll Keep It with Mine,"

"She's Your Lover Now," "I Shall Be Released," "Santa-Fe," "If Not for You," "Wallflower," "Nobody 'Cept You," "Tangled Up in Blue," "Call Letter Blues," "Idiot Wind," "If You See Her Say Hello," "Golden Loom," "Catfish," "Seven Days," "Ye Shall Be Changed," "Every Grain of Sand," "You Changed My Life," "Need a Woman," "Angelina," "Someone's Got a Hold of My Heart," "Tell Me," "Lord Protect My Child," "Fool of Pride," "Blind Willie McTell," "When the Night Comes Falling from the Sky," "Series of Dreams"

March 28

Dylan is interviewed for 20 minutes on the phone by Joe Queenan, for an upcoming feature in the *New York Times Magazine.* However, Queenan's piece is rejected by the magazine and the interview ends up appearing in the down-market *Spy* magazine. Dylan once again admits that he has very little interest in making videos and that he intends to tour until he drops. Not an important interview, unlike . . .

April 4

Dylan is interviewed in a bungalow of the Beverly Hills Hotel (the first time in 26 years) by Paul Zollo for *Song Talk,* the magazine of the National Academy of Songwriters. In a surprisingly lucid mood, Dylan attempts to articulate what motivates him as a songwriter and the whole piece comes across as almost an update on his interview with Bill Flanagan in March 1985. Aside from talking about favorite keys (musical ones), and how the melodies in his head keep returning to Elizabethan ballads, he admits that, "[the] motivation behind any song is something you never know."

April 19, Saenger Performing Arts Center, New Orleans, LA

Dispensing with Diaz as second guitarist, Dylan resumes touring. Tonight's one surprise is the opening song, a live debut for "New Morning," though little of its original melody remains. Jo-El Sonnier joins in on accordion for the statutory encore of "Maggie's Farm." After the show, Dylan and members of his band go to a restaurant called Gautreau's.

April 20, Oak Mountain Amphitheatre, Pelham, AL

"Barbara Allen" makes a welcome reappearance in the acoustic set. Less welcome are the three songs attempted at the electric piano, "Gotta Serve Somebody," a typically discordant "Everything Is Broken," and "Under the Red Sky."

April 21, Memorial Auditorium, Greenville, SC

"Like a Rolling Stone" gets the electric piano treatment.

April 23, Fox Theatre, Atlanta, GA

Dylan performs "I Shall Be Released" at the piano.

April 24, City Auditorium, Macon, GA

"Mr. Tambourine Man" is introduced as "one of my anti-drug songs."

April 25, King Street Palace, Charleston, SC

April 27, Musical Theater, Sunrise, FL
During "Wiggle Wiggle," Dylan suggests that the audience all "stand in one spot and wiggle."

April 30, Civic Center, Savannah, GA

May 1, Township Auditorium, Columbia, SC
A curious trio—"Wiggle Wiggle," "I Shall Be Released," and "Highway 61 Revisited"—get the electric piano treatment tonight.

May 2, Civic Center, Salem, VA
"I Believe in You" gets a rare outing. "Man in the Long Black Coat" is given a most cryptic introduction: "A lot of people came down on me for writing this next song, but the truth just had to come out."

May 4, Lawrence Joel Veterans Memorial Coliseum, Winston-Salem, NC

May 5, Memorial Auditorium, Raleigh, NC

May 7, State University of New York, Stony Brook, NY

May 8, Palace Theatre, Albany, NY
After playing electric piano during an acoustic version of "Mr. Tambourine Man," Dylan delivers one of the weirdest performances of "Visions of Johanna" since 1974. At one point he sings "these visions of Madonna."

May 9, Northeastern University, Boston, MA
"She Belongs to Me," with Dylan on piano, opens the acoustic set.

May 11, Western CT State College, Danbury, CT
The show opens with an instrumental version of "Dixie." There is no encore, the stage having been rushed by several girls during "Like a Rolling Stone."

May 12, University of MA, Amherst, MA

June 6, Paleur, Rome, Italy
Dylan opens his second European tour of 1991 with the song originally set in the streets of Rome, "When I Paint My Masterpiece." In the acoustic set, Dylan does to "Homeward Bound" what he had done to "The Boxer" on *Self Portrait*. A second cover of the evening opens the second electric set, John Prine's "People Putting People Down." The support act for the three Italian shows is Van Morrison.

June 7, Parco Nord, Bologna, Italy

June 8, Palatrussardi di Milano, Milan, Italy
During Van Morrison's support slot, Dylan embellishes "Whenever God Shines His Light" and "Enlightenment" with some wayward harmonica. Dylan's own set contains no such surprises.

June 10, Centralni Stadion Bezigrad, Ljubljana, Yugoslavia

June 11, Stadion FK Zemun, Belgrade, Yugoslavia

"One More Cup of Coffee" makes a rare appearance, sandwiched between "Shooting Star" and "I Shall Be Released."

June 12

In the afternoon, Dylan is interviewed on the terrace of his suite at the Buda Penta Hotel by Brazilian journalist Eduardo Bueno. It is a very odd interview, Dylan seemingly tolerating some impertinent lines of questioning about angels, vampires, and Brazil itself.

June 12, Kisstadion, Budapest, Yugoslavia

Dylan opens the acoustic set with the traditional "When First Unto This Country," a fleeting reminder of Dylan the consummate folksinger. He is accompanied by just John Jackson.

June 14, Olympiahalle, Innsbruck, Austria

Having been savaged in acoustic form earlier in the month, "Homeward Bound" is tonight given an equally disrespectful electric arrangement.

June 15, Sportshalle, Linz, Austria

During a semi-acoustic rehearsal before the show, Dylan runs through some remnants from the summer 1990 set, "No More One More Time," "Old Rock & Roller," and "Let's Learn to Live and Love Again." However, the show itself is quite mundane.

June 16, Liederhalle, Stuttgart, Germany

A legendary show, more for Dylan's demeanor than the set list. An eight-minute "New Morning" contains no more than two lines from the song itself, eluding recognition even from diehard Bobcats. This sets the stage for one of the most shambolic, rambling performances ever given by a major artist.

June 18, Grugahalle, Essen, Germany

Eleven of the show's 18 songs are graced with Dylan's harmonica, alternating freely between the off-key and the inspired.

June 19, Stadthalle, Offenbach, Germany

"The Two Soldiers" opens the acoustic set, Dylan informing the audience, "That was a song from another place, another time."

June 21, Zirkus Krone, Munich, Germany

"Man Gave Name to All the Animals" closes the first electric set. "Don't Think Twice" is prefaced by a strange rap about someone getting run over by a streetcar: "There wasn't anything for me to do but go back and write this song." Huh?

June 22, Schlosshof, Bad Mergentheim, Germany

Dylan plays a solo "Barbara Allen," apparently in response to a request.

June 23, Stadtpark, Hamburg, Germany
"Man Gave Name to All the Animals" includes a surreal verse about an animal on a lake, "driving a truck, think I'll call it a duck."

June 25–26, Cirkus, Stockholm, Sweden

June 28, Kalvoya Festival, Sandvika, Norway

June 29, Midtfyn Rock Festival, Ringe, Denmark
Dylan introduces "Positively Fourth Street" as "one of my songs about friendship."

July 1
The probable date of a show by Les Paul at Fat Tuesday's in New York attended by Dylan.

July 4, Tanglewood Music Shed, Lenox, MA

July 5, Great Woods Performing Arts Center, Mansfield, MA

July 6, Holman Field, Nashua, NH
"Lakes of Pontchartrain" opens the acoustic set.

July 9, New York State Fairgrounds, Syracuse, NY

July 10, Champlain Valley Fairgrounds, Essex Junction, VT
The second song tonight is Johnny Cash's "Folsom Prison Blues," a highlight of the summer '91 shows.

July 11, Jones Beach Theatre, Wantagh, NY

July 13, Garden State Arts Center, Holmdel, NJ

July 16, Melody Tent Amphitheatre, Pittsburgh, PA
A rare version of "Joey" is introduced as "kind of a gangster song." After "When I Paint My Masterpiece," Dylan says he should "apologize to Neil Young for stealing his harmonica riff," and, after "Folsom Prison Blues," says, of Cash, "if he's not in the Rock & Roll Hall of Fame, there shouldn't be a Rock & Roll Hall of Fame."

July 17, Nautica Stage Theatre, Cleveland, OH
Includes "Pancho and Lefty," Dylan informing the audience that it is the only song in his repertoire that mentions the city of "Cleveland."

July 19–20, Wolf Trap Farm Park, Vienna, VA

July 21, Kings Dominion Amusement Park, Doswell, VA

July 24, US Coast Guard Academy, Groton, CT

July 26, Kingswood Music Theatre, Maple, Ontario
"Visions of Johanna" comes after "Trail of the Buffalo" at tonight's show.

July 27, Darien Lake Amusement Park, Corfu, NY

August 8–10, 1 Obras Sanitarias Hall, Buenos Aires, Argentina
The first night includes an electric "People Get Ready" after the statutory "New Morning" opener.

On the final night, the second song is a one-off cover of Chuck Willis's "It's Too Late." In the acoustic set, Dylan performs "Ring Them Bells," which works surprisingly well.

August 12, Cilindro Municipal Stadium, Montevideo, Uruguay
"When Did You Leave Heaven?" appears as the second song.

August 13
Dylan is interviewed briefly by a local reporter in Porto Allegre, managing to redefine the word noncommittal in the process.

August 14, Gigantinho, Puerto Alegre, Brazil

August 16–17, Palace Theatre, Sao Paulo, Brazil
"People Putting People Down" makes its second and last appearance of the tour on the 17th.

August 19, Minetrinho, Belo Horizonte, Brazil
The acoustic "Ring Them Bells" makes another appearance.

August 21, Imperator, Rio de Janeiro, Brazil

Late August
Dylan, accompanied by Victor Maimudes and Carole Childs, spends a few days in Miami.

September 6–20(?)
Dylan's band convenes in Los Angeles for rehearsals with Dylan that are expected to last a couple of weeks. Although there are no details of what these rehearsals produced, the remarkable improvement in the band on the Fall 1991 tour suggests a serious rethink took place.

September 15
Dylan makes a third appearance on the Chabad telethon, accompanying Kinky Friedman on guitar for "Sold American."

October 2
Dylan attends Sting's 40th birthday party in Los Angeles.

October 15
Dylan arrives in Seville for the Guitar Greats Festival, accompanied by his son, Jesse. He stays at the Colon Hotel, as do most of the other performers attending the festival.

October 17
In the afternoon, Dylan soundchecks with Keith Richards and his band,

working on several songs, all of which he ends up vetoing. Instead, he decides to ask Richards Thompson of Fairport Convention fame to accompany him on an acoustic set.

October 17, Guitar Greats Festival, Auditorio de la Cartuja, Seville, Spain

The organizers, having stretched a point by including Dylan at a festival of guitar greats, are rewarded with a superb three-song acoustic set. A slightly-at-a-loss Richard Thompson embellishes Dylan's plaintive singing and light strumming with some virtuoso acoustic guitar work. If "Boots of Spanish Leather" may seem an obvious choice, covers of "Across the Borderline" and "Answer Me" transcend their original selves. In bathetic contrast, the two electric songs that bookend the acoustic set, "All Along the Watchtower" with Jack Bruce and his band, and "Shake, Rattle and Roll" with Keith Richards's band, are painfully amateurish, all nuance tossed to the hot Spanish wind.

October 24, Bayfront Auditorium, Corpus Christi, TX

October 25, City Coliseum, Austin, TX

Dylan pulls out all the stops tonight, performing "Pancho and Lefty" and "Friend of the Devil" in the electric sets and the obscure "20/20 Vision" and an ever-improving "Trail of the Buffalo" in the acoustic set.

October 26, Sunken Garden Theatre, San Antonio, TX

The lovely "Answer Me," first performed in Seville, reappears in the acoustic set, along with a magnificent "Visions of Johanna."

October 28, Memorial Civic Center, Lubbock, TX

October 30, Brady Theatre, Tulsa, OK

Steve Ripley, a guitarist in Dylan's 1981 band, joins the band for the second electric set. "Early Morning Rain" makes a rare appearance in the first electric set.

October 31, Convention Hall, Wichita, KS

After some very grim shows in 1991, the fall 1991 tour is shaping up to be one of the great Dylan tours. Tonight Dylan introduces a superb, stripped-down rendition of Eddy Arnold's "You Don't Know Me" as well as opening the acoustic set with the hoary Child ballad, "Golden Vanity," magnetically performed. "Girl from the North Country," "Answer Me," and "Visions of Johanna" all help make for a particularly fine acoustic set, while Little Feat's "Willing" makes a welcome return in the first electric set.

November 1, Midland Theatre, Kansas City, MO

Van Morrison's "One Irish Rover" makes a reappearance.

November 2, Iowa State University, Ames, IA

A beautiful, electric arrangement of "Across the Borderline" features some uncharacteristically sensitive playing from John Jackson. "Two Soldiers" is in the acoustic set.

November 4, Northwestern University, Evanston, IL
"Golden Vanity" is back in the acoustic set, while "Answer Me" makes its one appearance in an electric guise. Backstage tonight is *Los Angeles Times* reporter Robert Hilburn. After the show, Hilburn joins Dylan at the Ambassador East in Chicago and they head on to a blues club and then dinner. They talk about Dylan's relentless touring and his audience. Dylan admits, "A lot of people [in the past] were coming out to see The Legend, and I was trying to just get on stage and play music."

November 5, Dane County Memorial Coliseum, Madison, WI
The highlight of this fine show is a unique acoustic performance of "That Lucky Ol' Sun," a worthy kin to the "Farm Aid" version. Hilburn is again backstage tonight and, after the show, boards the bus with Dylan, where he continues to interview the man for a cover feature in the *LA Times*'s Sunday magazine, published the following February. Dylan, though dissatisfied with tonight's concert, responds well to Hilburn's subtle probings, admitting that, "there was a time when the songs would come three or four at the same time, but those days are long gone." Hilburn is dropped off at a motel near Chicago's O'Hare Airport as Dylan's bus heads for South Bend.

November 6, Morris Civic Auditorium, South Bend, IN
Dylan returns to his playful ways, singing a hilarious "Rainy Day Women" while the band are playing "Watching the River Flow." The playfulness continues as he introduces "All Along the Watchtower" by asking, "Anybody heard of U2? They recorded this song, but they did it with the wrong words. These are the correct words. All about business men. All about people getting on with the business of their lives." The traditional acoustic cover tonight is a magnificent "I'm a Rovin' Gambler."

November 8, Kentucky Center for the Performing Arts, Louisville, Kentucky

November 9, Memorial Hall, Dayton, OH
"Confidential to Me" is in a new electric guise.

November 10, Murat Theatre, Indianapolis, IN
Opening the second electric set, Dylan performs a song from *Street-Legal* for the first time on the "Never Ending Tour," and this "Senor," although a tad hesitant, has a forcefulness all its own. An acoustic "Every Grain of Sand" was one of the alternatives on the acoustic set list, although it is not performed.

November 12, Fox Theatre, Detroit, MI
A powerful "Tears of Rage" and a stomp through Elmore James's "Dust My Broom" are tonight's surprises.

1991

November 13, University of Akron, Akron, OH
"Simple Twist of Fate," has been a highlight of nearly every show on this leg, invariably stretched to a dramatic eight minutes. Dylan concludes the song tonight by calling it his "invasion of privacy song."

November 15, EM Kirby Center for the Performing Arts, Wilkes-Barre, PA

November 16, Yale University, New Haven, CT
Dylan prefaces "Gotta Serve Somebody" with a very odd rap, "You know about the saying, "Thou shalt not murder. It doesn't say, Thou shalt not kill." Actually it does.

November 18, Stanley Performing Arts Center, Utica, NY

November 19, Civic Center, Erie, PA
Dylan introduces the most incongruous cover of the fall '91 tour, that cloying smoocher, "Moondance," given the sort of perfunctory treatment it has long deserved.

November 20, University of VA, Charlottesville, VA
A remarkable tour ends in subdued fashion, although Dylan still raises "Queen Jane Approximately" from the dead for the second electric set.

10/11

Maggies
MAN iN ME
WATCHTower
F Confidential
Riverflow
Serve
SHELter
Alone With You
Desolation
Boots
HATTiE / Every Grain
One too Many
SENOR / Devil
Broken
BABy Tonite
Hwy 61
Long Black / Rainy Day

1992

1992 [Winter/Spring]

Dylan records his harmonica part in a Los Angeles studio for a version of "Boots of Spanish Leather" by Nanci Griffith. The take appears on Nanci Griffith's 1993 album, *Other Voices, Other Rooms.*

Early January

Dylan conducts some rehearsals in Los Angeles in the first week of January. Among songs he is rumored to have rehearsed are "Desperado" and a couple of Steve Miller tunes. Drummer Jim Keltner was possibly one of the musicians involved in these rehearsals.

January 17

Dylan rehearses at Radio City Hall for tomorrow's 10th anniversary "Late Night with David Letterman." Aside from working on "Like a Rolling Stone," Dylan also apparently attempts a version of Jimi Hendrix's "Dolly Dagger."

January 18

As part of the 10th anniversary edition of the mystifyingly popular "Late Night with David Letterman," Dylan agrees to perform "Like a Rolling Stone" with an all-star band that includes five backing singers of such stellar credentials as Mavis Staples, Rosanne Cash, Michelle Shocked, Emmylou Harris, and Nanci Griffith. Dylan performs the song twice and murders the song twice.

February 13–19

Dylan attends most, if not all, of Neil Young's six shows (the 16th being a night off) at the Beacon Theatre in New York. Before one of the performances, he talks with Victoria Williams, who is playing the support slot at these shows. One evening, Dylan and Young visit the Bitter End to catch one of David Bromberg's late shows. The rudeness of the Beacon audiences may well have dissuaded Dylan from considering an acoustic tour himself, a long-mooted option throughout the "Never Ending Tour."

March 9

Dylan and his band, now augmented by Bucky Baxter, are rehearsing at the Leeds Rehearsal Facility in Hollywood, presumably one of several days rehearsals prior to the Australian tour.

March 13

Dylan is interviewed on the phone by esteemed Aussie journalist Stuart Coupe, but seems determined to sleepwalk through the conversation until Coupe refers to his version of Townes Van Zandt's "Pancho and Lefty." Dylan, suddenly wide awake, asks our man, "May I ask where you heard that?"

March 18, 21, Entertainment Center, Perth, Australia

The opening show of 1992 suggests that much of the promise of the fall '91 shows remains intact. The band has been augmented by the pedal-steel player from Steve Earle's band, Bucky Baxter, who has a tendency to over-embellish at some of these early shows. Returning to surprising opening shows, Dylan pulls out two one-off electric covers. If the traditional "Little Maggie" remains an obvious favorite of folkies, a faithful rendition of Jimi Hendrix's "Dolly Dagger" definitely qualifies as offbeat. The Dead also rear their ugly repertoire, Dylan including "West LA Fadeaway." Although all three covers soon fall by the wayside, one "new" Dylan original debuted tonight—"Cat's in the Well"—holds its own for most of the tour.

Dylan continues to ring the changes on the 21st. An electric "Most of the Time," minus most of its lyrics, but with dollops of pedal-steel, needs further work. More welcome is Dylan playing the first two songs of the acoustic set solo. "Love Minus Zero" and the traditional "Little Moses" tend to be showstoppers most nights. Tonight Dylan also unveils the even more arcane "Female Rambling Sailor" during the acoustic set, accompanied by Tony Garnier on upright bass. Dylan concludes with a solo "Blowin' in the Wind," rather fine but damn predictable.

March 23–25, State Theatre, Sydney, Australia

On the 23rd, Dylan starts using Bucky Baxter more intelligently, bringing him in on mandolin on "The Times They Are a-Changin'" and electric slide on "Highway 61 Revisited." The second night features a shuffling, electric "She Belongs to Me."

March 29, Royal Theatre, Canberra, Australia

April 1–3, 5–7, Palais Theatre, Melbourne, Australia

After the first show, Dylan is interviewed in his dressing room by Peter Wilmoth of *The Age*. The interview apparently lasts half an hour and, once again, Dylan insists he plays the older songs because "the vision is still quite focused."

• Just as the sets seem to have settled into a comfortable pattern, Dylan pulls three surprises on a stunned Melbourne crowd on the second night. "Absolutely Sweet Marie" returns to favor, and "Tonight I'll Be Staying Here with You" becomes a welcome addition to this band's repertoire, but neither prepares fans for the second song of the second electric set, truly the resurrection of "Idiot Wind." Thankfully, Dylan perseveres with the song, which survives the transition to the States in May, although the third verse is lost somewhere in Hawaii. Nevertheless, the intensity of his performances rarely wanes.

• On the 6th, Dylan continues to mine the Grateful Dead's repertoire, performing a deep, dark "Black Muddy River." "Golden Vanity" also makes its first appearance of 1992.

April 8–9 (10?)
Dylan takes the overnight ferry to Tasmania, where he spends a couple of days looking around the island before returning in time for his show in Launceston.

April 10, Silver Dome, Launceston, Australia
"Visions of Johanna" appears in semi-acoustic form during the second electric set.

April 11, Derwent Entertainment Center, Hobart, Australia.
The first electric set features rare '92 performances of "I Want You" and "John Brown."

April 13, State Theatre, Sydney, Australia
Dylan opens with the bluesy "Don't Let Your Deal Go Down" on the first night.

April 14, State Theatre, Sydney, Australia
The acoustic finale on the 14th is not "Blowin' in the Wind." Instead Dylan performs a word-perfect version of the traditional "Lady of Carlisle" (also known as "The Bold Lieutenant"), a song he last sang in 1961. Dylan also bookends the first set with two songs from *New Morning,* opening with the title track and concluding with the live debut of "If Not for You," Baxter adding some appropriate pedal steel.

April 15, State Theatre, Sydney, Australia
The second song on the 15th is an electric arrangement of Blind Willie McTell's "Delia." Sadly, it is destined to be one of only two such performances.

April 16, State Theatre, Sydney, Australia
For the closing show, Dylan introduces two of his more obscure '80s recordings the first electric set, "Sally Sue Brown" and "Union Sundown."

April 18, Super Pop Tent, Auckland, New Zealand
For once "Visions of Johanna" is an unwelcome inclusion in the acoustic set. The alternate on the cue sheet had been a semi-acoustic "Ballad of Frankie Lee & Judas Priest," a prospect never realized.

April 22, Royal Lahaina Tennis Stadium, Maui, Hawaii

April 24, Waikiki Shell, Waikiki, Hawaii
During the acoustic set, Dylan responds to several inaudible shouts from the audience with, "This one's got all that stuff in it, you'll see, it's got all that and more," playing the final "Golden Vanity" to date.

April 27–28, Paramount Northwest Theatre, Seattle, WA

A second drummer joins the band in Seattle, Charlie Quintana adding a whole new dynamic to Wallace's more pedestrian approach. "Sally Sue Brown" fills the second-song slot on the 28th.

April 30, Hult Auditorium, Eugene, OR

Second up tonight is "Black Muddy River," a surprise quickly eclipsed by the first-ever live performance of "Drifter's Escape." Coming hard on the heels of reports of rioting following the verdict in the Rodney King trial in LA, it is tempting to view its inclusion as intentionally apposite. Although the song reappears a few shows later in the style of Hendrix, this is a unique, country-tinged rendition.

May 1, Sun County Fairgrounds, Red Bluff, CA

May 2, Sonoma County Fairgrounds, Santa Rosa, CA

During "Mr. Tambourine Man," a woman jumps onstage and begins to sing into the mike. Dylan steps back and, although she tries to get him to join her at the mike, only returns to the song after she is finally led off by security.

May 4–5, Warfield Theatre, San Francisco, CA

Dylan opens his first show at the Warfield in 12 years with an instrumental "Rainy Day Women." On the 5th, Jerry Garcia joins Dylan for "Cat's in the Well" and an extraordinary "Idiot Wind," culminating in a blistering harmonica break from Dylan.

May 7–8, Community Theatre, Berkeley, CA

A newly rocked-up "Drifter's Escape" returns to the set in Berkeley. Dylan also performs an acoustic "Visions of Johanna" in the venue where he had debuted the song 27 years earlier.

• For the first time on the "Never Ending Tour," Dylan duplicates the set on both nights, although the second night is a very different show, in front of a far more recalcitrant crowd.

May 9, State University, San Jose, CA

Perhaps the best of the West Coast shows features the last "Most of the Time," Dylan's face beaded with sweat, visibly living each phrase.

May 11, Arlington Theatre, Santa Barbara, CA

An anthemic "Queen Jane Approximately" is tonight's highlight.

May 13–14, 16–17, 19–21, Pantages Theatre, Hollywood, CA

The variable on these dates occurs in the second-song slot: On the 14th, the second and last "Delia" of 1992 appears there; "Friend of the Devil" is song number two on the 16th; "Black Muddy River" fills the slot next; and "That Lucky Ol' Sun" is featured on the 19th. On the 21st, the audience sings a slightly premature "Happy Birthday" before the first encore, "Lenny Bruce."

May 23, Bally's Goldwyn Events Center, Las Vegas, NV

In this gamblers' haven, Dylan can't resist performing "Joey." After two months on the road, Dylan needs a break.

June 4–(21?)

Dylan spends a couple of weeks at the Acme Recording Studio in Chicago working on an album of electric "folk" covers with David Bromberg, the nominal producer of the sessions. Dylan records some 26 songs, of which 15 are mixed down. Some eight song titles are known, including two of Bromberg's own compositions, "Catskills Serenade" and "World of Fools," Tim Hardin's "The Lady Came from Baltimore," the blues standard "Nobody's Fault but Mine," and the contemporary Christian ballad "Rise Again" (recorded with a local choir). Also cut at these sessions are the traditional "Polly Vaughn," "Casey Jones," and "Duncan and Brady." After the sessions, Dylan heads for New York and then onto Europe.

June 26, Sjoslaget, Norra Hamnea, Lulea, Sweden

A sedate start to an 11-date European tour, with Dylan struggling to overcome monitor problems. A 10-minute "Mr. Tambourine Man" concludes an excellent acoustic set that also features a first acoustic "West LA Fadeaway."

June 28, Tradgards Foreningen, Gothenburg, Sweden

Opening with the traditional "Don't Let Your Deal Go Down," Dylan replaces "The Girl on the Green Briar Shore" with "Little Moses."

June 30, Cote D'Opale Festival, Kursaal, Dunkirk, France

Dylan opens with "Don't Let Your Deal Go Down." "Idiot Wind" makes its last regular appearance, Dylan having run out of steam in the last couple of shows. The song that will take its place in the set is also debuted tonight, "I and I."

July 1, Parc Des Expositions, Reims, France

A powerful show opens with Paul Simon's "A Hazy Shade of Winter." However, the highlight of the show is a solo performance of the English broadside ballad, "Roving Blade" (aka "Newlyn Town").

July 2, Les Eurockennes De Belfort, Belfort, France

July 4, Porta Siberia, Genoa, Italy

July 5, Festa Communale Unita, Correggio, Italy

Dylan opens with a largely unintelligible "Two by Two" that segues into "I Believe in You." "Folsom Prison Blues" also makes its only appearance of 1992.

July 7, Hippodrome Di Maia, Merano, Italy

Tonight's opening set continues to throw surprises at the crowd. "Two by Two" is more recognizable, "Pretty Peggy-O" is simply excellent, and "I Dreamed I Saw St. Augustine" makes its first appearance since Toad's Place (see January 12, 1990).

July 8, Arene Croix Noire, Aosta, Italy

July 10, Centre Des Sports, Leysin, Switzerland
Tonight's opening trio of songs are "Friend of the Devil" into "Just Like Tom Thumb's Blues" into Chuck Berry's "Around and Around."

July 12, Pinede De Juan Les Pins, Antibes, France
Continuing to open with incongruous covers, Dylan attempts "Hey Joe."

Late July to Early August
At his own garage studio in Malibu, Dylan reevaluates the tracks cut with David Bromberg in Chicago and decides to record some acoustic songs. The process quickly takes over, and he ends up recording the entire *Good as I Been to You* album in a matter of afternoons, with a minimum of fuss, attended by just Debbie Gold, who is producing, and an engineer. Aside from the 13 songs on *Good as I Been to You,* at least one outtake is finished. "You Belong to Me" subsequently appears in the cliched setting of Oliver Stone's movie, *Natural Born Killers* (it is somewhat more audible on the soundtrack album).

August 17–18, Massey Hall, Toronto, Ontario
Dylan kicks off another leg of the "Never Ending Tour" with "Wiggle Wiggle," followed by an unusual "Heart of Mine." Dylan also temporarily revives "Female Rambling Sailor" and, closing out the main set, "Idiot Wind." "Tears of Rage" makes a rare appearance on the second night.

August 20, Conneaut Lake Park, Meadville, PA

August 21, Hamilton Place, Hamilton, Ontario

August 22, Lansdowne Stadium, Ottawa, Ontario
"Unbelievable" usurps "Cat's in the Well" in the second electric set.

August 24, Arena, Sudbury, Ontario

August 25, Memorial Gardens, Sault Ste. Marie, Ontario

August 27, Fort William Gardens, Thunder Bay, Ontario

August 29–31, September 2–3, Historic Orpheum Theatre, Minneapolis, MN
The five shows at the Orpheum, despite the lack of debut performances, are perhaps Dylan's most consistent residency since the G. E. Smith heyday. They also represent a fitting end to an inspired four months of touring with Charlie Quintana, who is due to leave after Minneapolis to join Izzy Stradlin, formerly of Guns'n'Roses, on his first solo tour. He particularly shines on the 2nd, driving the band through epic versions of "Friend of the Devil," "Tangled Up in Blue," and "Simple Twist of Fate." On the final night, Dylan's mother and brother are sitting in the fifth row as he sings two reminders of his gospel years, "I Believe in You" and "Every Grain of Sand," the latter

suitably embellished by mouth harp. "Idiot Wind" makes its final tour appearance of 1992 on the second night of this residency.

September 5, Orpheum Theatre, Omaha, NE
Quintana's last show.

September 6, Liberty Memorial Park, Kansas City, MO
The inexperienced Winston Watson takes over from Quintana.

September 8, Joseph Taylor Robinson Memorial Auditorium, Little Rock, AK
The old rock & roller Billy Lee Riley joins Dylan onstage to sing his own "Red Hot."

September 9, Municipal Auditorium, Jackson, MS

September 11, Oak Mountain Amphitheatre, Pelham, AL

September 12, Bayfront Auditorium, Pensacola, FL

September 13, Heymann Performing Arts Center, Lafayette, LA
"It's Alright, Ma" is the acoustic set's finale.

October 9, Duquesne University, Pittsburgh, PA

October 10, University of PA, Lock Haven, PA

October 11, Eastman Theatre, Rochester, NY

October 12, Broome County Forum, Binghampton, NY
As a precursor of things to come, Winston Watson is the sole beatmaster tonight. Watson does not attempt anything too ambitious, although Dylan does attempt "Pretty Peggy-O" and "Queen Jane Approximately" to test his mettle.

Mid-October (12–14?)
Rehearsals for the 30th Anniversary bash at Madison Square Garden take place at an old film studio in Long Island City.

October 15–16
Rehearsals for Dylan's 30th Anniversary bash relocate to Madison Square Garden.

October 18, Madison Square Garden, NY
There is an afternoon dress rehearsal for the event, billed on the tickets as "Columbia Records Celebrates the Music of Bob Dylan," at Madison Square Garden itself. Dylan does attend the dress rehearsal and is filmed rehearsing "It Takes a Lot to Laugh" with Eric Clapton—Dylan and Clapton trading verses and Dylan playing some inspired harmonica. However, the song is cut from the final running-order because of timing difficulties, i.e., Co-

lumbia's need to sneak in a couple more talentless no-hopers from their roster (Sophie B. Hawkins take a bow!) onto the bill. Dylan is apparently not amused.

The show itself commences on time at 8 PM. After two hours of performances by every hung-up person in the whole wide universe, Dylan finally takes to the stage and croaks his way through "Song to Woody" and "It's Alright, Ma." Seemingly in need of a little help tonight, Dylan is then joined by Roger McGuinn, Tom Petty, Neil Young, Eric Clapton, and George Harrison for an ultra-lame "My Back Pages," and everybody else for an equally perfunctory "Knockin' on Heaven's Door." Then, with his usual sense of timing, Dylan closes the show with a tender "Girl from the North Country" just as the credits are rolling on the live pay-per-view TV broadcast. Although the show is released as a double CD some months later, and Dylan is several hundred thousand /a couple of million dollars richer (take your pick) after the evening, on any kind of musical level the show has only served to remind that nobody sings Dylan like Dylan, and even he on occasion doesn't sing Dylan like Dylan.

• After the show, Dylan and assorted fellow performers retire to Tommy Makem's Irish Pavilion, where Dylan purportedly joins Liam Clancy, Ron Wood, and Eddie Vedder on assorted Irish ballads, presumably a la the "Friends of Chile" concert (see May 9, 1974), until the cold, gray dawn.

October 19
Dylan records his vocal for the song "Heartland," which he has cowritten with Willie Nelson. The session is produced by Don Was at the Power Station, NY.

October 23, University of DE, Newark, DE

October 24, University of CT, Storrs, CT

October 25, Civic Center, Providence, RI
Once again, Dylan shakes things up, hoping to keep the shows from becoming routine. Opening with Muddy Waters's "I Can't Be Satisfied," Dylan also debuts a *John Wesley Harding* masterpiece, "Dear Landlord," after extensive soundcheck rehearsals prior to the last couple of shows. The arrangement really is quite elaborate for this band, and the song is beyond Dylan's vocal capabilities at this point. Also replacing a world-weary "Little Moses" is a fine "Mama, You Been on My Mind," tightly wound around some fine harmonica work.

October 27, Memorial Auditorium, Burlington, VT

October 28, Paramount Theatre, Springfield, MA
Tonight Dylan opens with "I Can't Be Satisfied" and a resurrected "Hang Me, Oh Hang Me."

October 30, Endicott College, Beverly, MA

November 1, EM Kirby Center for Performing Arts, Wilkes-Barre, PA

Tonight "West LA Fadeaway" and "Pretty Peggy-O" kick off the gig in style.

November 2, Stanbaugh Auditorium, Youngstown, OH

If Dylan still can't be satisfied, the fourth electric song tonight is a brave stab at a miner's lament, "Farewell to the Gold," a song Dylan presumably learned from British folksinger Nic Jones's *Penguin Eggs* album. The band displays little imagination, but Dylan's forceful vocal still makes for a powerful performance.

November 3, Music Hall, Cincinnati, OH

> *Good as I Been to You* (CK 53200): "Frankie and Albert," "Jim Jones," "Blackjack Davy," "Canadee-I-O," "Sittin' on Top of the World," "Little Maggie," "Hard Times," "Step It Up," "Tomorrow Night," "Arthur McBride," "You're Gonna Quit Me," "Diamond Joe," "Froggie Went a-Courtin'"

November 6, University of FL, Gainesville, FL

November 8, University of Miami, Coral Gables, FL

November 9, Van Wezel Performing Arts Center, Sarasota, FL

In wet but intimate surroundings, Dylan plays his final versions of "I Can't Be Satisfied" and "Dear Landlord."

November 11, Ruth Eckerd Hall, Clearwater, FL

Dylan performs his first "Disease of Conceit" with this band. The show also features rare outings for "When I Paint My Masterpiece," "Senor," and "I Dreamed I Saw St. Augustine."

November 12, University of Central FL Arena, Orlando, FL

A venomous "Disease of Conceit" makes its second and last appearance of 1992, Dylan spitting the words at an unenthusiastic audience.

November 13, Musical Center, Sunrise, FL

"Willing" makes a rare appearance. Dylan also jams out on "I and I," a worrying indication of things to come.

November 15, South FL Fairgrounds, West Palm Beach, FL

Although two songs short of the usual 18-song set, this is an epic show. Dylan is unable to contain himself at this final show of the year, playing some of his most adventurous harmonica work in a long time. Among the first 11 songs in the set, just three escape harmonica workouts. "Stuck Inside of Mobile" and "Mama, You Been on My Mind" come in for particular attention. It has been a very good year on the road: 93 shows, a monumental schedule for a 51-year-old man.

Late November to Early December

Dylan overdubs a new vocal for the ensemble "My Back Pages" at the Madison Square Garden tribute, after his garbled live vocal is deemed unusable. The session is presumably at Sony Studios, NY.

December 23

Dylan is seen boarding an 11:30 AM flight for Minneapolis at Los Angeles International Airport. He is accompanied by his son Jakob and an unidentified blonde.

1993

January (?)
Dylan contributes backing vocals to a version of "Trust Yourself" recorded by Carlene Carter at Huh Studio, Los Angeles.

January 13
Dylan duets with Willie Nelson on the jointly composed "Heartland" for a CBS-TV production, "A Country Music Celebration." It is filmed at CBS Studios in Nashville.

January 17
In a surprising endorsement, Dylan joins the celebrations surrounding Bill Clinton's inauguration as president, performing a barely comprehensible "Chimes of Freedom" at the Lincoln Memorial in the afternoon. In the evening, Dylan even appears at an exclusive event for campaign workers, the "Absolutely Unofficial Blue Jeans Bash," at the National Building Museum, joining members of the Band on the opening song, "To Be Alone with You," and then playing a little perfunctory guitar on "Key to the Highway," "I Shall Be Released," and "(I Don't Want to) Hang Up My Rock & Roll Shoes."

February 3–4
Dylan and his band rehearse at the Factory in Ringsend, Dublin. The rehearsals apparently last around 10 hours on both days.

February 5, The Point Depot, Dublin, Ireland
Returning to the British Isles for the first time since a horrific winter '91 London residency, little remains of the energy, passion, and commitment of 1992. If the absence of the deadbeat drum sound of Ian Wallace should have given the band a certain sense of release, there is precious little evidence at The Point. Just two songs from the recently released *Good as I Been to You*, "Tomorrow Night" and "Jim Jones," are debuted and both will grow nightly in stature. After the show, Dylan, Elvis Costello, Chrissie Hynde, Bono, the Edge, and others retire to the Restaurant Tosca.

February 6
Dylan stays an extra day in Dublin, attending Van Morrison's own show at The Point. He can't resist joining Van for the usual disastrous "It's All Over Now, Baby Blue."

1993

February 7–9, 11–13, Hammersmith Apollo, London, England
Opening night introduces a chilling "I and I," which soon becomes a Winston Watson tour de force (at the expense of the song), and a hilarious "Don't Think Twice, It's All Right," in which Dylan lets Garnier play a bass solo—which he completely fouls up—leading Dylan to insist to the crowd, "This has been rehearsed a hundred times." For the last show, Dave Stewart, a guitarist of no fixed renown, joins Dylan on "Highway 61 Revisited" as another disappointing Hammersmith residency splutters to a conclusion.

February 15, Vredenburg, Utrecht, Netherlands
After six London shows without a single notable variant, Dylan opens tonight with Hank Snow's "I'm Moving On."

February 16, Vredenburg, Utrecht, Netherlands

February 17, Muziek Centrum, Eindhoven, Netherlands
Tonight Dylan opens with "Folsom Prison Blues." On "The Times They Are a-Changin'," Dylan is joined by a lady from the audience, one Liz Souissi, who duets with him on the song. At the end, she gives him a hug and a kiss before leaving the stage.

February 18, Musikhalle, Hanover, Germany

February 20, Rhein-Main-Halle, Wiesbaden, Germany

February 21, Centre Sportif, Petange, Luxembourg.

February 23, Le Zenith, Paris, France.

February 25, Maysfield Leisure Center, Belfast, N. Ireland
At the final show of a very disappointing tour, Dylan finally pulls out something to get the fans' pulses quickening, a live debut for the beautiful "Born in Time." Although he stumbles over some of the lyrics, it has an intensity missing from most songs performed on this tour. After the show, Dylan heads south for a holiday, staying in County Kildare, presumably at Ron Wood's home there.

April 12, Kentucky Center for the Performing Arts, Louisville, KY
The first electric set opens with another song from *Good as I Been to You*, the world-weary "Hard Times," performed in a semi-acoustic form. Dylan also attempts "Born in Time" again, along with a one-off "License to Kill."

April 13–14, TN Performing Arts Centre, Nashville, TN
"Disease of Conceit" supersedes "License to Kill."

April 16, Radford University, Radford, VA

April 17, General James White Memorial Coliseum, Knoxville, TN

April 18, Civic Centre, Asheville, NC

April 19, Civic Centre, Huntsville, AL

April 21, Civic Centre Theatre, Monroe, LA

April 23, Jazzfest, Fairgrounds Racetrack, New Orleans, LA
Dylan headlines the first Friday of Jazzfest to some 30,000 festival goers on
the Ray-Ban stage and rewards them with the tightest show of the year. The
acoustic set features particularly fine versions of "Jim Jones" and "Tomorrow Night," as well as a strong "Mr. Tambourine Man," while the Allman
Brothers's Dickie Betts adds some stinging lead guitar to "Cat's in the Well"
and "Everything Is Broken" in the second electric set. Dylan even goes over-
time to give the crowd a full three-song encore.

Late April
At some point in 1993, presumably during his stay in Austin, Dylan cowrites
a song with Texan singer-songwriter Jude Johnston. The song, "Howlin' at
My Window," does not suggest any significant Dylan input.

April 25
Dylan attends "For the Sake of the Song," the Texas Music Association's tribute to Townes Van Zandt at La Zona Rosa in Austin, TX. He does not perform and leaves early after he is recognized.

April 28
Dylan contributes to an hour-long TV special to celebrate Willie Nelson's
60th birthday. "Willie Nelson: The Big Six-O" is filmed at KRLU Studios
in Austin, and Dylan duets with Nelson on a quite magnificent "Pancho and
Lefty" and then delivers an equally effective "Hard Times" with his current
band. "Hard Times" apparently requires three or four takes.

May 19
Dylan records a new version of "Ballad of Hollis Brown," with Mike Seeger
accompanying on banjo, at Grandma's Warehouse in Los Angeles. The song
subsequently appears on Seeger's *Third Annual Farewell Reunion* album.

May
Dylan decides to repeat the *Good as I Been to You* experiment. With Debbie
Gold again producing, Dylan records another album's worth of acoustic cov-
ers in record time at his Malibu home. Taking just a few days, he records
14 songs, 10 of which make up *World Gone Wrong*. The four outtakes are
"Twenty One Years," a song Dylan referred to back in 1963 in his letter to
Dave Glover, Robert Johnson's "32.20 Blues," "Goodnight My Love," and
A.P. Carter's "Hello Stranger."

Early June
Dylan supposedly spends a few days in Ireland enjoying himself.

June 12, Fleadh Festival, Finsbury Park, London, England
Aside from mangling "One Irish Rover" with coheadliner Van Morrison, this is a very perfunctory set.

June 13
Dylan arrives at Tel Aviv airport where he signs autographs as he waits at passport control.

June 17, Mann Auditorium, Tel Aviv, Israel

June 19, Amphitheatre Dimoi, Beersheeba, Israel

June 20, Harbour Blues Festival, Port of Haifa, Haifa, Israel
A semi-acoustic "Little Moses" becomes an occasional alternate to "Jim Jones."

June 22–23, Lycabettus Theatre, Athens, Greece

June 24
Dylan is briefly interviewed by three Italian journalists, presumably for articles advertising his three Italian shows. However, Dylan's answers once again suggest a man thinking about his next appointment.

June 25, Tenda Partenope, Naples, Italy

June 26, Campo Sportivo, Pisa, Italy

June 27, Palatrussardi, Milan, Italy

June 29, Palais Des Sport, Marseilles, France

June 30, Palais Des Sport, Toulouse, France

July 1, Des Poble Espanyol Des Montjuic, Barcelona, Spain

July 2, El Pabellon Araba De Vitoria, Vitoria, Spain

July 4, Fleadh Festival, Tramore Racehorse, Waterford, Ireland

July 6, Plaza De Toros, Huesca, Spain

July 8, Plaza De Toros, Gijon, Spain

July 9, Riazor Stadium, Xacobe Festival, La Coruna, Spain

July 10, Coliseu, Porto, Portugal

July 12, Teatro Romano, Merida, Portugal

July 13, Pavilhao, Cascais, Portugal

July 14–16
Dylan cancels a show in Lyon on the day of the show (the 16th). Despite a history of back trouble, this is the first documented instance of Dylan canceling a show on health grounds. Apparently unable to travel to Lyon, Dylan had been in bed in Lisbon for three days, but flew to Zurich on the evening of the 16th.

July 17, Gurten Festival, Berner Hausberg, Bern, Switzerland
An abbreviated 13-song set ends one of the most uneventful of "Never Ending Tour" legs. After the show, there is a post-tour party at the Grand Hotelin Zurich that Dylan attends.

July 18
Dylan attends a Neil Young show in Bad Mergentheim. Young is playing with Booker T and the MGs. Booker T apparently attempted to persuade Dylan to join them onstage but without success.

July 21
Dylan makes a surprise appearance at Camden Lock market, an open-air market in Camden Town, London, where he is filmed in a restaurant called Fluke's Cradle and walking around in a top hat and frock coat by ex-Eurythmic Dave Stewart. The resultant footage appears as a promotional video for "Blood in My Eye," cleverly lip-synched and intercut with shots of Dylan signing autographs and walking among the crowds. Dylan is accompanied by his regular bodyguard, Jim Callaghan, but remains very approachable throughout the afternoon, even when dining at the restaurant.

July 22
Dylan visits a five-bedroomed house in Crouch End around 3 PM. He is apparently considering purchasing the property. However, the story of his visit is leaked to the press, thus presumably scuppering any possible sale. He leaves London for the States the same evening.

Early- to Mid-August
Dylan allows himself to be interviewed by a couple of American journalists, presumably to publicize his forthcoming joint tour with Santana. Greg Kot of the *Chicago Tribune* seems to have been the first to get to him, although only by telephone, in a three-way hookup with Dylan and Santana. The *New York Post* interview, on the other hand, conducted by Jennifer Bowles, takes place in "a small, stuffy room at his management office" in Los Angeles. Aside from a bizarre comparison between Wagner and Beethoven, Dylan seems to have very little to say, although there is the usual guff about playing live as the meaning of life.

August 20, Memorial Coliseum, Portland, OR
The first show in a two-month stint with Santana—meaning necessarily abbreviated sets and poor value for money—includes "Emotionally Yours," presumably resurrected because of the O'Jays's recent cover of the song, and a "God Knows" that quickly becomes an excuse to just rock out.

August 21
Dylan is briefly interviewed by Dennis Michael for "Entertainment Tonight" before tonight's show. Once again, Dylan insists he tours because he enjoys it: "It's not like it's a hardship to do it."

August 21, Waterfront, Seattle, WA
"Emotionally Yours" makes its second and last performance of the tour, extended to nine minutes by two harmonica breaks.

August 22, Pacific Coliseum, Vancouver, BC
"Hard Times" is replaced by "You're Gonna Quit Me."

August 25, Fiddlers Green, Denver, CO

August 27, MN State Fair, St. Paul, MN

August 28, Marcus Amphitheatre, Milwaukee, WI

August 29, World Music Theatre, Chicago, IL

August 31, Pine Knob Music Theatre, Clarkston, MI
For one show only, Dylan abandons the semiacoustic opener in favor of the battlecry "Like a Rolling Stone." The first encore is equally unusual, "One More Cup of Coffee."

September 2, Canadian National Exhibition, Toronto, Ontario

September 3, New York State Fairgrounds, Syracuse, NY

September 4, Performing Arts Center, Saratoga Springs, NY
"Blackjack Davey" becomes the fifth song from *Good as I Been to You* to be performed in 1993 when it replaces "Little Moses."

September 5, Montage Mountain Ski/Summer Resort, Scranton, PA
Supposedly Dylan turned up for this afternoon's soundcheck, a rare event indeed these days. They work on "Series of Dreams," "Pretty Peggy-O," "What Good Am I?," "Just Like Tom Thumb's Blues," "When I Paint My Masterpiece," and "All Along the Watchtower." "Series of Dreams" has been soundchecked several times previously, but without Dylan's input.

September 8, Wolf Trap Farm Park, Vienna, VA
The standout set of the Dylan/Santana tour, tonight's show features perhaps the best "Born in Time," an atmospheric "Blackjack Davey," and, most important of all, a live debut for "Series of Dreams," which had been soundchecked several times in Europe. Although Dylan takes a while to warm to the song, he puts everything he can into the last couple of verses, even deliberately reworking a couple of the weaker lines. After such an intense moment, Dylan begins singing "Boots of Spanish Leather," a song he had already sung in its entirety four songs earlier, rather than the scheduled "It Ain't Me, Babe." Realizing his mistake, he mumbles an apology, something

about "well, it's the same chords," before seguing into the correct song. A priceless moment, although it probably cost fans the opportunity of further performances of "Series of Dreams" at subsequent Dylan/Santana shows.

September 9, Wolf Trap Farm Park, Vienna, VA

September 10–11, Jones Beach Theatre, Wantagh, NY

September 13, Great Woods Performing Arts Center, Mansfield, MA

September 14, Garden State Arts Center, Holmdel, NJ

September 17, Blockbuster Pavilion, Charlotte, NC

September 18, Chastain Memorial Park Amphitheatre, Atlanta, GA

September 19, Walnut Creek Amphitheatre, Raleigh, NC
"Just Like Tom Thumb's Blues" and "One More Cup of Coffee" are two unusual inclusions at tonight's show.

September 21, Sundome, Tampa, FL

September 22, James L. Knight Center, Miami, FL

September 23, Auditorium, West Palm Beach, FL

October 1, Pacific Auditorium, Costa Mesa, CA

October 2, Hollywood Bowl, Hollywood, CA

October 3
Dylan is interviewed in his San Diego hotel by Gary Hill for the news agency Reuters. Although ostensibly intended to promote his new album, *World Gone Wrong,* Dylan says little about the album, except that the songs "are personal but . . . very universal."

October 3, Sports Arena, San Diego, CA

October 5, Glen Helen Blockbuster Pavilion, Devore, CA

October 7, Pavilion, Concord, CA

October 8, Cal Expo Amphitheatre, Sacramento, CA

October 9, Shoreline Amphitheatre, Mountain View, CA
Neil Young joins Dylan for the final song of the last Dylan/Santana show, hamming it up on guitar during "Leopard-Skin Pill-Box Hat." The tour, though, has done almost nothing for Dylan's commercial or critical standing, being a case of atrophy by association.

> October 26: *World Gone Wrong* (CK 57590): "World Gone Wrong," "Love Henry," "Ragged & Dirty," "Blood in My Eyes," "Broke Down Engine," "Delia," "Stack-a-lee," "Two Soldiers," "Jack-a-roe," "Lone Pilgrim"

November 9–12(?)

Dylan and the band rehearse some additions to the repertoire for a couple of rumored shows at a secret location. These initial rehearsals probably take place at Studio Instrument Rentals in New York.

November 13–16

Dylan and the band relocate to the Supper Club now that the secret is out, and set about honing the songs Dylan plans to record (and film) for a TV special. Rehearsals continue even on the afternoon of the show, although no songs are apparently rehearsed on the 16th that do not appear at the subsequent shows.

November 16, The Supper Club, NY

After a year of shows that have spanned the full gamut from tepid to lackluster, Dylan plays the first two of four shows at the intimate midtown Supper Club. With tickets distributed free at the downtown Tower Records store the previous Sunday, the four shows—two per night—are being filmed at Dylan's expense for a TV special along the lines of MTV's highly popular "Unplugged." Although he is backed by his usual four-piece band, they are required to take something of a muted role, restricted to acoustic instruments and, in Winston Watson's case, playing simple backbeats. The opening show starts a little ropey, with unfocused versions of "Absolutely Sweet Marie" and "Lay, Lady, Lay" but once Dylan debuts "Blood In My Eye" things start to gel. "Queen Jane Approximately" and "Tight Connection to My Heart" are both effective, without matching their G.E. Smith arrangements. "Disease of Conceit" is no more than pleasant, as is "I Want You." However, the final three songs are all good, and all sung with an intensity all too often lacking in recent shows, "Ring Them Bells," "My Back Pages" (minus its Bobfest meanderings), and "Forever Young" close a set that leaves the lucky attendees waiting anxiously for the 11 PM show. As it is, the late show this Tuesday evening is on an entirely different plane. With this second set, fans begin to realize just how fortunate they are to see these shows. Although only four songs—songs one, three, five, and six—are different from the first set, three are magnificent. "Ragged and Dirty" opens the show, "Jack A-Roe" puts the album version to shame, and "One Too Many Mornings" is as tender as can be. "I'll Be Your Baby Tonight" shuffles pleasantly enough, but the real highlights at this show are "Queen Jane Approximately," which maintains a natural ebb and flow for a good eight minutes, and possibly the finest-ever "Ring Them Bells," impassioned without being too ornamental, in a subtle semiacoustic arrangement.

November 17, The Supper Club, NY

The second night at New York's Supper Club, and both shows surpass their respective yesterday-twins. The first show includes just one song not performed at the previous two shows, "One More Cup of Coffee," which Dylan is clearly stumped by at the outset until a lady in the front row shouts out the first line. Although a commendable stab at a difficult song, it never hits the heights. However, the remaining eight songs—seven of which duplicate the previous night's early set—are all delivered with a fiery enthusiasm from Dylan and the band alike. However, it is tonight's late show that raises the stakes once more. After the best "Ragged and Dirty," a fine "Lay, Lady, Lay," and a more convincing "Tight Connection to My Heart," Dylan pulls out three surprises, one after the other, and each of them is a knock-'em-dead performance. First he conjures up Blind Boy Fuller's "Weeping Willow," complete with an "Aw, shucks!," a one-off performance. Then comes the only semi-acoustic "Delia" to date, which again puts the *World Gone Wrong* version in its proper place, and finally a gripping "Jim Jones," the solitary performance from *Good as I Been to You* at these shows. "Queen Jane Approximately," "Ring Them Bells" and "Jack A-Roe" maintain the momentum, temporarily lost with "Forever Young." However, this time Dylan returns for an encore, walks up to the lady who had helped him out on "One More Cup of Coffee" and asks her for the opening line of "I Shall Be Released," which he proceeds to perform. All in all, a remarkable series of shows that remain unseen and (save for bootleg audience tapes) unheard to this day (versions of "Queen Jane Approximately" and "One Too Many Mornings" appear on the *Highway 61 Interactive* CD-ROM but are all but unwatchable).

November 18

After his successful Supper Club stint, Dylan agrees to appear on "Late Night With David Letterman" for a third time. During the afternoon, Dylan and his band rehearse "Forever Young," which starts out some nine minutes long. After some musical pruning, they tape the song around teatime and without any major hiccups.

December 1993 to Early January 1994

Dylan spends some time viewing the footage from the four Supper Club shows. Apparently dissatisfied with the way he comes across visually, he ends up scrapping the project. However, he does not abandon the idea of a Dylan *Unplugged*.

Fall 1993 to Winter 1994

Dylan contributes to another less-than-impressive cover of one of his better songs, adding guitar and harmonica to Stevie Nicks's idea of "Just Like a Woman," presumably recorded in an LA studio during his annual respite from touring.

1994

January

Dylan is asked to provide a brief verbal tribute to Van Morrison, who is due to receive the BPI (British Phonographic Industry)'s equivalent of the Grammys' Lifetime Achievement. He manages to babble a couple of appropriate platitudes.

February 3

Dylan arrives at Narita Airport, Japan.

February 4

Dylan is interviewed by Japanese journalist Akihiko Yamamoto for *Crossbeat* magazine. The interview apparently lasts 40 minutes, Dylan informing the reporter that, "the sixties ended as early as 1965." Asked why he had released two acoustic albums of covers, he replies, "The songs I chose are very important to me. . . . They are the basis of my music."

February 5, Sun Palace, Sendai, Japan

Although Dylan fails to revamp his tired ol' repertoire, tonight's opening show does have two grand surprises at the very start. "Jokerman" makes a long-awaited return as opener, where it remains throughout 1994. "If You See Her, Say Hello" is an even more welcome resurrection, although it will be some months before the song's arrangement comes into its own. In both instances, the Japanese not only recognize these additions, but enthusiastically cheer their inclusion.

February 7, Bunka Taiikukan, Yokohama, Japan

February 8–9, Budokan Hall, Tokyo, Japan

On the second night, "Series of Dreams" returns to favor, although with a very odd arrangement and some atonal singing by the man himself. And yet Dylan seems to know exactly what he is trying to do. He is word perfect and pushing himself vocally.

February 11, Century Hall, Nagoya, Japan

The cue sheet for tonight's show lists a Gordon Lightfoot song, "I'm Not Supposed to Care," as an alternate for song number six. Sadly, it is never performed, although Dylan does record the song in a Memphis studio in May.

February 12, Castle Hall, Osaka, Japan

"Ring Them Bells" makes its only appearance of 1994 during the first electric set.

February 14–15, Kausei-Nenkin Hall, Kokura, Japan

February 16, Koseinekin Hall, Hiroshima, Japan

Tonight's show features one of Dylan's most dramatic statements in recent years, a brooding acoustic version of "Masters of War" that has the crowd on the edge of their seats. The significance of the song's introduction at this show is not lost on them, and they accord Dylan a fitting ovation. The song becomes a highlight of many 1994 shows.

February 18, Cultural Center, Urawa, Japan

February 20, NHK Hall, Tokyo, Japan

February 22, Putra World Trade Center, Kuala Lumpur, Malaysia

February 24, Indoor Stadium, Singapore

February 26, Coliseum, Victoria, Hong Kong

March 10

Dylan attends a tribute to Jack Nicholson at a plush Hollywood theater.

March 23

Dylan is a surprise guest at a charity show at the Universal Amphitheatre in Hollywood. Billed as "Rhythm, Country and Blues," the show features Dylan and Trisha Yearwood dueting on "Tomorrow Night," an idea that sounds last minute (at best).

Early April

Dylan is interviewed for the *St. Louis Post-Dispatch,* presumably by phone. It is not a long interview, and the only question that gets more than a one-sentence reply relates to his last two albums, which he insists, "were necessary for me to do."

April 5, Sangamon State University, Springfield, IL

April 6, Adler Theatre, Davenport, IA

Dylan debuts a song he had recorded in 1992, Tim Hardin's "The Lady Came from Baltimore," as part of the first electric set.

April 7, IA State University, Ames, IA

April 9, Lied Center, Lawrence, KS

April 10, Fox Theatre, St. Louis, MO

April 11
Dylan reads in the local Rockwood paper about a parent campaign in Rockford to build a playground at Page Park School for handicapped children. Seven days later his office sends a $20,000 donation.

April 12, Caronado Theatre, Rockford, IL

April 13, Civic Center, Peoria, IL

April 15, Brown County Arena, Green Bay, WI

April 16, University, Valparaiso, IN

April 17–18, Riviera Theatre, Chicago, IL

April 20, University of IL, Champaign, IL

April 22, Memorial Coliseum, Fort Wayne, IN

April 23, Riverside Theatre, Milwaukee, WI

April 24, Mayo Civic Center, Rochester, MN

April 26, Municipal Auditorium, Sioux City, IA

April 27, University of NV-Lincoln, Lincoln, NV

April 28, Performing Arts Center, Topeka, KS
"Silvio" is performed for the only time in 1994.

April 30, Southwest MO State, Springfield, MO

May 1, Jesse Auditorium, Columbia, MO

May 3, Roberts Stadium, Evansville, IN

May 5, University of TN, Bristol, TN

May 6, Memorial Auditorium, Spartanburg, SC

May 7, Memorial Auditorium, Chattanooga, TN

May 8, Beals Street Blues Festival, Memphis, TN

May 9–11
Dylan and his touring band record their first joint sessions at Ardent Studios in Memphis. The sessions result in five tracks, all covers. "Boogie Woogie Country Girl" subsequently appears on Rhino's *Tribute to Doc Pomus.* "Blue-Eyed Jane" appears in snippet form on the *Highway 61 Interactive* CD-ROM. "I'm Not Supposed to Care," "One Night of Sin," and "Easy Rider (Don't Deny My Name)" remain unreleased in any form.

May 20–22
Dylan performs at "The Great Music Experience," held in the grounds of the Todaiji Temple in Nara City, Japan. He is accompanied by Jim Keltner, percussionist Ray Cooper, and a Japanese orchestra, conducted by Michael Kamen. On all three nights, the three songs he performs are "A Hard Rain's a-Gonna Fall," "I Shall Be Released," and "Ring Them Bells." Not surprisingly, when Dylan is required to follow an arrangement and is not held back by a band of no fixed talent, the songs work extremely well and for once Dylan gains fans with a TV broadcast, rather than losing them. All three songs are broadcast on European TV, along with an ensemble encore of "I Shall Be Released" from either the 21st (most of Europe) or the 22nd (the BBC). Dylan and Joni Mitchell share a mike on the finale. "A Hard Rain's a-Gonna Fall" is subsequently released on assorted versions of the "Dignity" CD-single.

July 3, Le Parc Du Bourget, Paris, France
For once, "Jokerman" is replaced as opener by "To Be Alone With You."

July 4, Palais Des Sports, Besancon, France

July 5, Theatre Antique de Fourviere, Lyon, France

July 7, Stadio Communale, San Remo, Italy

July 8, Sornovia '94, Milan, Italy

July 9, Messegelande, Balingen, Germany

July 10, Tanzbrunnen, Cologne, Germany

July 12, Stravinsky Hall, Montreux, Switzerland

July 14, S.F.Z., Graz, Austria

July 15, Hohe Warte Stadion, Wien, Austria

July 16, Sportovni Hala Praha-Vystaviste,
Prague, Czech Republic

July 17, Stadion Cracovia, Krakow, Poland

July 19, Sala Krongresova PKiN, Warsaw, Poland

July 21, Freilichtbuhne am Elbufer, Dresden, Germany

July 23, Freilichtbuhne Peissnitz, Halle, Germany

July 24, Schloss Frieddenstein, Gotha, Germany

July 25, Ostseehalle, Kiel, Germany

July 26
Dylan arrives back in Los Angeles around 3 PM, accompanied by a blonde female companion.

August 10, State Theater, Portland, ME

August 11, Birch Concert Pavilion, Patterson, NY

August 12, Stratton Mountain Ski Resort, Stratton, VT

August 14, Woodstock II, Winston Farm, Saugerties, NY
Dylan performs for around three hundred thousand mud-soaked masochists plus a few million watching on a live pay-per-view cable broadcast of the event, designed to celebrate the 25th anniversary of the original Woodstock. For once, Dylan responds to the importance of the event by delivering a tight, powerful set. Although stripped of song surprises, Dylan's vocal commitment certainly surprises many watching on TV. "Just Like a Woman" has a sense of purpose often lacking, "Highway 61 Revisited" almost returns the song to its G. E. Smith heyday, and the acoustic set shows Dylan's nerve as a performer to be very much intact. "Masters of War" retains its menacing quality all the way from Hiroshima, but it is a 10-minute "It's All Over Now, Baby Blue" that has most of the young audience listening with a certain reverence as Dylan teases out the words while Garnier plays standup bass, bow in hand.

August 16, Artpark, Lewiston, NY

August 17, Hershey Park Stadium, Hershey, PA

August 19, Station Square/IC Tent, Pittsburgh, PA

August 20, Nautica Stage, Cleveland, OH

August 21, OH State Fair, Columbus, OH

August 23, Palace Theatre, Louisville, KY

August 24, Morris Theatre, South Bend, IN

August 26, Star Plaza Theater, Merriville, IN
Includes the only "Just Like Tom Thumb's Blues" of 1994, as part of the first electric set.

August 2, State Theater, Kalamazoo, MI

August 29, State Fairgrounds, Detroit, MI

September 30
Dylan returns to Sony Studios in New York, with Don Was producing, to cut three songs for a possible Elvis Presley tribute CD. The versions of "Lawdy Miss Clawdy" and "Money Honey" are fairly nondescript. However, the final vocal take of "Anyway You Want Me (Is How I Will Be)" is

really quite spectacular, Dylan delivering one of his most convincing vocals in years.

October 1, Ben Light Gymnasium, Ithaca College, Ithaca, NY

October 2, Le Frac Gymnasium, Amherst, MA

October 4–5, State Theatre, Portland, ME
"Ballad of Hollis Brown" makes a solitary 1994 appearance on the second night.

October 7–9, Orpheum Theatre, Boston, MA
Dylan performs the only "Two Soldiers" of 1994 on the closing night, presumably because of its opening line, "He was just a blue-eyed Boston boy. . . . "

October 11, Flynn Theater, Burlington, VT

October 12, Performing Arts Center, Providence, RI

October 14, Palace Theater, Albany, NY

October 15, Eisenhower Hall Theater, Military Academy, West Point, NY

October 16, Palace Theater, New Haven, CT

Mid-October
According to the *New York Post,* Dylan has been seen sparring at Geraldo's boxing gymnasium in the city.

October 17
Dylan joins the Grateful Dead for a perfunctory "Rainy Day Women" during their six-night residency at Madison Square Garden.

October 18, Roseland Ballroom, NY

October 19, Roseland Ballroom, NY

October 20, Roseland Ballroom, NY
A disappointing New York residency concludes with an extended encore. After a "My Back Pages," which bears all the irony the intervening years can bring, Dylan leaves the stage while the roadies hastily set up two more guitar inputs. When he returns it is in the company of Neil Young and Bruce Springsteen, with whom he performs two obligatory golden oldies, "Rainy Day Women" and "Highway 61 Revisited." If Young manages to eke something audible out of his guitar, Springsteen seems to spend most of both songs trying to get to know Dylan's guitarist, J. J. Jackson.

October 22, Auditorium Theater, Rochester, NY

October 23, Landmark Theater, Syracuse, NY

October 25, The F.M. Kirby Center for the Performing Arts, Wilkes-Barre, PA

October 26, Wicomico City Civic Center, Salisbury, MD

October 27–28, Tower Theatre, Upper Darby, PA

October 29–30, Warner Theatre, Washington, DC

November 1, Chrysler Hall, Norfolk, VA

November 2, Civic Center Auditorium, Roanoke, VA

November 4, GA Mountains Center, Gainesville, GA

November 5, TN Theater, Knoxville, TN

November 6, Thomas Wolfe Auditorium, Civic Center, Asheville, NC

November 8–9, Ryman Auditorium, Nashville, TN
Dylan plays the newly restored home of the *Grand Ole Opry* for the first time, the highlight of the opening show being a delicate "Born in Time."

November 10, Oman Arena, Jackson, TN

November 12–13, House of Blues, New Orleans, LA

November 16
Dylan and his band, augmented by producer Brendan O'Brien on keyboards, rehearse at Sony Studios in New York for their forthcoming "Unplugged" appearances. The songs rehearsed are "Absolutely Sweet Marie," "Don't Think Twice, It's All Right," "Desolation Row," "Tonight I'll Be Staying Here with You," "Hazel," "Everything Is Broken," "The Times They Are a-Changin'," "Love Minus Zero/No Limit," "Dignity," and "With God on Our Side." There is then a break, after which Dylan resumes work on the yet-to-be-unveiled "Dignity" before reverting to "Desolation Row,"

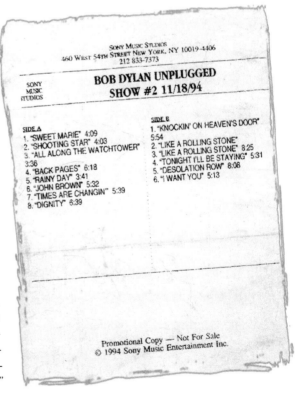

SONY MUSIC STUDIOS
460 WEST 54TH STREET NEW YORK, NY 10019-4406
212 833-7373

SONY
MUSIC
STUDIOS

BOB DYLAN UNPLUGGED
SHOW #2 11/18/94

SIDE A
1. "SWEET MARIE" 4:09
2. "SHOOTING STAR" 4:03
3. "ALL ALONG THE WATCHTOWER" 3:36
4. "BACK PAGES" 6:18
5. "RAINY DAY" 3:41
6. "JOHN BROWN" 5:32
7. "TIMES ARE CHANGIN'" 5:39
8. "DIGNITY" 6:39

SIDE B
1. "KNOCKIN' ON HEAVEN'S DOOR" 5:54
2. "LIKE A ROLLING STONE"
3. "LIKE A ROLLING STONE" 8:25
4. "TONIGHT I'LL BE STAYING" 5:31
5. "DESOLATION ROW" 8:08
6. "I WANT YOU" 5:13

Promotional Copy — Not For Sale
© 1994 Sony Music Entertainment Inc.

"Knockin' on Heaven's Door," "Tombstone Blues," "I Pity the Poor Immigrant," "Shooting Star," and "Tombstone Blues." "I Pity the Poor Immigrant,"last performed live in 1976, is not included at either "Unplugged" performance.

November 17

Rehearsals continue in the afternoon for this evening's first performance at Sony Studios. However, Dylan seems thoroughly uncomfortable with the setup and at the evening performance, in front of one of those dreaded "invited audiences," performs the entire show with dark sunglasses blocking out the lights, making a mockery of MTV's efforts to film the show. Nevertheless, the set lasts one hour and despite a faltering opening with "Tombstone Blues," contains a beautiful, slow "I Want You" (far more effective than 1978), "Hazel" and "Dignity," both of which have Dylan tripping over the first couple of lines before getting to grips with each song, and an atmospheric "With God on Our Side," the only song from tonight used in the MTV "Unplugged" broadcast.

November 18

In one great concession to MTV and its audience, Dylan returns to Sony Studios for his second "Unplugged" show, and this time gives them what they want, a largely undiluted greatest hits show. With hired moppets shaking their tousled airheads down front, Dylan—still donning his shades—plays a 90-minute set that repeats just four songs from the first show, "The Times They Are a-Changin'," "Dignity," "Desolation Row," and "I Want You." "Dignity" finally clicks and even O'Brien's organ vamps seem to fit as Dylan awakens to the song's challenge. "I Want You" is once again rather fine, although neither take will make the TV special or "Unplugged" album. Nor will tonight's opener, an effective "Absolutely Sweet Marie" or a word-perfect "My Back Pages." The semiacoustic "Like a Rolling Stone" does appear in the TV special, although cunningly edited to suggest the briefest of false starts. In fact, Dylan was a good two minutes into the world's slowest "Like a Rolling Stone" before he abandons the experiment and reverts to a somewhat more uptempo arrangement. Although Dylan evidently enjoys himself far more tonight than last night, neither show compares well with the Supper Club performances and it remains a mystery why these should be preferred, not only for broadcast but for official release.

Early December

Although he seems to have had little input into the editing of "Unplugged," Dylan is given final say on the version to be broadcast.

• While in New York Dylan is seen backstage at the play, *Blood Brothers,* in the company of Carole King.

1995

January to February

Dylan is interviewed for *Newsweek,* ostensibly about a recently published collection of his sketches, *Drawn Blank.* Comparing his art with his music he suggests, "These drawings, they kind of go with my primitive style of music." Certainly the word for some of the sketches in *Drawn Blank* is primitive. He also addresses the usual query about what motivates him to keep going, "I'd rather live in the moment. . . . People are mainlining nostalgia like it was morphine." Uh-huh.

Winter

Dylan is interviewed twice by a *Rolling Stone* reporter for a possible cover story to coincide with the release of "Unplugged." However, neither of the interviews is very satisfactory and when Dylan's people start making a series of unreasonable demands, the feature is scrapped.

March 10

After flying in to Prague on the ninth, Dylan gets struck down by some 48-hour flu bug that renders him unable to perform for the second time in a year. Tonight's show is rescheduled for the 13th, previously a rest day.

March 11, Congress Hall, Palac Kultury, Prague, Czech Republic

Dylan opens the year with one of the most remarkable performances of the "Never Ending Tour," despite still visibly suffering the after effects of the bug (at several points he sits on the drum rise, scrunched up in some discomfort). Opening with a song he has performed exactly once live, "Down in the Flood," the shock of the evening is not his song selection, which, after the opener, is mundane in the extreme, but the fact that he performs almost the entire show without a guitar (except for a two-minute guitar jam between him and Jackson on "Watching the River Flow"), harmonica in hand, making strange shadow-boxing movements, cupping the harmonica to his mouth on nearly every song, and blowing his sweetest harp breaks in years. The (anywhere up to) two-minute-plus harmonica solos on songs like "Just Like a Woman," "All Along Watchtower," and "Tangled Up In Blue" salvage the over-familiar and make them anew. However, it is in the acoustic set that the new setup really comes into its own. Hunched over the mike, Dylan exercises some tonal breath control on "Mr.Tambourine Man," "Boots of Spanish Leather," and an "It's All Over Now, Baby Blue" that suggests a whole new vocal approach is revealed in the 10 minutes it takes Dylan to relive the song. The harmonica solos that bookend the final verse share the same sense of danger as Dylan teeters on the brink, finally bringing the song home safe and sound, to a standing ovation. In the second half, Dylan seems at various points desperately tired but continues to push himself through new arrangements of "Man in the Long Black Coat" and, as first encore, "Shelter from the Storm." The drawn-out "Shelter from the Storm" may have been the result of a nervous band and a tired Dylan, but it works far better than subsequent attempts to revitalize it. Finally, Dylan performs "It Ain't Me Babe," on which he is joined by a girl from the audience, who sits behind him throughout the song until Dylan suggests she play the guitar. She declines and Dylan plays one final soaring harmonica break and then it is over and he can at last return to his bed.

March 12, Congress Hall, Palac Kultury, Prague, Czech Republic
After the drama of the opening show, the second show is inevitably something of an anticlimax. "Down in the Flood" is retained as opener, as indeed it is for most of the year, but with more harmonica work and Dylan determined to punch the words out. However, at various points in the evening, Dylan can't resist picking up the guitar. Although the acoustic set survives relatively unscathed, Dylan plays a beautiful harmonica intro to "Desolation Row" and then insists on playing a guitar, losing the whole thread of the song in the process. The acoustic sets at the European shows will continue to be remarkable, but more and more songs will feature Dylan with guitar in hand. Since he has evidently misplaced his harmonica rack, only the songs minus Dylan's guitar feature harmonica.

March 13, Congress Hall, Palac Kultury, Prague, Czech Republic
The final night includes a rare "License to Kill."

March 14, Stadthalle, Furth, Germany
Includes "Unbelievable" in the first electric set.

March 15, Unterfrankenhalle, Aschaffenburg, Germany

March 16, Stadthalle, Bielefeld, Germany
After assorted soundchecks and two performances to invited audiences, "Dignity" makes it's first performance in fully fledged electric guise. Needless to say, the 1995 version eclipses the "Unplugged" renditions.

March 18, Martinihal, Groningen, Netherlands.

March 19, Rodahal, Kerkrade, Netherlands

March 20, Musiek Centrum, Utrecht, Netherlands.

March 22, Lille, France

March 23, Vorst National, Brussels, Belgium

March 24, Le Zenith, Paris, France

March 26, Brighton Centre, Brighton, England

By this point on the European tour, Dylan is only performing the first two songs of the show and the first two songs of the acoustic set minus guitar. These are invariably the highlights of the shows, especially "Mr. Tambourine Man," which now includes the "ragged clown behind" verse, not sung in live performance since the '60s, as well as a lovely harmonica coda.

March 27, Cardiff International Arena, Cardiff, Wales

Tonight's highlight is a remarkable "Desolation Row," running to seven verses rather than the usual five, leading into a fiery "Dignity."

March 29–31, Brixton Academy, London, England

After a very poor opening night, Dylan pulls out a couple of favorites from the gospel years, "Every Grain of Sand" and "I Believe in You," on the second night. At the end of the show, Elvis Costello, who is playing acoustic support slots at the Paris, London, and Dublin shows, trades verses with Dylan on a hilarious "I Shall Be Released."

Night number 3, the day they bury East-End gangster Reggie Kray, Dylan closes the main set with his own paean to a hoodlum, "Joey." He also debuts a fine electric "Tombstone Blues," which becomes a highlight of 1995 sets. Costello again joins Dylan for an equally rambunctious "I Shall Be Released" and an even looser "Rainy Day Women," Carole King and Chrissie Hynde adding their own backing vocals on the latter.

> April 1995: *Unplugged* (CK 67000): "Tombstone Blues," "Shooting Star," "All Along the Watchtower," "The Times They Are a-Changin'," "John Brown," "Rainy Day Women Nos. 10 & 35," "Desolation Row," "Dignity," "Knockin' on Heaven's Door," "Like a Rolling Stone," "With God on Our Side"

April 2, Aston Villa Leisure Centre, Birmingham, England

Having seemingly woken up—halfway through the European tour—to the fans' desire for more varied sets, Dylan is now ransacking his "Never Ending Tour" repertoire night after night. Tonight sees "Just Like Tom Thumb's Blues," "Tears of Rage," and a disastrous "Lenny Bruce" all gaining temporary favor. "To Ramona" also makes a rare appearance in the acoustic set.

April 3, Labatts Apollo, Manchester, England

Twenty-nine years after some Mancunian misfit called him a "Judas," Dylan returns to the fair city and performs an acoustic set worthy of that night in May 1966. "Mr. Tambourine Man" receives a rhapsodic response, and tonight's "Gates of Eden" is the definitive performance. Also surprisingly exhumed is a splendid "Where Teardrops Fall," as song number two, complete with harmonica.

April 4, Labatts Apollo, Manchester, England

Barely two weeks after its electric debut, "Dignity" receives its final live outing on the second night. Although the band self-evidently enjoys playing the song, Dylan presumably finally despaired of getting the lyrics right in concert.

April 5, Labatts Apollo, Manchester, England

Responding to another ecstatic Manchester crowd, Dylan delivers a memorable final show at the Apollo. "A Hard Rain's a-Gonna Fall," the third song of the acoustic set, comes close to the intensity of "Gates of Eden" two nights earlier. During the electric sets, Dylan actually unstraps his guitar twice to pick up the harmonica and play impromptu harp breaks, concluding "Knockin' on Heaven's Door" and "Rainy Day Women" in this fashion.

April 6–7, Playhouse, Edinburgh, Scotland

"What Was It You Wanted?" and "Disease of Conceit" are featured on opening night; "Everything Is Broken" appears on the 7th.

April 9, Scottish Exhibition Centre, Glasgow, Scotland

April 10, King's Hall, Belfast, N. Ireland

An electric "Ring Them Bells" makes for the eighth *Oh Mercy* song to be performed on the British leg of this tour.

April 11, The Point Depot, Dublin, Ireland

The final show of a very good European tour features many of the highlights of previous shows: "Where Teardrops Fall," "Ring Them Bells," "Mr. Tambourine Man," and "Tombstone Blues" are all outstanding. Dylan is joined for the second electric set by Carole King on keyboards, who remains stubbornly inaudible. Then, after the obligatory acoustic encore, Dylan is joined by Van Morrison for Van's own "Real, Real Gone," on which Dylan also sings a full verse, by Elvis Costello (and Van) for "I Shall Be Released," and Costello, Morrison, *and* King for "Rainy Day Women." Dylan is clearly enjoying himself as he wraps up a two-hour show surrounded by fellow singer-songwriters.

Early May

Dylan is interviewed by Edna Gundersen for *USA Today,* presumably by phone, ostensibly to promote the recently released "Unplugged" album, although he quickly dismisses the project, "I felt like . . . I delivered something that was preconceived for me." He also dismisses Woodstock II as "just another show," and insists that he has written "a whole bunch of songs" but has no plans to record them.

May 10, Embarcadero Marina, San Diego, CA

Tonight's only surprise is the reintroduction of "Seeing the Real You At Last."

May 12–13, Casino, Hard Rock Hotel, Las Vegas, NV

May 15, McCallum Theatre, Palm Springs, CA
The second set tonight includes one of only three songs from *Blonde on Blonde* never previously performed live, "Obviously Five Believers" (it had been on set lists throughout the European tour), and the second-ever performance of the less-than-sublime "Never Gonna Be the Same Again."

May 17–19, Hollywood Palladium, Hollywood, CA
The opening night set includes "Pledging My Time"; "Ring Them Bells" is added to the second night's program. Dylan performs a bonus encore of "I Shall Be Released" with female pop star Sheryl Crow for the final show.

May 20, County Bowl, Santa Barbara, CA

May 22–23, Warfield Theatre, San Francisco, CA
On opening night, "Man in the Long Black Coat" makes its only appearance in the number-two slot, where it is graced with a powerful, extended harmonica break at song's end.

May 25–26, Community Theater, Berkeley, CA

May 27, Laguna Beach, Big Sur, CA

May 28, Reno Hilton, Reno, NV

May 31, Hult Center for the Performing Arts, Eugene, OR

June 2–4, Paramount Northwest Theatre, Seattle, WA
"Cat's in the Well" is the closing night's first encore.

June 6, Arlene Schnitzer Concert Hall, Portland, OR

June 7, Riverfront Park, Spokane, WA

June 15, Franklin County Airport, Highgate, VT
Dylan supports the Grateful Dead.

June 16, Harbor Lights, Boston, MA

June 18–19, Giants Stadium, East Rutherford, NJ
Dylan supports the Grateful Dead.

June 21, The Theatre of Living Arts, Philadelphia, PA
With a four-day gap between support slots with the Dead, Dylan slips in two shows at the 700-capacity T.L.A. at short notice. In the opening show, he introduces "Unplugged"-style versions of perhaps his two most perfect songs, "Visions of Johanna" and, as the acoustic encore, "Tangled Up In Blue." Although "Visions of Johanna" remains a one-off, "Tangled Up In Blue" becomes a regular part of the acoustic set. "Unbelievable" concludes the main set tonight.

June 22, The Theatre of Living Arts, Philadelphia, PA
"Drifter's Escape" opens the second show. It is retained as an occasional alternate to "Down in the Flood," although it lacks that song's immediacy.

June 24–25, RFK Stadium, Washington, DC
Dylan supports the Grateful Dead.

June 29, Spektrum, Oslo, Norway

June 30, Festival Tent, Roskilde, Denmark

July 2, Stadtpark, Hamburg, Germany

July 3, Music Hall, Hannover, Germany

July 4, Tempodrom, Berlin, Germany.
Includes "Cat's in the Well."

July 7, Freilichtbuhne, Glauchau, Germany

July 8, Terminal One, Munchen, Germany

July 10, Leiderhalle, Beethovensaal, Stuttgart, Germany

July 11, Kockelschbaur Ice-Rink, Luxembourg City, Luxembourg

July 12, Westfalenhalle 2, Dortmund, Germany

July 14, Phoenix Festival, Long Marston Airfield, Stratford-on-Avon

July 16, La Plaza de Toros de Vista Alegre, Bilbao, Spain

July 19, La Riviera, Madrid, Spain

July 20, El Coto, Cartagena, Spain

July 21, Velodromo Luis Puig, Valencia, Spain

July 24, Plaza Mayor del Poble Espanyol de Montjuic, Barcelona, Spain

July 25, El Palacio de Deportes, Zaragoza, Spain.
Includes "When I Paint My Masterpiece."

July 27, Espace Grammont, Montpellier, France
Agreeing to support the Rolling Stones at the last minute, Dylan delivers a contemptuously perfunctory nine-song set. He does, however, joins the Stones on "Like a Rolling Stone," a regular feature of the Stones's European tour, although even his presence cannot salvage the song from a crass arrangement.

July 28, Theatre Antique, Vienne, near Lyons, France
Includes "Ring Them Bells."

July 30, Paleo-Nyon Festival, Nyon, near Geneva, Switzerland

August 9: Jerry Garcia is found dead at a Californian drug rehab clinic.

August 10
Elliot Mintz releases a statement from Dylan regarding the loss of Jerry Garcia: "There's no way to measure his greatness or magnitude as a person or as a player. I don't think eulogizing will do him justice. He was that great, much more than a superb musician with an uncanny ear and dexterity. He is the very spirit personified of whatever is Muddy River Country at its core and screams up into the spheres. He really had no equal. To me he wasn't only a musician and friend, he was more like a big brother who taught and showed me more than he'll ever know. There's a lot of spaces and advances between the Carter family and, say, Ornette Coleman, a lot of universes, but he filled them all without being a member of any school. His playing was moody, awesome, sophisticated, hypnotic, and subtle. There's no way to convey the loss. It just digs down really deep."
  • Dylan attends Garcia's funeral at St. Stephen's Church in San Francisco. The funeral is restricted to close friends and families.

Mid- to Late August
In San Francisco to attend the funeral of Jerry Garcia, Dylan spends several days at the house of Dead lyricist Robert Hunter. They apparently work on some songs together.

September 2, Cleveland Stadium, Cleveland, OH
Dylan and his touring band are part of a four-hour pay-per-view broadcast to commemorate the opening of the Rock & Roll Hall of Fame in Cleveland. It is a tired performance and the choice of songs—"All Along the Watchtower," "Just Like a Woman," "Seeing the Real You at Last," and "Highway 61 Revisited"—unadventurous in the extreme. After a short break, Bruce Springsteen joins Dylan and his band on a slightly more spirited "Forever Young," freely trading lines with Dylan. However, Dylan's association with such a lame idea, couched solely in terms of America's impact on rock, does no one any favors.

September 23, The Edge, Fort Lauderdale, FL
After a couple of days rehearsing with the band in Florida, Dylan decides to play a free gig at a small club to a select audience of two hundred. Providing a stark contrast to the shows proper, tonight's set is top-heavy with covers, opening with Van the Man's 1980 ditty "Real, Real Gone." Although there are no "Never Ending Tour" debuts, "Real, Real Gone," "Key to the Highway," Chuck Willis's "It's Too Late," "That Lucky Ol' Sun," and "With God on Our Side" are all songs performed just once in the last six years. Dy-

lan also tips his hat to the recently demised Mr. Garcia with spirited versions of "Friend of the Devil" and "West LA Fadeaway" as well as new arrangements of the likes of "Silvio" and "Maggie's Farm." The emphasis, though, is firmly on non-Dylan works. When he is asked, a couple of days later, about one of these, "Confidential," he replies, "You won't hear that again," implying that there are rehearsals and there are crowd-pleasing concerts.

September 25 or 26
Dylan is interviewed around midnight by the Arts & Features Editor of the *Fort Lauderdale Sun-Sentinel,* John Dolen. The interview, by phone, lasts nearly an hour and Dolen, clearly a Dylan fan, asks a couple of great questions. Asked about the song, "Slow Train," Dylan admits, "Just writing a song like that probably emancipated me from other kind of illusions." At the end of the interview, Dylan even comes out with a remarkable discourse on time: "I don't think the human mind can comprehend the past and the future. They are both just illusions that can manipulate you into thinking there's some kind of change. But after you've been around a while, they both seem unnatural."

September 27, Lee County Civic Center, Fort Myers, FL

September 28, Sunrise Musical Theatre, Sunrise, FL

September 29, Sunrise Musical Theatre, Sunrise, FL
Tonight Bob Dylan pulls out a most welcome surprise, the live debut (if we discount Mr. Hawkins hogging the mike on June 6, 1990) of "One More Night," with support act Alison Krauss playing fiddle as Dylan sings.

September 30, Sundome, Tampa, FL
Dykan is joined by the Allman Brothers' guitarist Dickie Betts for the last third of the show. In deference to Betts, the first encore tonight is "Ramblin' Man."

October 2, St. Lucie Civic Center, Fort Pierce, FL

October 5, University of Central FL Arena, Orlando, FL

October 6, Riverview Music Shed, Jacksonville, FL
Another Grateful Dead song is added to the repertoire. "Alabama Getaway" remains the standard first encore for the remainder of '95

October 7, King Street Palace, Charleston, SC

October 9, The Johnny Mercer Theater, Civic Center, Savannah, GA

October 10, Bell Auditorium, Augusta, GA

October 11, Fox Theatre, Atlanta, GA

October 12, Civic Center, Dothan AL

October 14, Gulf Coast Coliseum, Biloxi, MS

October 15, Civic Center, Thibodaux, LA

October 16, McAllister Auditorium, Tulane University,
New Orleans, LA

October 18, Alabama Theater, Birmingham, AL

October 19, Mud Island Amphitheatre, Memphis, TN

October 24, Target Center, Rockford, IL

October 26, University of IN Auditorium, Bloomington, IN

October 27, American Theater, St. Louis, MO

October 29, Juanita K. Hammons Hall, Springfield, MO

October 30, Robinson Center Music Hall,
Little Rock, AR

November 1, Music Hall, Houston, TX

November 3, Majestic Theater, San Antonio, TX
John Jackson plays banjo on "To Ramona" tonight.

November 4, Music Hall, Austin, TX
Charlie Sexton is tonight's special guest, playing the usual inaudible guitar
on the last three songs of the main set and the two electric encores.

November 5, Music Hall, Austin, TX
Doug Sahm is tonight's guest guitarist at the show's end.

November 7, Dallas Music Complex, Dallas, TX

November 9, Symphony Hall, Phoenix, AZ
Stevie Nicks lends her voice to the "I Shall Be Released" encore.

November 10, The Joint, Hard Rock Hotel & Casino,
Las Vegas, NV
Dylan opens with Van the Man's "Real, Real Gone" at his third Vegas show
in six months.

November 19, Shrine Auditorium, Los Angeles, CA
Dylan is part of an all-star cast who have convened at the Shrine to celebrate
Frank Sinatra's eightieth birthday. While cameras roll and Sinatra is
seated in A18, Dylan unveils a remarkable version of "Restless Farewell," all
five verses sung with a nervy precision, accompanied by his usual musical
misfits and a string quartet. The whole thing is actually rather moving, as

is Sinatra's seemingly genuine enthusiasm for the performance, which is subsequently broadcast on cable TV.

December 7, O'Neill Center, Danbury, CT
Dylan breaks one of his rules—not touring in December—to play ten East Coast dates with "Special guest" Patti Smith, playing her first Patti Smith Group shows in sixteen years. Though Smith's presence seems to enervate Dylan, the sets remain ever-familiar.

December 8, Worcester Auditorium, Worcester, MA
A rare "I and I" is the highlight of one of the better late '95 shows.

December 9, Orpheum Theatre, Boston, MA

December 10, Orpheum Theatre, Boston, MA
After much speculation, Patti Smith finally joins Dylan during his set for a duet on the long-ignored "Dark Eyes," a song she has been performing at her solo shows. The first night Dylan repeatedly stumbles over the words, though the vibe is remarkable. Dylan and Smith persevere with the song for the remaining shows, their harmonies growing closer and closer until, by Philadelphia, they are almost singing the same song.

December 11, Beacon Theatre, New York, NY

December 13, Stabler Arena, Lehigh University, Bethlehem, PA
An astonishing "Desolation Row," Dylan even singing the "Nero's Neptune" verse, almost wakes up the audience from Nodsville.

December 14, Beacon Theatre, New York, NY
G. E. Smith joins Dylan for the final encore of "Rainy Day Women Nos. 12 & 35" but is frustratingly low in the mix.

December 15, Electric Factory, Philadelphia, PA

December 16, Electric Factory, Philadelphia, PA
The best show in many months features the sporadically impressive '95 arrangement of "Shelter from the Storm," a lively "I Want You," and, best of all, as the final song of the main set, a rather fine full electric "Forever Young," Dylan bending the words with all the old flair.

December 17, Electric Factory, Philadelphia, PA
After a record-breaking 118 shows in a single year—an extraordinary physical display for a fifty-four-year-old man—Dylan wraps it up with a three-song encore comprising "West LA Fadeaway" (light relief after nine "Alabama Getaway's"), "Knockin' on Heaven's Door" with Patti Smith taking a verse and a couple of joint choruses before Dylan goes a-doodling, and "Rainy Day Women," on which the band is joined by ex-guitar technician Cesar Diaz.

Bibliography

This bibliography purports to include just about every pamphlet or book written on Dylan in the English language, as well as a few select titles that have some major form of Dylan content but have a more general outlook (these are marked with an asterisk). There are many privately published items herein (marked pp), which may or may not be available through the two specialist Dylan mail-order companies. With these items I have indicated country of origin, although not date of publication since in a fair few cases it would be purely speculative on my part. With books published in the conventional way, the US publisher and year of publication is noted, as well as the country of publication if I am unaware of an American edition. I have included a list of both current and defunct Dylan fanzines, and the addresses of the various fan-related services at the end of the bibliography.

Anon. *The Bob Dylan File '63–'69* (pp, UK).

_____.*Step into the Arena* (pp, UK).

_____. *Looking for Some Answers: The Bob Dylan Quiz Book* (pp, UK).

. *The Fiddler Now Upspoke* Vol. 1 (pp, UK).

_____. *The Fiddler Now Upspoke* Vol. 2 (pp, UK).

Anderson, Dennis. *The Hollow Horn* (Hobo Press, 1981).

Auschlag, Hermann. *Small Talk* (pp, Germany).

*Balfour, Victoria. *Rock Wives* (Beech Tree, 1986).

Bauldie, John. *Bob Dylan and Desire* (Wanted Man, 1984).

_____. *The Ghost of Electricity* (pp, UK).

_____, ed. *Positively The Dream & other assorted interviews and tall tales* (pp, UK).

_____, ed. *Wanted Man: In Search of Bob Dylan* (Citadel, 1991).

_____, and Gray, Michael, eds. *All Across the Telegraph* (Sedgwick & Jackson [UK], 1987).

*Baez, Joan. *And A Voice to Sing With* (Summit, 1987).

Bergerau, E. *Every Grain of Sand* (pp, Germany).

Bicker, Stewart P. *The Red Rose and the Briar: A Commentary on Renaldo and Clara* (pp, UK).

_____, ed. *Friends & Other Strangers: Bob Dylan in Other People's Words* (pp, UK).

_____, ed. *Talkin' Bob Dylan 1984 & 1985 (Some Educated Rap)* (pp, UK).

Bowden, Betsy. *Performing Literature: Words and Music by Bob Dylan* (IN University Press, 1982).

Cable, Paul. *Bob Dylan: His Unreleased Recordings* (Schirmer, 1980).

Cartwright, Bert. *The Bible in the Lyrics of Bob Dylan* (Wanted Man, 1985 [revised ed. 1993]).

Cooper, Chris and Marsh, Keith. *The Circus Is in Town: England 1965* (pp, UK).

Cott, Jonathan. *Dylan* (Doubleday, 1984).

Crowe, Cameron. *Biograph* [book accompanying CBS boxed-set] (CBS, 1985).

*Davis, Clive. *Clive: Inside the Record Business* (Ballantine, 1974).

Day, Aidan. *Bob Dylan: Escaping on the Run* (Wanted Man, 1984).

_____. *Jokerman: Reading the Lyrics of Bob Dylan* (Blackwell, 1988).

De Somogyi, Nick. *Jokermen & Thieves: Bob Dylan and the Ballad Tradition* (Wanted Man, 1986).

*DeTurk, David A., and Poulin, A., Jr., eds. *The American Folk Scene: Dimensions of the Folksong Revival* (Dell, 1967).

Dergoth, Jonas. *Renaldo and Clara: A Concise Synopsis* (pp, Netherlands).

Diddle, Gavin. *Images and Assorted Facts: A Peek Behind the Picture Frame* (pp, UK).

_____, ed. *Talkin' Bob Dylan 1978* (pp, UK).

_____, ed. *Talkin' Bob Dylan 1984* (pp, UK).

Dorman, James E. *Recorded Dylan: A Critical Review and Discography* (Soma Press, 1982).

Dowley, Tim, and Dunnage, Barry. *Bob Dylan: From A Hard Rain to A Slow Train* (Hippocrene Books, 1982).

Dreau, Jean-Louis, and Schlockoff, Robert. *Hypnotist Collectors: An International Illustrated Discography* (pp, France).

Dundas, Glen. *Tangled Up in Tapes: The Recordings of Bob Dylan* (pp, Canada [three eds. 1987, 1990, 1994]).

Dunn, Tim. *I Just Write 'Em as They Come* (pp, US).

Dylan, Bob. *Tarantula* (Macmillan, 1971).

_____. *Writings and Drawings* (Knopf, 1973).

_____. *The Songs of Bob Dylan from 1966 through 1975* (Knopf, 1976).

_____. *Lyrics 1962–1985* (Knopf, 1986).

_____. *Drawn Blank* (Random House, 1994).

_____. [anon. ed.] *In His Own Write* (pp, Denmark).

_____. [anon. ed.] *I Can Change, I Swear: The Alternate Blood on the Tracks Lyrics* (pp, UK).

_____. [anon. ed.] *Some Other Kind of Songs (I'm Not There 1986)* (pp, UK).

_____. [anon. ed.] *Get Your Rocks Off* (pp, Netherlands).

_____. [anon. ed.] *Words to His Songs* (pp, Netherlands).

_____. [anon. ed.] *Words Fill My Head 1960–1990* (pp, Sweden).

*Eisen, Jonathan, ed. *The Age of Rock: Sounds of the American Cultural Revolution, A Reader* (Vintage/Random House, 1969).

*_____. *The Age of Rock 2* (Random House, 1970).

*Elliot, Marc. *Death of a Rebel* (Anchor, 1979).

*Flanagan, Bill. *Written in My Soul* (Contemporary, 1987).

*Fong-Torres, Ben, ed. *The Rolling Stone Rock & Roll Reader* (Bantam, 1974).

Gans, Terry Alexander. *What's Real and What Is Not: Bob Dylan Through 1964* (Hobo Press, 1983).

Gant, Sandy. *A Discography of Bob Dylan* (pp, US).

Garrett, B. *My Back Pages* (pp, UK).

Gilbert, Joel. *The Acoustic Bob Dylan* (pp, US).

Gray, Michael. *Song & Dance Man: The Art of Bob Dylan* (E.P. Dutton, 1972).

_____. *The Art of Bob Dylan: Song & Dance Man* [revised ed. of above] (St. Martin's Press, 1981).

Gross, Michael. *Bob Dylan: An Illustrated History* (Elm Tree [UK], 1978).

*Hampton, Wayne. *Guerilla Minstrels: John Lennon, Joe Hill, Woody Guthrie, and Bob Dylan* (Univ. of TN Press, 1986).

Hansen, Larry. *A Million Faces at My Feet: 1986 True Confessions Tour* (pp, US).

*Helm, Levon, with Davies, Stephen. *The Wheel's on Fire* (William Morrow, 1993).

Herdman, John. *Voice Without Restraint* (Paul Harris [UK], 1982).

Heylin, Clinton. *The Bob Dylan Interviews: A List* (pp, UK).

_____. *Rain Unravelled Tales (The Nightingale's Code Examined): A Rumourography* (pp, UK).

_____. *More Rain Unravelled Tales (The Nightingale's Code Re-examined): Another Rumourography* (pp, UK).

_____. *Bob Dylan Stolen Moments* (Wanted Man, 1988).

_____. *To Live Outside the Law: A Guide to Bob Dylan Bootlegs* (pp, UK).

_____. *Bob Dylan: Behind the Shades* (Summit, 1991).

_____. *Bob Dylan: The Recording Sessions 1960–1994* (St. Martin's Press, 1995).

_____, ed. *Saved! The Gospel Speeches of Bob Dylan* (Hanuman, 1990).

Hinchey, John. *Bob Dylan's Slow Train* (Wanted Man, 1983).

Hoggard, Stuart, and Jim Shields. *Bob Dylan: An Illustrated Discography* (Transmedia Express, 1978).

*Hoskyns, Barney. *Across the Great Divide* (Hyperion, 1993).

Humphries, Patrick, and Bauldie, John. *Absolutely Dylan* [pub. in UK as *Oh No! Not Another Bob Dylan Book*] (Viking Studio, 1992).

Jansen, Gerhard, ed. *Slow Train Coming* (pp, Netherlands).

_____. *Pressing On* (pp, Netherlands).

_____. *Shot of Love* (pp, Netherlands).

Karpel, Craig. *The Tarantula in Me: Behind Bob Dylan's Novel* (pp, US)

*Kooper, Al. *Backstage Passes* (Stein & Day, 1977).

Kramer, Daniel. *Bob Dylan* (Citadel, 1967).

Krogsgaard, Michael. *Twenty Years of Recording: The Bob Dylan Reference Book* (SSRR, Denmark, 1981).

_____. *Master of the Tracks: The Bob Dylan Reference Book of Recording* [revised ed. of above] (SSRR, Denmark, 1988).

_____. *Positively Bob Dylan: A 30-Year Discography* [revised ed. of above] (Popular Culture Inc., 1992).

*Landy, Elliot. *Woodstock Visions* (Continuum Publishing Co., 1994).

Lawlan, Val, and Brian. *Steppin' Out* (pp, UK).

Ledbury, John. *Mysteriously Saved: An Astrological Investigation into Bob Dylan's Conversion to American Fundamentalism* (pp, UK)

Liff, Dennis. *Raging Glory* (pp, US).

Lindley, John. *Seven Days* (pp, UK).

*Marcus, Greil. *Mystery Train: Images of America in Rock & Roll Music* (E.P. Dutton, 1976 [revised ed. 1982]).

McGregor, Craig. *Bob Dylan: A Retrospective* (William Morrow, 1972 [republished: De Capo, 1990]).

McKeen, William. *Dylan: A Bio-Bibliography* (Greenwood, 1993).

Mellers, Wilfred. *A Darker Shade of Pale* (Faber & Faber, 198?).

Michel, Steve. *The Bob Dylan Concordance* (pp, US).

Miles, Barry. *Bob Dylan* (Big O, 1978).

_____, ed. *Bob Dylan In His Own Words* (Quick Fox, 1978).

Milne, Larry. *Hearts of Fire* (NEL, 1987).

Pennebaker, D. A., ed. *Don't Look Back* (Ballantine, 1967).

Percival, Dave. *The Dust of Rumour* (pp, UK).

_____. *This Wasn't Written in Tin Pan Alley* (pp, UK).

_____. *Just A Personal Tendency* (pp, UK).

_____. *Dylan Songs: A Listing* (pp, UK).

_____. *The Concert Charts* (pp, UK).

_____. *Love Plus Zero/With Limits* (pp, UK).

*Pichaske, David R. *The Poetry of Rock: The Golden Years* (Ellis Press, 1981).

Pickering, Stephen. *Dylan: A Commemoration* (pp, US).

_____. *Praxis: One* (pp, US).

_____. *Tour 1974* (pp, US).

_____. *Bob Dylan Approximately: A Portrait of the Jewish Poet in Search of God* (McKay, 1975).

Rawlins, Adrian. *Dylan Through the Looking Glass* (pp, Australia).

Ribakove, Sy, and Barbara. *Folk Rock: The Bob Dylan Story* (Dell, 1966).

Riley, Tim. *Hard Rain: A Dylan Commentary* (Knopf, 1992).

Rinzler, Alan. *Bob Dylan: The Illustrated Record* (Harmony, 1978).

Roberts, John. *Mixed Up Confusion: The Krogsgaard Companion* (pp, UK).

Rolling Stone, eds. *Knockin' on Dylan's Door: On the Road in '74* (Pocket Books, 1974).

_____. *The Rolling Stone Interviews: 1967–1980* (St. Martin's Press, 1981).

Roques, Dominique. *The Great White Answers: The Bob Dylan Bootleg Records* (pp, France).

Rowley, Chris. *Blood on the Tracks* (Proteus, 1984).

Russell, Alex. *Flagging Down the "Double E": Dylan with Allusions* (pp, UK).

Sarlin, Bob. *Turn It Up! I Can't Hear the Words* (Simon & Schuster, 1973).

Scaduto, Anthony. *Bob Dylan: An Intimate Biography* (Grosset and Dunlap, 1971, [revised ed.] [Signet, 1973]).

Scobie, Stephen. *Alias Bob Dylan* (Red Deer College Press [Canada], 1991).

Shelton, Robert. *No Direction Home* (Beech Tree, 1986).

Shepard, Sam. *Rolling Thunder Logbook* (Viking, 1977).

Sloman, Larry. *On the Road with Bob Dylan: Rolling with the Thunder* (Bantam, 1978).

Spitz, Bob. *Bob Dylan: A Biography* (McGraw-Hill, 1989).

Stein, Georg. *Bob Dylan: Temples in Flames* (Palmyra [Germany], 1989).

Stone, Lee Anderson. *Temptation?* (pp, Germany).

_____. *Who's Gonna Go to Hell for Anybody* (pp, Germany).

Styche, Geoff. *A Discography of Bob Dylan* (pp, UK).

Thompson, Toby. *Positively Main Street: An Unorthodox View of Bob Dylan* (Coward-McCann, 1971).

Thomson, Elizabeth M., ed. *Conclusions on the Wall: New Essays on Bob Dylan* (Thin Man, 1980).

_____, and Gutman, David. *The Dylan Companion* (Macmillan [UK], 1990).

Townshend, Phil. *Strangers and Prophets Vol. 1* (pp, UK).

Townshend, Phil. *Strangers and Prophets Vol. 2* (pp, UK).

Van Estrik, Robert. *Concerted Efforts* (pp, Netherlands).

*Vassal, Jacques. *Electric Children* (Taplinger Publishing Co., 1976)

*Von Schmidt, Eric, and Rooney, Jim. *Baby, Let Me Follow You Down* (Anchor Press, 1979).

*Walker, Bob. *Hot Wacks XV: The Last Wacks* (Blue Flake, 1992).

Way, John B. *Hungry As a Raccoon (Bob Dylan Talks to His Fans & Other Strangers)* (pp, UK).

*Wexler, Jerry, and Ritz, David. *Rhythm and the Blues: A Life in American Music* (Knopf, 1993).

Williams, Alan. *Whaaat?: The Original Playboy Interview* (pp, UK).

Williams, Chris. *Bob Dylan: In His Own Words, Vol. 2* (Omnibus Press).

Williams, Don. *The Man, The Music, The Message* (Revell, 1985).

*Williams, Paul. *Outlaw Blues: A Book of Rock Music* (E.P. Dutton, 1969).

_____. *Dylan: What Happened?* (Entwhistle, 1979).

_____. *Dylan: One Year Later* (pp, US).

_____. *Performing Artist: The Music of Bob Dylan Vol. 1 (1960–1973)* (Underwood-Miller, 1990).

_____. *Performing Artist: The Middle Years Vol. 2 (1974–1986)* (Underwood-Miller, 1992).

Williams, Richard. *Dylan: A Man Called Alias* (Bloomsbury).

Wilson, Keith. *Bob Dylan: A Listing* (pp, Canada).

Wissolik, David. *Bob Dylan: American Poet & Singer—An Annotated Bibliography* (pp, US).

Witting, Robin. *Isiah on Guitar: A Guide to John Wesley Harding.* (pp, UK).

_____. *The Cracked Bells: A Guide to* Tarantula (pp, UK).

_____. *Orpheus Revisited: A Celebration of* Highway 61 Revisited (pp, UK).

Woliver, Robbie. *Bringing It All Back Home: Twenty Five Years of American Music at Folk City* (Pantheon Books, 1986).

Woodward, Ian. *Back of the Tapestry* (pp, UK).

Worrell, Denise. *Icons: Intimate Portraits* (Atlantic Monthly Press, 1989).

Wraith, John, and Wyvill, Mike. *Still on the Road: 1991 Tourbook* (Wanted Man, 1992).

_____. *Heading for Another Joint: 1992 Tourbook* (Wanted Man, 1993).

_____. *Down the Highway: 1993 Tourbook* (Wanted Man, 1994).

_____. *From Town to Town: 1994 Tourbook* (Wanted Man, 1995).

Wurlitzer, Rudy. *Pat Garrett & Billy the Kid* (Signet, 1973).

Yenne, Bill. *One Foot on the Highway: Bob Dylan on Tour 1974* (pp, US).

Current Dylan Fanzines

The Telegraph [ed. John Bauldie]—[52 issues] (UK) (included for a time the *Rolling Telegraph Supplement*).

Isis [ed. Derek Barker]—[62 issues] (UK)

On the Tracks [ed. Mick Mchouston]—[6 issues] (US)

Defunct Dylan Fanzines

Endless Road [ed. John Welburn]—[7 issues] (UK)

Fourth Time Around [ed. Chris Hockenhull]—[4 issues] (UK)

Look Back [eds. various]—[21 issues] (US)

Zimmerman Blues [ed. Brian Stibal]—[10 issues] (US)

Dylan [ed. Pete Hoffman]—[11 issues] (Germany)

Occasionally [ed. Ian Woodward]—[5 issues] (UK)

Homer the Slut [ed. Andy Muir]—[12 issues] (UK)

Dylan Book Services

MY BACK PAGES, P.O. Box 117, Carlisle, CA1 2UL, UK

ROLLING TOMES, P.O. Box 1943, Grand Junction, CO 81502, USA

WANTED MAN, P.O. Box 307, Richmond, Surrey TW10 5AQ, UK

Newport 1963

Index